Controlling CRIME

Crime, Order and Social Control Course Team

The Open University

Mandy Anton	*Graphic Designer*
Sally Baker	*Subject Librarian, Education and Social Sciences*
Hilary Canneaux	*Course Manager*
John Clarke	*Professor of Social Policy*
Jonathan Davies	*Graphic Design Co-ordinator*
Margaret Dickens	*Print Buying Co-ordinator*
Clive Emsley	*Professor of History, Arts*
Janis Gilbert	*Graphic Artist*
Peggotty Graham	*Staff Tutor, Social Sciences*
Fiona Harris	*Editor, Social Sciences*
Celia Hart	*Picture Researcher*
Gordon Hughes	*Lecturer in Social Policy*
Liz Freeman	*Copublishing Adviser*
Nicole Jones	*Course Secretary*
Mary Langan	*Senior Lecturer in Social Policy*
Patti Langton	*Producer, BBC/OUPC*
Eugene McLaughlin	*Senior Lecturer in Criminology and Social Policy*
John Muncie	*Senior Lecturer in Criminology and Social Policy (Course Team Chair)*
Doreen Pendlebury	*Course Secretary*
Winifred Power	*Editor, Social Sciences*
Roger Sapsford	*Reader in Psychology, University of Teesside*
Esther Saraga	*Staff Tutor, Social Sciences*
Mercia Seminara	*Producer, BBC/OUPC*
Richard Skellington	*Project Officer, Social Sciences*
Alison Tucker	*Producer, BBC/OUPC*
Emma Wheeler	*Project Control*
Chris Wooldridge	*Editor, Social Sciences*

Consultant Authors

Sean Damer	*Honorary Research Fellow, University of Glasgow*
Loraine Gelsthorpe	*Lecturer in Criminology, University of Cambridge*
Paul Gordon	*Academic Consultant, London*
Victor Jupp	*Head of Sociology, University of Northumbria*
Jim Sharpe	*Professor of History, University of York*
Richard Sparks	*Professor of Criminology, University of Keele*
Sandra Walklate	*Professor of Sociology, Manchester Metropolitan University*
Louise Westmarland	*Lecturer in Criminology, Scarman Centre, University of Leicester*

External Assessors and Examiners

Pat Carlen	*Professor of Criminology, University of Bath (Course Assessor: 1st editions)*
Victor Jupp	*Head of Sociology, University of Northumbria (Book Assessor)*
Tony Jefferson	*Professor of Criminology, University of Keele (Course Assessor: 2nd editions)*
Ken Pease	*Professor of Criminology, University of Huddersfield (Course Examiner)*
Sandra Walklate	*Professor of Sociology, Manchester Metropolitan University (Course Examiner)*

Tutor Panel

Tom Burden	*Policy Research Unit, Leeds Metropolitan University*
Hilary Hiram	*School of Law, University of Glasgow*
Marilyn Woolfson	*Open University Associate Lecturer, London*

Controlling
CRIME

Edited by

Eugene McLaughlin
and John Muncie

Los Angeles | London | New Delhi
Singapore | Washington DC

in association with

The Open
University

This book is the second in a series published by Sage Publications in association with
The Open University.

The Problem of Crime
edited by John Muncie and Eugene McLaughlin

Controlling Crime
edited by Eugene McLaughlin and John Muncie

Criminological Perspectives: A Reader
edited by John Muncie, Eugene McLaughlin and Mary Langan

The books are part of The Open University course D315 *Crime, Order and Social Control.* Details
of this and other Open University courses can be obtained from the Call Centre, PO Box 724,
The Open University, Milton Keynes MK7 6ZS, United Kingdom: tel. +44(0)1908-653231,
e-mail ces-gen@open.ac.uk. Alternatively, you may visit The Open University website at
http://www.open.ac.uk where you can learn more about the wide range of courses and packs offered
at all levels by The Open University. For availability of other course components, including video- and
audio-cassette materials, contact Open University Worldwide Ltd, The Berrill Building, Walton Hall,
Milton Keynes MK7 6AA, United Kingdom: tel. +44 (0) 1908 858785; fax +44 (0) 1908-858787; e-mail
ouwenq@open.ac.uk; website http://www.ouw.co.uk.

SAGE Publications Ltd
1 Oliver's Yard
55 City Road
London EC1Y 1SP

SAGE Publications Inc.
2455 Teller Road
Thousand Oaks, California 91320

SAGE Publications India Pvt Ltd
B 1/I 1 Mohan Cooperative Industrial Area
Mathura Road
New Delhi 110 044

SAGE Publications Asia-Pacific Pte Ltd
33 Pekin Street #02-01
Far East Square
Singapore 048763

British Library Cataloguing in Publication data
A catalogue record for this book is available from The British Library.

ISBN 978-0-7619-6972-3
ISBN 978-0-7619-6973-0 (pbk)

Library of Congress Cataloging-in-Publication data
A catalogue record for this book has been requested.

Edited, designed and typeset by The Open University.

Printed by CPI Antony Rowe, Chippenham, Wiltshire

Mixed Sources
Product group from well-managed
forests and other controlled sources
www.fsc.org Cert no. SGS-COC-2953
© 1996 Forest Stewardship Council
FSC

Contents

Preface

This second edition of *Controlling Crime* is the second of three volumes in a series of criminology texts published by Sage in association with The Open University. The series, entitled *Crime, Order and Social Control*, explores key issues in the study of crime and criminal justice by examining the diverse and contested nature of crime, the varied formal and informal means designed to effect its control, and the multiplicity of approaches and interpretations that criminologists have brought to bear on this study. Each volume introduces readers to different aspects of the complex bodies of knowledge that make up contemporary criminology. By emphasizing diversity – both in the nature of criminological knowledge and in its object of study – the series engages with stereotypical representations of the extent and causes of crime and of the rationales and practices of criminal justice. Above all, we maintain that the study of crime cannot be divorced from the study of how the social is ordered and reproduced. Definitions of crime, and the ways in which it is understood and responded to, are contingent on the interplay of social, political and economic circumstances.

The main aim of these second editions is to continue to chart and re-conceptualize the parameters of a contemporary criminological imagination. They provide an interdisciplinary overview of 'classic' and current scholarly work in crime, criminal justice and criminology by drawing on the approaches and modes of analysis found in such subjects as sociology, social policy, psychology, socio-legal studies, gender studies, social geography and political science. This again alerts us to the potentially disparate and diverse nature of our subject matter and to ongoing disputes about the 'proper' constitution of the discipline of criminology.

The first volume, *The Problem of Crime*, is a critical and comprehensive examination of the complex and multi-faceted ways in which 'crime' is defined and theorized. This volume, *Controlling Crime*, offers detailed consideration of the changing and expanding parameters of criminal justice. The third, *Criminological Perspectives: A Reader*, narrates and explores the interdisciplinary bodies of knowledge that are constitutive of criminology and is designed as an essential sourcebook for the other volumes. Each is distinctive, not only in its chosen subject matter, but also because, unlike a majority of edited collections, it is primarily intended as a resource to facilitate student understanding of the distinctiveness of criminology as an academic discipline and its relations with other social sciences.

To this end, this volume has been designed as a fully illustrated interactive teaching text. The chapters should be read sequentially, as each builds on those that have gone before, and each concludes with suggestions for further and more in-depth reading. The following features have also been built into the overall structure of the book:

- activities: these are exercises to encourage students to work through the text, in order to test their understanding and develop skills in critical thinking.

- review questions: these are designed to encourage the reader to pause and reflect back on what has just been studied;

- key concepts: concepts that are core to each chapter and central to the study of criminology are highlighted in the margins.

In addition, the majority of chapters include a number of readings – topical newspaper articles and extracts from important academic books and articles – which are integral to the discussion as it develops and are designed both to encourage self-reflection and to aid in the application of central criminological ideas and concepts to contemporary issues, debates and trends. While each volume in the series is self-contained, there are also a number of references back and forward to the other volumes, and for those readers who wish to use the books for an integrated exploration of issues in crime, criminal justice and criminology, the references to chapters in the other volumes are printed in bold type. The aim of all these organizational features is to help readers to examine and think through the principal arguments not only of each chapter, but of each book and the series as a whole.

The form and content of this volume – and the series – have been made possible not simply through the work of its editors and chapter authors, but through the collective endeavours of an Open University Course Team. Each chapter has been substantially revised from the first edition whereby content and argument have been updated and teaching strategy modified and refined. In this respect, we are indebted to our consultants, tutor-testers and assessors who have given invaluable advice; a course manager who, against all the odds, has ensured that all our efforts have been co-ordinated and that deadlines have been met; course secretaries who have suffered more than most from being asked to do the impossible; and a supportive team of production editors, designers, graphic artists and media librarians who have made sure that the quality of the first editions has been maintained and enhanced. Gillian Stern and Miranda Nunhofer at Sage have been a constant source of support and encouragement. We thank them all.

John Muncie
(on behalf of The Open University Course Team)

Introduction:
the shifting parameters of crime control

Eugene McLaughlin and John Muncie

In the UK in the period immediately following the Second World War, concerted efforts were made to remove the highly emotive question of what to do about crime from the formal political arena. In the wake of this depoliticization it was left to a group of professional experts to formulate what might be described as the social democratic welfarist 'canon' of effective crime control. This perspective proclaimed that the state should concentrate on tackling the societal roots of crime, most notably poverty, unemployment, poor housing, educational disadvantage and dysfunctional family and community formations. Diversion, decriminalization, welfare, treatment and rehabilitation, rather than criminalization, imprisonment and punishment, would be the 'domain assumptions' guiding the criminal justice system (see Chapter 6). This would apply particularly to juvenile offenders who were viewed, by and large, as victims of circumstances beyond their control. Despite the fact that the various agencies were encased in Victorian bureaucratic structures (see Chapters 1 and 4), radical systemic reform was ruled out. Rather, they would undergo a process of pragmatic, gradual and incremental rationalization and professionalization for three reasons. First, it was still believed that the British criminal justice system was the fairest in the world. Second, radical structural reform could upset all notions of operational autonomy and political impartiality. And, finally, the criminal justice agencies would have a limited role to play as the UK made the transition towards a projected 'golden age' of civic order, stability and pro-social behaviour.

With the unfolding of the 1960s and 1970s – the decades of discontent – the social democratic vision of a crime-free society turned into a quagmire of watered-down policies, uneasy compromises, professional disagreements, organizational rivalries, unintended consequences, trenchant critiques and disappointing outcomes. Radical criminology questioned the 'foundational truths' of the social democratic model by arguing that the state interventions constituted more of a problem than a solution to the question of crime. Those promising effective crime control were raising false societal hopes and expectations that could never be fulfilled. The market for formal crime control was significantly determined by public reporting and police investigative and recording practices. These practices constructed and maintained the parameters of 'crime'. To the extent that such identification of crime was partial and highly selective, formal crime control reproduced the fiction that it was in the business of controlling all crime. Self-evidently, the energies and resources of the state's 'control system' constituted a narrowly focused spotlight on particular types of offence and offender. Furthermore, state interventions inevitably (if unintentionally) labelled and stigmatized, setting in process further deviance and criminality which justified, in turn, the expansion of the boundaries and capacities of a multi-layered 'social control' apparatus.

During the 1970s, 'crime', in a variety of guises, was repoliticized and increasingly came to occupy a central place in public consciousness and political discourse. For example, the recorded crime rate in England and Wales, driven by young offenders, almost doubled. There was serious public disorder in the form of repeated clashes between extra-parliamentary right and left and the anarchistic actions of a confrontational counter-culture. Trade unions defied court rulings and caused turmoil by mounting unofficial wildcat strikes. Every major city developed racially defined localities which, it was argued, were beyond the rule of the law. The IRA's bombing campaign introduced new unpredictable risks to public safety. All of this fed into broader fears and concerns about a society whose citizenry was being repeatedly victimized by vandalism, incivilities, indiscipline, rowdiness and extremism. Public commentary began to link these disparate issues and to present a picture of a brutalized, forbidding society teetering on the verge of collapse, with the state seemingly paralysed, incapable or unwilling to reimpose law and order and protect the rights and freedoms of law-abiding individuals.

The run-up to the 1979 general election witnessed the construction of an 'authoritarian populist' 'New Right' discourse which rested on cherished memories of a safer, more orderly society and a hard-hitting analysis on how to wrest society back from the criminals, terrorists, strikers, muggers and hooligans. The root causes of crime and disorder were located firmly with the criminal 'other' who had been aided and abetted by the 'sugar spin' storylines of the so-called experts and professionals. These 'social engineers' were blamed for promulgating irresponsible policies which had sought to erase all notions of human wickedness, right and wrong, self-discipline, personal responsibility and shame; and undermined the core institutional arrangements and cultural precepts that were the essential source of social order, discipline and shared moral meaning. The Conservative Party made crime control an ideological battleground by promising that if elected they would, as a matter of priority:

- restore the 'rule of law' to its rightful position in British society;
- recentre individual free-will, guilt, just deserts, deterrence and punishment;
- rebalance the interests and needs of victims of crime against the rights of offenders;
- replace the welfarist 'culture of excuses', which positively encouraged criminality and violence, with a common-sense moral code which would condemn law-breaking without exception;
- roll back the morass of moral relativism and re-establish the absolute boundary between right and wrong;
- free the criminal justice agencies from the disempowering influences of welfare professionals and ideologies, and provide them with powers, resources and state patronage necessary to unleash a war against crime.

There is no doubt that the Conservatives' election pledge of 1979 was honoured in full. The New Right ideology that elsewhere stipulated that state intervention in the public sphere (for example, in housing, health and welfare) was misguided, because it acted to deny self-responsibility and violated individual rights, remained absent initially from debates about criminal justice. There is considerable evidence to give substance to the claim that law and order was the hallowed no-go area for public expenditure cuts. In the first half of the 1980s total funding on the police increased by almost 40 per cent. An extra 14,000 personnel were recruited by police forces and individual officers were awarded pay rises of approximately 16 per cent in real terms. In the same time period there was an 85 per cent increase in prison expenditure; prison-building was earmarked as a government growth area with the commitment to build 16 new penal institutions at a cost of £360 million.

Unprecedented systemic empowerment was also forthcoming under Conservative patronage. The police were equipped with contentious powers (see Chapter 2). Magisterial powers, in determining type and length of custodial sentence (particularly for juveniles), were increased by the Criminal Justice Acts of 1982 and 1988 (see Chapters 3 and 6). The courts were encouraged to hand out longer sentences and the adult prison population in England and Wales first peaked at 50,000 in 1988: thus ensuring the highest rate of imprisonment per capita in Europe (see Chapter 5). It was because of such developments, and the promise that the strong state would erect a 'barrier of steel' to protect the honest citizen from the nefarious 'enemies within', that the 1980s have been characterized by radical and liberal criminologists as a period of increasing authoritarianism, coercion, repression and criminalization.

Despite the emphasis on law and order and the vigorous crusade to cut crime, it is difficult to regard the outcome of such hardline policies as a success. The rhetoric and policies of 'discipline and punishment' seemed to do little to halt a 'rising tide' of criminality and lawlessness. The recorded crime rate escalated to an unprecedented level during the 1980s, whilst the police clear-up rate fell. The inability of criminal justice policy to reduce the crime rate was also highlighted by failures in the 'deterrent' value of a punitive prison system. Despite tougher sentences – epitomized by the 'short, sharp shock' – just under a half of adult prisoners and two-thirds of young prisoners were reconvicted within two years of release. The first years of Conservative rule also witnessed nationwide inner-city riots and clashes between police and trade unionists in various industrial disputes.

UK society became painfully aware of the economic costs of crime. Legitimate businesses complained about the impact of a flourishing illegal economy in stolen goods. Hospitals, general practitioners and employers protested about the costs of supporting victims of crime. Local authorities had to divert scarce resources to combating vandalism on public housing estates. House and car owners were confronted with spiralling insurance premiums to cover escalating theft and burglary. Fear of crime and communal insecurity became just as important a public reality as crime itself.

There was a corresponding 'loss of faith' in the fairness and impartiality of the criminal justice system, particularly in the aftermath of the Guildford Four, Maguire Seven, Birmingham Six, Tottenham Three and Cardiff Three acquittals. Surveys reported that such miscarriages of justice had caused the public to lose confidence in the police and to believe that the judiciary was unrepresentative and out of touch with society and that it discriminated against defendants from minority ethnic backgrounds. At a more everyday level, concern was also expressed about the lack of sentencing consistency in the courts, with reports pointing out that the chance of immediate imprisonment depended not so much on the offence, but on the ethnic background and gender of the defendant and on where in the country the case was heard. By the beginning of the 1990s, with the appointment of a Royal Commission, it was the criminal justice system itself that was on trial (see Chapter 3).

The political reverberations of this 'failure to deliver' and downward spiral of support for the criminal justice system compelled the Conservative government to rethink its law and order policies and the uncritical public support it had traditionally given to the prison-centred criminal justice system. As a result, a strategy was unveiled which attempted to redefine the ownership of the crime problem and promote managerialist solutions.

Part of the response to the failure of a tough law and order stance was a gradual withdrawal from wider philosophical and macro-level debates about the causes of crime and the purpose of criminal justice policies. Home Office officials informed the public at every opportunity that extreme caution was needed in 'reading' crime statistics because, despite media representations, most crime is petty in nature and the UK remains a relatively crime-free society. In addition, a certain level of crime was viewed as normal and inevitable and it was therefore seen as unrealistic to expect any set of policies to reduce the crime rate drastically. What governments could do, according to this new 'normalization of crime' orthodoxy, was to work with the community in order to lessen the opportunistic crime rate, and the fear of crime, to manageable and acceptable levels. As a consequence, the message was that the public and other social agencies would have to 'join up' in the war against preventable crime.

The public was told that it must recognize that the sources of crime and its control lie, first and foremost, in the actions of individual citizens and local communities. Shared responsibility and individual self-discipline and self-help were stressed through the 'target hardening' and fortification of homes and businesses and in the presumed greater security offered by membership of Neighbourhood Watch schemes. With the emergence of community safety, police community liaison and community punishment, responsibility for crime control was relocated to the realm of private citizenship (see Chapters 6 and 7). Primary blame was attached to 'careless' victims, especially repeat victims, who were lax in their efforts to prevent crime (whether it was a failure to protect their property adequately, or in learning to avoid dangerous situations) and to an anti-social 'underclass' who were failing to meet their moral obligations as parents and citizens. There was also the suggestion that the fight against the criminal 'other' could be the basis for the creation and maintenance of local social solidarity.

By the late 1980s private self-help efforts were also supplemented and augmented by inter-agency approaches to crime and prevention. The Home Office redoubled its efforts to devolve and disperse frontline management of crime to other social agencies. Safer Cities and Crime Concern projects had as their common aim, for example, the creation of partnerships between local authorities, local businesses, voluntary organizations and statutory agencies, which would restructure institutional knowledge in order to identify patterns and trends and prepare effective policies and localized micro-level strategies to design out crime and reduce the fear of some crime (see Chapter 7). These shifts in rhetoric and practice revealed both a reworking of state responsibility for crime control matters and the attempted removal of questions of crime, criminality and punishment from the political and moral arena.

Given the nature of this strategy, it looked initially as if the criminal justice agencies would remain immune from public demands that they be held to account for their self-evident failures in preventing or controlling crime. However, by the late 1980s the seeming incapability or unwillingness of the various agencies to respond to increasing criticism and to put their own houses in order persuaded the Conservatives to open up the criminal justice system to the investigations of the Public Accounts Committee, the National Audit Office and the Audit Commission. As a consequence, law and order would no longer be exempted from the processes of fiscal accountability, performance measurements and strict controls on expenditure (see Chapters 2, 3, 5 and 6).

A series of managerial, actuarial and legislative reviews and directives in the late 1980s and early 1990s signalled the Conservatives' commitment to this approach. By the mid-1990s numerous Audit Commission reports had been completed on various aspects of police structure and practice, the probation service, the magistrates' courts, the Crown Prosecution Service, the youth justice system, Legal Aid schemes and the Prison Service. The recommendations emanating from these sector-by-sector reviews acted as a stimulus for further inquiries because they uncovered the need for ever deeper change to resolve problems of chronic under-management. Reform and reinvention were to be achieved within an overall framework of *continuous* organizational and operational restructuring, fiscal accountability and rationalization. The different agencies would have to justify their existence and re-imagine themselves in terms of competitiveness, core competencies, resource control, customer responsiveness, quality of service and cost-effectiveness. As a consequence, certain activities and tasks would be centralized while others would be devolved. Since the requirement for market testing and innovation would be ever present, some activities would be contracted out, 'disaggregated' or privatized (see Chapters 2 and 5). Such changes had considerable implications for working practices and, perhaps more significantly, the conditions of service of the workforce, in core criminal justice agencies, because they necessitated the displacement of the old quasi-military models of public administration on which the criminal justice system was founded (see Chapters 1 and 4). Instead, 'transparent' management systems would be put in place internally and strenuous efforts made to managerialize the different agencies involved. This transformatory process involved introducing new conceptions and strategies of control and disciplining of the workforce and new managerial ideas about how to produce and manage organizational and cultural change.

The overall purpose of this ongoing sea change in policy was to create a cost-effective, efficient and dovetailed criminal justice system where strategic and operational roles, responsibilities and accountabilities were clarified. Within this overarching 'task environment' the professional remit of the agencies would be to work together within nationally agreed sets of guidelines and standards to deliver a specific product — 'justice' – for their customers, whilst also ensuring that demands for the product were kept within economically manageable levels. Hence, the police, the Crown Prosecution Service and the courts would have the role of ensuring the detection and conviction of the guilty by meeting strict procedural rules of evidence (see Chapters 2 and 3); the private and public Prison Service would treat prisoners with humanity and decency (see Chapter 5); and the probation service and youth justice workers should deliver cheaper but tough and effective sentences in the community (see Chapter 6). A start to such rationalization was made in the 1991 Criminal Justice Act which formalized 'just deserts', proportionate sentencing and community-based sentences as the most effective and justifiable means to achieve 'economy and justice' (see Chapters 3 and 6). A focus on 'deeds' rather than 'needs' formally expunged many of the last vestiges of social democratic welfarism from the system, but at least held the promise of a new era of rational policy making and consistent practices.

However, even before the new 'settlement' was put into practice it came under intense attack. Senior members of the judiciary, magistrates and police officers voiced grave misgivings about the removal of professional discretion. Not surprisingly, the attempt to inject new managerial ideas also provoked considerable resistance from criminal justice professionals who argued that criminal justice – a public sector good – could not be run or managed like a business selling products to customers in a competitive market. During 1992–93 the nature of the law and order debate in Britain shifted dramatically. Against the backdrop of the highest recorded crime levels in western Europe, an escalating tabloid panic about the seemingly relentless surge in youth crime, and increasingly conflictual relations between the Conservatives and core criminal justice professionals, Tony Blair, then shadow Home Secretary, found the critical political and moral space to present New Labour as the party of law and order.

In January 1993, in the context of a media panic about 'Britain's deepening law and order crisis', the sound bite 'tough on crime and tough on the causes of crime' was coined by Blair to signal a new (later termed 'Third Way') approach to law and order. In various speeches and position papers presented in the aftermath of the James Bulger murder, the importance of moving beyond ideologically blinkered old left and New Right understandings of the problem of crime was spelt out. Blair argued that rising crime rates were not inevitable and that the restoration of law and order could be achieved by rebuilding the foundations of a strong civic society through self-regulating and re-moralized, cohesive communities. Central to this was the re-establishment of the communitarian values of mutual obligation, self-discipline and parental responsibility (see Chapter 6). 'Old' Labour's liberal and welfarist thinking on penal affairs would have to be 'modernized' by giving equal rights to victims and witnesses and the needs of law-abiding citizens. Individuals would be held responsible for their own behaviour and be given their 'just deserts' if they committed a criminal offence. Blair's determination to play the crime card for electoral advantage in a highly volatile political context stoked an emergent Conservative backlash. At the Conservative Party conference in October 1993, the ever-more-desperate Home Secretary Michael Howard vacated the centre ground of British criminal justice politics and shifted government policy resolutely to the right, unveiling a 27-point law and order package of new criminal sanctions, tough minimum sentences and mass incarceration. With the appointment of Jack Straw as shadow Home Secretary in 1994 it became apparent that New Labour was willing to go to considerable lengths to 'out-tough' the Conservative government on law and order issues. For example, in order to undercut politically the impact of the recorded crime rate which had begun to fall in 1994 (and continued to do so for much of the decade), Straw attempted to expand the debate about the 'crime crisis' by highlighting the need to implement 'zero-tolerance' policing strategies to tackle what he described as a rising tide of 'low level' disorder, incivility and anti-social behaviour (see Chapter 2). Furthermore, New Labour lent tacit parliamentary support to increasingly illiberal Conservative proposals contained in the Crime (Sentences) Act 1997 and the Police Act 1997. The reward for this 'new realist' crusade against crime and disorder and the tailoring of its policies towards 'Middle England' was a series of opinion polls which indicated that, for the first time in the post-war period, New Labour was consistently ahead of the Conservatives on the issue of law and order.

On coming to power in 1997, New Labour's approach to governance was epitomized by the concept of 'modernization'. New Labour took on board the thesis that the capacities of the nation state must be 'modernized' so that it can manage and regulate, rather than be submerged by, the social, cultural and economic changes wrought by the 'new global order'. New Labour's long-term programme of state reform acknowledged that the Conservatives' managerial reform process of the late 1980s and early 1990s was a necessary act of modernization that improved productivity and delivered better value for money and enhanced quality of service. As a result it instigated a 'new wave' of managerialism across the public sector. In the case of criminal justice, a deepening of managerialization was necessary for two reasons: first, to 'resolve' the contradictions and tensions generated by the Conservatives' uneven and differentiated criminal justice reform project; and second, to ensure that its 'flagship' criminal justice legislation, the 1998 Crime and Disorder Act, could stand as the basis for 'the most coordinated and coherent attack on crime in a generation' (see Chapters 3 and 6). The objectives for the criminal justice system as established in the 1998 Act were to:

■ draw a line under the 'failures' of past decades;

■ reduce crime and disorder and fear of crime and disorder and their social and economic costs;

■ dispense justice fairly and efficiently and promote confidence in the rule of law;

■ establish a defining principle of the criminal justice system to prevent offending and re-offending, particularly of children and young persons;

■ force young offenders and their parents to take responsibility for offending behaviour;

■ deploy early proactive interventions for those thought likely to offend;

■ implement fast-track, efficient procedures from arrest to sentence;

■ build partnerships both between the various criminal and youth justice agencies and between these agencies and other public, private and voluntary organizations.

Virtually every Home Office document stressed that this would be achieved through continual auditing, setting priorities and targets, monitoring, evaluation and inspection. 'Modernization', then, institutionalized the processes of managerialism established by the Conservatives. The criminal justice system was subjected to an unprecedented expenditure review and forced to operate with strategic and business plans with specified aims, objectives, performance measures, efficiency targets and clearly defined outcomes. League tables on various aspects of police performance became commonplace. Local authorities were empowered by law to audit their crime and disorder reduction strategies and budgets to comply with the new ethos of 'best value'. Individual police forces were set five-year targets to reduce burglary and car crime. Further resources were made contingent on such targets being met (see Chapter 2). Courts were ordered to reduce the time taken between the prosecution and sentencing of offenders (see Chapter 3). New penal establishments were to be built with private money and run by the private sector (see Chapter 5). All of this was intended to raise levels of performance and monitoring within a new conception of criminal justice based on 'what works'. As a result, in place of 'old' criminal justice bureau professionalism, New Labour hoped that a series of realigned operational agencies would emerge whose performance was dominated by the requirements to produce measurable and quantifiable outputs and outcomes.

New Labour's first term in office was also marked by re-inventions of some familiar themes of the past. As well as managerialism, New Labour's crime control politics incorporated:

- *just deserts* – the erosion of mitigating circumstances (such as age) by focusing on the gravity of the offence and formulating a proportionate response;

- *risk assessment* – acting on the possibility of future crime and on the non-criminal as well as the criminal, thus drawing younger populations into formal systems of control;

- *community responsibilization* – maintaining that certain families and communities are implicated in criminality and that they have a responsibility to put their own houses in order. If they 'fail', then stringent and intrusive community penalties are warranted, delivered by community-based multi-agency partnerships;

- *authoritarian populism* – the resort to criminalization and penalization to respond to and channel perceptions of public punitiveness for the purposes of political expediency and electoral gain;

- *restorative justice* – the attempt to increase offender awareness and ensure that offenders make amends to victims and communities.

Because of these disparate – and conflicting – aims it will not be possible to assess the full impact of New Labour's criminal justice reform programme for several years. It is certainly not clear how the strains within and between managerialism, community responsibilization, restorative justice and authoritarian populism will play out. As the chapters in this book indicate, criminal justice in the UK also faces a series of unprecedented challenges. The criminal justice system is now in the process of institutionalizing complex crime problems such as domestic, sexual and racist violence. However, it will also have to incorporate emergent social harms brought to public attention by victims' interest groups. In the same moment it will have to respond constructively to ongoing campaigns for the decriminalization and depenalization of certain forms of 'consensual' action and behaviour. Criminal justice will also have to be provided with a coherent philosophical framework that can underpin practices appropriate for and representative of a multi-ethnic society. Finally, criminal justice will have to be reconnected to broader questions of social justice and human rights if the socio-economic causes of crime are to be addressed in a comprehensive and inclusive manner.

Further reading

Audit Commission (1996) *Misspent Youth: Young People and Crime*, Abingdon, Audit Commission Publications.

Audit Commission (1999) *Safety in Numbers: Promoting Community Safety*, Abingdon, Audit Commission Publications.

Bottoms, A. and Stevenson, S. (1992) 'What went wrong? Criminal justice policy in England and Wales, 1945–70', in Downes, D. (ed.) *Unravelling Criminal Justice*, London, Macmillan.

Bowling, B. (1999) *Violent Racism*, Oxford, Clarendon Press.

Brake, M. and Hale, C. (1992) *Public Order and Private Lives: The Politics of Law and Order*, London, Routledge.

Campbell, B. (1993) *Goliath: Britain's Dangerous Places*, London, Methuen.

Criminal Justice Review Group (2000) *Review of the Criminal Justice System in Northern Ireland*, Belfast, Stationery Office.

Downes, D. (1998) 'Toughing it out: from Labour opposition to Labour government', *Policy Studies*, vol.19, nos 3/4, pp.173–85.

Duff, P. and Hutton, N. (eds) (1999) *Criminal Justice in Scotland*, Aldershot, Ashgate/Dartmouth.

Goldblatt, P. and Lewis, C. (eds) (1998) *Reducing Offending: An Assessment of Research Evidence on Ways of Dealing with Offending Behaviour*, London, Home Office Research Study No.187.

Hall, S., Critcher, C., Jefferson, T., Clarke, J. and Roberts, B. (1978) *Policing the Crisis: Mugging, the State and Law and Order*, London, Macmillan.

Independent Commission on Policing for Northern Ireland (1999) *A New Beginning: Policing in Northern Ireland*, Belfast, Stationery Office.

Macpherson, Sir W. (1999) *The Stephen Lawrence Inquiry: Report of an Inquiry by Sir William Macpherson of Cluny*, Cm4262-I, London, Stationery Office.

Morris, T. (1989) *Crime and Criminal Justice in Britain Since 1945*, Oxford, Blackwell.

Muncie, J. (1999) *Youth and Crime: A Critical Introduction*, London, Sage.

Radford, J., Friedberg, M. and Harne, L. (eds) (2000) *Women, Violence and Strategies for Action*, Milton Keynes, Open University Press.

Reiner, R. (2000) 'Crime and control in Britain', *Sociology*, vol.34, no.1, pp.71–94.

Runnymede Trust (2000) *The Future of Multi-Ethnic Britain*, London, Profile Books.

Scraton, P. (ed.) (1987) *Law, Order and the Authoritarian State*, Milton Keynes, Open University Press.

Young, P. and Young, M. (1996) *Crime and Criminal Justice in Scotland*, Edinburgh, Scottish Office.

CHAPTER I

The Origins and Development of the Police

by Clive Emsley

Contents

1   Introduction

After working through this chapter, you should be able to make your own informed assessment of: first, the reasons behind the creation of police forces in Britain, particularly England and Wales; second, the role of these forces once created and the shifting patterns of local and central control; and third, the extent to which police development in Britain has been unique. You should note at the beginning of this discussion that using the generic term 'the police' can sometimes obscure the fact that there has never been a single police force in England, let alone Britain as a whole.

2   The origins of the British police

2.1   Contrasting interpretations

There is no single school of police history; the divisions between the different interpretations of the origins and development of the police in Britain tend to reflect the way in which different individuals and competing theoretical positions regard the police and their role in society. The modern, bureaucratic police had their origins in political debates and discussions, which inevitably ended in some compromises. The police developed partly as a result of legislation, as well as through administrative decisions and the emergence of working practices and strategic policies. Many of the contemporary debates about police accountability and policework that you will encounter in Chapter 2 have their origins in these earlier compromises and decisions.

ACTIVITY 1.1

Extract 1.1 shows how one of the earliest and most influential historians of the police in Britain accounts for their origins in terms of progress and advancement at the beginning of the nineteenth century. Extract 1.2, by contrast, adopts an alternative theoretical position that is more concerned with control and disciplinary aspects of the police role.

Read the two extracts now. As you do so, make notes on how Reith's interpretation of the origins of the police in Extract 1.1 differs from that of Storch in Extract 1.2.

Extract 1.1 Reith: 'The police idea'

… authority [was] faced at the [beginning of the nineteenth century] with the menace of increase of crime, part of the problem of which, in London alone, was the army of the homeless children, estimated at eight thousand, who lived by stealing and begging. Worse still was the constant menace of mob disorder, and the knowledge that the 'thin red line' of the Guards was all that stood, from day to day, between order and chaos, and that the dangers of using it as a defence made it unable to save the dignity of Parliament and its members from one humiliation after another, whenever the mobs of the town found occasion to assemble in its neighbourhood. The reports [of parliamentary committees] confirmed emphatically and unhelpfully, the corruption, disunity, and utter uselessness of the rabble of beadles, watchmen, deputy-constables, and undisciplined police officers whose function was the maintenance of order, and rejected with strong and forceful language the controlled organization which was the obvious and only remedy. …

Meanwhile, the state of affairs in London, serious as it was, had become only an item of the problem of crime and disorder which menaced authority from every part of the kingdom. The new town concentrations of population had become Londons of lesser size, with the same poverty and destitution, the same potential explosive properties, and the same deficiencies of power for the maintenance of order and the preservation of life and property. Both in towns and in the country-side the centuries-old organization of independent magistrate and parish constable was under pressure of the new phenomenon of vast mobs of desperate and starving men and women, springing up now here, now there, whenever a sudden jolt in the creaking and badly oiled new machinery of the Industrial Revolution deprived them of mass livelihood and drove them to mass despair.

(Reith, 1938, pp.188–9)

Extract 1.2 Storch: 'The policeman as domestic missionary'

Historians of the police, public order, and the criminal law have understandably concentrated on the role of the police in the repression of crime, public disorder, and popular political movements or have studied the police from the point of view of social administration. The police had a broader mission in the nineteenth century, however – to act as an all-purpose lever of urban discipline. The imposition of the police brought the arm of municipal and state authority directly to bear upon key institutions of daily life in working-class neighbourhoods, touching off a running battle with local custom and popular culture which lasted at least until the end of the century. Riots and strikes are by definition ephemeral episodes, but the monitoring and control of the streets, pubs, racecourses, wakes, and popular fêtes was a daily function of the 'new police'. It was in some part on this terrain that the quality of police–community relations in the second half of the nineteenth century was determined. In northern industrial towns of England these police functions must be viewed as a direct complement to the attempts of urban middle-class elites – by means of sabbath, educational, temperance, and recreational reform – to mould a labouring class amenable to new disciplines of work and leisure. The other side of the coin of middle-class voluntaristic moral and social reform (even when sheathed) was the policeman's truncheon. In this respect the policeman was perhaps every bit as important a 'domestic missionary' as the earnest and often sympathetic men high-minded Unitarians dispatched into darkest Leeds or Manchester in the 1830s and 1840s.

(Storch, 1976, p.481)

Reith was arguing the need for the establishment of an organized police force (namely the Metropolitan Police), though we might be tempted to suggest that 'mobs of desperate starving men and women' needed something rather different, and that menaces to 'authority' and threats to the 'dignity of Parliament' were less important than social problems such as poverty, destitution and unemployment. Reith's view of the origins of the police in Britain, though not that of a professional, academic historian, was in keeping with the Whig historiography of the period in which he was writing. Essentially this saw history as progressive, and for the Whig historians (and essentially this was a British school) the liberal British state and its institutions were at the forefront of progress. History was also largely concerned with 'great men'; in British history this meant those who were liberal, humanitarian, and farsighted enough to see how to develop progressive and necessary institutions. The nineteenth century was a particularly notable time for such men in the criminal justice system; they reformed the 'Bloody Code' of the eighteenth century, reformed the prisons, and established the police. Sir Robert Peel, the Tory Home Secretary for much of the 1820s and later prime minister, stood out among these 'great men' for his legal reforms and his creation of the Metropolitan Police in 1829.

There is no mention by Storch of any menace to authority or the dignity of parliament; the emphasis is on the need to control the new urban population – Reith's 'desperate and starving men and women' perhaps. While Reith sees the problem as one of crime and disorder, Storch describes the police as an institution established as another element in a broad strategy of 'control'.

Storch was the first of a generation of academic social historians to address the origins of the police and to develop a revisionist view. It might be argued against him that the parliamentary debates on policing in the first half of the century generally focused on the issues of public disorder and, above all, on the perception of increasing crime. Moreover, elites in several of the biggest industrial cities were, initially at least, strongly opposed to any suggestion from Westminster that they reorganize their policing systems along Metropolitan lines. Storch shows that the police played the role of 'domestic missionary' once they were on the streets, but it is not clear that this was a key reason for them being put on the streets in the first place.

Before the establishment of the police, policing depended on active magistrates, parish constables and night watchmen. These received a bad press from many nineteenth-century police reformers, and Reith, you will note from the paragraphs quoted above, accepted this criticism. Nor was Reith alone in this; for many years it was common for historians of the police to quote extracts from Shakespeare's comic constables – Dogberry and Verges in *Much Ado About Nothing* and Elbow in *Measure for Measure* – to imply, first, that Shakespeare was telling it how it was (rather than creating comic characters for dramatic effect) and, second, that nothing much changed, and rarely for the better, between 1600 and 1800. There were feeble magistrates, watchmen and constables in the seventeenth and eighteenth centuries, but there were also significant developments that took place over a longer time-scale than the old Whig school would have had us believe.

At the centre of these developments was London. It was a thriving capital and commercial city regarded with great pride, but also with increasing fear. Much of this fear was the result of London's size. This almost doubled during the eighteenth century, by the end of which it had a million inhabitants. This was almost a tenth

Whig historiography

revisionism

of the English population and made London roughly twice as big as Paris, the capital of a country with almost 30 million people. There were teeming slums within London's sprawl, and it was these that provoked fears of crime and disorder. No crime statistics were collected for Britain as a whole or for London in particular before 1810, but there was a belief among some leading magistrates, politicians and social commentators that crime was increasing and that the inhabitants of the poorer districts preferred idleness, with occasional expeditions for plunder to fulfil their desire for luxury, rather than an honest, frugal existence based on the proceeds of hard work.

In the middle of the eighteenth century Henry Fielding, the Bow Street magistrate perhaps better known as a novelist, differentiated between those who could not work and those who would not. At the end of the century Patrick Colquhoun, an active stipendiary magistrate lauded by the Whig historians of the police, fulminated against the 'extravagance, idleness and profligacy' of the poor, which they supported by 'gambling, cheating and thieving' (quoted in Emsley, 1996a, p.62). Coincidental with the fear of crime, there seems to have been an increasing belief that a new level of order and decorum needed to be established. Such a belief was linked with the emergent political economy espoused by a significant section of the ruling elite, which refused any sympathy for the old moral economy of the crowd. Popular disorder in the shape of a demonstration over the high cost of food was no longer seen as community political action, with the crowd drawing their social superiors' attention to their plight and the elite responding with subscriptions to reduce prices and the prosecution of hoarders and profiteers. Political economy demanded that the market be allowed to work freely, and that disorder be suppressed and not be understood and met half way: this meant that community action, while not legal before, was increasingly stigmatized as criminal (see **Sharpe, 2001**). The week-long mayhem of the Gordon Riots in London in 1780 was exceptional, but it burned itself into the memory of the respectable classes of what crowd action could become, and this memory was aggravated in the decade following 1789 both by the lurid accounts of massacres in Paris during the French Revolution and the appearance of British Jacobins urging reform on the French model.

Charles Rowe, a London watchman. Note the lantern, staff, cutlass and the rattle tucked into his cutlass strap. While Rowe is rather old in this picture, it must have been photographed some time after his retirement and the end of the watchmen in London – there were no photographs in 1829. Contrary to the declarations of the police reformers and Whig historians, some eighteenth- and early nineteenth-century vestries and parishes ensured that their watchmen were young and fit

Legislation in the early eighteenth century allowed parishes to reorganize their night watch. Increasingly, the metropolitan parishes took advantage of this to establish watches recruited from fit, relatively young men, and by the turn of the century the wealthier parishes actually had watchmen patrolling beats in greater numbers than the 'new police' when they were introduced (Paley, 1989).

Yet the best known of the eighteenth-century developments is the system established by Henry Fielding and his brother Sir John in Bow Street, with its thief-takers (the Bow Street Runners), patrols, information gathering and diffusion; there were also the police offices, stipendiary magistrates and their constables created for London in 1792 on the Bow Street model. However, it is wrong to assume, as the traditional Whig historians did, that the eighteenth-century developments led logically and inevitably to the Metropolitan Police. The Metropolitan Police's three thousand uniformed men, organized in a centralized, hierarchical and rigid body, were very different from the plain-clothes constables responsible to magistrates working out of the police offices, or the plain-clothes watchmen recruited by, answerable to, and paid for by local parishes. Parish watches in London were abolished with the creation of the 'new police', but the old police offices continued to function for another decade, and there was considerable friction throughout the 1830s between the stipendiaries and their constables on the one hand and Metropolitan policemen on the other (Reynolds, 1998).

2.2 Creating the Metropolitan Police

Sir Robert Peel:
'I want to teach people that liberty does not consist in having your house robbed by organized gangs of thieves and in leaving the principal streets of London in the nightly possession of drunken women and vagabonds'

If the gradual changes in policing during the eighteenth century in London can be said to be the result of a new threshold for public order and increasing anxiety about the city's growth and its poorer inhabitants, there is still the need to explain the actual occasion of the creation of the very new style of police in 1829. Without subscribing to the 'great man' view of history, it can be argued that Peel's role was critical.

When Peel was appointed Home Secretary in 1822 he expressed his determination to rationalize and reform the criminal code. He already had experience of organizing a police system in the very different circumstances of Ireland, and he made it clear that he considered the creation of a preventive police force for England as central to any reform of the justice system. Key legal reforms were carried through by the middle of the 1820s, but police reform was delayed by suspicion of the idea of police. However, Peel persevered and limited to London what appear to have been original hopes for a national system. He created some uniformed constables for Bow Street in 1822, and in 1828 established a parliamentary select committee with men who shared his ideas. Not surprisingly the committee recommended in favour of a police force for London. Astute politician that he was, Peel adjusted the proposal by omitting the square mile of the

City of London from the subsequent Bill – the powerful men of the commercial capital were jealous of their independence and might well have wielded enough political clout to defeat it. In his speech introducing the Bill, Peel argued that a preventive police was needed to stem the increase in crime, yet it is possible that the figures for committals which he cited (there were no figures for 'reported crime') showed an increase because his legal reforms were making prosecution easier and were consequently bringing more people before the courts. Nevertheless, parliament was convinced, the Bill became law, and the first Metropolitan constables began patrolling the streets in September 1829.

The new threshold of order was not something confined to the thinking of men in London: most government ministers responsible for fostering the new political economy had their country seats and sometimes served as county magistrates. But they also had a faith in the superiority of English institutions, and they rejected the notions of centralization to be found both in the France of the old regime, which had served as the model state for most of the absolutist monarchs of eighteenth-century Europe, and in the France of the Revolution and Napoleon, which provided a model for administrators even in those states of continental Europe which fought Napoleon. Large police organizations existed both under the old regime and under Napoleon, and these included significant political and military elements, both of which were anathema to the English ruling elite's perception of English liberty and constitutionalism. The concerns about spies and militarized *gendarmes* continued to underpin much hostility to the idea of police in England, and also influenced the way in which the English police developed.

Cartoon from The Political Drama, *no. 11, June–July 1833. The original caption read: 'Reviewing the Blue Devils, alias the Raw Lobsters, alias the Bludgeon Men'*

2.3   Creating the provincial police

The Whig interpretation argues that the Metropolitan Police were such a success that the model was introduced into the incorporated boroughs by the Municipal Corporations Act of 1835 and into the counties by the Rural Constabulary Acts of 1839 and 1840. Certainly the Metropolitan Police did provide a model for provincial police reformers during the 1830s and 1840s, but it was only one model among several. These reformers were motivated by similar concerns to those in London, and there were experiments even before the creation of the Metropolitan Police.

An Act of parliament in 1829, predating the Metropolitan Police Act, established a system of professional constables for Cheshire designed to work under the county magistrates, to supervise the parish constables and to link with the police systems of the nearby industrial areas. Unemployment and disturbances among miners in Shropshire led the Quarter Sessions of that county to consider following Cheshire's lead in 1830 and 1831. Associations for the prosecution of felons and some small units of local government were also recruiting professional constables to carry out patrols and pursue offenders. It could be argued that the clauses of the Municipal Corporations Act which required the creation of watch committees to establish and supervise police forces were, like the rest of the Act, simply rationalizing the system of local government. Mayors and corporations had always had responsibility for policing their city or town; some had taken the responsibility more seriously than others and had already established police patrols under special legislation or general Acts. The Act of 1835 required that they all organize along the same lines.

The legislation of 1839 and 1840 followed on the heels of the Report of the Royal Commission on Constabulary (1836–39), which had recommended the creation of a national police. The traditional view has always been that the driving force behind police reform during the 1830s were the Benthamite reformers and, in particular, Edwin Chadwick, who was a key figure in both the inquiry into the Poor Law, which reported in 1834, and the Royal Commission on Constabulary. However, recent research shows that the government of Lord Grey, which came to power in 1830, went so far as to draw up a Bill for a national police system in 1832. The Bill eventually sank under the weight of events surrounding the Great Reform Act of that year, together with doubts about the ability of persuading parliament and local authorities to accept it, particularly the costs associated with a national system and the impact on local autonomy (Philips and Storch, 1994). The 1839 Act, and the amending Act of 1840, ignored both the national proposals of 1832 and those of the Royal Commission, and left matters to the magistrates who ran local government. It empowered county benches to create a

Manchester police on parade, 1845

constabulary if they so wished. Some did, but others did not, and during the 1840s there were continuing experiments to develop and improve the old parish constable system, most notably with the creation of professional superintendents to oversee and co-ordinate.

1839 was also a year of Chartist disorder. It is possible that this acted as a spur to the reforms overall, and it did have an influence in the development of policing systems in three burgeoning industrial urban areas which, since they were not incorporated boroughs, had been uninfluenced by the 1835 requirements. Three separate Acts of parliament established police in Birmingham, Bolton and Manchester, where Chartism appeared a powerful force and where local administrative rivalries had brought at worst friction and at best inertia. The police in the three towns were organized, initially, under government-appointed commissioners. They were passed on to local government control in the early 1840s when they were felt to be running efficiently and effectively.

By the middle of the nineteenth century there were several different models of police functioning in England, ranging from the Metropolitan Police in London to the revived parish constables in some counties who were now supervised by professional superintendents. **models of police**

Further legislation was enacted in 1856 in the form of the County and Borough Police Act. This Act made it obligatory for all counties and boroughs to set up uniformed, bureaucratic, hierarchical police forces rather than reorganize the traditional parish system (a few of the smaller incorporated boroughs had still not complied with the 1835 legislation) and it established a national inspectorate to assess the efficiency of the forces once created.

Another forceful Home Secretary was behind the 1856 Act. Lord Palmerston served only briefly at the Home Office before becoming prime minister and handing over to Sir George Grey, but it was long enough for him to support the appointment of a select committee on police whose membership and witnesses appear, in general, to have been men sympathetic to the new models. It is perhaps significant that while the county of Kent had been the driving force behind the legislation reforming and reorganizing the old parish constable system, there were no witnesses called from Kent; however, the chair of the committee, the member for the Kentish port of Dover, was strongly in favour of the new police. Yet the reformers did not have it all their own way. The initial Bill brought forward by Palmerston in 1854 provoked massive hostility in the boroughs by proposing that henceforth the Home Secretary draw up their police regulations and that the smaller forces be amalgamated with the surrounding counties; the proposed amalgamation of the police of the five smallest counties with their larger neighbours also provoked fury. The offending clauses were dropped from the Bill introduced by Grey two years later. The second Bill also won support with its proposal that the central government would contribute one quarter of the cost of pay and clothing for forces deemed efficient by a new police inspectorate. It is probable that other events contributed to the Bill's success, though any precise assessment is, of course, impossible. For example, transportation had virtually ended in 1853, and there was concern about dangerous offenders who had once been shipped to the other side of the world now being released from prison into the community on a ticket-of-leave. The fall of Sebastopol in September 1855 meant the end of the Crimean War, with the return of much of the army to Britain, and while Victorians may have gloried in the feats of British redcoats overseas, they could be equally concerned about their habits at home, especially when demobilized.

2.4 Policing the Celts

Wales had been fully integrated with England since the Tudors, and the police legislation described above was equally applicable there. Police reform in Scotland followed a similar pattern, though there had been organized, military-style police in Edinburgh and Glasgow from the beginning of the nineteenth century, and Scottish law continued to maintain its separate identity.

Ireland, united with the British crown in 1801, was different. In England the magistracy prided itself on its independence, its ability to run local affairs and to cope in times of disorder. While as a last resort they might call in troops to suppress disorder, they were also known to meet and negotiate with rioters and to persuade them to return to their homes. The Irish gentry modelled themselves on their English counterparts, but their circumstances were very different. Often, though not always, they were divided from those who worked the land by both religion and language. They, like most of their English counterparts, regarded the Irish peasantry as a primitive race. But unlike the English rural magistracy, the Irish gentry showed themselves totally incapable of responding to, and coping with, disorder; and disorder in Ireland in the shape of occasional full-scale rebellion as well as continual agrarian unrest – sometimes manifesting itself in appalling violence – seemed endemic. The close of the eighteenth century saw a succession of policing experiments in both Dublin and the countryside. Disorder in the early part of the nineteenth century led Peel, as Chief Secretary for Ireland, to establish the Peace Preservation Force, which was gradually reshaped into the centralized, armed, *gendarmerie*-style Royal Irish Constabulary. Dublin was excluded from this system, but it too was given a centralized police. The concern here was not an ineffective gentry, but the influence of Catholic priests and 'demagogues' who, it was feared, might gain control of the police if Dublin were permitted the local government control allowed in the English and Scottish boroughs.

Was it inevitable that a professional police force would be established in the early nineteenth century? Was the root cause for the creation of the police: crime; fear of disorder/revolution; or was it a logical development of the expanding role of the state? The smug historian's response is that nothing is inevitable in history. Furthermore, it might be argued that there was no reason why police reform took the direction it did.

Why wasn't there greater interest in, and reorganization of, the old parish constable system? Why wasn't there a determined decision to take the bull by the horns and create a national police? Of course, we cannot measure any precise increase in crime or disorder, though fear that these were increasing probably fed into decisions to reform the police. So, too, did changing perceptions of what was acceptable behaviour on the streets. A case might also be made for state development (even allowing for the fact that the nineteenth-century British model was a very decentralized version). Increasingly, the state was involving itself in everyday life, introducing factory legislation, Poor Law reform and census enumeration, so we might well ask why it didn't also take a greater degree of responsibility for the maintenance of law and order?

Table 1.1 summarizes the development of policing in England and Ireland in the latter half of the eighteenth and the first half of the nineteenth centuries.

Table 1.1   The establishment of police forces in England and Ireland, 1750–1856

England Description of force	Location	Year	Location	Ireland Description of force
Bow Street Police Office. Magistrate and four thief takers. *C/F/N*	London	**1750**		
Short-lived, eight-man Bow Street Horse Patrol. *C/F S?/N*	London	**1763–64**		
Small Bow Street Foot Patrol. Initial size unknown, 70 men by 1797. *C/F S/N*	London	**1773**	Counties	Tiny, scattered baronial police. *L/D/N*
		1778	Dublin	City-wide force, constables and watch, totalling 425 men. *L/D/N*
		1786	Dublin	450-man new police. *C/F/U*
		1787	Counties	Originally in disturbed Cork, Kerry, Kilkenny, Tipperary; from 1795 in 11 counties. Lapses, *c.*1800. *C/F/U (motley)*
Seven Police Offices. Twenty-one magistrates and 42 constables. *C/D/N*	London	**1792**	Counties	Small forces in 15 counties other than those policed by the 1787 Act. *L/F/N*
		1795	Dublin	Local force restored, 1786 police abolished. *L/D/U*
		1799	Dublin	Centralized police replaces 1795 force. Fifty peace officers and 500 watchmen. *C/F & S/U*
Thames River Police. Three magistrates and a 60-man patrol. *C/S/N*	London	**1800**		
Bow Street [Mounted] Horse Patrol re-established. Fifty men ('Redbreasts'). *C/F & S/U*	London	**1805**		
		1808	Dublin	Consolidation of 1799 police and addition of Horse Patrol (50 men) and Foot Patrol (100). *C/F & S/U*
		1814	Counties	Peel's Peace Preservation Force. Initially in Tipperary; by 1822, 2,300 Peelers in 16 disturbed counties. *C/F & S/U (motley)*
'Dismounted' Horse Patrol [foot patrol]. Ninety men. *C/F & S/U*	London	**1821**		
		1822	Counties	Irish constabulary. Compulsory in all counties. Mostly replaces, or in a few counties supplements, the Peelers. Initially 4,800 men; 7,500 by 1836. *C, L/F & S/U*
Peel's 3,200-man Metropolitan Police. Bow Street Patrols and Thames Police abolished, 1839. *C/D/U*	London	**1829**		
Police forces begin to replace constables and watch in incorporated towns. *L/D/U*	Boroughs	**1835**		
		1836	Counties	Constabulary reformed and Peelers (1814 force) abolished. Force grows to 12,000 men by 1850. *C/F & S/U*
		1837	Dublin	1,100-man police replaces force established in 1808. *C/D/U*
Optional police forces; adopted in 15 whole counties by 1842 (a total of 1,900 men) and in 19 by 1856 (3,300 men). *L/D/U some S*	Counties	**1839**		
Temporary government-controlled police. *C/D/U*	Manchester Birmingham Bolton	**1839–42**		
Compulsory forces in all counties. *L, C/D/U*	Counties	**1856**		

Note: London = the metropolis, not the City of London.

Key: *C* Central (i.e. government) control   *N* No uniform   *F* Armed with firearms
        D Disarmed: staff or truncheon only   *L* Local control   *S* Armed with short sword or cutlass   *U* Uniformed

Source: Adapted from Palmer, 1988, p.32

3 Control and management

3.1 Accountability

Following the establishment of the new police, other individuals and groups continued to undertake 'policing' tasks. For example, the old parish constables were not automatically abolished – indeed, many continued to be appointed until well into the twentieth century. Gamekeepers and private watchmen continued to function on private property, and for much of the nineteenth century it was possible for landowners or businesses to pay for additional constables in their local police who would concentrate on guarding their property. Docks had their own police, though these were often speedily incorporated into new, local town forces. The railway companies continued to run their own police until their nationalization in 1948, which brought about the creation of a single British Transport Police, the only force authorized to act on both sides of the Anglo-Scottish border. The period since the Second World War has seen a considerable growth in private security companies for guarding premises and a variety of other tasks.

The number of police forces in England, Wales and Scotland varied throughout the nineteenth and twentieth centuries. A peak was reached towards the end of the 1850s, after which the numbers increasingly declined as the smaller forces either found it convenient, or were compelled, to amalgamate with their larger neighbours. In 1860 there were 226 forces in England and Wales; on the eve of the First World War there were still 188; and a series of amalgamations at the end of the Second World War brought the number down to 131.

These forces were of three different kinds – the London Metropolitan Police, borough or city police, and county police – and each kind had a different administrative and organizational structure. From the outset, the commissioners of the Metropolitan Police were directly accountable to the Home Secretary. This incensed many of the representatives of local government in London.

ACTIVITY 1.2

The petition of the Parish of Marylebone to Viscount Melbourne, the Whig government's Home Secretary, in December 1832 was one of the more reasoned and restrained of such initial complaints. Part of this is reproduced in Extract 1.3 opposite. Read the extract and consider the following questions:

1 What is the constitutional concern expressed in the petition?
2 What do you understand from this document to be the difference between the financing of the old Marylebone Watch and that of the new Metropolitan Police?

militarism

The petitioners are concerned that this is a military-style organization directly responsible to central government and with no local control. It could, therefore, be used against the people by an unscrupulous government. The old Marylebone Watch was financed and directed by the parish; the new Metropolitan Police continues to be financed by the London parishes, but they have no control over its operations.

Extract 1.3 'Petition of the Parish of Marylebone to the Home Secretary, 1832'

Your Memorialists respectfully beg leave now to approach that part of the subject the most delicate ...,
viz., whether the Force, as at present constituted and governed, is, or is not, accordant with the spirit of
the Constitution and the Freedom of the Subject; a Force which will most likely, 'ere long, pervade the
whole Kingdom, formed upon a Military System, regulated and directed by persons appointed by the
Government, and altogether uncontrolled by those who pay for it, and the protection of whose persons
and property is the presumed object of its formation.

It will require no power of argument or deduction of reason to satisfy a mind, constituted like your
Lordship's, that a Force such as this must be incompatible with the Liberty of the Subject. It differs from
a Military Force only in the name, and ... [with] all the attributes and powers of any army, it may, at any
moment of public excitement, be called out, at the will of the then existing government, in array against
the people, from whom its members derive their daily pay ...

Your Memorialists ... admit that so long as the Helm of the State is guided by those tried Friends of the
People [the Whigs] who ... have for nearly half a century steadily pursued an undeviating course ...
[toward] restoring to the People their long-usurped Rights, they have nothing to fear, but my Lord, ... it
is not enough that the political integrity of the present Government is a guarantee to the people of the
abuse of such a Force ...

(quoted in Palmer, 1988, p.307)

These arguments were to flare up again and again during the nineteenth and
twentieth centuries. In 1888, for example, when legislation was introduced to
establish the London County Council, Liberals and Radicals urged that control
of the police should be passed to the new body – after all, the constituent parts
of London were paying for the police through their rates. The government's
line, however, was that the Metropolitan Police had 'imperial' as well as 'local'
tasks such as protecting the royal family and parliament. One government
apologist warned: 'It is undeniable that if the London County Council held the
control of the police, it would wield a weapon that might be handled with
deadly effect against a weak Government, if the majority of the Council chose
to make use of it for political purposes.' He went on to wonder whether 'any
reasonable person [could] assert that there will never be a majority of extreme
Radicals and Socialists on the County Council?' (Evans, 1889, p.449). The
comment brought predictable outrage: 'This ... is the first time that I have ever
heard the claim set up in England that the police are a body for the protection of
the Government against the citizens.' It also brought the complaint that London
was now the only place in Britain 'where a charge falls permanently on the
rates ... and where those who manage the expenditure of that charge are not
themselves responsible to the ratepayers' (Stuart, 1889, pp.629 and 626). But
outrage and complaint did not sway the legislators or bring about any
amendments. In the aftermath of the First World War the issue flared up again
when the Labour majority on Poplar Council refused to pay their precepts for
the Metropolitan Police, arguing that money was short and would be better
spent on solving social distress and problems in the district; several council
leaders were imprisoned as a result.

The Municipal Corporations Act of 1835 obliged incorporated boroughs to
establish watch committees, which in turn were to appoint head constables
and police forces. At the beginning these committees took a very serious interest
in policing matters and gave precise operational details to their head constable

on the deployment of his men; moreover the committees possessed the authority to hire, fire and discipline. Often, as the century progressed, an accommodation was reached between a committee and its head constable. Busy local politicians found less and less time to devote to police matters and were content to let their 'expert' get on with it. In some instances the small size of the police force – a few borough forces had less than two dozen men well into the twentieth century – and the consequent lowly origin of the head constable ensured that he remained very obviously the servant of the local politicians. But even the head constable of a very large urban force could find himself compelled to obey operational instructions from his watch committee which he regarded as ill-conceived. Liverpool, for example, had the largest provincial urban force in England during the 1890s. The watch committee became dominated by a group of moral reformers determined to stamp out prostitution, and the head constable was instructed to close down the city's brothels. Captain Nott-Bowyer, the head constable, advised against the policy, warning that it would not stamp out prostitution, merely move it, and that once the offence had moved it would take up a significant amount of police time pursuing it. His advice was ignored, and he was required to administer the policy, with precisely the results he had predicted. However, as will be explained in section 3.2 below, the authority of the watch committee was gradually undermined by Whitehall's growing professionalism, by the responses to a succession of emergencies, and by debatable legal rulings.

The chief constables of county police forces had much greater independence from the beginning. They were appointed by their police committees, but the Home Secretary approved the appointment. Generally during the nineteenth century they were drawn from the same social class as the county magistrates; in the second half of the century an increasing number were former military officers. Until the Act of 1888 which established county councils, they were in some measure answerable to the police committees of magistrates appointed by the county bench. The 1888 Act established standing joint committees made up of an equal number of magistrates and elected county councillors, although there were those who had argued that the police should be directly responsible to the new county councils. However, as with the London County Council, the government was wary and some of its supporters were outspoken in their fears of what might happen if trade unionists or socialists should gain control of a county and hence of its police.

3.2   Creeping centralization

centralization   There had been little in the way of centralization before the 1856 County and Borough Police Act, but this does not mean that the police forces did not have much in common. Indeed, as men moved from one force to another, especially as the new forces sought cadres of officers from those already in existence, particularly from London, they probably developed more and more similarities. The 1856 Act, by offering Treasury money to 'efficient' forces and by establishing inspectors who would assess that efficiency, gave the Home Office new and significant leverage over the development of the provincial police. A few proud boroughs maintained their independence and refused the Treasury grant, yet this was not the kind of policy to ensure a council's popularity with ratepayers at the polls, and even these few soon fell into line. In 1874 the Treasury grant was increased to one half the cost of pay and uniforms, and in the aftermath of the First World War this was raised to half the total cost of the force.

In addition to the leverage which the Home Office acquired through its financial involvement with the provincial police, there were other factors at work which served to undermine local control. Examinations for the Civil Service, introduced in the second half of the nineteenth century, led to an increasingly professional elite of bureaucrats in Whitehall. At the same time policemen were acquiring more knowledge of their trade and increasingly perceived themselves as the experts in matters of law and order, while new legislation dealing with, among other things, explosives and adulterated food gave direct executive power to the police with no reference to the local police committees. There was therefore no sudden change, but gradually senior police officers, particularly those of the larger forces, and Home Office bureaucrats began by-passing local government 'laymen'. This situation gathered pace at the turn of the century as the result of industrial disputes and spy scares; the First World War and the Russian Revolution accelerated the process. Government ministers and their advisers reasoned that big industrial disputes required a greater response than a single police force could often provide. A miners' strike in the West Riding in 1893 found the county police hopelessly stretched, not least because the dispute coincided with the policing demands of the Doncaster races. Troops were deployed, and at Ackton Hall Colliery, Featherstone, two miners were shot dead and fourteen others wounded. The Home Office urged police forces to enter into mutual aid agreements. At the close of the following decade the dynamic young Liberal Home Secretary, Winston Churchill, pushed the constitutional position to the limit, and probably legally exceeded his authority, by moving police and troops around the country as he saw fit. Churchill also urged the creation of police reserves to supplement the forces when stretched; some police committees took up the idea, but some boroughs refused, protesting that the Home Office was encroaching on their authority.

Immediately before the First World War there was a succession of spy scares, as a result of which chief and head constables were brought into contact with the embryonic secret service. The war itself strengthened such links, and again to the detriment of local control, since Labour and Independent Labour Party activists were often on the lists of anti-war suspects. The war emergency led to the creation of Authorized Competent Military Authorities – military officers responsible for the wartime management and supervision of their nominated regions; these officers liaised directly with senior police officers, again by-passing the lay police committees. The Authorized Competent Military Authorities were abolished at the end of the war, but, at the same time, closer links were forged between the police and the Home Office by a succession of conferences, circulars discussing how the police were to respond in future emergencies, and, finally, by the Emergency Powers Act of 1919. The latter authorized the executive to make 'regulations for the preservation of the public peace' and 'for any other purposes essential to the public safety and the life of the community'. The Act was untouched by the Labour government of 1924, and provided the basis for the management of the General Strike of 1926. Sir Arthur Dixon, one of the civil servants responsible for the Police Division of the Home Office during the 1920s, concluded that these developments and experiences 'established the [Police] Service in what was virtually a new, and certainly important, role as an executive Force, efficient, trustworthy and versatile, and ready at a call to guide, assist or restrain the civil population in a wide variety of ways' (quoted in Emsley, 1996b, p.138).

The First World War exerted enormous pressures on those policemen who were not recruited into the military: the numbers of police declined, their average age increased, they were given a multitude of new, specifically wartime tasks, their leave and rest days were reduced, and their pay fell way behind with the

unionization impact of wartime inflation. Unionization of an *ad hoc* kind had emerged among different forces during the nineteenth century, and shortly before the war a national police trade union had been established. The experience of the war provided a considerable boost to membership, and in 1918 and again in 1919 the union brought its members out on strike – in the first instance essentially over pay and conditions, but on the second occasion for the very existence of the union. The second strike was a disaster for the union and for all those men who participated, some of whom had upwards of twenty years' service; the union was destroyed, and the strikers were dismissed and never reinstated. However, the strikes prompted the government to create a committee, chaired by Lord Desborough, whose recommendations with reference to conditions, pay and uniforms brought a much greater unity to the hundred or so forces then in existence. The recommendation that the smaller forces be amalgamated with their larger neighbours was viewed sympathetically by successive governments, by the Inspectors of Constabulary and by civil servants in the Home Office, but proposals for requiring such amalgamations brought the usual chorus of protest from the boroughs.

3.3   Twentieth-century redefinitions

Although the smaller boroughs, backed by the larger, were able to hang on to their own police forces, the relationship between them and their policemen was being redefined. During the nineteenth century borough policemen in particular were commonly regarded as the servants of local government. I have described above how the head constable of Liverpool gave way to the directives of his watch committee in 1890. Increasingly during the 1920s, however, official and semi-official voices began to deny that the relationship between policeman and police committee was one of master and servant. One of the clearest such statements was made by O.F. Dowson, a barrister and Assistant Legal Adviser to the Home Office, in a series of articles published in the journal *Justice of the Peace* in 1928.

> … every police officer, irrespective of the authority under whom he is serving, possesses powers and is required to carry out duties at common law which seem at first sight, at any rate to be inconsistent with any theory that he is a mere servant of the police authority. Apart from the public character of his office he is clothed with functions and powers which, though exercisable locally only, are not dependent upon or under the complete control of the authority under whose management he is placed and at whose cost he is paid (apart from the Exchequer grant) …
>
> (*Justice of the Peace*, 13 October 1928, p.663)

The argument was given judicial force two years later with the ruling of Justice McCardie in *Fisher* v. *Oldham*. A man named Fisher was wrongly arrested by a policeman from the Borough of Oldham and, on his release, he brought an action for false imprisonment against the borough. The judge's ruling that a policeman 'is a Servant of the State, a ministerial officer of the central power, though subject in some respects to local supervision and local regulation' (quoted in Emsley, 1996b, p.164) has been hotly debated and disputed, but it has become a crucial underpinning of the argument that the police have, and always have had, operational independence from local politicians.

operational independence

While it would be unwise to detect a conspiracy on the part of central government to forge greater links between itself, in the shape of the Home Office, and the police, it is true that during the inter-war period central government always backed chief constables in dispute with their police committees. Such disputes were not to be found in great numbers, but where they did occur the reason was invariably political. A few chief constables, particularly a trio in South Wales, insisted that they were upholding a non-political, British way of life against alien creeds; the police committees with whom they clashed had large numbers of Labour, and occasionally a few Communist, councillors.

The chief constables of counties had always had more freedom of action than those of boroughs; theoretically, if increasingly less in practice, the latter remained directly responsible to the local watch committee. But the 1920s also witnessed a serious conflict between a borough head constable and his watch committee which ultimately involved the Home Office. A.R. Ellerington, the head constable of St. Helens since 1905, had been given a virtual free hand in operational matters for twenty years, but friction developed in 1926 when he brought in police from Liverpool to assist his men during industrial trouble. Watch committee meetings became the scenes of ferocious arguments. The committee sought Ellerington's dismissal, but the Home Office ordered his reinstatement. Accusations were made about misconduct, but an inquiry found in Ellerington's favour and again the watch committee was instructed by the Home Office to reinstate him and maintain proper relations with him. Some thirty years later, in 1959, a similar conflict erupted in Nottingham after the chief constable, Captain Athelstan Popkess, launched an investigation into corruption in the city government. The Director of Public Prosecutions advised that no action should be taken, at which point the watch committee, hearing of the investigations for the first time, demanded a report from Popkess. He refused on the grounds that criminal investigation was his duty and no concern of the committee. The committee suspended him, but the Home Secretary insisted on his reinstatement. The Popkess affair was one of several incidents which led the government to establish a Royal Commission in January 1960. The principal question which the Royal Commission found itself having to confront was precisely where the ultimate control of the provincial police should reside.

In Scotland the increasing links between the police and central government, at the expense of local government, appear to have followed a pattern largely similar to that south of the border, though the history of Scottish policing is far less researched. In Ireland, as noted above, the bureaucratic police organizations developed during the nineteenth century, namely the Royal Irish Constabulary (RIC) and the Dublin Metropolitan Police, were always centrally directed. When, following partition in 1922, the RIC was replaced in the north by the Royal Ulster Constabulary and in the south by the *garda siochana* ('people's guard') the influence of the organization of the old force remained significant, especially on the former. Both of the new forces were made responsible, first and foremost, to government ministers. But in Northern Ireland, a fiercely Protestant state with a significant Catholic minority and a large Catholic neighbour, a major part of policing concerned the preservation of the border. This led to the creation of a Special Constabulary, heavily armed and quite unlike any other force in the United Kingdom.

All of this leads to the key question: are the police in Britain 'political' or above politics? The official line has always been that the police in Britain are not political, yet, as Reiner has pointed out: 'This notion … rests on an entirely untenable narrow conception of "the political", restricting it to "the administrative apparatus of state and party organization" … In a broader sense all relationships which have a power dimension are political' (Reiner, 1992, pp.1–2). During the nineteenth century some borough police were political in an even narrower sense of obeying the directives of the political members of the watch committee. This position shifted, especially during the inter-war years, but it brought senior police officers much more within the supervision and direction of central government.

4 Police efficiency and effectiveness

4.1 The prevention of crime

The 'New Police Instructions' issued to the London Metropolitan Police in 1829 declared:

> It should be understood at the outset, that the object to be attained is 'the prevention of crime'. To this great end every effort of the police is to be directed. The security of person and property, the preservation of the public tranquillity, and all other objects of a police establishment, will thus be better effected than by the detection and punishment of the offender after he has succeeded in committing the crime. This should constantly be kept in mind by every member of the police force, as the guide for his own conduct. Officers and constables should endeavour to distinguish themselves by such vigilance and activity as may render it impossible for any one to commit a crime within that portion of the town under their charge.
>
> (*The Times*, 25 September 1829)

The instructions above were often used, word for word, by provincial forces established later in the century. But there are unfortunately major difficulties in assessing the effectiveness of this strategy of prevention. If you take the absence of crime and disorder as the measure of success, how can you differentiate between general 'good' behaviour on the part of the public and good behaviour created by the presence of the police? What other bench-mark could be used to assess police effectiveness? The number of arrests? If you rely on the latter, could an increase in arrests (and convictions) mean (a) better policing; (b) more aggressive policing, which might not necessarily be better, but could be the targeting of 'easy' offences, and 'known offenders' picked up and even 'fitted up'; or (c) more crime and disorder? An increase in arrests and convictions might also be taken to imply a failure of 'prevention'.

prevention   Prevention became an article of faith for the police, but the problems associated with it were soon apparent. There were certain kinds of offenders who could be picked up with relative ease. Drunks are an obvious example, though the stories are legion of drunks being moved by one constable to his neighbour's beat so that he could go to bed after a long night shift rather than having to take the offender back to his station, possibly having his uniform fouled on the way, and then having to hang around in the magistrates' court waiting for the case to be heard. Vagrants were another easy target. Statistics showing large numbers of vagrants thrown into borough or county gaols during the nineteenth century are a dubious guide to the incidence of vagrancy – more probably they were the result of orders to the police from a magistrates' police committee, a watch committee, or a head or chief constable to clamp down on itinerants. Catching thieves and burglars was rather more problematic; no-one produced any yardstick showing the extent to which their activities were, or could be, prevented by men in uniform.

In 1842 the belief that the new county police forces in particular were not achieving what they had promised in terms of efficiency and effectiveness, in spite of costing a considerable amount of money, led to campaigns by ratepayers across the country. Some demanded that the new police be reduced in size or even disbanded. The campaigns were cut short by a new wave of Chartist demonstrations, but not before the Lancashire Constabulary had been reduced from 502 to 355 men.

The founders of the Metropolitan Police believed that the primary responsibility of the police was the prevention of crime and the maintenance of public order – not the detection of crime. However, in 1842 a detective branch was established and reformed as CID in the late 1870s. The photograph shows Limehouse CID investigating dope smuggling in disguise, c.1911

It is possible, of course, that the appearance of policemen on beats did reduce some opportunist crime. Furthermore, while on their beats, policemen were expected to check the preventive measures of shopkeepers and others. Constables checked for open windows and gates, and they 'shook hands with the doorknobs' to ensure that doors were properly closed and locked. Failure to report an open window, gate or door, especially if this led to 'failure' in 'preventing' a crime, could lead to a reprimand and punishment. Rewards often came as a result of arrests, and chances of promotion could be improved. Harry Daley, who joined the Metropolitan Police in 1925 and served for a quarter of a century, recalled how, in his first police station, the inspector approved of the 'snatchers' who arrested or summonsed any and everyone, since they made his district look active and important.

> He held up the snatchers as examples to others and threatened to delay promotion unless more work was done. When other detrimental factors were present, he occasionally carried out his threat. This pressure to make young policemen work – to summons and arrest people – was always denied when questions were asked in Parliament …

> The Metropolitan Police Act entitles 'any constable to stop, search and detain any person reasonably suspected of being in possession of stolen property'. In my early days I made perfect use of this Act. As I stood in a doorway in the dead of night I heard hurrying footsteps and, peeping out, saw a man with a heavy bag which clinked with metal as he got closer. With heart in mouth I stopped a doctor carrying his instruments, returning from a nearby emergency call. Hearty laughter and a friendly parting, of course.

> Snatchers ignored the words 'reasonably suspected' and by stopping everyone with a bag or parcel occasionally caught thieves carrying stolen property. They antagonised hundreds of innocent people and those almost innocent – such as workmen carrying home wood or paint which had been 'left over'. At night they interfered unnecessarily with happy drunks and made them drunk and disorderlies and assaults on police.

> (Daley, 1986, pp.100–1)

4.2 Police strategies

targeting Prevention arguably led to the targeting of 'criminal' areas and of particular individuals and social groups. The first commissioners of the Metropolitan Police spoke in terms of protecting the elegant, wealthy district of St. James by watching the slum of St. Giles. The St. Giles 'rookery' was demolished as one of a series of urban improvements in the middle of the nineteenth century, as much to remove the 'criminal class' from the centre of the city as to provide the wide new thoroughfare of New Oxford Street. Other rookeries met similar fates: in Manchester, for example, the building of the Central Railway Station and the widening of Deansgate provided the opportunity for demolishing part of one of the worst slums. The inhabitants of these districts then moved elsewhere, and the police maintained their surveillance of the new 'criminal' districts.

Of course, there were people living in the rookeries who did commit offences, but it is unlikely that everyone there could be labelled as a 'criminal'. Many of the inhabitants of these and other poor, stigmatized districts were casual labourers dependent on an uncertain job market. Parts of these districts were crammed with Irish immigrants who brought with them rural habits and the rough traditions of the faction fight. Irish districts in the Victorian city became notorious as 'criminal', yet it does not seem to have been property crime which singled out the Irish, but interpersonal violence, commonly committed among themselves, or else directed against the police. Paradoxically, while the police tended to equate 'Irishman' with 'criminal', a very high percentage of recruits to the police forces in those cities with large Irish populations were themselves Irish.

Another example of police 'labelling' during the nineteenth century was the way that a large number of women arrested for petty theft or as drunk and disorderly were listed by the police as 'prostitutes'. The situation was aggravated during the period when the Contagious Diseases Acts were in force (1864–83). These enabled the Metropolitan Police and the police of garrison towns to arrest women suspected of being prostitutes and have them medically examined. The Acts put any young working-class woman out alone, especially after dark, at risk from an over-zealous policeman. Even after their abolition the problem of such police officers apprehending young women on suspicion continued. This, together with the surveillance of the poor districts and the identification of certain districts as 'criminal', did not endear the police to the 'suspect' working class.

While crime statistics are notoriously difficult to use, those that we have for the nineteenth century suggest a general levelling out of most property crime (with the notable exception of burglary) and crimes against the person after about 1850. It is possible that the new police had some impact here; the spread of policing across the whole country, with the uniformed constables pounding their beats at the regulation two and a half miles an hour, may have deterred some of the opportunist crime. But it would be difficult to prove conclusively. Whatever their impact on crime statistics, the new police were probably only one of several reasons for this levelling out. Furthermore, changes in leisure habits, linked with developments in technology, presented a challenge to the strategies adopted by the new police.

For much of the nineteenth century the working classes, and particularly the poorer elements who were identified by the police as the objects for surveillance, took much of their leisure on the street. They would sit in the street, eat in the street, gamble in the street, argue and fight in the street. Organized sports – particularly with the development of football stadiums and dog tracks – provided new outlets. So too did the cinema. In addition to the leisure opportunities provided by new, specially designed public spaces, the twentieth century brought better housing provision for the working classes, together with new forms of home leisure provided by new technologies – the radio and the gramophone. But as the working classes gradually moved off the streets, so, again courtesy of the new technology, the traditionally respectable classes, who had never been the objects of police surveillance, moved on to the roads in their motor cars. The decade before the First World War witnessed nasty confrontations between motorists and the police, with a new pressure group, the Automobile Association, being founded to provide 'scouts', who would warn members of police speed traps, and legal assistance in court cases. By the middle of the inter-war period motoring offences were clogging the magistrates' courts, and concerns were being expressed about motoring legislation poisoning the hitherto good relations between the police and the public.

4.3   Public order

The statistics of riot and disorder are as difficult to assess, perhaps more so, as those of crime. However, most historians of popular disorder and riot suggest that there was a decline in the incidence of riot during the nineteenth century, together with a shift from the reactive riot inspired by legitimizing notions (food riots, recruiting riots, anti-enclosure riots, anti-Poor Law riots) to the proactive demonstrations organized by groups such as the new trade unions. The role of the police in this shift is difficult to estimate. As the century wore on police forces began more and more to replace the army in dealing with disorder. In part this was simply because there were more police available, and at times before 1856 the Home Office specifically instructed local authorities fearful of riot not to expect military support but to recruit a police force.

crowd control

Policemen were less likely to kill people involved in disorder than soldiers, in as much as they were usually only armed with truncheons rather than the edged weapons and firearms of the military. Nevertheless it took the police some time to develop sensible crowd control techniques. Some of the techniques employed early in the century may have served to exacerbate violence rather than reduce it. For example, a political demonstration in Gray's Inn Road, London, in May 1833 saw the Metropolitan Police seal off streets to the sides of the crowds, thus cutting off lines of retreat and dispersal, while they charged the crowds with drawn batons from the front. The only fatality in this instance was a police constable who was stabbed in the chest; but the coroner's jury which sat on the case brought in a verdict of justifiable homicide on the following grounds:

> that no Riot Act was read nor any proclamation advising the people to disperse; that the Government did not take proper precautions to prevent the meeting from assembling and that the conduct of the police was ferocious, brutal and unprovoked by the people. And we, moreover, express our anxious hope that the Government will, in future, take better precautions to prevent the recurrence of such disgraceful transactions in the Metropolis.

(quoted in Tobias, 1979, p.89)

While the authorities were outraged, the jury itself was celebrated in banners and medals, and the foreman was presented with a silver cup. Later in the century there were reports of policemen setting about crowds, including women and children, with their batons. The 1868 General Election was marred in Bromley, Kent, by the death of 78-year-old William Walter, trampled in a police baton charge. Questions remain about the incident: why were 200 Metropolitan Police brought in when there had been no violence or vandalism before the election day, and why were the local police sent home for the day? The Liberals, mounting a strong challenge to the local Conservatives who controlled the district, complained that the police were brought in by Tory JPs, but neither the police nor the magistrates admitted this. However, at the trials of twenty residents accused of assaulting the police, any witness giving testimony critical of the police was ordered from the court on the grounds that: 'The Bench was bound to believe the evidence of the police'. At the inquest on Walter, the solicitor who asked the local coroner if he might present evidence of police violence was informed that: 'You had better not say such things; because the police are a body whose duty it is to keep the peace, and when soldiers or police were brought into a town, they came to keep the peace and not to break it' (both quotations from Conley, 1991, p.39). Violent police behaviour during a strike at Silksworth Colliery in County Durham in 1891 was celebrated with a pastiche of Tennyson's 'The Charge of the Light Brigade':

> Down the hill, down the hill
> Fifty yards onward,
> All among the flying folk
> Ran the half hundred.
> 'Forward the 'Cop's' Brigade!
> Charge for the lot!' he said;
> Into the scattr'ing crowd
> Ran the half hundred.
> Old men to the right of them,
> Women to the left of them,
> Bairns right in front of them,
> Bolted and wonder'd;
> Left free to have their way,
> Nimbly their staves did play,
> Into the fleeing crowd,
> Into the roaring fun
> Plunged the half hundred.
>
> (Sunderland *Daily Echo*, 28 February 1891)

There are instances from the inter-war years when the police appear to have been the principal cause of violence in street demonstrations, either because of over-reaction or fear. The belief of some senior officers, and perhaps also some of their men, that they had a responsibility to protect the British way of life against alien creeds, and the identification of the National Association of Unemployed Workers with the Communist Party, may have contributed to some of the over-reaction. For example, in 1921 *The Police Chronicle*, a newspaper aimed at policemen, declared: 'There never was a time when public interests stood more in need of a police independent and uninfluenced by party politics … The Bolshies in this country must be reckoned with and their defeat is assured only if we see to it' (quoted in Weinberger, 1987, pp.157–8).

One officer of the Metropolitan Police described ordering a crowd of hunger marchers to break up in the Edgware Road in November 1932, 'as it was about to become disorderly' (quoted in Stevenson and Cook, 1977, p.231). In September the same year police in Birkenhead appear to have got completely out of control in poor working-class districts of the town after a demonstration against the Means Test. There were no public inquiries into these events. As the chief constable of Liverpool put it to the Home Secretary after a baton charge to disperse a meeting of the unemployed in September 1921:

> With regard to the advisability of holding any inquiry, I may say that we are at the present time passing through the most serious period of unrest in Liverpool. The unemployed trouble is being used by a gang of extreme Communists (all known to Sir Basil Thomson [the head of Special Branch]) for the purpose of a propaganda of violence. They are a self-selected committee acting as leaders of the unemployed and nothing but very firm measures in dealing with them can prevent serious trouble and disorder … My considered opinion is that any inquiry into the question of whether the police used undue violence in quelling an unlawful assembly … would seriously

weaken the authority of the police at a time when it needs every possible support ... If the sworn evidence of ... experienced police superintendents ... is called into question how can they be expected to act with the necessary firmness when another occasion arises in which force may be necessary, and this may occur at any moment.

(quoted in Weinberger, 1987, p.160)

From the moment of their creation the police became involved in contests between labour and capital. The Master and Servant Act of 1824 made breach of contract by an employer a matter for civil law, while breach of contract by an employee could be pursued through the criminal courts. This meant that workers breaking a contract could be, and were, pursued by the police – another factor contributing to the potential for hostility between the working class and the police. The Master and Servant legislation was amended in the second half of the century, by which time organized labour and strike activity was becoming increasingly permissible within the framework of the law. But problems remained. How could the police appear neutral during a strike if called upon to protect bailiffs seeking to eject strikers from company housing (as was the case in the Silksworth Colliery disorder), or if called on to protect what employers called 'free labour' and what strikers called 'blacklegs' or 'scabs'? Legislation of 1875 and 1906 authorized 'peaceful picketing', but the definition of this remained obscure. It would appear that, following a Home Office circular issued in 1911 and again in 1913 which stated that a non-striker was only to be approached by one 'persuader' at a time, the Metropolitan Police decided not to allow more than one man as a picket. During the General Strike of 1926 some chief constables negotiated closely with strike committees to ensure the maintenance of the peace; others strongly resisted any such inclinations and regarded strikers with, at best, suspicion. The chief constable of Manchester complained that:

In effect there is no such thing as 'peaceful picketing'. What is known as 'peaceful picketing' leads to more trouble than anything else the Police have to deal with in trade disputes, as pickets, when they see a favourable opportunity, will and do resort to means which certainly cannot be regarded as peaceful.

(quoted in Emsley, 1996b, p.141, n.58)

Special constables in London during the 1926 General Strike. More than 226,000 specials were recruited to help police the country, including 70,000 in the capital alone, although the majority were not uniformed

Traditional histories of the police have put great stress on the football matches played by police and strikers: violent confrontation was probably the exception rather than the rule, and where it did occur it appears often to have been the work of undisciplined special constables sworn in for the duration of the emergency. However, there were violent incidents, as the police reward for 'little Kathleen Baggott' testifies (see the photograph below).

Illustration from On and Off Duty, *July 1926, p.103. The original caption read: 'Little Kathleen Baggott, a twelve-year-old heroine of the general strike, receiving at Leigh, Lancashire, a gold wrist watch, given in recognition of her bravery in finding a means of escape from rioters for P.S. Cooper. She let him into her mother's house, and locked the door. The mob smashed the windows, but dispersed when police reinforcements arrived'*

4.4   Miscellaneous duties

While there is a common assumption that police duties are essentially crime fighting and the maintenance of public order, it is worth noting that during the nineteenth century the police acquired a variety of tasks often only loosely connected to these duties. In boroughs, particularly the smaller ones, policemen were required to assume a variety of petty responsibilities, from acting as mace-bearers on civic occasions to collecting market tolls. The town worthies reasoned that, if they were paying their police for one task, they might just as well perform another. The Education Act of 1870 resulted in constables being required to act as School Attendance Officers, pursuing parents who did not send their children to school. Policemen were appointed to act as inspectors of weights and measures, inspectors of lodging houses, and Poor Law relieving officers. Such duties may have brought them into contact with suspect individuals, but again it seems the reason for the acquisition of these duties was primarily that the policemen were already available and being paid, at least partly, out of local government coffers. In the early 1950s the Burrell Committee on Police

Extraneous Duties issued a report listing a whole series of tasks which, it considered, the police should not be expected to perform; yet a decade later there were still forces where the men were required to change street signs, collect money due under maintenance orders, keep registers of domestic servants, license and inspect hackney carriages, and act as civic mace-bearers, court ushers, market inspectors, and mortuary attendants. It is, of course, impossible to assess the extent to which such tasks impeded the policeman's efficiency in the maintenance of order or as a crime-fighter. It is also worth considering the extent to which some of these duties may have provided part of the basis for police legitimacy.

5   Recruits, recruitment and police culture

5.1   Recruitment policies

It was Robert Peel's decision in 1829 that his Metropolitan policemen should come from the working class, and should be able to rise in rank through their own efforts. The commissioners of the new force were selected from 'gentlemen', but other ranks were to be open to ordinary working men who showed talent and merit. Similar policies were adopted by the provincial forces: the counties and the major cities generally chose their chief constables from gentlemen, at least until the Second World War, but all other ranks, including that of head constable in the smaller towns, were open to men who had first enlisted at the lowest grade of constable.

A cross-section of men generally from the unskilled and semi-skilled working class made up the bulk of recruits between 1840 and 1940. Large numbers were listed in the recruitment books simply as 'labourers'. This has been taken to mean agricultural labourer, and certainly there was a feeling among certain senior officers during the Victorian period that a man straight from the plough would be fit, tough and deferential to his superiors; but 'labourer' was a catch-all term, and recruits came from a much broader range of trades than simply those of the countryside. Furthermore, different forces had different recruitment policies. There were some large towns where chief constables refused to accept local men on the grounds that they would have difficulty carrying out some tasks if they found themselves having to deal with relatives and people with whom they had grown up. But there were other forces, particularly county ones, where the overwhelming majority of recruits were local men. Some chief constables in the Victorian period were reluctant to take former soldiers, suspecting that they might have become too fond of drink. But others had a predilection for former soldiers, considering them as disciplined and smart. In the economically difficult inter-war years some young men joined the army on three-year contracts with the specific aim of joining the police at the end of their service. It would appear also that, probably as a result of the economic depression during the inter-war years as well as improved educational opportunities, recruits were generally better educated and more likely to perceive the police as a career.

5.2   The recruit's aspirations

Many of the early recruits to the police joined to tide themselves over a period of unemployment, and they clearly had little idea of what the job would entail. Many men loathed it because of the ferocious discipline, the night-work (two-thirds of all nineteenth- and early twentieth-century beats were worked at night) and the exhausting and physically dangerous nature of the job. The turnover of recruits in the early years was enormous, but not just because of resignations by men who could not stand the life; a very large number were dismissed for disciplinary offences – particularly drinking or drunkenness on duty.

Until the Second World War men were required to ask permission to marry, and their prospective wives had their characters investigated to ensure that they were 'suitable' to be a policeman's wife. During the nineteenth century, and in some forces for part of the twentieth century, a policeman's wife was not allowed to take any form of paid employment. This had an obvious impact on the family budget since working-class wives commonly sought some kind of work. In police houses in the countryside the policeman's wife was expected to act as his auxiliary, taking messages when he was on patrol and, subsequently, answering the telephone; she was also expected to keep the police house in a high state of cleanliness. The policeman was held responsible for his wife's behaviour, and should she get into debt with local tradesmen, or commit any kind of offence (not necessarily 'criminal'), then her husband was called before his superior officers to explain.

However, there were some advantages to the job: a uniform was provided; some forces offered a degree of health care, even for a man's family; accommodation was found for some, though it was not free; and rent allowances were introduced at the beginning of the twentieth century. Most attractive, however, and a great rarity for working-class occupations in the nineteenth and early twentieth centuries, there was a pension. This pension was not guaranteed until 1890, but it provided a great incentive for a man who was in the job, and might also have been the prompt for some young men to join.

5.3   The culture of the job

The policeman's life was tough. Most patrolling was done at night, and it did not stop whatever the weather. In addition to the sickness brought on by exposure to the elements, policemen were commonly assaulted: during the 1890s, when assaults on police were on the decline, an annual average of some 12,000 individuals were brought before summary courts charged with assaulting policemen. The tough life appears to have contributed to a tough, masculine culture. Police autobiographies of the Victorian period and the early twentieth century commonly reveal the author taking a pride in his physical prowess and his ability to 'look after' himself in a fight. Victorian and Edwardian biographies are not the places to find discussions of sexual prowess, yet other evidence suggests that pride in vigorous heterosexual ability could be part and parcel of this tough masculinity.

police culture

There was an *esprit de corps*, which possibly had part of its origins in the police 'barracks' or section houses where the recruit constables to the London and other urban forces commonly began their careers; the horse-play and practical joking of the barrack was even known to spill over to the beat. From early on policemen were known to back each other up when in trouble from attacks on the street, from complaints by the public, and from discipline charges by their superiors.

By the mid nineteenth century this *esprit de corps* was also linked with an emerging corporate consciousness and pride in the job. Individual forces petitioned, and even took industrial action, over pay and conditions. 'Trade' newspapers, *The Police Service Advertiser* (from 1866) and *The Police Review* (from 1893), fostered this consciousness. While the *Review* itself objected to a police union with the right to strike, this corporate consciousness contributed to the movement for a police trade union in the years before the First World War. The self-help ethos of the police newspapers, with their educational pages and their inspirational biographies of men who had made good in the service, was very similar to that of other self-consciously respectable working-class organizations, notably the trade unions.

Craft consciousness and pride instil the practitioners of a skill with the notion of being the 'experts' and the 'professionals' in that skill. Of course these practitioners are 'experts', and problems arise when this expertise is questioned by a layperson or when there appears a threat of dilution. While the evidence is sparse, it appears that some nineteenth-century bobbies, rather than maintaining an even temper whatever the provocation, even bridled at members of the middle class who dared to question their authority. The stigmatized slum-dweller doubtless reasoned that he stood more chance on the streets than in the courts if he challenged a 'crusher' (the costermonger's slang for policeman) and responded accordingly.

The exigencies of world war led to the rapid training of the unskilled for certain skilled trades; the dilution of their trade craft was more or less grudgingly accepted by the skilled, but only for the duration of the war. Gaps in police ranks created by wartime military demands led to men being kept on beyond retirement age and to the recruitment of special constables. But war also boosted the demand for women police – a demand articulated, from the closing years of the Victorian period, by different feminist groups. During the First World War large, temporary military camps were thought to attract prostitutes and were feared as potential corrupters of other young women, while at the same time munitions factories brought together large numbers of young female workers. **women police** Women police were employed primarily to patrol and protect women in these areas. Generally the recruits were from a different social class to the male police; they were socially privileged and often well-educated. A few had links with feminist and suffragette activists, but the early women police were much more concerned with social purity than political and social change. The women police had an ambiguous position and, significantly, while they were required to have a knowledge of the duties of a constable, they were denied his key prerogative – that of arrest. If a woman police officer witnessed a breach of the law, it was her duty to enlist the help of the nearest male constable in the vicinity.

Some chief constables were prepared to maintain small numbers of women constables after the war to deal with problems involving women and children only. Others could not wait to dispense with women police, convinced that policework was man's work. There has been no study of what the rank and file

A woman police officer chasing children caught bathing in the Serpentine in London's Hyde Park, c.1926

thought of the few women officers who served in the First World War and the inter-war period, and the rather larger number that began to be recruited during the Second World War. However, it is probably indicative that the Police Federation only agreed to accept women as full and equal members in 1949.

There are several key issues emerging from this. Was policing just another working-class occupation? If not, in what respects was it different? Did a tough police culture develop as a result of the job, or did the recruits bring it with them? Only very recently have such questions begun to be addressed by historians. Traditional historians of the police have tended to stress the developing professionalism of the police, while labour historians have rarely considered the police as anything other than the body deployed against strikers and the organized working class. There were obvious differences between the job of the policeman and most working-class jobs – the regimentation and strict discipline is the most obvious. Yet the aspirations of the policeman as a worker were not that different from those of other workers. A tough, masculine culture may have gained something from the job, but it also drew on the broader cultural context; plenty of other male jobs developed an aggressive, self-consciously tough masculine element in their workplace sociability. The recruitment of ex-soldiers (as well as the military-style discipline) probably contributed to the police culture. Perhaps, too, the Victorian and Edwardian police attracted a particular form of personality, but this would be extremely difficult to prove.

6 A comparative perspective

6.1 'The best police in the world'

Notwithstanding the fact that they do not do everything they should, I believe that the Metropolitan Police, after the City [of London] Police, are the best police force in the world.

(John Burns, Independent Radical MP, *Hansard*, 13 July 1900, col.1559)

[Captain Nott-Bower, Chief Constable of the City of London] remarked that on the testimony of foreign countries, England was, in police matters, *facile princeps* [easily the best].

(*The Times*, 19 May 1906)

'Robert's ... wonderful faculty for combining official integrity and detachment with the part of a man and a brother ... has made the English policeman the envy of the civilized world.'

(*Justice of the Peace*, 13 February 1926, p.112)

It was commonly stated by members of parliament, policemen, journalists and others, at least from the close of the nineteenth century, that the English (sometimes the 'British') police were the best in the world. The criteria for the boast, however, were not always apparent. Charles Reith attempted an explanation based on his Whiggish understanding of national development by identifying two forms of police: 'the kin police or Anglo-Saxon police system, and the ruler-appointed gendarmerie, or despotic totalitarian police system. The first represents, basically, force exercised indirectly, by the people, from below upwards. The other represents force exercised, by authority, from above, downwards' (Reith, 1952, p.20). During the inter-war years refugees from Europe boosted such notions by contrasting their experiences of police in their own countries with such meetings as they had with polite bobbies; while few American film stars seem to have met the British press without commenting, 'Gee, I think your police are wonderful!'. The strikers at Silksworth Colliery and men marching on a demonstration of the National Union of Unemployed Workers probably took a very different view.

ACTIVITY 1.3

Look at the illustrations (opposite) of the German *Schutzmann*, the French *gendarme*, and the English bobby c.1890–1910. Are there any apparent differences in uniform and equipment? Does this suggest anything different about them?

We could have chosen other illustrations here which might have given a rather different image: for example, some English police forces had spikes on their helmets similar to the German policeman's *Pickehaube* (and similar to the parade uniform helmets of British infantry regiments at the end of the nineteenth and beginning of the twentieth centuries). Furthermore, some English policemen on particularly lonely or dangerous beats were authorized to carry revolvers on belts on the outside of their uniforms from the mid 1880s, and on occasions, in the middle of the century, cutlasses were issued for similar beats or for dealing with riots. Yet the non-military/military contrast between the bobby and his European counterparts remains valid in many respects.

German Schutzmann (left), French gendarme (centre), and English bobby (right)

6.2   The origins of continental police forces

It is important to note that Britain was a 'late developer' with regard to the establishment of a formal police institution. During the eighteenth century, police forces were developing in continental Europe, and these generally were based on the systems established in France. The absolutist princes of eighteenth-century Europe admired most things French and sought to model themselves and their institutions on the monarchs at Versailles. French models were specifically rejected by the English as being inimical to the unique form of 'liberty' which, it was claimed, had been established by the Glorious Revolution of 1688. The roads of provincial France were patrolled by the *maréchaussée*, literally the men of the marshals of France. This force was never particularly large – it reached about 4,000 men on the eve of the French Revolution – but it increasingly acquired a good reputation and early on in the Revolution it was virtually doubled in size and renamed the *gendarmerie nationale*. What specifically led the English to reject the *maréchaussée*, and later the *gendarmerie*, as a model for police reform was the military nature of the force. The men were recruited from former soldiers, they were uniformed and equipped like soldiers, and in matters of administration and discipline they were responsible to the minister of war. The wars of the French Revolution and then Napoleon extended the impact of French models by bringing, often at bayonet point, the physical experience of French administration to many of the states of Europe; when Napoleon was finally defeated the general effectiveness of his administration remained in men's minds. *Gendarmes* followed the French armies to police the troops, and *gendarmeries* were established by the French in the Low Countries, in Italy and in parts of Germany. When the French left, some of their reforms were ripped up by the roots, but the new *gendarmeries* remained. In other states, some of which had been among Napoleon's most determined opponents, the *gendarmerie* model was adopted for rural districts either during the French wars or subsequently. The Kingdom of Prussia established its *gendarmerie* in 1812; Spain created the *gardia civil* in 1844; the Austrian Empire inherited a Napoleonic *gendarmerie* in part of its north Italian provinces and later established a force to cover all its territories. But the *gendarmes* were not simply policemen; they also had a role in state-building. The map of Europe that emerged at the Congress of Vienna in 1815, following the fall of Napoleon, was rather different from that which had existed two decades before at the outset of the wars. In 1815 there were fewer states and they were bigger. The populations of these states were largely peasants, for many of whom the state meant nothing; they did not always even speak the national language. The small brigades of *gendarmes*, usually four to six men, in their village or small-town barracks over which flew the national flag, were one of the principal physical manifestations of the nation-state in the countryside. The *gendarmes* were there, the state maintained, to keep the peace and to protect the rural dwellers from bandits and brigands; but they were also there to ensure that the peasants paid their dues to the nation-state in the form of taxes and the annual quota of military conscripts.

While notions of English liberty kept ideas of police reforms along the *gendarmerie* model at bay, it is also arguable that nineteenth-century England did not need a *gendarmerie* of the European variety. There were no bandits or brigands comparable with those of southern Europe. There was no conscription and no violent unrest over taxes. There was no independent peasant class like that of rural Europe. English was the common language, and even if the understanding of the British state was shaky among the working classes, it appears to have been firmer than similar perceptions in much of rural Europe. But this is not to deny that, on occasions, English policing came close to resembling that of the *gendarmerie*. Serious rioting in south-west Wales between 1839 and 1844 led to the deployment of Metropolitan Police and troops, who carried out joint, armed patrols in the disturbed districts. During the 1850s and 1860s a succession of chief constables proposed having their men armed and trained as an auxiliary military force in case of war with, and invasion by, France. The restraining influence throughout these years was the Home Office. In the 1880s Sir Charles Warren, a former army officer appointed to be Commissioner of the Metropolitan Police, completely revised the police training book on the lines of the infantry training manual. Warren sought to keep the Home Office at arm's length, and he responded to criticism of his militarization of the force with a counterblast to his critics, including politicians, in *Murray's Magazine*.

The outcry which this provoked, together with the failure of his men to make any headway with the 'Jack the Ripper' murders in London's Whitechapel district, forced his resignation.

Across the Irish Sea the British government did create a *gendarmerie*. The rural detachments of the Royal Irish Constabulary (RIC) lived in small barracks and carried out armed patrols of their districts. Indeed, *gendarmerie*-style police were developed across the British Empire: in Canada the French title for the Royal Canadian Mounted Police is still today *La Gendarmerie Royale du Canada*, and when the force was first established in the 1870s to colonize the Canadian west, the only thing that can really be said to have differentiated it from a regiment of light cavalry was the name 'police'.

It has been commonly and popularly asserted that the RIC provided the model for Britain's imperial police, but, as ever, the reality is rather more complex. Certainly men destined to command imperial forces did attend the RIC training school, and many former members of the Irish force served in other imperial forces. But the men who governed the empire tended to be pragmatic in the way that they drew on policing strategies according to immediate circumstances. When England's rural constabularies were established in the 1840s the magistrates of some county benches looked to the Irish Constabulary for their officer cadres, reasoning that the Metropolitan Police had been created for a city and that the Irish model, designed for the countryside, was rather more relevant to their needs – though this did not lead to small barracks and armed patrols. Alongside the former army officers recruited to command county police forces in England after 1856, there were also men who had been officers in the British imperial *gendarmeries*. Moreover, RIC men patrolling in Irish urban districts were, by the end of the century, little different from their English counterparts, and did not regard themselves as different.

6.3   Urban police and political police

There is a popular misconception in contemporary Britain that all French policemen are *gendarmes*. This is not, and never has been, the case. *Gendarmes* patrolled the countryside, while in French towns there were, and are, different policemen. Although the *maréchaussée* was seen as a model by some European princes during the eighteenth century, even more effective in their eyes were the Paris police. In London around 1750 the Fieldings had their dozen or so Bow Street Runners, and the different parishes had their constables and watches of varying numbers and varying degrees of efficiency. In contrast, the *Lieutenant Général de Police de Paris* had some 3,000 men directly under his command. These men had a variety of tasks relating to the eighteenth-century European understanding of the word 'police' (*police* in French; *polizey*, in a variety of spellings, in German). During the seventeenth and eighteenth centuries 'police' was commonly used as a synonym for government, particularly the government and administration of a city. The model police of eighteenth-century Paris were thus not only responsible for the prevention and detection of crime and the basic maintenance of public order, but also for supervising everything from markets to street lighting, to wet-nurses and beyond. They maintained surveillance of beggars and vagabonds, and also of those higher up the social scale who were critical of the existing order. A belief in the existence of thousands of active police spies convinced many in England that a police force meant a spy force.

political policing

Political policing was given a further boost by the French Revolution. In France, as well as in countries numbered among its ideological enemies, spies were employed by governments to inform on those who were politically suspect. Even in Britain during the 1790s an internal spy network was developed within a section of the Home Office responsible for checking aliens.

The fall of Napoleon left a legacy of problems in continental Europe. There was the fear of liberalism, which menaced the restored monarchs with its ideas of the career open to talent. Nationalism threatened the independence of monarchs and princes in Italy and Germany – both of which were 'geographical expressions' rather than united national states; it also threatened the existence of the Austrian Empire which contained Czechs, Germans, Italians, Magyars, Poles, Slovaks and others. In France a variety of groups claimed the right to govern: royalists (and after 1830 there were two kinds of royalist), Bonapartists, and republicans of a variety of different hues. These problems ensured that governments maintained political police to keep a surveillance of both the ideas and the rivals. At times the police did rather more than this, employing *agents provocateurs*; the police chiefs in Paris during the 1820s acquired a particularly unenviable reputation in this respect. Revolutionary disorders in 1820–21, 1830 and 1848 convinced European governments of the necessity of political surveillance.

Britain stood aside from much of this. Of course, the police were expected to keep an eye on political radicals, notably the Chartists, but political surveillance was never developed in the way it was in continental Europe. British governments and political commentators noted smugly that while they might have experienced Chartism, unlike the rest of Europe, nineteenth-century Britain had not had to contend with revolution. Opponents of the new police had objected to the idea of police as spies, and it appears that successive governments, both Whig and Tory, were largely in sympathy with such objections. The revelation that a Metropolitan Police sergeant had exceeded his authority in investigating a radical group in the early 1830s led to a parliamentary inquiry and the man's dismissal. Forty years later, in the aftermath of the Paris commune, a permanent secretary at the Home Office could boast to a colleague in the Foreign Office that: 'We can safely rely on the good sense of the great bulk of our working-classes to check and defeat the wild and impracticable designs of the few' (quoted in Porter, 1987, p.10). Furthermore, when it was felt necessary to make some enquiries into the International Workingmen's Association, the Home Office decided that the best way was to write for information to that body's secretary – Karl Marx. This kind of innocence was not to continue.

The turning point in Britain came with the Fenian bombing campaign in the early 1880s. To meet the threat the Special Irish Branch was created within the Metropolitan Police. At the conclusion of the scare the new department was continued, and gradually the 'Irish' part of the title was dropped.

Simultaneously the British government found itself under pressure from its continental neighbours to do something about the political refugees to whom it had opened its doors. Earlier in the century British governments had resisted such pressure, but anarchist bombings and murders in Europe, together with concerns that Britain was losing its industrial dominance and that the British 'race' was being undermined by an exceptionally high birth rate among the residuum in city slums, combined to make the government more prepared to develop a political police. It remained a relatively small-scale affair compared with most of its European counterparts. But even in continental Europe in the last quarter of the nineteenth century political policing was rather more restrained than it had been after the fall of Napoleon; the great exception was Russia, where the secret police (the *ochrana*) became a law unto itself and engaged in a savage war of terror and counter-terror against anarchists, nihilists, social revolutionaries and virtually anyone else to whom they took a dislike.

Shortly before the First World War it was still possible to find the British Home Secretary reacting furiously in parliament to the suggestion that the Special Branch was a 'political police', but the run-up to the war with its succession of spy scares had brought significant developments in links between provincial chief constables and the embryonic secret service. The war itself, and then the Russian Revolution, cemented these links and brought British political surveillance more in line with that in Europe. Of course, there was no *Gestapo* in Britain, but the traditional, popular image of *Gestapo* terror as all-pervading is itself fanciful. Recent research into surviving *Gestapo* files has demonstrated that this was a relatively small organization which put great reliance on support and information received from the general public (Gellately, 1990).

This discussion of political police has diverted me, as it diverted and obsessed many of the early opponents of the Metropolitan Police, from the subject of capital city police, though it remains closely linked. Political policing was not the only kind of policing regarded necessary in the capital cities of eighteenth- and nineteenth-century Europe. On 1 March 1828 a senior officer in the Prefecture of Police in Paris issued a circular:

> The essential object of our municipal police is the safety of the inhabitants of Paris ... Safety by day and night, free traffic movement, clean streets, the supervision of, and precaution against, accidents, the maintenance of order in public places, the seeking out of offences and their perpetrators ... The municipal police is a paternal police; that is the intention of the Prefect.
>
> (quoted in Tulard, 1976, pp.436–7)

Napoleon had created the Prefect of Police to replace the *Lieutenant-Général*, who had disappeared along with the rest of the old regime's administrative structure during the Revolution. The description of this 'paternal police' might have fitted that of the *Lieutenant-Général*. Moreover, the year after this circular, in an attempt to improve the low standing of the Paris police following the employment of *agents provocateurs* and sensational revelations about the detective department, a new, reforming Prefect, Louis Debelleyme, created a new kind of uniformed patrolman – the *sergent de ville*. While far fewer in numbers than the constables of the Metropolitan Police, the *sergents* were lionized by their supporters in much the same way. 'The *sergent de ville* of Paris', according to one commentator in the early 1840s, is the guardian angel of the peaceable citizen, the terror of criminals. Without him your wives, your mothers, your sisters would, at every instant, be exposed to the coarseness of every lout. In the streets in your absence, to whom do they turn to bring an end to these vile insults? To the *sergent de ville* alone, *for this man is the law in uniform.*

For these agents hard labours, weariness, unpleasantness; for us happiness and pleasure. When Paris enjoys the fine days of summer; when festivals and dances follow each other; when, in the public halls, carnival unravels its long chain of masks; when all Paris dances in the transports of feverish excitement, a single man remains impassive in the midst of turbulence. On his feet, immovable, throughout the long night he sees pleasure flit before him and laugh around him, without ever being able to take part himself.

(Birroteau, 1840–42)

In the 1850s Napoleon III set out to improve the *sergents* by introducing various practices that he had witnessed at first hand among the London police, notably a regular beat system and numbers on the men's collars to make them instantly identifiable. Yet for all the praise heaped on the *sergents* (renamed, later in the century, *gardiens de la paix*), they never acquired the popularity of the London bobby among the respectable classes. At the end of the century Prefect Louis Lépine introduced another package of reforms to get rid of brutal and undesirable men and improve the public standing of the rest. The problem is how to explain the reasons for the different perceptions.

It would appear that, immediately before Lépine's appointment in 1893, discipline in the Paris police was poor, which may account for the brutality towards demonstrators and the cavalier treatment of bystanders, and that there was intense rivalry and hostility between different departments. Earlier I gave examples of brutal treatment meted out by London policemen during the nineteenth and early twentieth centuries; nevertheless, while there were criticisms and concerns expressed at times, the overall image of the Metropolitan Police does not appear to have reached the depths of that experienced by the *gardiens*. The only explanation I can offer is linked to the overtly political role of the Paris police and the differing attitudes held by articulate and influential members of society in Britain and France towards elements of constitutional government. Articulate and influential men in Victorian Britain rarely came into contact with policemen – remember, the police guarded St. James by watching St. Giles. In France, since such men could be Bonapartists, royalists or republicans, it was quite likely that they could find themselves, at some point in their lives, under police suspicion and surveillance. The French might have been proud to have given the world the idea of the rights of man, yet they recognized that this had not given them secure or stable government. In Victorian Britain, however, men took pride in a secure and stable government which had escaped the revolutionary upheavals of the continent; they criticized the political party to which they were opposed, but they did not criticize the constitutional and administrative system that was taken to be a model for others to follow. By the 1850s at the latest, the Metropolitan Police, and subsequently other police forces, appears to have been accepted as an integral part of the constitutional structure.

Outside of Paris the municipalities of France were policed by a mixture of state-appointed and locally appointed men. Legislation passed early in the French Revolution required every town with a population of 5,000 or more to have a *commissaire*. Under Napoleon the *commissaires* became central government appointees; larger towns acquired more than one, and in 1854 the post of chief *commissaire* was established in 23 major cities and towns with several such officers – Marseilles, for example, with a population of 198,000 in 1855 had one central and 18 other *commissaires*; Bordeaux, population 90,900, had one and 12 respectively. The *commissaires* had the usual police roles, but were also expected to keep in touch with, and pass information to, central government in Paris. However, the rank-and-file policemen who worked under the *commissaires* were appointed by the municipalities, and a complicated system of command and control could develop. When a local municipality was of a very different political complexion to the government in Paris, friction between the local mayor and the *commissaire* could become acute. The police of a few cities and towns were brought under the direct control of a departmental prefect. Lyon was the first of these in 1851; the city was notorious for its radical working class, which launched two full-scale insurrections (1831 and 1834) and was a constant worry throughout the revolution of 1848 and the short-lived (1848–52) Second Republic. It was believed that the Prefect of the Department of the Rhône – a government functionary with overall responsibility for the administration of the department – would have a better overall control of the police than the mayor. But more than fifty years were to elapse before another French city had its police taken over in such a manner (Marseilles in 1908), and the municipal police of France were not brought into a national organization until the Vichy regime in 1941.

I have largely stressed the Anglo-French comparisons in this discussion primarily because they provide significant models which others sought to follow. Liberals in nineteenth-century Europe looked to what they understood to be the Metropolitan Police model to develop a police system, but they generally lacked the political and social environment in which such a police could take root. Italian liberals, for example, were impressed by the English police, but equally their concerns for agrarian uprisings, anarchist bombs, socialist demonstrations and southern brigands ensured that they maintained their militarized *carabinieri* and developed a national civilian police in the shape of the *guardie di città* (or *guardie di pubblica sicurezza*). Yet, at the same time, many of the states which are generally assumed to have been far more centralized than nineteenth-century Britain continued to have urban police linked closely with the mayors and municipalities rather than central government. Towards the end of the nineteenth century in Italy, for example, there were about 10,000 *guardie municipali* responsible to local government. It was not until the 1890s that the Prussian state began seriously to contemplate taking over the municipal police in its various territories; this was partly because of concerns about democratized municipalities choosing left-wing mayors who were not considered the kinds of individual to be entrusted with the supervision of police forces.

Table 1.2 overleaf summarizes the development of policing and the establishment of police forces across Europe.

Table 1.2   The establishment of modern police in Europe and the United States to 1860

Urban police	Year	District or national police
	1536	France (*maréchaussée*)
Paris	*1667*	
Police Commissioners		
St. Petersburg	*1718*	
Berlin	*1742*	
Vienna	*1751*	
Dublin	*1786*[1]	
	1787[2]	Ireland (partial: disturbed counties)
	1791	France (*commissaires* for French towns with population of 5 000+; *gendarmerie*): subsequently spreading throughout the Napoleonic Empire in Northern Italy, the Rhineland and the Low Countries
Glasgow	*1800*	
Edinburgh	*1805*	
	1812	Prussia; Bavaria
	1814[3]	Ireland (partial: disturbed counties)
	1814	Piedmont, Italy (forerunner of *carabinieri*; other Italian states followed suit)
	1822	Ireland (all counties: compulsory)
	1826	Russia
London	*1829*	
Scottish burghs (enabling Act; subsequent Acts 1847 and 1850)	*1833*	Greece
English boroughs (incorporated towns)	*1835*	
	1836	Ireland (reformed)
Dublin (reformed)	*1837*	
	1839/40	England and Scotland (partial) (enabling Acts for counties)
	1844	Spain
New York	*1845*	
Berlin	*1848*	
	1849	Austria
Turin, Italy	*1852*	
Paris (reformed)	*1854*	
Boston, Chicago, Philadelphia	*1855*	
	1856	England (all counties and boroughs: compulsory)
	1857	Scotland (all counties and burghs: compulsory)

1   This centralized police was abolished in 1795, revived in 1799, and reformed in 1808.
2   Experiment lapsed *c.*1800.
3   This force was abolished in 1836.
Source: based on Palmer, 1988, p.17

6.4   The US alternative

A further, and final, comparison needs to be brought in here. The democratic nature of the United States kept police forces closely bound to the elected officials who ran urban government. Some police chiefs (in the shape of sheriffs) were themselves elected; elected mayors appointed others. In some nineteenth-century cities the bosses of electoral wards appointed police captains and even patrolmen. The system could ensure close links between the police and their communities: thus, there were occasions when local police refused to protect blackleg labour during strikes, especially if the employer was based out of town. But where the local mayor and corporation were employers, the police could find themselves deployed in an unashamedly partisan fashion against strikers, particularly when the latter were immigrants and could easily be labelled as un-American. The municipal police in the USA could be used in an equally blatant way at election time on the part of the faction in power. Yet the openness of US society meant also that the police were regularly under scrutiny in the courts and in the press. William McAdoo, a former chief of the New York Police, visited London in 1909 and was astonished by the difference between the police of the two cities:

> The internal workings of the machinery are not exposed to public view. Transfers of policemen and police officials are not noticed in the public prints …

> The press praises the police on every possible occasion. The press has no means of knowing of the daily volume of crime except through the courts or the reports of persons made directly to the newspapers, so the police are not held to the same direct accounting as in New York, where the statistics are inspected every hour, or, at least were under my administration …

> The [police] court treated the policeman as part of the machinery of the law, and as partners with it in the doing of substantial justice. Their intercourse is characterized by mutual respect and goodwill … Not a single policeman was reprimanded or criticized in any case, even when the court made prompt acquittals as against the charge of the constables.

(McAdoo, 1909, pp.658–9 and 661)

All of which brings us back to the central question: in what respects are the British police different from police in other countries? There is a problem establishing just what is meant by 'different' or 'unique'. In one sense every national police system is different or unique – there are clear organizational and structural differences between the British police and others. However, what they did and do on the ground is probably very similar – remember that the London Metropolitan Police system of beat patrols became a model for other states. What most commentators, politicians and policemen appear to be alluding to when they speak of 'difference' relates to the ethos of policing in Britain. The police are, allegedly if not practically, non-political; the system espouses a philosophy of 'policing with consent'; and, as a general rule, police officers have only rarely been armed. Of course, it can be argued that much, even most, of the difference is the result of contingency and good fortune, rather than design.

7   Conclusion

This brief history of the coming of the new police has highlighted the following issues. First, there was protracted resistance in England to the very *idea* of a police force on the grounds that such an instrument of government would invariably interfere with revered constitutional freedoms and liberties and disturb the peace of the country. Political opposition obliged the police reformers to drop all hopes of creating a national police force. Instead, a bewildering assortment of forces gradually took to the streets alongside a number of other individuals and groups who were performing local policing functions. While the differences must not be overemphasized, it nevertheless remains the case that three different types of police force gradually emerged in England and Wales, namely the Metropolitan Police, the borough constabularies and the county forces.

Second, during their formative period, numerous questions were raised about the precise purpose of the new forces. Questions of cost-effectiveness and efficiency surfaced repeatedly, particularly in relation to their crime prevention function, and eventually proactive strategies were developed in an attempt to curb crime. However, it was acknowledged by key sections of English society that a disciplined police *force* was manifestly useful when it came to industrial disputes, large-scale demonstrations and bringing some semblance of routine order to public thoroughfares.

Third, as the century wore on, discussion of the police centred on the vexed question of the precise nature of the political and legal relations governing policework and the constitutional implications of the claims by a growing number of chief police officers that they were operationally independent.

Finally, despite being strictly organized in a hierarchical bureaucracy, the English bobby on his beat enjoyed a considerable degree of legally mandated discretion in deciding how to respond to different offenders. How that discretion was exercised became a key question in the policing of different neighbourhoods and social groups.

As the next chapter makes clear, criminologists are still debating virtually all of the issues and controversies bequeathed by the creation of the new police.

Review questions

- What at the origins of the word 'police'?
- Why is it important to study the historical origins of the modern police?
- 'The prevention of crime is the key function of the modern police.' Discuss.
- Should the police be constitutionally autonomous or subject to political control?
- What makes the British police different from other police forces?

Further reading

The most recent thorough historical overview of the police in England is Emsley (1996b). Palmer (1988) is an enormous, comprehensive study which compares the very different origins of modern police in England and Ireland.

Philips and Storch (1999) provide a detailed and original analysis of the reform of the policing of provincial England and Reynolds (1998) presents a revisionist history of the state of policing in London prior to 1829. Carson and Idzikowska (1989) document and analyse the main structural processes underpinning the emergence and growth of the 'new police' in Scotland. The contributors to Anderson and Killingray (1991) examine how colonial policework was organized in various political, legal, administrative and anthropological contexts. Emsley and Weinberger (1991) detail how police forces in Western European states were constituted and how they worked within different political and legal mandates and developed distinctive policing styles and self-images. For a seminal analysis of the differences between the new urban police in England and the United States see Miller (1999).

References

Anderson, D.M. and Killingray, D. (eds) (1991) *Policing the Empire: Government, Authority and Control, 1830–1940*, Manchester, Manchester University Press.

Birroteau, C. (1840–42) 'Le sergent de ville', in *Les français peints par eux-mêmes*, Paris.

Carson, K. and Idzikowska, H. (1989) 'The social production of Scottish policing, 1795–1900', in Hay, D. and Snyder, F. (eds) *Policing and Prosecution in Britain, 1750–1850*, Oxford, Clarendon Press.

Conley, C.A. (1991) *The Unwritten Law: Criminal Justice in Victorian Kent*, Oxford, Oxford University Press.

Daley, H. (1986) *This Small Cloud: A Personal Memoir*, London, Weidenfeld and Nicolson.

Emsley, C. (1996a) *Crime and Society in England 1750–1900* (2nd. edn), London, Longman.

Emsley, C. (1996b) *The English Police: A Political and Social History* (2nd. edn), London, Longman.

Emsley, C. and Weinberger, B. (eds) (1991) *Policing Western Europe: Politics, Professionalism and Public Order, 1850–1940*, New York and London, Greenwood Press.

Evans, H. (1889) 'The London County Council and the police', *Contemporary Review*, vol.LV, March, pp.445–61.

Gellately, R. (1990) *The Gestapo and German Society: Enforcing Racial Policy, 1933–1945*, Oxford, Clarendon Press.

McAdoo, W. (1909) 'The London police from a New York point of view', *Century Magazine*, no.LXXVIII, September, pp.649–70.

Miller, W.R. (1999) *Cops and Bobbies: Police Authority in New York and London, 1830–1870* (2nd edn), Columbus, OH, Ohio State University Press.

Paley, R (1989) '"An imperfect, inadequate and wretched system?" Policing London before Peel', *Criminal Justice History*, vol.10, pp.950–80.

Palmer, S.H. (1988) *Police and Protest in England and Ireland 1780–1850*, Cambridge, Cambridge University Press.

Philips, D. and Storch, R.D. (1994) 'Whigs and coppers: the Grey ministry's national police scheme, 1832', *Historical Research*, vol.LXVII, no.1, pp.75–90.

Philips, D and Storch R (1999) *Policing Provincial England 1829–1856*, Leicester, Leicester University Press.

Porter, B. (1987) *The Origins of the Vigilant State: The London Metropolitan Police Special Branch before the First World War*, London, Weidenfeld and Nicolson.

Reiner, R. (1992) *The Politics of the Police* (2nd. edn), Hemel Hempstead, Harvester Wheatsheaf.

Reith, C. (1938) *The Police Idea*, Oxford, Oxford University Press.

Reith, C. (1952) *The Blind Eye of History*, London, Faber and Faber.

Reynolds, E. (1998) *Before the Bobbies: The Nightwatch and Police Reform in Metropolitan London, 1720–1830*, Stanford, CA, Stanford University Press.

Sharpe, J. (2001) 'Crime, order and historical change', in Muncie, J. and McLaughlin, E. (eds) *The Problem of Crime* (2nd edn), London, Sage in association with The Open University.

Stevenson, J. and Cook, C. (1977) *The Slump: Society and Politics During the Depression*, London, Jonathan Cape.

Storch, R.D. (1976) 'The policeman as domestic missionary: urban discipline and popular culture in Northern England, 1850–1880', *Journal of Social History*, vol.9, no.4, pp.481–509.

Stuart, J. (1889) 'The Metropolitan Police', *Contemporary Review*, vol.LV, April, pp.622–36.

Tobias, J.J. (1979) *Crime and Police in England 1700–1900*, New York, St Martins Press.

Tulard, J. (1976) *Paris et son administration (1800–1830)*, Paris, Ville de Paris Commission des Travaux Historiques.

Weinberger, B. (1987) 'Police perceptions of labour in the inter-war period: the case of the unemployed and of miners on strike', in Snyder, F. and Hay, D. (eds) *Labour, Law and Crime: An Historical Perspective*, London, Tavistock.

CHAPTER 2

Key issues in policework

by Eugene McLaughlin

Contents

1   Introduction

A significant reshaping of the British police is underway and some commentators argue that the changes are so profound in implication that they amount to a paradigmatic revolution. To evaluate this viewpoint, this chapter analyses trends in policework, the re-imagining of the cultural identity of police officers, the use of police powers on the street, and the changing structure of police governance. Throughout the chapter a sense of perspective can be gained by keeping the following in mind:

■   A society's need for social order does not require the establishment or maintenance of an organized police institution. Policing is socially necessary, but state-structured policework is not. The formation of a police bureaucracy in the UK, as discussed in Chapter 1, was not inevitable but contingent on a political elite's vision of what an orderly, disciplined metropolis might look like.

■   In many parts of the UK this vision of social order and authority was contested and resisted. From the outset, each new policework regime struggled to establish the legitimacy to operate in the existing local framework of public, communal and private social controls.

■   The new modality of policework was thus negotiated with different audiences, and multiple versions of policing were produced, each with particular symbolic and instrumental meanings for specific social groups.

■   Societies have reorganized or even discarded previously hegemonic police bureaucracies when they outlived their political usefulness, or as a result of public disenchantment.

■   The police institution is both constrained by temporal and spatial factors and able actively to influence the context within which it operates and to define its own development.

■   Police officers as individuals are involved in a complex struggle to reconcile the policies of the organization, legal procedures and public expectations with their own idea of what is meaningful policework.

■   No segment of the criminal justice system has a more visible and complicated mandate than the police.

2   The boundaries of policework

According to Jerome Skolnick (1966, p.1) any serious consideration of public policing must start with the question: 'For what social purpose do police exist?'

ACTIVITY 2.1

Examine Figure 2.1 to familiarize yourself with the nature of the police task. Try to rank the key areas of policework on a scale of 1 to 5 according to what you think the core should be. Do you think that these activities should be a police responsibility?

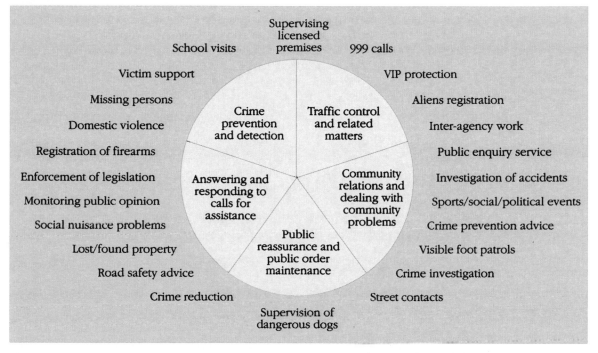

Figure 2.1   *The five key areas of policework (Source: Association of Chief Police Officers, 1993, p.2)*

2.1   Order maintenance

Research suggests that the popular image of people making contact with the police to report serious violations of the criminal law is overstated. It has been estimated that, over a full 24-hour period, calls for help about crime take up approximately 30 per cent of police time. The other 70 per cent of policework consists of reassuring the public; giving advice and assistance on a wide range of issues; taking control of and regulating problematic personal, interpersonal and communal situations; dispute management; and dealing with miscellaneous social problems, the responsibility for which has been historically imposed on the police. This picture of policework lends support to those who argue that the police are, first and foremost, a multipurpose 24-hour 'order maintenance' service. The core puzzle is why people think that calling the police will help. Bittner (1970) argues that the arrival of the police creates the dramatic appearance of an authoritative order (see Extract 2.1). In this sense the police officer is the symbolic representative of the state and of the rule of law.

order maintainance

Extract 2.1 Bittner: 'Non-negotiable coercion'

Police intervention means above all making use of the capacity and authority to overpower resistance to an attempted solution in the native habitat of the problem. There can be no doubt that this feature of policework is uppermost in the minds of people who solicit police aid or direct the attention of the police to problems, that persons against whom the police proceed have this feature in mind and conduct themselves accordingly and that every conceivable police intervention projects the message that force may be, and may have to be, used to achieve a desired objective. It does not matter whether the persons who seek police help are private citizens or other government officials, nor does it matter whether the problem in hand involves some aspect of law enforcement or is totally unconnected with it.

It must be emphasized, however, that the conception of the centrality of the capacity to use force in the police role does not entail the conclusion that the ordinary occupational routines consist of the actual exercise of this capacity ... the actual use of physical coercion and restraint is rare for all policemen and ... many policemen are virtually never in the position of having to resort to it. What matters is that police procedure is defined by the feature that it may not be opposed in its course, and that force can be used if it is opposed. This is what the existence of the police makes available to society. Accordingly, the question, 'What are policemen supposed to do?' is almost completely identical with the question, 'What kinds of situations require remedies that are non-negotiably coercible?'

(Bittner, 1970, pp.40–1)

If we accept that the police are primarily involved in 'order maintenance' and that people call the police because of the nature of the 'force' that officers are mandated to bring to bear on a problematic situation, we are left with three intriguing questions:

- What is the nature of the 'social order' the police are maintaining?
- In what situations and against which individuals will 'non-negotiable force' be employed?
- How is 'non-negotiable force' regulated and controlled?

2.2 Crime control

Thinking about the role of the police in controlling crime immediately conjures up images of the uniformed officer on the beat, acting as a deterrent and reassuring the public; of the police car rushing to the crime scene and of detectives involved in the painstaking process of working out 'whodunit'. However, research carried out on these cornerstones of policework has called their effectiveness into question (see Table 2.1).

2.2.1 Patrol work

The constable on the beat, as Chapter 1 has indicated, has always been presented as the backbone of the police, and in most forces the majority of officers are formally assigned to patrol work. However, because of specialization and factors including the shift system, holidays, training, sick leave, paper work, and time

Table 2.1   Possible police strategies for reducing crime

Strategy	Underlying hypothesis	Summary of research indications about the underlying hypothesis
1 Increase the numbers of police.	The more police a city employs, the less crime it will have.	Effect of overall numbers is unclear.
2 Random patrol.	The more random patrol a city receives, the more a perceived 'omnipresence' of the police will deter crime in public places.	Not effective.
3 Increase the use of the police power of arrest.	The more arrests police make in response to reported or observed offences of any kind, the less crime there will be.	Effective in some domestic violence situations: counterproductive for juveniles.
4 Contact with the community in general.	The greater quantity and better quality of contacts between police and citizens, the less crime.	Not generally effective except where the objective is to increase police 'legitimacy' with the public.
5 Informal contact with children.	Informal contact between police and young people will dissuade those likely to offend from doing so.	Not generally effective.
6 Respond quickly to emergency calls.	The shorter the police travel time from assignment to arrival at a crime scene, the less crime there will be.	Mixed evidence. US research finds it ineffective, but indications from UK work are that it may yield a marginal improvement in clear ups for burglary.
7 Target high profile crimes or criminals.	The higher the police-initiated arrest rate for high-risk offenders and offences, the lower the rates of serious or violent crime.	Targeting repeat offenders appears to be worthwhile, but targeting drug markets is less effective.
8 Directed patrol.	The more precisely patrol presence is concentrated at the 'hot spots' and 'hot times' of criminal activity, the less crime there will be in those places and times.	US evidence is that this is an effective strategy for dealing with local problems.
9 Targeting repeat victims.	Crime can be reduced by protecting victims from further crime.	UK research indicates that this can effect a significant reduction in certain types of crime.
10 Inter-agency working.	The police can prevent crime by working in partnership with, or providing crime-related information to, other agencies, mainly local authorities but, with the intention of informing the national effort to reduce crime, perhaps also the DETR, DfEE, Probation Service, etc.	UK evidence is that this can be a very useful mode of working for the police.
11 Problem-orientated Policing.	If police can identify specific patterns of crime and analyse the underlying problems in the community, they are more likely to come up with solutions that reduce the number of criminal incidents.	The main tenet of this rational approach has been tested on a small scale, but formal evaluation of the impact on crime in a wider implementation is awaited.

Source: Jordan, 1998, pp.65–6.

spent interviewing prisoners, uniformed constables spend between only one-half and two-thirds of their time outside the police station and approximately only one-third of that time actually patrolling. Moreover, routine unsupervised patrol work appears to have minimal impact on local crime levels:

> Set in temporal and geographical contexts, crimes are rare events, and are committed stealthily – as often as not in places out of reach of patrols. The chances of patrols catching offenders red-handed are therefore small, and even if these are somewhat increased, law breakers may not notice or may not care. An average foot beat in a large British city covers a square half-mile, with 4–5 miles of public roadway and a population of about 4,000. Thus, given present burglary rates and evenly distributed patrol coverage, a patrolling policeman in London could expect to pass within 100 yards of a burglary in progress roughly once every eight years – but not necessarily to catch the burglar or even realize that the crime was taking place.
>
> (Clarke and Hough, 1984, pp.6–7)

According to the Goldblatt and Lewis (1998), increasing the number of officers on the beat would not necessarily reduce the crime rate, nor would it constitute an effective use of resources. From this perspective, then, the constable on the beat is little more than an expensive public relations exercise.

Vehicle patrols fare no better. Available research suggests that increasing the speed with which patrols respond to calls from the public is unlikely to achieve much:

PC George Dixon of Dock Green became the fictional embodiment of the English bobby on the beat and has come to represent a golden age of policing that lacks the uncertainties and pressures that plague present-day policework

> Police officers attending to calls from the victims of crime might travel fast and hopefully, but more often than not their arrival signals the beginning of a mundane, routinized and often frustrating course of activity. They usually arrive after the critical incident has occurred and so have to make do with a mere report of it. They must rely upon external sources to find an adequate 'trace' of what has happened, and so their active role is minimal beyond the routine checking of such sources. Furthermore, because they are now dealing with history, it is seldom critical for them to uncover quickly more evidence. The officer attending the scene of an undisturbed and successfully accomplished midnight burglary the morning after will usually gain little more from interviewing the neighbours instantly rather than later. Neither his [nor her] own personal situation, nor that of the victim, nor in most cases that of the offender, will be much affected by instant action … In most … cases the role of the police, apart from giving advice and consolation would be little more than that of information processors, compilers of a formal record of what happened.
>
> (Bradley *et al.*, 1986, p.174)

The decision to concentrate officers in vehicles brings with it a whole series of unintended consequences. It effectively isolates the police by removing the need for officers to walk through neighbourhoods and cuts out access to the rhythms of the neighbourhood and gossip:

What the patrol car officer sees is familiar buildings with unfamiliar people around them. What the public sees is a familiar police car with an unfamiliar officer in it. The public has little chance to tell the officer what is going on in the community: who is angry at whom about what, whose children are running wild, what threats have been made, and who is suddenly living above his apparent means. Stripped of this contextual knowledge, the patrol officer sees, but cannot truly observe.

(Sherman, 1983, p.149)

The skill of negotiating with the public is also lost. Police officers who find themselves in a difficult public encounter can request immediate 'back-up' from police vehicles cruising in the area. As a result, the potential for conflictual police–public encounters increases. Moreover, it encourages adrenalin-driven policework as certain officers look for thrilling chases and 'trouble'. In this version of policework, walking the beat has been left to the most junior and inexperienced officers or becomes a punishment posting for those who run foul of the organization.

2.2.2 Detective work

In the period following the Second World War, detective work underwent significant developments with the establishment of specialist local, regional and national crime squads to deal with new forms of organized crime (see Hobbs, 1988; Maguire and Norris, 1992). It was also during this period that two conceptions of detective work captured the public imagination. First, there was the image of the 'hard-boiled' detective called to the scene of the crime who, in the process of attempting to answer the question of 'whodunit', used considerable organizational autonomy and professional skills to work out the logic and rationale of the criminal. The investigation unfolded: the results of

Crime analysis computer programmes, team-working, quality of service and performance league tables will leave little room for maverick detectives like Inspector Morse

forensic evidence were analysed; victims and witnesses questioned; the 'modus operandi' of particular criminals matched against the facts of the case; professional hunches followed; informants' hints and leads methodically enquired into and the usual suspects rounded up and questioned. The second image was even more dramatic, with elite squads of detectives, such as the Flying Squad, putting together sophisticated pro-active operations to catch professional criminal gangs in the act or to break multi-million pound crime rackets. Both images confirmed the idea that plain-clothes detectives were the direct heirs to the eighteenth-century 'thief-taker', spending a hectic working life putting dangerous criminals behind bars (see **Clarke, 2001**).

However, on several counts, such popular representations are hardly consistent with the reality of detective work. First, only 40–45 per cent of detective time is devoted to investigating crime. The rest of the time is spent on report writing, attending court, and miscellaneous duties. Second, detectives spend a considerable amount of time on 'relatively minor crime matters' which could be handled by uniformed officers. Third, a significant number of offences are 'self-detecting' in nature. The offender's identity is apparent from the outset; victims or witnesses know who did it, or the offender is caught red-handed or clearly implicated in some other way.

Finally, there is the ever-present opportunity for detectives to manipulate the clear-up rates. To clear the books, detectives have depended heavily on criminals and convicted prisoners confessing to other offences (Davies, 1999; **Muncie, 2001**). Such practices demonstrate that there are serious problems with using the clear-up rate as an accurate indicator of police performance and success. At the very least, researchers argue, police forces need to distinguish between *primary* clear-up rates, based on actual charges and cautions, and *secondary* ones, based on prison visits and offenders 'asking' for other offences to be taken into consideration (Walker, 1992; Audit Commission, 1990). The overall negative picture of traditional forms of policework is represented clearly in Figure 2.2.

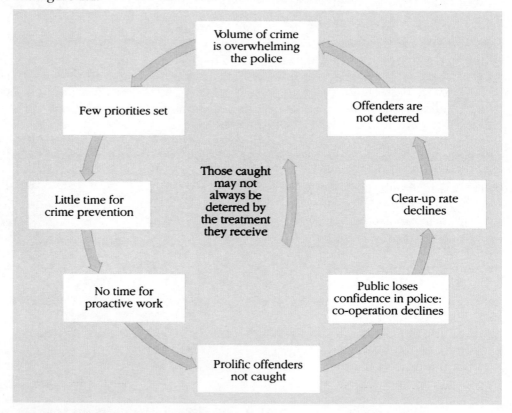

Figure 2.2   The vicious circle of crime control: the police and the rest of the criminal justice system are caught in a vicious circle of reactive policing in which crime threatens to overwhelm them (Source: Audit Commission, 1993, p.40)

2.3   Managing crime effectively

The problem of developing effective crime control strategies has presented the police with a fundamental dilemma. On the one hand, Klockars warns senior officers that controlling crime will always be a highly problematic mandate:

> The fact is that the 'war on crime' is a war police not only cannot win, but cannot in any real sense fight. They cannot win it because it is simply not within their power to change those things – such as unemployment, the age distribution of the population, moral education, freedom, civil liberties, ambitions, and the social economic opportunities to realize them – that influence the amount of crime in any society. Moreover, any kind of real war on crime is something no democratic society would be prepared to let its police fight. We would simply be unwilling to tolerate the kind of abuses to the civil liberties of innocent citizens – to us – that fighting any real war on crime would inevitably involve.
>
> (Klockars, 1988, p.241)

From this perspective the police should be careful not to represent themselves solely as professional crime fighters or to make promises to politicians and the public on which they cannot deliver. On the other hand, the public, politicians, media and, indeed, rank-and-file officers *need* to believe that the police are or can become effective crime fighters. Thus the organization has been compelled to rethink, at a variety of levels, its entire approach to this core task.

2.3.1   Localization: the co-production of crime reduction and community safety

Lord Scarman's report into the 1981 'riots' stressed to senior officers that all aspects of policework should be premised upon active community consent and participation. He argued that the police working on their own could not make a significant impact on local crime problems, and that effective crime prevention was the responsibility of the whole community. In the course of the 1980s and 1990s, police forces underwent the painful process of attempting to move towards community-centred policing by adjusting structurally to take account of local people's perceptions, priorities and expectations. They began to forge proactive problem-oriented policing styles and strategies which were sensitive to the needs of different groups and which would, hopefully, tackle rising crime rates and the fear of crime. Neighbourhood officers advised communities on how they could take responsibility for their own safety and reduce the threat and fear of crime by setting up Neighbourhood Watch schemes, joining the Special Constabulary, 'target hardening' their property and becoming more security conscious (see **Clarke, 1980**). Perhaps most significantly, the police have also as a result of the Crime and Disorder Act, 1998, entered into statutory multi-agency crime reduction partnerships with local authorities and local businesses, sharing expertise and resources, to tackle specific local crime problems (see Chapter 7 of this volume). To improve clear-up rates forces are employing upgraded intelligence networks, paid informants, decoys, new surveillance technologies, crime analysis packages and forensic techniques in an effort to put the right people in court and ensure their conviction (Audit

problem-oriented policing

Commission, 1996a, 1996b). This problem-solving approach is represented as the 'virtuous circle' (see Figure 2.3).

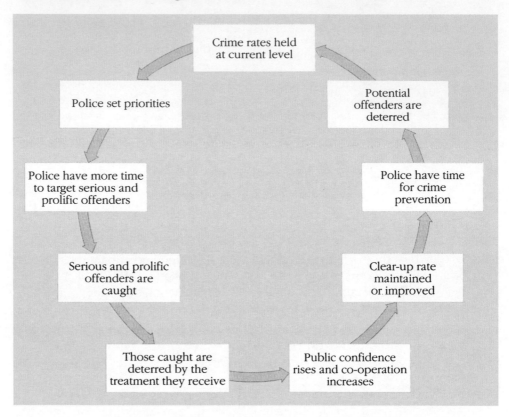

Figure 2.3 The virtuous circle of crime control: clearer prioritization, emphasis on prevention and more resources moved into proactive work could produce a virtuous circle (Source: Audit Commission, 1993, p.49)

The approach to crime victims has been overhauled generally and particular attention is paid to the impact of 'serial victimization' and the specific needs of victims of domestic and sexual violence and homophobic and racist violence. In these cases, the police have conceded that the traditional approach was characterized by delayed responses; inadequate recording; aversion to investigation; refusal to arrest, charge and prosecute; unwillingness to afford adequate protection and, in certain instances, outright hostility to complainants. Critics drew a stark contrast between the lack of time devoted to these categories of serious crime and the considerable energy and resources expended on policing victimless crimes and harassing certain communities. This response illustrated how the critical question of 'what is policed and what is not?' is gendered and racialized. In the case of domestic violence, campaigns by women's groups pressurized forces to overhaul their recording procedures, set up specialist units to deal with domestic violence, and move from a 'mediation' to an 'interventionist' stance with more emphasis on arrest, charging and prosecuting offenders (see Gregory and Lees, 1999; Hoyle and Sanders, 2000;

Saraga, 2001). It was not until the publication of the report into the racist murder of Stephen Lawrence in February 1999 and the finding of 'institutional racism' that police forces committed themselves to recognizing the particular needs of victims of racial violence; developing training appropriate to investigating racial violence; implementing pro-active strategies to tackle racial violence and involving community representatives to ensure that policies and practices are appropriate and 'race sensitive'.

Specialist community safety units were established to tackle hate crimes in the aftermath of the publication of the Macpherson Report (1999)

2.3.2   Zero-tolerance policing: law and order or social order?

zero-tolerance policing

Police forces have also periodically responded to the problem of the ineffectiveness of traditional methods by launching high profile offensives against street crime, robbery and burglary. 'Lawless' inner-city neighbourhoods and crime 'hotspots' are, without warning, flooded with officers and special 'hit squads' who stop, search and question pedestrians, set up roadblocks, raid premises and engage in intensive plain-clothes surveillance. When combined with a 'broken windows' or NYPD style 'zero-tolerance' philosophy, even the most minor misdemeanours are pursued with the same vigour as more serious crimes to create a 'maximum deterrence' effect (Wilson and Kelling, 1982; Bratton, 1997; Kelling and Coles, 1997).

ACTIVITY 2.2

Draw up a list of what you regard as the possible short-term advantages and disadvantages of zero-tolerance law-enforcement strategies. Try to assess how the various groups or audiences affected by the strategy might perceive it, and consider potential long-term outcomes for police–community relations.

Senior police officers hope that high visibility operations will: garner valuable information about the movements of local criminals; produce hard and fast evidence by catching criminals 'red-handed'; deter potential criminals; boost the morale of officers; reassure potential victims; create a local image of police 'omnipresence'; and prove to the public that the police are capable of fighting crime. However, the strategy can also generate serious problems for the police. First, it can be perceived by those on the receiving end as a crude and heavy-handed exercise of power and authority which tends not to discriminate very effectively between the innocent and the guilty. Everyone in a given locale who corresponds to stereotypical representations of 'the criminal' is treated as suspect, which can cause widespread individual resentment and distrust, particularly among young people. Second, whole communities and neighbourhoods may begin to complain vociferously of civil rights violations and blanket criminalization. Communities can contrast this over-policing with the lack of an adequate police response and 'under-protection' when they report incidents. Finally, police–community relations in certain areas may deteriorate to such a degree that both sides come to expect and prepare for conflictual contacts. Fighting the war against crime can transform these neighbourhoods into 'front-lines' where the police lose the 'hearts and minds' of people. Furthermore, it is not clear that a zero-tolerance policing operation does diminish street crime, drug dealing or prostitution: it may well only be displaced elsewhere.

2.3.3   Private and para-policing

Despite proactive initiatives, insecure and frustrated communities continue to make vociferous demands for an increased police presence to act as a visible deterrent. When police forces declare that it is unrealistic to expect 24-hour police patrols and that constables on the beat are not an effective use of scarce resources, disillusioned communities have taken direct action to prevent crime.

There has also been the development of a thriving private security infrastructure **private policing**
and the establishment of local government community safety teams and
constabularies, and neighbourhood wardens schemes (see Chapter 7 of this.
volume). These developments raise a fundamental question: Should the public
police have a monopoly over patrol work? Police Federation spokespersons
emphasize that patrolling is the foundation stone for the entire edifice of
professional policework (order maintenance, law enforcement, intelligence
gathering, instilling public confidence) and a potent source of legitimacy and
authority. The Federation has warned that *de facto* privatization and
commodification of policing services is socially divisive and destabilizing
because, if the experience of North America is typical, the wealthy will benefit
disproportionately. In its view, the government needs to re-establish the
boundaries of public work by providing extra resources to put more
professionally trained police officers on the beat.

However, certain chief police officers argue that the police should take
responsibility for training, licensing and managing the private security firms
patrolling public spaces. Ian Blair, the then chief constable of Surrey, has
presented the case for proactive engagement with 'para-policing' initiatives in
the following terms:

> We stand at a turning point in the history of policing in Britain. The past 50 years
> have seen an accelerated loss of our share of the security market – the loss of guarding
> of cash in transit, the monopoly of control of sports events, prisoner escorts, and
> above all, the subtle redefinition of what was once public space – the High Streets
> – into private spaces in the form of shopping centres, patrolled by private security.
> This tide will continue. Within 10 years it is possible that a substantial proportion of
> the police function may be absorbed by other local authorities and an unregulated
> private security sector.
>
> Alternatively, the police service can put itself forward as the central point both of
> co-operation to strengthen communities, and of patrol services carried out by a
> mixture of police, volunteer, local authority and private sources. It is not abandoning
> a monopoly of patrol. It is admitting that we haven't had one for years. The bobby
> on patrol, alone, has been seen as, somehow the point of the service. Yet you and
> I know the very small number of police officers who are actually patrolling. Chief
> officers and police authorities are simply choosing not to spend particularly heavily
> on patrolling officers …
>
> Community security should not, however, merely be left to a matter of consumer
> choice. I would want local constables to co-ordinate all that activity. We already
> train and accredit door supervision – 'bouncers' – who carry out a much more
> confrontational task. Why shouldn't we do the same with private security and local
> authority patrols?
>
> (Blair, 1998, p.18)

This debate about private security and para-policing has forced the police,
politicians and criminologists to think about whether the notion of a holistic
constabulary with a universalistic core mandate and monopoly market position
is an anachronism in an increasingly pluralistic, diverse and fragmented society
(Jones and Newburn, 1998). If we refer back to Figure 2.1 and Activity 2.1, we
might conclude that communities and a variety of public and private agencies
could undertake, not just patrolling, but many of the routine tasks presently
under the jurisdiction of the public police.

2.3.4   Nationalization and transnationalization

From the late 1980s, across the European Union senior police officers and transnationalization politicians began to argue that the nationalization and transnationalization of certain policing functions was necessary to keep pace with the de-territorialization of serious organized crime. In the UK, after considerable internal debate, the National Crime Intelligence Service (NCIS) commenced work in 1992, absorbing the national drugs and football intelligence units as well as the UK Interpol office and collecting, processing and distributing high-level intelligence relating to all aspects of serious crime across force boundaries. But it was given no powers of arrest or surveillance and could not instruct either regional crime squads or local forces. If NCIS is to develop into an effective FBI-style national police agency, Parliament will have to place it on a statutory basis and chief police officers will have to allocate it full operational capabilities.

The UK police have also become involved in politically sensitive discussions about how to develop and strengthen European police co-operation and whether a pan-European police force is feasible. Representatives of European police forces are networking, both informally and through various multilateral and bilateral agreements instituted to facilitate extradition processes and foster cross-border collaboration against terrorism, espionage, drug trafficking, asylum and immigration and other threats to national security (Anderson *et al.*, 1995; Hoogenboom *et al.*, 1997). Concerted efforts have been made by government and police representatives to co-ordinate, harmonize and institutionalize these largely piecemeal, haphazard and overlapping initiatives. For example, the Schengen group of European Union member states has created a core zone within the European Union which is free of internal frontier identity checks. To stop this open border policy becoming what was described as 'a criminals' charter', the states established the right of 'hot pursuit', stronger and stricter external border controls and the Schengen Information System (SIS) (a database of Euro-criminals and 'undesirables') which can be accessed by relevant police forces of the signatories to the agreement. In its first years of operation, the UK police were not allowed full access to the databank because the government refused to give up its border controls, arguing that they were essential to controlling illegal immigration, drug trafficking and terrorism (Abott, 2000).

However, the UK police played a more central part in the establishment of Europol, which became fully operational on 1 July 1999. Although in the early stages its remit was limited to collecting, processing, analysing and exchanging intelligence about major drug dealers and associated money launderers, its supporters successfully argued for a convention that would allow it to establish a database with permanent access to information on Europe's most menacing criminals. They also argued that eventually it should be given an operational wing, which would have the right to cross national borders and, if necessary, override local forces.

The practical difficulties of establishing a fully operational Europol or meaningful compatible cross-border policing arrangements cannot be overstated. Each state has a different and shifting vision of what type of Euro-policing is needed, how it should be achieved and resourced, and what its priorities should be. Each has different constitutional, police and legal frameworks and operational philosophies; delicate questions of sovereignty still abound and there remain very basic communication problems. It has also yet to be settled within each nation state which police agencies will take the lead role in the rapidly expanding business of national and transnational policing. In the UK, for example, MI5 and MI6, the

Figure 2.4   Police forces of the United Kingdom

political policing

state's traditional 'political policing' departments, are playing a more central role in investigating drug trafficking, money laundering, computer hacking and commercial espionage. In addition to the meshing of 'normal' and 'political' policing at national level, the European Union is also exploring the possibility of establishing a rapid reaction corp combining fully operational paramilitary police and civilian police functions.

ACTIVITY 2.3

Turn back to the beginning of section 2.3, and consider again the quotation from Klockars, bearing in mind the following questions:

1   Are those politicians and policing agencies who advocate a Europe-wide, and indeed global, war on organized crime being realistic?

2   What are the implications of this stretching of the boundaries of conventional policework? In responding to this question, you may want to consider aspects such as the relationship between localization, nationalization and transnationalization.

2.4   Public order

It has been argued that the core mandate of the police officer is to enforce dominant conceptions of public order. No matter what other roles officers adopt, if the status quo is challenged they will be called upon to defend it. Indeed radical critics such as Scraton (1985) maintain that the reason why the police are unable to do anything about crime is because crime fighting has never been their real function. Their usefulness to the state has been as a standing army to deal with collective threats to the socio-economic and political order.

public order policing

Public order policing is a particularly politically sensitive role which highlights the fundamental dilemma of how a democratic society can strike a balance between the right to peaceful assembly and public protest, and the right to public order and tranquillity. A police force which uses excessive force to suppress popular dissent or discontent runs the real risk of being characterized as a state police rather than a public police; and, relying upon its monopoly of force among an alienated populace, it risks losing legitimacy and public sympathy.

2.4.1   The golden age of tranquillity

It was believed that maintaining public order in the post-war social democratic UK would not be a particularly significant or controversial aspect of policing for three reasons. First, serious public disorder would not be a feature of British life – the social democratic settlement ruled out the need to resort to violence to resolve political differences or achieve political goals; public protests and demonstrations would be orderly and peaceful. Second, on the rare occasion when the police would be called upon to maintain public order, they would do so in a manner that would not unnecessarily antagonize protesters, demonstrators or the wider public. Police officers would adhere, even if provoked, to the unique principles of British policing: consent; maximum tolerance; the use of local officers; 'minimum force'; and steadfast neutrality. Finally, the public knew that the 'thin blue line' was unarmed and restrained and the police would 'win by appearing to lose'; if officers were attacked by demonstrators or strikers there would be a public outcry. The police would thus be able to control public order situations with minimum difficulty.

This golden moment of social democratic consensus never materialized, and the 1970s and 1980s were characterized by increasing industrial conflict, urban riots and political confrontations. Waddington has argued that during this period 'the police stopped "winning by appearing to lose" and started to actually "lose" and the response was to introduce changes designed to "win"' (Waddington, 1991, p.129). In the aftermath of the 1980s' riots, a reshaping and considerable strengthening of public order policing has taken place. As an alternative to the formation of a separate continental-style riot police, local forces established specialist public order units. A national public order policing capacity also exists and organizational structures have been developed to deploy and direct officers from every constabulary. New equipment, weaponry and surveillance technology have been made available and new public order powers granted, allowing the police to exercise much tighter control over organizers and demonstrators. Officers have also been trained in new public order tactics and strategies.

2.4.2 The case against paramilitarization

Commentators such as Jefferson (1990) reflected on the long-term consequences of these changes for British policing and argued that paramilitarization had taken **paramilitarization** place, a 'fatal attraction' because the coercive policing styles and cast of thinking that emanate from it fundamentally redefine the nature of police–community relations. Such approaches, it is argued, can seep insidiously into other policing styles. New tactics or strategies can move quickly from being exceptional, reactive measures to being the normal police response. Because serious public disorder is not a regular occurrence, specialist units may be deployed on normal policing duties or be used to spearhead drives against certain forms of 'crime' and 'criminals'. And given the nature of their training and their deployment as 'trouble-shooters', they can have an adverse effect on local police–community relations. At a more general level, ordinary officers mobilized in riot control/public disorder situations find it difficult to readjust to normal duty because they experience considerable role conflict.

Once these systems are operational they can be deployed in situations where there is little real risk of serious disorder. Shows of force can constitute an overreaction that provokes serious disturbances which prove that the initial deployment was necessary. The 1990s were littered with examples where the 'new public

'Senior officers privately conclude that once a baton charge is initiated, it is largely beyond their control to direct. The police are out of control' (Waddington, 1991, p.177)

order policing' led to various highly controversial 'battles' between the police and new age travellers, peace protestors, poll tax demonstrators and 'ravers'. Such incidents suggest that when riot police are sent in, unpredictable forces are released.

Finally, Jefferson argues, once the paramilitary pathway is taken, it is difficult to turn back. The 'mindset' of officers and forces becomes locked into these strategies, tactics and weaponry and new elite squads are created which are committed to developing public order policing from an art to a science. In addition, there is every possibility that those in conflict with the police will develop aggressive counter-tactics to meet the anticipated police response. If this 'mirror dance' happens, front-line police officers will demand more public order powers and further paramilitarization. Rules drawn up by the Association of Chief Police Officers in 1999 allow police officers in violent public order situations to fire plastic baton rounds to protect themselves or members of the emergency services. According to Jefferson, it should be drilled into officers that the real skill in public order policing is avoiding trouble and limiting the deployment of riot squads (Jefferson, 1990, p.143).

2.4.3 The need for the strong arm of the law

Other writers, most notably Waddington (1991, 1999a), argue that, whether we like it or not, we need the police to maintain a democratic social order; it is the police who furnish a sense of public security and facilitate free elections, freedom of speech, and freedom of movement and assembly. Waddington also asks us to keep the following points in mind. First, under the heading 'public order' are gathered very different situations – industrial disputes, football crowds, rallies, marches, meetings, communal riots, pop festivals and 'low level' disorder associated with night clubs, pubs etc. The police tactics employed in any given situation are linked to the nature of the specific event and careful assessment of the risk of trouble. Second, the police spend a considerable amount of time informally negotiating with groups and organizers and planning events to minimize the possibility of violent confrontation rather than invoking public order legislation. Third, the vast majority of public order situations pass off peacefully, but the media and the critics prefer to focus on instances of disorder and violence. Fourth, police officers, at every level, try to avoid confrontation and trouble in public order situations because they know that media images of police violence will lead to calls for public inquiries and investigations. Fifth, we need to recognize that there are criminally minded

Anarchy in the UK: police officers baton charge protesters during the 'Carnival Against Capitalism' in June 1999

groups in British society who hijack public events to 'have a go' at the police, and society has a duty to provide its police with adequate protection from these extremist elements. Finally, if large-scale public disorder or violent criminality occurs as a result of 'softly-softly' tactics, the police will face heavy criticism in the news media.

Waddington accepts that the creation of paramilitary units makes the police a more formidable force, but argues that such units have specialist training and rules governing their use. This improves discipline and control and makes it more probable that the principles of 'graded response' and 'minimum force' will be maintained. Officers acting on their own in a disorganized manner are more liable to lose control and to lash out indiscriminately, whereas:

> More sophisticated tactics allow the police more options. If 'pushing and shoving' becomes too vigorous for the traditional cordon, the development of the 'chorus line' enables the cordon to be maintained and avoids the need for a more forceful police response. If serious disorder erupts and dispersal becomes necessary, then the use of CS smoke, in preference to the baton charge, eliminates the possibility of people in the crowd being arbitrarily struck. If a street is ablaze, with burning barricades obstructing movement and a hail of missiles preventing police intervention … then arsonists can be stopped from committing possibly murderous actions by an incapacitating baton round, instead of the use of lethal force – gunfire.
>
> (Waddington, 1991, p.216)

Waddington also maintains that the police cannot be held primarily responsible for any paramilitarization that has taken place: 'It was not the police who abandoned consent in favour of coercion. The acquisition of this technology has been, at every stage, a *reaction* to the violence with which the police have been faced' (Waddington, 1991, p.217). He is convinced that the police and general public need to accept that police officers should be professionally trained to use 'force' in a disciplined manner. He also emphasizes that, in the final instance, facing the 'new public order police' is preferable to facing the army, as happens in many other countries.

It is very difficult to reach a definitive conclusion on public order policing because in many respects it depends on where one stands politically, theoretically and, indeed, on which side of a public order situation. Furthermore, one of the problems in studying this aspect of policework is that 'public order' is not a static condition, but constantly shifting. What is very evident is that forms of public protest and public disorder policing will become increasingly complex and sophisticated (HMIC, 1999).

2.4.4 Deadly force

Although there are widely differing views on the changing nature of public order policing, one point is agreed upon: that the routine arming of police officers would mark an irreversible transformation of British police and an irrevocable departure from custom and practice. But there is evidence to suggest that this consensus might not last for much longer. During the 1970s, there was a significant nationwide increase in firearms training for rank-and-file officers and the creation of specialist firearms support units. In the course of the 1980s, as a result of highly controversial police shootings, the police revised their policy and decided that a small number of officers should receive specialist training, to minimize the possibility of accidental shootings. Consequently, the number of officers authorized to carry guns was reduced, with the majority being attached to specialist protection squads. The remainder were either based in elite firearms teams, or patrolled in armed response vehicles (ARVs) which were introduced in the late 1980s. The rules of engagement, screening processes and training were also tightened up.

However, in the 1990s, after the murder of several police officers, further steps were taken towards the general arming of police officers. In 1994, ACPO recommended that the decision to issue weapons to non-specialist officers would no longer have to be taken by a senior officer and that specialist firearms officers staffing ARVs would be overtly armed whilst on patrol. A more low-level form of rearming also took place to offer greater protection to police officers who face a plethora of potentially violent situations in routine policework. Officers are allowed to carry side-handled batons and gas canisters/sprays and wear body armour. Police forces are also testing a variety of other 'non-lethal' forms of weaponry that are used in other countries.

At the beginning of the twenty-first century it was not clear whether the UK police would make the transition to being fully armed or whether elite, paramilitary, US-style SWAT squads would emerge as an alternative. However, there is a growing feeling among many younger, urban police officers that they should be armed because of perceptions that the UK is becoming a more violent society in which criminals are more willing to carry and use firearms.

Given his overall perspective on public order policing, it is interesting to note that Waddington cautions police officers against campaigning for routine arming (see his article reproduced opposite).

There is little public discussion about the arming of the police because it is defined as an operational matter for chief constables

History has kept officers unarmed – to their benefit, **says Peter Waddington**

Guns won't protect the police

... When Robert Peel started the 'New Police' in 1829, the idea faced profound and widespread hostility. Peel and his colleagues realized that the police could not defeat the mass of the population by force. Policing by consent was the only option, even if that consent was grudgingly offered by the lower social classes. That was why he consciously decided that the 'bobbies', unlike the Bow Street Runners and other *ad hoc* groups of constables, should be unarmed. Even the truncheon was to be hidden away, lest it should appear offensive.

The doctrine of 'minimum force' came to mean that there was a ceiling on the weapons to which the police had access – and a low ceiling at that. When a serious threat presented itself, the military was called in.

The vulnerability of the police was turned to advantage. When PC Culley was stabbed to death during a riot in 1833, and the inquest jury returned a verdict of 'justifiable homicide', there was public outrage and the verdict was overturned on appeal. Periodically since then, the murder of police officers has aroused public sympathy; the more vulnerable the officer and the more callous the murder, the greater the public outcry.

The image of an unarmed police force has been nurtured throughout the past 160 years, even when the reality was very different. Following a spate of armed burglaries in the 1880s, the Metropolitan Police allowed officers to carry a pistol on night duty if they wished. This policy was kept secret and officers were instructed to keep the gun hidden. Even today, uniformed armed officers on diplomatic protection keep their guns out of sight. When officers were allowed to carry carbines openly at Heathrow and other airports in 1987, much of the debate revolved around the effect this change would have on the public image of the police.

Rather than be accused of 'tooling up', the police made little attempt to train officers in the use of firearms, relying instead on officers who had received military training. It was only in the 1960s that such training began to be taken seriously. A few other countries have taken the same course. When Ireland became independent in the 1920s, the Garda Siochana – the police who replaced the Royal Irish Constabulary – were unarmed. This was intended to signal the change from a colonial to a post-colonial regime. New Zealand made a similar declaration by disarming the paramilitary police who had fought the Maori wars.

The colonial tradition has normally been less benign. Colonialism entails the suppression of the native population, who do not qualify as citizens. The relationship between them and the police tends to be that between an army and the 'enemy within'. This relationship is reflected in the use of military tactics and weaponry designed to inflict maximum injury, or death, not minimum force. Thus, the South African police still arm their officers with automatic rifles and train them in the use of hand grenades and mortars.

In countries where the police were armed, it was not because they faced greater dangers than the early Victorian British police, but because their origins lay in the military. On the Continent, civil policing evolved through paramilitary police, who had (and continue to have) a military and a police function. The French gendarmerie, for example, have light tanks and are expected to fight within France in time of war.

Do our police, facing gun-toting drug dealers, pay the price of a historical legacy of minimum force? Probably not: the vast majority of the world's police forces are armed and the murder of, and attacks on, the police vary enormously from one jurisdiction to another. It seems pretty clear that arming the police has little effect on their safety or on crime levels generally. The police are always vulnerable, no matter how heavily armed they are. The police must *react* to threat; the initiative, therefore, lies with the 'bad guys'. The FBI (Federal Bureau of Investigation) estimates that, in 50 per cent of police murders in the United States, the officer does not have time even to draw his gun.

Throughout the world, whatever the present level of arming, officers seek enhanced weaponry ... In other countries, officers demand 'quick draw' holsters and more powerful weapons and ammunition. In the US, the reliable six-shot revolver is being traded in for mechanically complex 'semi-automatics' that carry up to 18 rounds but are more difficult to use. This is despite evidence that, in most shootings involving the police, no more than three shots are fired. Recognising their vulnerability, police officers seek 'the edge', but they never have the edge, because they rarely have the initiative.

This is so even in a pre-planned armed operation. In 1984, PC Brian Bishop and his armed colleagues confronted an armed man in Frinton, Essex. PC Bishop called on the suspect to surrender, but the man fired two blasts from inside a bag he was carrying. Bishop was killed and a colleague seriously wounded. Fire was returned and the assailant seriously injured, but by then it was too late. Desperate, deranged and drugged adversaries are not necessarily deterred by armed police.

Nowhere in the developed world are armed police as well protected as their unarmed British counterparts. Genuine protection is not offered by weaponry, but by the conditions in which the police carry out their task. Instead of arming the police, we should attend to how order and justice can be maintained and enhanced.

(*The Independent on Sunday,* 24 October 1993)

3 Police culture and identity

It is frequently argued that police officers have a distinctive set of mutually reinforcing traits that set them apart from the public. One view maintains that, because of the nature of the work, a police career attracts recruits with an authoritarian disposition. The second perspective, which this chapter examines, stresses that it is group socialization, the work environment and institutional **canteen culture** routines that generate a very strong occupational culture ('cop culture' or 'canteen culture'). The concept is used to describe the corpus of values and associated actions that guide routine policework (Holdaway, 1996; Chan, 1997; Waddington, 1999b).

ACTIVITY 2.4

Review and categorize the various aspects of policework that we have explored so far. What types of individual coping strategies and occupational culture might be engendered by working as a police officer?

The process of becoming a police officer takes place inside an institution whose probationers have to come to terms with being located at the bottom of a hierarchical, military-style rank structure. But, despite being part of a quasi-military bureaucracy which stresses command, discipline, regimentation and following orders, as 'sworn' police officers they also possess considerable autonomy and space from the organization for three reasons. First, the office of constable is original not delegated (see Chapter 1). Second, 'law enforcement' is a complicated activity. Many laws are general, ambiguous and some are **discretion** ludicrously antiquated. Officers have to exercise their discretion as to whether in any given situation a criminal or disorderly act has taken or is taking place. In essence, they must transform 'written law' into 'law in action' and in so doing act as key decision-makers or gatekeepers to the criminal justice systems:

> A superficial look at police work is enough to show that any patrolling police officer ignores a large number of offences or potential offences on every working day. In central London he walks past many illegally parked vehicles, drives behind speeding cars, walks past shops openly selling hard-core pornography, sees prostitutes soliciting, knows of many clubs selling liquor and providing gaming facilities without a licence, goes past unlicensed street traders, and so on, usually without taking any immediate action. Where he does take action over any one of these matters, this will usually occupy him for a considerable period, so that in the meantime he can do nothing about the others. This means that, far from 'enforcing the law' in a straightforward way, every police officer must constantly make decisions about which particular offences he should do something about.
>
> (Smith and Gray, 1985, p.14)

Third, significant parts of their working life will be spent in situations of low visibility, with little direct supervision or monitoring by senior officers.

The crucial question is: What are the key determinants governing an officer's action or non-action in a given situation? Many sociologists of the police argue that the occupational culture is the principal guide to action.

Under the guidance and control of experienced officers, probationers are encultured into the real world of 'practical' policework, the territorial structures, working rules and folklore of a particular force, division, and immediate peer group. Researchers argue that it is in the canteen and in the patrol car, in both the quiet and the chaotic moments of the shift, and in the locker room that junior officers learn about the realities of 'the job', the extra-legal tricks of the trade, and the maxims for dealing with and 'solving' the highly problematic organizational and public situations they will encounter in the course of their working lives. They develop the ability to see and feel, almost instinctively, when something or someone is not right. And just as crucially, they learn how to employ mediation and conciliation and when to use the full force of the law.

Junior officers develop their own common-sense theories of 'justice', crime causation and solutions and come to distinguish between 'real' policework ('feeling collars' and 'getting figures') and 'rubbish' or 'dead-end' work (the rest) (Young, 1991). Officers learn how to identify and classify offenders and suspects and the defining features and characteristics of a typical crime. New officers also undergo various rites of passage and 'blooding' to test loyalty and trustworthiness and to cultivate group identity and team solidarity.

Because of the ever-present possibility of being abused, threatened, provoked and physically attacked, officers become hypersensitive to aspects of daily life of which civilians are largely unaware. But there are other moral dangers: there is always the temptation of corruption or of becoming emotionally over-involved with victims. And because procedural violations can lead to criminal charges, civil actions, reprimands, lost cases, demotion or dismissal, officers learn to watch their backs, protect their superiors from embarrassing information and, when necessary, raise the blue wall against outsiders:

> Their sense of security is not with the force, or the area, or even the station – it is only with their relief. They know that reporting on the actions of another PC may even help their promotion in future, but it might put them beyond the pale of their colleagues' trust and company for as long as they remain a PC. Wherever they might go in a move to another station, their reputation will follow them.
>
> (Graef, 1989, p.241)

This working personality is also suspicious of and mistrusts the motives of outsiders, particularly those who can challenge their version of reality, advocate change or voice criticism. The problem for police officers is that, while they have the task of enforcing the law through arrests, they cannot straightforwardly control the outcome of their efforts. They also complain about being humiliated as a result of aggressive and unfair cross-examination by 'bent' or 'slick' lawyers and let down by incompetent prosecutors, gullible juries and liberal judges (Graef, 1989; Young, 1991, 1993).

Police officers also experience a process of depersonalization. They come to expect to be viewed by many members of the public as uniforms rather than as individuals and to be routinely called 'pigs' and 'the filth' by some sections of society. In order to do their job 'objectively' officers must also depersonalize the public by 'stereotyping' them. The public are separated and labelled into those deemed to be deserving of police help – the community – and 'others' who are discursively excluded, the 'toe-rags', 'slags', 'scrotes', 'scum' and 'animals'. Researchers argue that in certain important respects these highly moralistic stereotypes drive the day-to-day nature and pattern of policework (Smith and Gray, 1985; Young, 1991, 1993).

There is also a tendency to think that the community does not appreciate the difficulties of their task or provide them with the necessary amount of support and/or respect they need to do their job properly. And, as Neiderhoffer (1967, p.9) first pointed out, many officers, given the realities of their working environment, develop a deep cynicism, losing faith in people, society and eventually themselves. In their Hobbesian view the world becomes a jungle in which crime, corruption, complicities and brutality are normal features of the terrain.

Smith and Gray (1985) found that a discourse of violence was central to the occupational culture, even though it was rare for officers to experience actual violence:

> This is partly because the central meaning of the job for most officers is the exercise of authority, and force (rather than knowledge or understanding) is for them the main *symbol* of authority and power, even if they actually impose their authority in other ways. Also, it is because many police officers see violence as a source of excitement and glamour.

(Smith and Gray, 1985, p.369)

It has been noted in several studies how the defining features of this culture generate many pernicious problems for the organization. The baleful attitudes of the culture towards the public in general and particular groups are the source of many unnecessarily conflictual and counterproductive encounters with citizens. The occupational culture also has the capacity to resist or subvert any 'top-down' management initiative that plays down the 'crime control' function or attempts to restrict officers' autonomy. Senior officers have had to recognize that they are, to a degree, prisoners of the culture and that control over the work situation is pragmatic and 'bottom-up' rather than strategic and 'top-down'. Many well-publicized 'liberal' plans for reforming the organization have been neutralized by rank-and-file resistance or 'cynical obedience', or 'reworked' by officers to ensure that they do not threaten the status quo.

Furthermore, the shared definition of situations, group solidarity and an ever-alert 'grapevine' provides officers with the means to 'close ranks' effectively against those officers who are deviant or different. Officers contemplating blowing the whistle on malpractice are aware that, if they are found out, they will face a very lonely and extremely vulnerable working life.

One point to make clear is that the occupational culture is not static or monolithic. There is not one police force in the UK but many, all with their own distinctive histories and cultural inflections (see Figure 2.4 in section 2.3.4). Within these forces different ranks have their own 'take' on the canteen culture. Various elite departments, different divisions, shifts or sectors develop their own distinctive sub-cultural orientations. Each new generation of officers also brings with it different attitudes, values and concerns, some of which will be absorbed into or even refocus core aspects of the occupational culture. Finally, the culture has to adapt to new laws and rules, shifts in formal working practices and policing styles and a changing social context (see Dixon, 1997; Chan, 1997; Waddington, 1999b). Questions of gender, sexuality, race and ethnicity also have to be taken into account in any serious discussions of the defining features of the organizational culture.

3.1   Issues of gender and sexuality

It is argued that the police organization as a whole, and the canteen cul\[ture in\] particular, 'represents' and projects a particular type of masculinity:

> in the emphasis on remaining dominant in any encounter and not losing face\[, the\] emphasis placed on masculine solidarity and on backing up other men in the gr\[oup\] especially when they are in the wrong, the stress on drinking as a test of manlin\[ess\] and a basis for good fellowship, the importance given to physical courage and t\[he\] glamour attached to violence. This set of attitudes and norms amounts to a 'cult \[of\] masculinity' which also has a strong influence on policemen's behaviour toward\[s\] women, towards victims of sexual offences and towards sexual offenders.
>
> (Smith and Gray, 1985, p.372)

In the post-war period, the police became one of the last occupations where the ideology of the full-time, single-occupation, male breadwinner, who worked outside the home providing for his family, had real meaning. This had considerable implications for women officers.

The Sex Discrimination Act of 1975 compelled a deeply reluctant force to abolish separate policewomen's departments. Women found themselves in an institution that believed they would undermine the *essential* masculinity of the organization because:

- They did not have the necessary physical stamina needed to engage in routine policework.

- Their presence in violent situations would put their male colleagues at risk.

- They would not be an economic investment because marriage and family would inevitably come before careers and commitment.

- They would present a discipline problem. Supervisors would be less strict with female officers over deployment and shifts, and would have difficulty controlling male officers because of the sexual dynamic introduced into an intimate working environment.

Women suffered considerably as a result of integration into what Campbell (1993, p.20) has described as 'the most masculinized enclave in civil society'. They endured stereotyping, derogatory banter, intrusive questioning about marital status or sexual orientation, unwanted sexual advances and outright harassment. They were excluded and side-lined from specialist departments which were crucial 'career fields'. Without operational command experience it was virtually impossible to progress through the ranks (Heidensohn, 1992). They also stood outside all-important 'old boy networks' and Freemason lodges. Women officers found themselves limited to administrative tasks because they had 'an instinct for tidiness' and/or looking after the victims of sexual offences, young offenders and children because of their supposedly compassionate nature (Brewer and Magee, 1991). There were also questions over whether the interests of women officers were adequately represented by the Police Federation, Superintendents' Association and ACPO.

Women fared badly when it came to promotion and there were considerable regional variations – several forces had no women in senior positions. Hence, for decades there was no 'critical mass' of senior women officers to provide patronage or support to junior women officers or to push for cultural change within the organization. Just around the time forces received Home Office Circular 87/1989, which stressed the importance of implementing equal opportunity policies, the issue of sexism at all levels in the police finally surfaced as a public issue. In 1990, Alison Halford, the Assistant Chief Constable of Merseyside and the then most senior woman officer in the country, brought a sex discrimination case against the force on the grounds that she was being repeatedly turned down for promotion while male officers with less experience and qualifications were being appointed.

Her decision to go public triggered a bitter dispute with her chief constable and the police authority (Halford, 1994). The senior officers of the force stood accused of ingrained hostility to female officers, chaotic and capricious management, and operating a promotion system premised not on merit but on corrupt patronage and whim. She was, in turn, suspended from duty, and accused of being promoted beyond her ability, of lacking professional judgement, not being a team player, neglect of duty, discreditable conduct and falsehood.

In 1992, after it was decided that the police authority had acted unfairly in opening disciplinary proceedings, and just before senior police officers were due to give evidence, the case was settled out of court. The police attempted to play down the significance of the Halford case by saying that her views and experiences were not representative. However, the issue did not go away. A Home Office study (1993) reported that nearly all the women officers surveyed had experienced some form of sexual harassment and this was at a significantly greater rate than that experienced by other women working within the police. A report by Her Majesty's Inspectorate in the same year concluded that breaches of equal opportunities policies were often instigated or defended by senior officers. Both reports concluded that many female officers were suffering from routine low-level harassment; and that when they brought it to the attention of their senior officers, they were likely to meet with hostility, prevarication and pressure to drop the complaint. The reports agreed that women officers spent a considerable amount of their personal resources managing male colleagues instead of doing their job. The result, in certain cases, was stress, poor performance, absenteeism and demoralization (see Figure 2.5).

The case of WPC Sarah Locker also provides us with an insight into what can happen to a police officer if she decides to pursue a case for workplace harassment. The Metropolitan Police made a public apology and settled an employment tribunal case for sex and race discrimination brought by WPC Locker in 1993. She initiated the case as a result of being subjected to hardcore pornographic material and derogatory comments about her Turkish origins. In June 2000, the Metropolitan Police agreed to pay Sarah Locker an out-of-court settlement package of an estimated £1 million. Locker was suing the force for breach of contract and negligence, arguing that it had broken the back-to-work agreement of 1993. She claimed that upon her return to work she was subjected to a hate campaign by colleagues, given no structured support by senior officers, and sidelined from meaningful policework. Commenting on the Metropolitan Police's refusal to admit liability despite the large pay out, Alison Halford pointed out that:

The publicity surrounding the case of WPC Sarah Locker undermined the efforts of the Metropolitan Police to address racism and sexism within the force

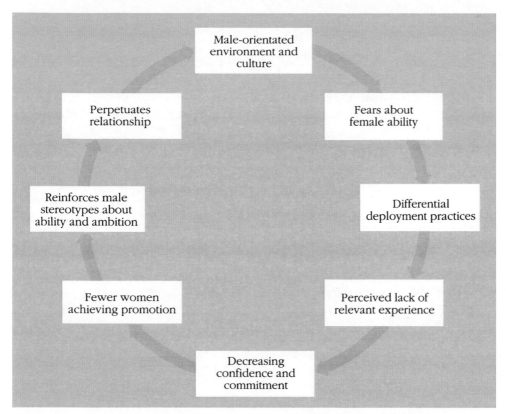

Figure 2.5   Causes and effects of discrimination (Source: adapted from Jones, 1986, p.109)

The Locker settlement is just the tip of the financial iceberg when all internal costs are calculated. Officers we pay to uphold the law use the public purse to resolve management failures. Senior officers walk away unscathed, and although the victim gains some recompense, nothing substantive changes. Chief officers will only amend their behaviour when faced with external pressure. Jack Straw must demand a Lawrence-type inquiry to establish the facts and bring about a commitment to resolve the ingrained culture of sexism in British police forces.

(*The Guardian*, 8 June 2000, p.8)

The sexuality of officers has also become an issue within the force. Many in the gay community viewed the police as an organization that: refused to respond effectively to 'queer bashing'; acted as agents provocateurs by loitering in public toilets known to be frequented by gay men; and targeted and raided gay bars and clubs. The police also stood accused of being openly hostile to the idea of gay police officers. Every time the question of anti-gay recruiting practices was raised, letters would appear in police publications claiming that gay men and lesbians should not be allowed to be police officers because they adversely affect the ability to:

- maintain discipline, morale and authority on the streets;
- foster mutual trust and confidence;
- ensure the moral integrity of the system;

- facilitate the assignment and deployment of officers who must work in close proximity with minimal privacy;
- prevent blackmail and corruption;
- sanction same sex body searches (see Burke, 1993; Leinen, 1993).

In 1991, a Lesbian and Gay Police Association covering every rank up to chief superintendent was launched and campaigned to make sexual orientation a mainstream issue within the force and to ensure there was no discrimination against lesbian and gay officers.

3.2   Issues of 'race' and ethnicity

Evidence has also surfaced of the difficulties black police officers face in an overwhelmingly white ethnocultural organization. In the aftermath of the 1981 riots, the police were forced to consider once more the implications of predominantly white forces patrolling ethnically diverse neighbourhoods. Various reasons were put forward to explain the under-representation of black officers. The police argued that there was no reason why people should be automatically interested in becoming a police officer and that many potential recruits feared being alienated from their own community. It was also suggested that white people would not take orders from a black officer. Black organizations argued that no sensible black person would think of joining an institutionally racist organization.

The Scarman Report recommended that renewed efforts be made to recruit from minority ethnic communities. However, senior officers were forced to realize that there was a high turnover among black officers as a result of racial prejudice and discrimination. Smith and Gray (1985) and Holdaway (1993) found that black officers were isolated and extremely vulnerable and had to work in an environment where racist jokes, stereotyping and banter were the norm. In 1994 the Black Police Association (BPA) was set up to act as a network group to improve the working environment for police officers and civil staff of African, African-Caribbean or Asian origins. The BPA in its written submission to the Stephen Lawrence inquiry in 1998 provided an insider's perspective on the relationship between 'institutional racism' and the occupational culture:

institutional racism

> A second source of institutional racism is our culture, our culture within the police service. Much has been said about our culture, the canteen culture, the occupational culture. How and why does that impact on individuals, black individuals on the street? Well we would say that the occupational culture within the police service, given the fact that the majority of police officers are white, tends to be the white experience, the white beliefs, the white values. Given the fact that these predominantly white officers only meet members of the black community in confrontational situations, they tend to stereotype black people in general. This can lead to all sorts of negative views and assumptions about black people, so we should not underestimate the occupational culture within the police service of institutional racism in the way we differentially treat black people.
>
> (cited in Macpherson, 1999, para. 6.28, p.25)

Issues of gender, 'race' and sexuality have challenged the occupational culture. For decades, senior officers and Home Office officials ignored, denied or downplayed allegations of prejudicial attitudes and discriminatory police behaviour in the public sphere; and so long as the ranks held together there was little possibility of addressing such complaints. However, once women, black and gay officers began to go public on their experience of the private world of the organization, one question above all others was bound to be posed: If this is how colleagues are discriminated against, what can the general public expect?

It was this uncomfortable reality that made equal opportunities an acknowledged organizational issue in the police. Various policy statements and strategy documents, circulating in the aftermath of the devastating report into the murder of Stephen Lawrence (Macpherson, 1999), stressed that the police would not tolerate a workplace ethos that is sexist, homophobic or racist or that harbours discriminatory working practices. As a result, targets were set for recruitment from under-represented groups and 'active career development' programmes put in place to ensure that all officers fulfil their potential (HMIC, 2000). However, each high-profile case of sexism, homophobia or racism undermines the much publicized commitment of police forces to equal opportunities and 'diversity'. Such cases also stand as a reminder of the strength of the occupational culture.

As part of its response to the Macpherson Report (1999) the Police Federation launched an advertising campaign to challenge racial stereotyping within the police

4 Police powers and human rights

Baldwin and Kinsey (1982) have argued that, in a democracy, there is an inherent tension between providing the police with the necessary powers to bring offenders to justice and ensuring that they use these laws impartially, responsibly and in a manner that is not an unwarranted infringement on civil liberties and human rights.

Any proposed review and change to the criminal law is likely to produce a predictable, often ritualistic exchange of charges and counter charges between the police and civil liberties groups. Police representatives tend towards a crime control/law and order stance, arguing that they are being forced to derogate from the rule of law and due process and that they need more powers and fewer restrictions to do their job properly. Periodically they raise a hue and cry about collusion between members of the legal profession and the criminal fraternity, argue that existing powers are antiquated and unworkable, that loopholes need to be closed to stop the acquittal of the guilty, and point out that law-abiding members of the public in a democratic society have nothing to fear from new police powers.

Human rights groups take a due process/rule of law line, maintaining that extensions of police power will inevitably be at the expense of the rights of the individual and that, for example, so-called technical loopholes are in fact rights and liberties that guard against the harassment and conviction of the innocent. From this viewpoint, each act of police empowerment legitimizes pre-existing extra-legal police practices, becomes the basis for further extension of powers, and results in the further erosion of civil liberties and human rights. Human rights groups argue that legislators pay more attention to empowering the police than to providing a legal framework which manifestly safeguards the rights of the individual. For example, public order legislation has never laid down statutory clauses which would place on a firm legal footing the right to participate in demonstrations, processions and assemblies. They believe that the police should have to prove, to an independent, democratically constituted review body, the contribution that a given power makes to the prevention and detection of crime. If proof is not forthcoming the power should be repealed or suspended. They also stress that the police have become a powerful and successful pressure group and accuse them of using media panics about crime and disorder to expand their powers and neutralize demands for accountability. As it is not possible in this chapter to discuss every aspect of the debate about police powers, we will concentrate on facets of 'stop and search' as it has been a constant source of conflict in police–community relations.

4.1 Stop and search: controlling the streets

reasonable suspicion

Stop-and-search powers, which are premised on the notoriously loose concept of 'reasonable suspicion', have been the source of controversy for many years. The police argue that the powers are the cornerstone of street policing which aid the detection of crime and arrest of offenders and allow for a crucial sifting or gate-keeping to take place prior to the decision to arrest.

However, there have been persistent allegations that highly discretionary street policing powers are not used primarily to assist crime detection but to collect information on individuals, control localities and discriminate against certain communities. For these reasons, stop-and-search practices have been a major cause of tensions between the police and minority ethnic communities. Smith and Gray (1985) found that officers:

> strongly tend to choose young males, especially young black males. Other groups that they tend to single out are people who look scruffy or poor ('slag'), people who have long hair or unconventional dress (who, they think, may use drugs) and homosexuals. We observed two cases where men were stopped purely because they appeared to be homosexual. In a few cases there appeared to be no criteria at all and the stop is completely random; this happens especially in the early hours of the morning when police officers tend to be bored.
>
> (Smith and Gray, 1985, p.496)

The Police and Criminal Evidence Act 1984 (PACE) provided all police officers with a general power to stop and search a person in a public place, if they had reasonable grounds for suspecting that they would find stolen goods or prohibited articles. It also laid down procedural safeguards to ensure that the powers were not used in an arbitrary or capricious manner. Police officers would be required to state the purpose of a search and their grounds for undertaking it, before a search could be carried out. A record of the search had to be made (detailing purpose, grounds, date and time, place and outcome) and be made available to the suspect. Codes of Practice accompanying the Act attempted to specify what constituted 'reasonable suspicion'. There had to be a firm basis for the officer's suspicion, not merely suspicion based on hunch, gut feeling or instinct:

> there must be some objective basis for it ... Reasonable suspicion can never be supported on the basis of personal factors alone without supporting intelligence or information. For example, a person's colour, age, hairstyle or manner of dress, or the fact that he is known to have a previous conviction for possession of an unlawful article, cannot be used alone or in combination with each other as the sole basis on which to search that person. Nor may it be founded on the basis of stereotyped images of certain persons or groups as more likely to be committing offences.
>
> (Home Office, 1991, pp.13–14)

This was an attempt to modify the organizationally invisible behaviour of officers on the street by focusing their attention on the need for an objectively verifiable stop. It was argued that the new inhibitory rules would ensure that stops were used more sparingly and any that did take place would be on stronger grounds leading to more arrests.

However, research suggested that problems would remain with the new approach. First, there is only a requirement to record where searches have taken place. Second, there is evidence to suggest that police officers have devised techniques and procedures that bypass or avoid the former safeguards (the 'ways and means' act). One way round the rules, for example, is to negotiate 'consensual' encounters. A significant number, if not the majority, of stops and searches are not recorded because members of the public consent to being questioned and searched. In such cases, PACE, particularly the requirement of 'reasonable suspicion' and legal constraints, does not apply. Hence, Bottomley *et al.* argue that much street policework happens in the 'grey area' between the clear exercise of coercive powers and the informed consent of citizens:

The co-operation of citizens, many of whom do not know about their rights and police powers, is a valuable resource for every police officer, who has little incentive to establish whether that co-operation represents 'true' informed consent. If many searches are done without co-operation, and outside PACE procedures, who can say with certainty that suspects' rights are being consistently safeguarded under new legislation?

(Bottomley *et al.*, 1991, p.40)

Third, there is considerable variation in the use of stop-and-search powers by different forces; whether the variations are due to differences in police policy or in recording practices is difficult to establish. Fourth, the arrest rates indicate that the 'hit rate' has not changed appreciably. Fifth, there is little meaningful monitoring of the stop-and-search records by supervising officers. There is no way of knowing, for example, whether the reason stated in the record is in fact the same as the original reason that led to the stop and search. As Smith (1986) has argued:

a policy like stop and search *cannot be effectively regulated through the law* and its embodiment in the criminal justice system. A law on stop and search is essentially permissive; like the law against obstructing a police officer it represents a resource that the police may use. We can argue about whether the police exceed their statutory power – I say they do – but this is ultimately irrelevant since there is no conceivable way in which such a vague (and necessarily vague) criterion as 'reasonable suspicion' can be made to constitute an effective constraint. In this field, the law is just a source of *presentational rules* which exist to put an acceptable face on practices we prefer not to look at squarely.

(Smith, 1986, p.93)

The inquiry into the murder of Stephen Lawrence was given testimony indicating that disproportionality in the use of stop and search remained a source of complaint in London's minority ethnic communities. The final report noted:

If there was one area of complaint which was universal it was the issue of 'stop and search'. Nobody in the minority ethnic communities believes that the complex arguments which are sometimes used to explain the figures as to stop and search are valid … It is not within our terms of reference to resolve the whole complex argument on this topic. Whilst there are other factors at play we are clear that the perception and experience of the minority communities that discrimination is a major element in the stop and search problem is correct.

(Macpherson, 1999, p.312)

The report concluded that 'the powers of the police under current legislation are required for the prevention and detection of crime and should remain unchanged' (*ibid.*, p.333). However, it is also recommended that:

- a record is made by police officers of all stops and stops and searches made under any legislative provision;
- non-statutory or voluntary stops also be recorded;
- the record include the reason for the stop, the outcome, and the self-defined ethnic identity of the person subjected to the stop;
- a copy of the record be given to the person;
- records be monitored, and analysed and reviewed;
- information and analysis be published;

■ police authorities be empowered to undertake publicity campaigns to ensure that the public is aware of 'stop-and-search' provisions and the right to receive a record in all circumstances.

In the aftermath of the publication of the report, strenuous efforts were made by the Metropolitan Police in particular to re-legitimate the power of stop and search. For example, in December 1999 the force published research findings which drew together the available evidence on S1 PACE stop-and-search powers (Fitzgerald, 1999). Whilst acknowledging that the power was a source of tension in police–community relations and that it could be abused by officers, the study reiterated that stop and search contributes to the detection and prevention of crime by producing arrests, especially for categories of crime such as possession of drugs, 'going equipped' and carrying offensive weapons; generating intelligence and information flows and acting as a general deterrent.

The study also argued that the debate on 'disproportionality' and 'fairness' was considerably more complex than had been previously acknowledged. A number of specific recommendations were presented to deal with the problems generated by conflictual stop and search. It also advocated a new approach which would encourage more professional use of the power within 'a clearly defined framework linked specifically to public concerns and police objectives', namely: local audits of the use of the power; jointly agreed plans for the use of the power in the context of local crime strategies; and publication of the plan along with information targeted at young people about the circumstances under which stop and search happens and what their rights are.

The study's main findings on the value of retaining the power and the other recommendations were enthusiastically received by the Metropolitan Police and the Home Office. As a result of the Macpherson Report, the debate about whether stop and search can be used in a much less discriminatory and conflictual manner is considerably more complex and open-ended (Bland *et al.*, 2000; Jordan, 2000). The police face the difficult task of explaining how racism has been institutionalized in their stop-and-search policies and practices, and identifying how they can construct an anti-racist street policing philosophy. If no progress can be made on the issues of disproportionality, fairness, effectiveness and public confidence, there will be renewed campaigns to tighten the legal framework that permits the use of stop and search or to abolish the power on the grounds that it violates the Human Rights Act.

5 The governance of policework

ACTIVITY 2.5

To what extent and to whom do you think the police should be accountable? In addressing these questions, you will need to consider:

1   What 'accountability' means.
2   Different modes and levels of accountability.
3   The difference between accountability and control.

4   Who should determine policing needs and priorities (for example, should it be the community? the police? politicians?).

5   From your reading of the first two chapters in this book, what do you think are the issues which might cause the notion of accountability to be a sensitive and complicated concept in policework?

Brogden *et al.* argue:

> police accountability becomes an issue when there is public concern that the arrangements for ensuring the police perform satisfactorily any part of their role are not working. Such concern may arise through dissatisfaction with … the biased use of powers and the wasteful deployment of resources to practices unacceptable to any section of the public: with anything, in short, which threatens to undermine any of their central obligations.
>
> (Brogden *et al.*, 1988, p.153)

accountability

Senior police officers assert that the police are one of the most accountable organizations in the country. Constables, it is argued, are accountable to the courts, to prosecutors who scrutinize all the paperwork involved in criminal cases, to internal supervisory systems, and to a disciplinary code under which serious complaints are investigated by an independent police complaints authority. Chief constables are constrained by the law and are accountable to police authorities and, ultimately, the Home Secretary for the running of their forces. Police representatives also argue that they are accountable to the community through a variety of consultative bodies and through the constant focus of a highly critical media. Critics of the present system stress, however, that we must distinguish between formal, paper modes of accountability and substantive meaningful ones.

5.1   Legal accountability

Being accountable to the courts can be regarded as the ultimate form of accountability because both statute and common law specify the powers available to the constable and establish the legal ground rules of policework. A court can exclude a confession where there was oppression or if anything has occurred to make it unreliable. It also has the discretion to exclude evidence that might influence the fairness of the trial. Police officers are also constrained by a panoply of pre-trial checks, such as the custody record, the tape recording of the interrogations, and prosecutors' demands for transparently credible and well-prepared cases. But questions remain about the capability of the legal system to police the police. Critics argue that the legal mode of accountability is *retrospective* and selective in that it tends to turn on technical points of law rather than critically scrutinizing the principles and processes of routine policework. And judges tend to work with a human error or 'rotten apple' theory of police malpractice rather than countenancing the idea of institutional or systematic rule-breaking. Furthermore, as Sanders and Young (1994) argue, judicial control only applies to those cases that are brought to trial; and since the vast majority of defendants plead guilty, the legal gaze can be remarkably limited.

5.1.1 The complaints process

Stenning has argued that:

> An effective process for handling public complaints against the police requires many things: a sound legislative foundation; dedicated, competent, experienced and/or trained personnel to administer it; a reasonable level of commitment and co-operation on the part of the police organizations and personnel to whom the process applies; an adequate degree of knowledge of, confidence in, and willingness to use the process, and good faith on the part of potential complainants in particular and the public more generally; and the commitment of adequate resources for full and effective implementation of the process.
>
> (cited in report of the Independent Commission on Policing for Northern Ireland, 1999, pp.36–7)

The Police Complaints Authority (PCA) was set up under PACE to supervise the investigation of serious complaints against police officers and also of cases not based on complaints but voluntarily referred to the PCA by a police force because they raise grave or exceptional issues. It was also mandated to review completed investigations, whether supervised or not, to decide whether police officers, below a certain rank, should face disciplinary charges. Supervision consisted of a PCA member approving the appointment of the investigating officers and then overseeing the conduct of the inquiry and examining the evidence as the inquiry takes shape. Once the investigation was concluded, the PCA issued a formal statement as to whether it has been satisfactory or not. If the final report suggested that a police officer may have committed a criminal offence, the report was passed to prosecutors who evaluated the evidence and decided whether to prosecute. If there was no criminal prosecution, the chief constable of the force involved had to decide whether a disciplinary charge would be appropriate.

From its inception, the PCA found itself embroiled in considerable controversy. Police officers denounced it as a body that had too many powers, touted unscrupulously for business, and victimized good people doing a messy job. Civil liberties campaigners condemned it because it depended on serving police officers to carry out the actual investigations and had few real powers. Both civil libertarians and rank-and-file police officers were united in their demands for it to be replaced by a fully independent and impartial complaints investigation body.

The PCA acknowledged that it faced a number of problems in carrying out its work effectively. For example, because most stops and searches or arrests are one-to-one, complainants had considerable difficulty in producing corroborative evidence, unless exceptional violence had been used by officers. Moreover, the PCA found in many important cases that very few officers were willing to give evidence against each other. Finally, many officers exercised their right of silence when questioned over alleged improprieties. Hence the Crown Prosecution Service was forwarded cases where there was not enough evidence to proceed.

Internal disciplinary proceedings were difficult to pursue because, as a result of rank-and-file campaigning, the standard of proof in police discipline cases was uniquely the same as that of a criminal trial; that is, proof beyond reasonable doubt, as opposed to that of a civil trial, the balance of probabilities. Additionally, criminal lawyers could be engaged by officers to refute disciplinary allegations, though not to substantiate them. Furthermore, the PCA found that officers under investigation could undermine the inquiry by leaving the force on medical grounds with full pension rights. This left a significant number of cases unresolved and pre-empted the outcome of disciplinary proceedings. Not surprisingly, given the obstacles that investigators faced, there were serious delays in bringing cases to court and important cases were thrown out by the courts. The PCA also complained about undue restrictions on the release of information about the progress of cases.

But perhaps the most fundamental problem remained the reluctance of many people with grievances to activate the formal complaints procedure because of cynicism towards a system where police officers investigate other police officers, and the potent threats of their evidence being subsequently used against them if their complaint failed or of harassment by colleagues of the police officers concerned. The PCA's lack of success in bringing manifestly corrupt and criminal officers to justice and lack of adequate explanation confirmed to many the pointlessness of using the formal complaints machinery. It is in this context that certain solicitors advised clients that private prosecutions and civil proceedings were more effective ways of seeking redress and justice. As a consequence, during the 1990s the Metropolitan Police, for example, paid out millions in settled actions following claims for wrongful arrest, false imprisonment and assault. However, critics argue that this was unsatisfactory because in such cases police forces did not have to admit liability or guilt, did not have to apologize and were under no obligation to take further disciplinary action against the officers involved.

Several potentially significant shifts in the investigation of police complaints took place in 1999–2000. Following the publication of the Home Office Affairs Committee Report into 'Police Disciplinary and Complaints Procedures', the Home Office declared its intention to introduce procedures to: deal with unsatisfactory performance (as distinct from misconduct); use a civil rather than criminal standard of proof at discipline hearings; and fast track the dismissal of officers in cases of serious criminal misconduct where the evidence is overwhelming. The Home Office also announced that, in line with Recommendation 58 of the Macpherson Report and to shore up public confidence in the police, it would give serious consideration to handing over investigations into complaints against the police to an independent investigation body (KPMG, 2000). In Northern Ireland, an official review of the police complaints system which was published in 1997 recommended an independent Police Ombudsman with an independent team of investigators and changes to the internal disciplinary code. The report of the Independent Commission on Policing for Northern Ireland (1999) supported the government's decision to implement the recommendations and proposed that the Police Ombudsman should: exercise the power to initiate investigations even if no specific complaint has been received; compile data on trends and patterns in complaints against the police; and investigate and comment on police policies and practices, where these are perceived to give rise to difficulties.

By 2001 there seemed to be a new consensus emerging in the UK that an independent police complaints system is vital to ensure police accountability to the law, public confidence in the police, and the protection of human rights (see also Runnymede Trust, 2000). In this context it is also worth noting that the

Council of Europe (1997) launched a special human rights programme for European police forces in order to: raise awareness of national, European and international standards for the protection of human rights; identify the role of the police in the protection of human rights; identify groups and individuals who are at risk and in need of support; and develop education and training initiatives that will inculcate respect for human rights in all officers.

5.2 Democratic accountability

The 1964 Police Act established a tripartite structure of police governance. Police authorities, composed of two-thirds local councillors and one-third magistrates, were given the responsibility to secure and maintain adequate and efficient local forces. They had the powers to appoint chief constables and could require their retirement on efficiency grounds. However, all major decisions made by the authorities were subject to the final approval of the Home Secretary who was also given the important fiscal responsibility for allocating a central grant, representing half of each force's annual budget. Police forces were placed under the direction and control of the chief constables. To ensure political impartiality, the Act enshrined the 'operational independence' of the chief constables from the police authorities and the Home Secretary, reiterating that they were not civil servants or local government employees and that they should be free from conventional processes of democratic accountability. Chief constables could be required to submit *ex post facto* reports on local policing matters, but could exercise discretion and refuse to do so if they considered the information not to be in the public interest or outside the authorities' remit. They could also appeal to the Home Secretary against such demands. Chief constables were also given responsibility for all appointments and promotions below assistant chief constable and the disciplinary authority for these ranks. The Home Secretary's supervisory powers spanned pay and regulations, the monitoring of force performance through an inspectorate of constabulary and, controversially, continuing to act as the police authority for the Metropolitan Police.

During the deliberations on this Act there were angry protests from local government representatives that the powers of both the Home Secretary and the chief constables were being clarified and enhanced at the expense of the local government police authorities. The Act, it was claimed, was not sustaining a tripartite but creating a bipartite structure of police governance. The police authorities would in any conflict be squeezed between the Home Secretary who had the power of veto and the chief constables who were constitutionally entitled to ignore them. Lord Denning put a final seal on the legal position of the chief constables, *vis-à-vis* the Home Secretary and the police authorities, when he proclaimed that the chief constable:

> is not the servant of anyone, save of the law itself. No Minister of the Crown can tell him that he must or must not prosecute this man or that one. Nor can any police authority tell him so. The responsibility for law enforcement lies on him. He is answerable to the law and to the law alone
>
> (Lord Denning, R V Commissioner of Police for the Metropolis, ex parte Blackburn, 1968, 2, QB. 118, p.136)

As Jefferson noted, chief constables were no longer constrained by police authorities, their operational independence was constitutionally guaranteed, and their professional status and power enhanced as the result of the creation of fewer and larger police bureaucracies in the latter half of the 1960s. They 'could debate with the Home Office as equals, with each "side" supported by its own army of professional advisers. Thus, professionalization not only penetrated deeply into the reshaped structure but augmented the power granted to both the Home Office and the chief constables under the 1964 Act' (Jefferson, 1987, p.18).

However, in the 1970s and 1980s, in response to increasing complaints about police racism, violence and corruption, and controversial public order policing strategies, certain community groups campaigned for police powers to be limited to those which were strictly necessary, discretionary powers to be curbed, a general tightening of policework rules and procedures, and the establishment of effective independent institutions to investigate police malpractice (**Hall, 1980**).

Communities also asked their elected representatives on local police authorities to explain how and why a particular course of police action had been decided on. Why had racists been allowed to march through a black neighbourhood when two weeks previously an anti-racism march had been banned? Why was 'cottaging' a force priority rather than domestic, racial or anti-gay violence? Why was the force pressing for a state-of-the-art riot training centre when neighbourhood police stations were being closed? Why had the residents of 'Jonesville' not seen a constable on the beat in two weeks when it had just been announced that the force was putting more officers back on the streets? Authority members had to declare that these were operational questions which were not open to deliberation.

The fact that virtually every question seemed to be covered by the term 'operational' generated campaigns of democratic renewal to move the police authorities away from a *subordinate and passive* relationship with their chief constables to a more equal and proactive one. Some argued that police authorities should be legally able to require chief constables to *account retrospectively* for their decisions by explaining and justifying particular policies and actions. Others argued for democratically reconstituted police committees which would have *prospective control* of the formulation of policing policies, patterns and priorities. They would also have responsibility for all appointments, disciplinary proceedings and promotions and be able to *require* reports and to inspect files and records. In this division of duties, chief constables

Community campaigns arising out of controversial police actions have a central role to play in any meaningful framework of democratic accountability

would be public servants, responsible for operationalizing and enforcing, in accordance with the rule of law, these democratically agreed policies and decisions. Democratization and the re-empowerment of police authorities would also make it clear to the community that answering the previously posed questions was political as well as legal in nature. Campaigners also pointed out that few democracies allowed police forces such organizational autonomy. Chief officers in the USA are subject to the formal electoral process whilst in Europe they are servants of Internal Ministers of Justice or municipal authorities, who are themselves democratically accountable. Senior police officers and the Conservative government made it clear during the 1980s that they would oppose any moves towards what they defined as the political control of the police because this would undermine the sacred principles of operational independence and impartiality.

5.3   The managerialization of accountability

In the early 1990s, the question of police accountability resurfaced. This time, however, it was what Reiner (1993) describes as 'calculative and contractual', rather than democratic, accountability that was foregrounded. A series of unprecedented official investigations into police effectiveness and efficiency evaluated virtually every aspect of the organization. They wanted to know whether the taxpayer was getting value for money and how the organization was managed.

Suddenly, senior police officers found themselves facing a set of seemingly non-political managerial questions:

managerialism

- Why has the force so many middle managers?
- Why are the lines of financial management blurred?
- How is effectiveness measured?
- How is performance evaluated?
- How can being a monopoly provider be justified?
- What is the core task?
- How is customer satisfaction with the level of service evaluated?
- Why are staffing levels fixed according to national rather than local needs?

The problem for the police was that the Audit Commission, the National Audit Office, and the Sheehy Inquiry (1993) into Police Responsibilities and Rewards managed to side-step the question of 'operational independence', to get inside the organization, and to establish that it was administered rather than managed. Various reports recommended a fundamental shake-up of the managerial and financial configuration, personnel policies, motivational rationales and working practices of the organization to promote sound management and cost-effectiveness.

After heated debate and many significant political compromises, the 1994 Police and Magistrates' Courts Act was passed, bringing with it yet another internal reorganization of the tripartite structure. From April 1995, free-standing, more business-like police authorities, with reduced memberships, were given responsibility for producing, in conjunction with the chief constable, an annual local policing plan which detailed crime control targets, objectives and expenditure. The police authorities also had a duty to set a lawful budget for the year. The Home Secretary's role was to lay down key national objectives and publish league tables over-viewing the performance of all forces and police authorities. She or he could also determine a variety of policy matters by issuing codes of practice and would have enhanced sanctions to give directions to police authorities in the case of an adverse report from the upgraded inspectorate of constabulary. The Home Secretary was also given the power to 'fast-track' force amalgamations. Finally, because police budgets were cash limited, detailed central government controls over police expenditure were relaxed and chief constables, who retained overall charge of operational matters, were given a degree of freedom to manage their budgets, personnel and resources. To facilitate personal accountability, senior police officers were also placed on fixed-term contracts and moved towards performance-related remuneration (Audit Commission, 1995).

This set of managerialist changes sparked a furious debate. On one side were those who argued that a final centralization of power was taking place which would lead eventually to a national police organization. The battery of powers and levers allocated to the Home Secretary would enable her or him to determine local police practices which would constitute a direct infringement on the operational independence of chief officers. The new police committees would be directly accountable to central government. Because of their size and composition, these quango-like committees could not be said to represent local interests in a democratically accountable manner. The foregrounding of crude, over-simplistic, quantitative plans and targets, which highlighted crime control as being the core police task, would be counterproductive and have an adverse effect on the overall quality of policing and police–community relationships. Forces would concentrate on those activities that could be easily identified and quantified and deliver immediate results. Officers would be forced to cut corners, bend the rules and twist the statistics to deliver their targets, resulting in a high level of wrongful convictions. Chief officers on fixed-term contracts and financial incentives would be forced to collude with central government to protect their jobs. Overall, the 'calculative and contractual' mode of accountability would corrupt the unique ethos of British policing by transforming the police from a local public service into a state-run 'crime control' business (see Reiner, 1995; Loader, 1996; and Walker, 1995).

Others argued that it would be necessary to study carefully the workings of the new regime because the reforms would generate new organizational pressure points, contradictions and strategic alliances. Decentralization and devolution as well as centralization could happen, because in order to deliver on the local policing plan, responsibility for operational policework would have to be located as near as possible to the point of service delivery. Performance targets, league tables and customer charters may be a crude starting-point, but as benchmarks they would compel police authorities and police forces to account publicly for differences in effectiveness in clearing up crime, efficiency, priorities and resourcing. Sophisticated quantitative and qualitative measurements of local policework could be constructed which foiled easy manipulation. In sum, managerial modes of accountability and the proper stewardship of public finances are crucial aspects of democratic accountability (Loveday, 1998; McLaughlin and Murji, 1995).

Under New Labour, managerialism remained central to the overall framework for enhancing and measuring police performance, not least because police performance was identified as a key driver in determining demands on the rest of the criminal justice system. New Labour sharpened the logics of the Police and Magistrates Courts Act to ensure that police force and police authority efforts are directed to realizing national crime reduction targets. It also extended this constitutional framework to the Metropolitan Police, the largest and most resource-intensive police force in the UK. The auditing and inspection regime was also strengthened. The Audit Commission, one of the key drivers of managerialization under the Conservatives, was charged with ensuring 'Best Value', a rolling system of audit to ensure that public services are delivering services to clear standards – covering both cost and quality – by the most economic, efficient and effective means available. To demonstrate 'Best Value' public authorities are required to publish annual performance charts and identify standards, priorities and targets. Because 'Best Value' became a statutory responsibility under the 1999 Local Government Act, this regime institutionalizes a performance framework that stresses continuous improvement and foregrounds the question of comparison with other similar providers across a range of performance indicators. Underlying this is a clear emphasis on competition as a means of securing efficient and effective service delivery based on performance targets agreed by consultation with stakeholders and sections of the community. In the case of the police, one of the most significant developments is that under the guise of 'joined-up inspection' the HMIC has been given the managerial authority to conduct 'Best Value' inspections that: develop the idea of continuous efficiency savings; inculcate a culture of continuous improvement; develop a diagnostic model based on risk assessment; and conduct local rather than force-wide inspections (see HMIC, 1998, 1999).

In informing the Superintendents' Association that the police were to be included within the 'Best Value' framework, Home Secretary Jack Straw said that: 'Best value will also have teeth, it will involve certification, audit and inspection and in those extreme cases where communities are not given the level of service they are entitled to, there will be provision for intervention, ultimately by the Secretary of State' (*The Independent*, 17 September 1998). He also threatened to 'name and shame' poorly performing forces and suggested that 'hit squads' could be sent in to run forces that failed to meet their targets. Individual police forces and their constituent Basic Command Units (BCUs) have been given specific crime reduction targets that are intended to narrow the gap between the best performing forces and those with a substandard track record on fighting crime. From 2001 the targets will be backed up by inspection of the BCUs, rather than just force-wide checks.

A further strand is New Labour's managerialism has been the promotion of an evidence-based approach to policework. *Reducing Offending*, the Home Office report published in July 1998 to coincide with the launch of New Labour's crime reduction strategy, stressed that there was no connection between increasing the number of police officers and lower crime rates. The report supported the development of strategic frameworks to deliver locally relevant strategies:

This calls for local crime audits, good intelligence systems, proper strategic management, monitoring of performance, responsiveness to the constantly changing crime picture and creativity ... The current drive to develop better routine performance measures for police also provides an opportunity to distinguish effective working practices more systematically. A package of police performance measures could be used to discriminate police management units at all levels, from force to beat, and relate the outcomes achieved more rigorously to styles and strategies.

(Jordan, 1998, p.74)

This links into the government's intention to use financial management tools to determine where resources can be deployed more effectively by: first, dropping initiatives and practices shown to offer poor value for money; second, redeploying resources saved to cost-effective activities; and third, developing more flexible funding arrangements to transfer funds between criminal justice agencies. Equally significantly, it leaves open the possibility of further rationalization of the functions of the police and the development of intermediate forms of policing.

The final plank of New Labour's strategy is to be found in the Crime and Disorder Act 1998. As was noted earlier in this chapter, this places new obligations on the police to co-operate in the development and implementation of local crime-reduction strategies. This renewed emphasis on partnership aims to instigate significant changes in the working practices of all the criminal justice agencies. As one of the main players – in terms of their resources as well as functions – the police have been required to develop mutual priorities both with other agencies and with local communities. This compels them to:

- conduct and publish local crime and disorder audits;
- undertake a consultation exercise based on the results of the audit;
- establish and publish objectives and targets for reducing crime and disorder;
- monitor the strategy and its inputs, processes and outputs;
- evaluate outcomes.

Local policework is being increasingly enmeshed in a complex network of overlapping relationships and interests. Localization complements and connects with inspection, audit and financial accountability in a network of processes that, taken together, compose New Labour's aim of creating and institutionalizing a new regulatory framework of performance measurement and review that will hold police forces to account for the resources they use and the outcomes they achieve. Not surprisingly, the discourses and techniques of managerialism remain constitutive of the whole process (McLaughlin and Murji, 2000).

6 Conclusion

The police had always asserted that if they were given the requisite powers and resources they could not only control but defeat crime. Both were forthcoming in the 1980s and the 1990s, and yet the crime rate, the fear of crime, and public disorder escalated and the clear-up rates and public confidence dropped. It was these realities, the accompanying research findings on 'what works', and public loss of faith resultant from a series of well-publicized controversies that induced the unveiling of a new wave of managerial reforms. The stated aim is to remake the public police for the twenty-first century and to refashion its culture, style and methods. The old administrative police force, which worked to the principle that effective crime control was dependent on the amount of public money spent on the police, is to be transformed into a new, professional, managerialized police service based on principles of flexibility, diversity, equity, transparency, representativeness and cost-effectiveness. Recent innovations in policework, particularly those associated with evidence-based and problem-orientated policing and new modes of managerial accountability, demand new levels of initiative and skill among police officers of all ranks. In the aftermath of the Macpherson Report the police will also have to unlearn the habits of decades and rethink the type of person most suitable to being a police officer. However, as we have seen in this chapter, there are special difficulties in reforming this particular public bureaucracy. It has shown itself to be inherently resistant to changes which threaten or infringe upon its professional autonomy or bind it into radical modernization projects. The rank and file has traditionally been sceptical of any changes that fundamentally interfere with working patterns, practices and conditions of service. Senior officers have dreaded changes which require them to take major managerial decisions for which they can be personally held to account. Moreover, because this public bureaucracy operates in such multifaceted task environments, it has been difficult to devise meaningful structures, processes and cultures of accountability. The gap between the need to change and resistance to change will only be closed if all the stakeholders affected by the changes participate in the decision-making process. This will require embracing new values and perspectives, instead of marginalizing everything but the interests of the organization. Only then can we think about the forms of policework appropriate to a multi-ethnic, pluralistic society.

Review questions

- Is it possible to distinguish between law enforcement, order maintenance and service functions of the police?
- What do you understand by the term 'occupational culture'?
- Why is police discretion such a central part of policework?
- Why has the relationship between the police and minority ethnic communities been a major source of tension and conflict?
- What is the most appropriate framework for evaluating police performance?

Further reading

The most accessible overviews of the UK police are Waddington (1999a) and Johnson (2000). Audit Commission and HMIC reports on policing provide an important insight into the managerialist perspective on the organization and core tasks of the public police. The Stephen Lawrence Report (Macpherson, 1999) is the most important official text on the racialization processes underpinning policework. The report of the Independent Commission on Policing for Northern Ireland (1999) is arguably the most sophisticated official report on policing ever produced in the UK. Chan (1997) presents an important analysis of the many meanings of police culture. Valuable sets of comparative papers are presented in Findlay and Zvekic (1993) and Brodeur (1998).

References

Abott, J. (2000) 'Breaking down the borders: the Schengen Agreement', *Nexus*, no.9, pp.12–14.

Anderson, M., Boer, M., Cullen, P. and Gilmore, W. (1995) *Policing The European Union*, Oxford, Clarendon Press.

Association of Chief Police Officers (1993) *Your Police: The Facts*, London, ACPO.

Audit Commission (1990) *Effective Policing: Performance Review of Provincial Police Forces*, London, HMSO.

Audit Commission (1993) *Helping with Enquiries: Tackling Crime Effectively*, London, Audit Commission.

Audit Commission (1995) *Cheques and Balances: A Framework for Improving Police Accountability*, London, Audit Commission.

Audit Commission (1996a) *Streetwise: Effective Police Patrol*, London, HMSO.

Audit Commission (1996b) *Detecting a Change: Progress in Tackling Crime*, London, HMSO.

Baldwin, R. and Kinsey, R. (1982) *Police Powers and Politics*, London, Quartet Books.

Bayley, D. (1994) *Police for the Future*, New York, Oxford University Press.

Bittner, E. (1970) *The Functions of the Police in Modern Society: A Review of Background Factors, Current Practices, and Possible Role Models*, Rockville, MD, National Institute of Mental Health.

Blair, I. (1998) 'Off beat solution', *The Guardian,* 17 July, p.21.

Bland, N., Miller, J. and Quinton, P. (2000) *Upping the PACE: An Evaluation of the Recommendations of the Stephen Lawrence Inquiry on Stops and Searches*, London, Home Office.

Bottomley, K., Coleman, C., Dixon, D., Gill, M. and Wall, D. (1991) *The Impact of PACE: Policing in a Northern Force*, Hull, University of Hull.

Bradley, D., Walker, N. and Wilkie, R. (1986) *Managing the Police: Law, Organisation and Democracy,* Brighton, Harvester.

Bratton, W.J. (1997) 'Crime is down in New York city: blame the police', in Dennis, N. (ed.) *Zero Tolerance: Policing A Free Society*, London, IEA.

Brewer, J.D. and Magee, K. (1991) *Inside the RUC: Routine Policing in a Divided Society,* Oxford, Oxford University Press.

Brodeur, J.P. (ed.) (1998) *How To Recognise Good Policing: Problems and Issues*, London, Sage.

Brogden, M., Jefferson, T. and Walklate, S. (1988) *Introducing Policework*, London, Unwin Hyman.

Burke, M. (1993) *Coming Out of the Blue: British Police Officers Talk about their Lives in "The Job" as Lesbians, Gays and Bisexuals*, London, Cassell.

Campbell, B. (1993) 'Too much of a woman for the boys in blue', *The Independent*, 1 June, p.20.

Chan, J. (1997) *Changing Police Culture: Policing in a Multi-Cultured Society*, Cambridge, Cambridge University Press.

Clarke, J. (2001) 'Crime and social order: interrogating the detective story', in Muncie and McLaughlin (2001).

Clarke, R. and Hough, M. (1984) *Crime and Police Effectiveness*, London, Home Office.

Clarke, R.V.G. (1980) '"Situational" crime prevention: theory and practice', *British Journal of Criminology*, vol.20, no.2, pp.136–47. (Extract reprinted in Muncie *et al.*, 1996.)

Council of Europe (1997) *Human Rights and The Police: Seminar Proceedings*, Strasburg, Council of Europe.

Davies, N. (1999) 'Watching the detectives: how the police cheat in the fight against crime', *The Guardian*, 18 March, p.12.

Dixon, D. (1997) *Law in Policing: Legal Regulations and Police Practice*, Oxford, Clarendon Press.

Findlay, M. and Zvekic, U. (eds) (1993) *Alternative Policing Styles*, Deventer, Kluwer.

Fitzgerald, M. (1999) *Stop and Search*, London, New Scotland Yard.

Goldblatt, P. and Lewis, C. (eds) (1998) *Reducing Offending: An Assessment of Research Evidence on Ways of Dealing with Offending Behaviour*, London, Home Office, Research Study No.187.

Graef, R. (1989) *Talking Blues: The Police in their Own Word,* London, Collins Harvill.

Gregory, J. and Lees, S. (1999) *Policing Sexual Assault*, London, Routledge.

Halford, A. (1994) *No Way Up the Greasy Pole*, London, Constable.

Hall, S. (1980) *Drifting into a Law and Order Society*, London, Cobden Trust. (Extract reprinted in Muncie *et al.*, 1996.)

Heidensohn, F. (1992) *Women in Control: The Role of Women in Law Enforcement*, Oxford, Clarendon.

Her Majesty's Inspectorate (1994) *Report of Her Majesty's Chief Inspector of Constabulary for the Year 1993*, London, HMSO.

HMIC (1998) *What Price Policing?*, London, Home Office.

HMIC (1999) *Keeping The Peace: Policing Disorder*, London, Home Office.

HMIC (2000) *Policing London: Winning Consent*, London, Home Office.

Hobbs, D. (1988) *Doing the Business,* Oxford, Clarendon.

Holdaway, S. (1993) *The Resignation of Black and Asian Officers from the Police Service*, London, Home Office.

Holdaway, S. (1996) *The Racialization of the British Police*, Basingstoke, Macmillan.

Home Office (1991) *Police and Criminal Evidence Act 1984 (s.66) Codes of Practice* (2nd edn), London, HMSO.

Home Office (1993) *Sex Discrimination in the Police Service in England and Wales,* London, HMSO.

Hoogenboom, A.B., Meiboom, M.J., Schoneveld, D. and Stoop, J. (eds) (1997) *Policing The Future*, Hague, Kluwer.

Hoyle, C. and Sanders, A. (2000) 'Police response to domestic violence', *British Journal of Criminology*, vol.40, no.2, pp.14–36.

Independent Commission on Policing for Northern Ireland (1999) *A New Beginning: Policing in Northern Ireland*, London, Stationery Office.

Jefferson, T. (1987) 'The police', in The Open University, D310 *Crime, Justice and Society,* Block 3, *Delivering Justice* Part 1A, Milton Keynes, The Open University.

Jefferson, T. (1990) *The Case Against Paramilitary Policing*, Buckingham, Open University Press.

Johnson, L. (2000) *Policing Britain: Risk, Security and Governance*, Harlow, Longman.

Jones, S. (1986) *Policewomen and Equality: Formal Policy versus Informal Practice,* London, Macmillan.

Jones, T. and Newburn, T. (1998) *Private Security and Public Policing*, Oxford, Clarendon Press.

Jordan, P. (1998) 'Effective strategies for reducing crime', in Goldblatt and Lewis (1998).

Jordan, P. (2000) *Stop/Search: Impact on Crime and Impact on Public Opinion*, London, Police Foundation.

Kelling, G.L. and Coles, C.M. (1997) *Fixing Broken Windows: Restoring Order and Reducing Crime in Our Communities*, New York, Touchstone Books.

Klockars, C.B. (1988) 'The rhetoric of community policing', in Green, J.R. and Mastrofski, S.D. (eds) *Community Policing: Rhetoric or Reality?*, New York, Praeger.

KPMG (2000) 'Feasibility of an independent system for investigating complaints against the police', London, Home Office, *Home Office Research Services Paper,* 122.

Leinen, S. (1993) *Gay Cops*, New Brunswick, NJ, Rutgers University Press.

Loader, I. (1996) *Youth, Policing and Democracy*, Basingstoke, Macmillan.

Loveday, B. (1998) 'Waving not drowning: chief constables and the new configuration of accountability in the provinces', *International Journal of Police Science and Management*, vol.1, no.2, pp.133–47.

Macpherson, Sir W. (1999) *The Stephen Lawrence Inquiry: Report of an Inquiry by Sir William Macpherson of Cluny*, Cm4262–I, London, Stationery Office.

Maguire, M. and Norris, C. (1992) *The Conduct and Supervision of Criminal Investigations*, London, Home Office.

McLaughlin, E. and Murji, K. (1995) 'The end of public policing? Police reform and the "new managerialism"', in Noaks, L., Levi, M. and Maguire, M. (eds) *Contemporary Issues in Criminology*, Cardiff, University of Wales.

McLaughlin, E. and Murji, K. (2000) 'Lost connections and new directions: neo-liberalism, new public managerialism and the "modernisation" of the British police', in Stenson, K. and Sullivan, R. (eds) *Crime, Risk and Justice: The Politics of Crime Prevention in Liberal Democracies*, Cambridge, Willan Publishing.

Muncie, J. (2001) 'The construction and deconstruction of crime', in Muncie and McLaughlin (2001).

Muncie, J. and McLaughlin, E. (eds) (2001) *The Problem of Crime*, London, Sage in association with The Open University.

Muncie, J., McLaughlin, E. and Langan, M. (eds) (1996) *Criminological Perspectives: A Reader*, London, Sage in association with The Open University.

Neiderhoffer, A. (1967) *Behind the Shield*, New York, Doubleday.

Reiner, R. (1993) 'Police accountability: principles, patterns and practices', in Reiner, R. and Spencer, S. (eds) *Accountable Policing*, London, IPPR.

Reiner, R. (1995) 'The perfidy of the paramour: how the police fell out of love with the Conservatives', *The Times Literary Supplement*, 1 September.

Runnymede Trust (2000) *The Future of Multi-Ethnic Britain*, London, Runnymede Trust.

Sanders, A. and Young, R. (1994) *Criminal Justice*, London, Butterworth.

Saraga, E. (2001) 'Dangerous places: the family as a site of crime', in Muncie and McLaughlin (2001).

Scarman, Lord (1981) *The Brixton Disorders 10–12 April 1981: Report of an Inquiry*, Cmnd 8427, London, HMSO.

Scraton, P. (1985) *The State of the Police*, London, Pluto.

Sherman, L. (1983) 'Patrol strategies for police', in Wilson, J.Q. (ed.) *Crime and Public Policy*, San Francisco, CA, ICS Press.

Skolnick, J. (1966) *Justice Without Trial*, New York, Wiley.

Smith, D.J. (1986) 'The framework of law and police practice', in Benyon, J. and Bourn, C. (eds) *The Police: Powers, Procedures and Proprieties*, Oxford, Pergamon.

Smith, D.J. and Gray, J. (1985) *Police and People in London: The PSI Report*, London, Gower.

Waddington, P.A.J. (1991) *The Strong Arm of the Law: Armed and Public Order Policing,* Oxford, Oxford University Press.

Waddington, P.A.J. (1999a) *Policing Citizens*, London, UCL Press.

Waddington, P.A.J. (1999b) 'Police (canteen) culture – an appreciation', *British Journal of Criminology*, vol.39, no.2, pp.286–309.

Walker, M.A. (1992) 'Do we need a clear up rate?', *Policing and Society*, vol.2, pp.293–306.

Walker, N. (1995) 'Defining core police tasks: the neglect of the symbolic dimension', *Policing and Society*, vol.6, pp.53–71.

Wilson, J.Q. and Kelling, G. (1982) 'Broken windows', *Atlantic Monthly*, March, pp.29–38.

Young, M. (1991) *An Inside Job: Policing and Police Culture in Britain*, Oxford, Oxford University Press.

Young, M. (1993) *In the Sticks,* Oxford, Oxford University Press.

CHAPTER 3

Critical Decisions and Processes in the Criminal Courts

by Loraine Gelsthorpe

Contents

1   Introduction

The criminal justice system is always in some degree of flux and any particular accounts of it are conditioned by its state at that time. Public concerns about criminal justice are relatively constant, but in the late 1980s the justice system provoked an unusual level of anxiety, particularly with respect to miscarriages of justice and instances of police malpractice, which culminated in the creation of a Royal Commission on Criminal Justice in the early 1990s. The murder of two-year-old James Bulger by two ten-year-old boys on 12 February 1993 in Bootle, Merseyside, received massive national and international media coverage and inspired an enormous amount of public and private debate about social decay, moral decline, and above all the ineffectiveness of the criminal justice system. The sentencing of the boys in Crown Court, the subsequent intervention on the part of the Home Secretary to increase the penalties, and the culmination of the case when the European Court declared the trial to be in contravention of human rights had drawn further attention to decisions and processes in the criminal courts (Gelsthorpe, 1999; Dyer and Travis, 1999).

The Stephen Lawrence Inquiry (Macpherson, 1999) also raised important questions about the delivery of criminal justice and in particular the role of the police and institutionalized racist policies and practices (see Chapter 2 of this volume). Further, in the past decade, awareness of an increasing politicization of criminal justice has been more widely recognized (James and Raine, 1998). Criminal justice, it seems, is invariably contentious.

There are two key aims in this chapter: firstly, to set out some theoretical considerations in an effort to establish what precisely is meant by 'criminal justice'; secondly, and more crucially, we examine some of the major issues that arise out of the operation of the criminal justice system. These include:

- Whether the judiciary and magistracy can truly be said to be impartial and how far their discretionary powers affect procedural justice.
- Whether the courts discriminate against particular social groups.
- Whether there is equality of access to justice.

While the chapter examines numerous empirical research-findings on these issues, its broader aim is to stimulate critical reflection on the processes through which 'justice' is delivered and whether indeed either 'impartiality' or 'discrimination' can ever be empirically 'proved'. The chapter concludes with a brief discussion of possible alternatives to formal and adversarial systems of justice. While the criminal justice system in England and Wales is used as a key point of reference throughout, the general issues we raise are of relevance to all formal systems that attempt to deliver 'justice'.

2   Questions of justice

ACTIVITY 3.1

What do you think are the main elements of 'justice'? Can these be realized in criminal justice systems?

Justicia: the figure of Justice surmounts the dome of the 1906 'Old Bailey' sessions-house in London

Look at the picture of the statue of Justicia (reproduced above) who stands blindfolded on top of the Old Bailey in London with the scales of justice in one hand and a sword in the other. What do you think she symbolizes?

The blindfold, the scales and the sword usually conjure up notions of *impartiality*, the scales the promise of a *fair* trial and the sword the *certainty of punishment* for wrongdoing. Justicia is an icon that symbolizes objectivity, neutrality, fairness and rectitude. 'Justice', however, is a concept that has been debated time and again in the history of ideas. It is a term that is easy to picture, but hard to grasp. The dimensions of the question 'What is justice?' are enormous. Do we mean fairness? Equal treatment? Just deserts? Furthermore, must the concept of justice depend on a particular social and political setting or set of social goals and conventions? Or is it something bigger and more universal than that, which can be instinctively divined? Indeed, we could ask, 'is there a natural or divine law from which our criminal and civil laws derive?'

A starting-point in trying to answer the question 'What is justice?' could be the familiar passage from Exodus in the Bible: 'an eye for an eye, a tooth for a tooth'. There is perhaps a basic urge for retribution: 'measure for measure'. The moral philosopher Immanuel Kant (1724–1804) argued that retribution – and retribution alone – necessitates and justifies punishment (see Kant, 1796–97). He contended that, even if there were no point in deterring future crime or curing the criminal or no practical purpose to expressing the authority of the state, it would still be necessary to punish offenders in order to repay crime with punishment.

justice

John Stuart Mill (1806–73), on the other hand, regarded social utility as the only justification for punishment and key to justice (see Mill, 1859). He speculated on a natural 'outgrowth' of two sentiments: self-defence and sympathy. Mill argued that we find it necessary as rational creatures to generalize from our own good to the good of all. This means that when it comes to matters of punishment we realize that 'any conduct that threatens the security of society generally is threatening to our own'. A desire for justice is thus the 'natural feeling of retaliation or vengeance'. The problem with depending on natural feelings of vengeance for meting out justice is that it can become uncontrollable. Mill recognized that, when we think through the implications of this, we can see that it is best to think in terms of resenting a hurt to society, not just to oneself. Vengeance then becomes constrained by the overarching principle that defines all moral action: the public interest, or 'the greatest good of the greatest number' (see also **Beccaria, 1764**).

More recent philosophical debates about justice have revolved around the widely acclaimed book *A Theory of Justice* (1971) by John Rawls. We assume that our courts give fair *and* just punishment, but Rawls argues that the concepts of justice and fairness are essentially the same. He tells a fairy story in which a group of men and women, who do not belong to any particular society, have come together in a kind of constitutional convention to choose fundamental rules for a new society. There is nothing particularly distinctive about these people; they have specific identities, weaknesses, strengths, and interests. They suffer from amnesia, however, and they have no idea who they are, whether they are young or old, black or white, talented or stupid. In particular (and crucial to Rawls's argument), they do not know what their own beliefs are regarding what is valuable in life. Each person has some sort of conception of what he or she wants life to be like, but no-one else knows. Indeed, they are separated from their own personalities by what Rawls calls a 'veil of ignorance'. Rawls contends that the construction of rules will reflect what people believe is best for them – as individuals. Each person would be interested in establishing the fairest rules possible because they would not be protected by social or any other advantages.

Rawls suggests that people would be likely to agree on two main principles. First, everyone would have basic liberties – such as equal liberty to speak, freedom of conscience, freedom to hold personal property, to be protected in your person, not to be arrested suddenly and without due cause, and so on. Indeed, these are what we might call conventional liberties. Rawls's second principle relates to wealth. He argues that no difference in wealth should be tolerated unless that difference works for the benefit of the worst-off group in the society. The first principle is of more relevance to us here because we can recognize that punishment might be used to protect liberties. It is likely that we would all look at the system from the standpoint of the least advantaged representative man or woman, in which case inequalities are only permissible when they maximize, or at least contribute to, the long-term expectations of the least fortunate group in society.

Subsequently, Rawls's theory has come under attack, not least from those who believe that the idea of a rational agent (person) situated behind 'the veil of ignorance' is faulty. There are also those who suggest that it is one thing to establish rules for a 'desert island' society, where wealth has somehow fallen from the sky and has to be divided out, but quite another in situations where there are differential entitlements. Nozick (1974), for instance, dismisses Rawls's focus on equality and stresses the importance of 'liberty'. Whilst Rawls may be trying to tie the principles of equality and liberty together, Nozick argues that they are fundamentally incompatible and if a choice is to be made, it must be for liberty. This is an inalienable right in Nozick's view, and the only right which the state can legitimately defend without interfering too much in people's lives. A clear implication of this view is that punishment must be restricted to those who have broken the law – it cannot extend to those who *might* break the law.

Where do these debates take us, and what have these broad perspectives on justice got to do with criminal justice and the operation of contemporary criminal justice systems? Such abstract discussions perhaps have limited utility in trying to understand the behaviour of the courts. As Foucault (1980) and others would argue, the pursuit of abstract ideas of justice can be futile: it may be more relevant to ask how the *discourse* of justice functions in society, and whose interests it works to perpetuate. They *are* important debates, of course, but not ones which are easily resolved; indeed, the rhetorical and controversial nature of the debates reminds us that 'justice' is a social and political issue. While it could be argued that the broad questions can provide a theoretical backcloth to all that takes place under the cloak of criminal justice, it is hard to imagine politicians and policy-makers sitting around discussing such grand conceptions of justice. Nevertheless, the criminal justice system cannot be separated from broader issues about the rules that govern society – indeed, the system gives the appearance of serving to defend the righteous, protect the innocent and punish offenders. Findlay (1999) comments that the issues are complicated further by globalization and an increased emphasis on the idea of justice in an international context. Philosophical debates about justice remind us that we need to think about the social and political *choices* involved in establishing legal rules. If the criminal justice system is concerned with those who break the rules, we need to question not only whether they are the 'right' rules (whose values and aims do they reflect?), but also the procedures of criminal justice through which it is assumed such rules are upheld and maintained.

3   Questions of criminal justice

What shapes and 'drives' the criminal justice system? What kinds of values and debates inform its operation? A common-sense view might be that what guides the criminal justice system is simply a desire to catch criminals, take them to court, judge them and, if they are found guilty, punish them. But this may be overly simplistic. It may be more useful to consider such questions in the light of six key perspectives on what shapes criminal justice systems (derived from Packer, 1969 and King, 1981). We can envisage these perspectives as 'windows' through which criminal justice and its processes can be viewed, each window providing a particular (though partial) view of what is 'driving' the criminal justice system.

1   A due process perspective emphasizes the need to administer justice according   **due process**
    to legal rules and procedures that are publicly known, fair and seen to be
    just. The main function of the criminal courts is to act as an impartial arbitrator
    of conflicts arising between the state and its citizens. Central to this perspective
    are the presumption of innocence, the restraints of arbitrary power and the
    inviolability of legal rules and procedures. Such procedures do not weight
    the process against the accused or in favour of those in power, but rather
    seek to guarantee a measure of judicial equality to all parties. Hence, a due
    process position stresses the absolute need to abide by strict and formal
    procedures to ensure that adherence to 'due process' results in a smooth-
    running, fair and impartial system (see **von Hirsch, 1976**).

crime control 2 A crime control perspective stresses that the primary function of the criminal courts is to punish offenders and, by so doing, to control crime. The aim of criminal justice is, first and foremost, to repress criminal conduct. The courts are thus more guardians of law and order than upholders of impartial justice. While a 'due process' position prioritizes civil liberties in order to ensure that the innocent are acquitted (even at the risk of acquitting some who are guilty), 'crime control' values stress the goal of convicting the guilty (even at the risk of convicting some who are innocent and of infringing some civil liberties). In a due process perspective, the actions of criminal justice agencies are tightly regulated; in a crime control perspective, formal rules of procedure are often seen as obstacles standing in the way of securing a defendant's conviction. As the ultimate aim is to punish offenders and to deter future crime, the criminal justice system cannot afford a high acquittal rate: 'In order to operate successfully the process must produce a high rate of apprehension and conviction … there must be a feeling of speed and finality' (Packer, 1969, p.159).

In England, the due process approach is frequently associated with the attitudes of the legal profession, particularly those involved in defence work, and with the aims of such organizations such as, for instance, the civil liberties group, Liberty. The crime control approach is more reflective of traditional conservative views of the proper function of the courts. The tension between these opposing perspectives is often viewed as the single most important source of conflict and contradiction in the operation of contemporary justice systems. It is the interplay between their respective goals that gives criminal justice its most clear and defining characteristics.

welfare 3 A welfare (and rehabilitative) perspective, gives us a third 'window' through which to view the criminal justice system. This stresses that the aim of criminal justice is not to deter or punish, but to restore defendants to a state of social health whereby the 'threat' they pose to society can be diminished. Working from positivist assumptions regarding the individual and social causes of crime, this perspective maintains that the courts' objectives should be to diagnose, treat and cure, on the basis of information gathered from a defendant's family background, work record, educational and medical history, and so on. Each case is thus individualized and a greater degree of discretion is afforded to decision-makers (judges and magistrates and also probation officers and social workers). Strict adherence to inflexible rules and principles is seen as misguided and inappropriate.

critical socio-legal studies 4 A critical socio-legal perspective views criminal justice as a means of legitimating and maintaining class and other forms of domination and of preserving existing patterns of social, economic and political power in society. In this perspective, 'due process', 'crime control' or 'welfare and rehabilitation' are all ways of meeting the same goal of giving legal and judicial justification to coercive and repressive social orders (Quinney, 1974). Much of this approach has dwelt on the social, economic and ideological origins of criminal law and criminal justice in the late eighteenth and early nineteenth centuries (Hay *et al.*, 1975; Thompson, 1975), noting in particular how the development of the nation state depended on the law to regulate social relationships, to coerce and to protect, and to bind society to the dominance of private property and market relations.

5   A bureaucratic perspective views the criminal justice system precisely 'as a **bureaucratic** system': a set of bureaucracies, governed by rules, roles and routines which control the way in which criminal justice is delivered. Criminal justice practice is dominated by 'what happens next in the process', rather than by grander goals and philosophical desires. As a result, increasing emphasis is placed on what might be termed 'formal justice' as opposed to 'substantive justice', an approach derived from Max Weber's analyses of types of legal thought (Weber, 1954). According to Weber, law can be irrational or rational and it can be formal or substantive in orientation. Law is rational to the extent that its operation is guided by general rules rather than by substantive reaction to individual cases, or by irrational formal means, such as oracles or ordeals. *Substantively rational law* is determined by general rules derived from extra-legal ideologies (such as a system of morality, a religion or a political ideology). *Formally rational law* is guided by general rules so that in both substantive and procedural matters only unambiguous general characteristics of the case are taken into account. There is, then, a close relationship between due process ideals and the bureaucratic perspective. However, whilst due process is designed to protect the individual against arbitrary power, the bureaucratic objective is simply to ensure that the system follows standard procedures and is operated as efficiently and effectively as possible, irrespective of any wider goals.

6   A closely related position to the bureaucratic perspective is the management model. This concerns the apparent dominance of 'managerial values'. The **managerialism** model

> ... is based on the insight that some crime is inevitable in any society and conceives the task as being to manage, reduce or prevent the amount of crime so as to make its occurrence as little damaging to society as possible. On this model the responsibility for devising ways of 'dealing' with crime falls largely to central administration, which has to measure the efficacy of any particular means of 'dealing' carried out by any of the agencies involved, and to extend or replace it according to its utilitarian value in reducing or preventing the kind of crime which damages society.
>
> (Tuck, 1991, pp.23–4)

Commenting on shifts in criminal justice in the 1980s and 1990s, McLaughlin and Muncie (1994) refer to the development of a mixed economy of criminal justice in which the state absolves itself of its traditional role as the natural provider of law and order. This is achieved in a variety of ways: through the privatization of various functions of the criminal justice system (for example, prisons); the increasing involvement of the public (with expectations that they will in some way 'police' and 'protect' themselves); and an enlarged role for voluntary organizations (for example, in the realm of community sentences and secure training orders for children). Again, the key concern is with matters of efficiency, tempered, however, by an overriding interest in cost effectiveness and in establishing new boundaries of state responsibility and new modes of regulation. Notable shifts to systemic managerialism in criminal justice are characterized, for instance, by 'performance indicators', 'quality service', and 'devolved budgets' (Jones, 1993; Bottoms, 1995; Loveday, 1999). McLaughlin and Muncie (2000) have added to these: the enhanced use of existing resources (cost effectiveness), evidence-based approaches to crime reduction (emphasis on 'what works') and consistent and mutually reinforcing aims and objectives (reflected in prison–probation partnerships, for instance, and in the creation of a national probation service to replace local services).

These six perspectives on the criminal justice system are not exhaustive. But they do remind us that there are competing models of criminal justice (just as there are competing models of justice and social order) which influence how the system is – or should be – run. Models are of course interpretations: we should not expect any *one* model to be fully implemented or to operate in isolation. Criminal justice systems are more an uneasy compromise between different models or even an adoption of contradictory elements. There are no simple 'facts' about criminal justice; it is a social, political and legal process, a contested and negotiated arena. This points *back* to the broader question of what justice is and how society should be governed: who defines the rules by which people live? What is the nature of legalized power and what constrains it? But it also points *forward* to the domain of controversies: how is injustice generated from justice systems? How does ideology penetrate the workings and operation of criminal justice?

It is to some of these controversies that we now turn in section 4.

4 The delivery of justice and injustices

ACTIVITY 3.2

From a range of newspapers (preferably both tabloid and broadsheet) from the past week, locate any articles that focus on criminal justice system practices (courts, prisons, probation, the legal profession):

1   Make a list of any general issues underlying these articles. (You might identify issues such as perceptions of 'justice' and 'injustice', the efficiency and costs of the system, public confidence in the system.) Are the articles critical of the system? Do they point forward to the need for reform?

2   Do the six perspectives discussed earlier shed any light on such debates and controversies?

When an activity such as this was undertaken with a group of students in 2000, a number of critical issues were raised:

■   The notion of disparity and discrimination in sentencing.

■   The potential erosion of the privilege against self-incrimination through the loss of the right to silence.

■   The possible unreliability of scientific evidence presented to the courts.

■   The failure to provide adequately for mentally disordered offenders.

■   The seeming reluctance to create access to justice in the court room for non-English speakers.

■   The fact that the concept of legal aid was under extreme threat which might have meant that some people would be disadvantaged in the court room.

■   The neglect of victims in the delivery of criminal justice.

Many of these issues can be seen to stem from the contradictions between 'due process', 'crime control' and 'managerial' perspectives. The abandonment of defendants' 'right to silence', for example, is reflective of a crime control approach, whilst the restriction on access to legal aid, because of its increasing costs, may suggest the primacy of 'managerial' objectives. The failure to provide for mentally disordered offenders could suggest a need for the injection of more overtly 'welfare and rehabilitative' ideals. Similarly, commenting on the unreliability of some scientific evidence may be a means of arguing that, for the purposes of 'due process', only reliable and sustainable 'evidence' should be entertained.

If 'criminal justice' is difficult to define, then it may help to examine perceived 'injustices'. The remainder of this chapter focuses on four general issues that illustrate the controversies we have discussed so far. These are based on suggestions that:

1   Magistrates' discretion in sentencing should be more tightly controlled.

2   The judiciary are not the impartial body they are supposed to be.

3   The jury system (a key feature of the English system) is under threat.

4   The criminal justice system (particularly the courts) is imbued with discriminatory attitudes and practices: sentencing appears to be arbitrary or even whimsical.

All four of the issues listed here suggest that there is a perceived, and very often real, injustice in the criminal justice system. An examination of these issues may lead us closer to a sense of what we mean by 'criminal justice'.

4.1   Disparities in sentencing

In 1764, Cesare Beccaria published *Dei Delitta e delle Pene* (On Crimes and Punishments): this provided a thorough and searching critique of the arbitrary and harsh criminal justice systems of Europe, and, along with others (Jeremy Bentham, for instance) in the so-called 'Classical School' of criminology, called for reform, for clarity in the law, and due process in criminal procedure, combined with certainty and regularity of punishment **(Beccaria, 1764/1963)**. Ever since those reforms, there have been attempts to establish some rational relationship between the seriousness of the offence and the severity of the punishment. This is known as the principle of proportionality; this means that **proportionality** the perceived seriousness of the offence should be dealt with by way of an appropriate penalty, one which is neither too lenient nor too severe, but is in proportion to the offence. It is because of this principle, for instance, that it is usually considered inappropriate to give custodial sentences to first-time petty property offenders.

It could be argued, however, that judicial discretion has prevailed and **sentencing** sentencing powers have been untrammelled. In the United Kingdom, the judiciary and Magistrates' Association have emphasized the use of discretion and *individual sentencing*. This is not to suggest that sentencers have been totally unfettered; indeed, various attempts have been made to constrain the use of discretion and to structure it by regulating its use in advance. It has also been checked in other ways. For example, under the 1982 Criminal Justice Act, the courts were directed to avoid passing custodial sentences on young offenders unless it appeared that no other sentence was available, and were required to check the case against three specific criteria:

1   the offender was 'unable or unwilling' to respond to non-custodial penalties

2   a custodial sentence was necessary for the 'protection of the public' or

3   the offence was so serious that a non-custodial sentence could not be justified.

Thomas's (1979) *Principles of Sentencing* also facilitated the checking of discretion by providing an accessible digest of general sentencing principles. This handbook, first produced in 1970, is informally referred to as the sentencers' Bible. The Court of Appeal, of course, has also served as a valuable check on judicial discretion, though some have argued that there has always remained a serious weakness in the self-regulatory capacity of this court (Cavadino and Dignan, 1997; Rozenberg, 1994; Zander, 1989).

While there has always been a certain degree of self-regulation practised by sentencers, until the mid 1990s wide discretion was the hallmark of the system. Since then, a series of governmental attempts have been made to ensure judicial consistency. These include both a shift towards mandatory sentencing for more serious crimes (in the Crime Sentences Act, 1997) and the introduction of judicial sentencing guidelines. For example, the Crime and Disorder Act 1998 places the Appeal Courts under a duty to consider framing guidelines or revising outdated guidelines whenever it hears an appeal against a sentence. In doing so, the court will also have to incorporate the views of the Sentencing Advisory Panel (launched 1 July, 1999). Previous attempts to change patterns of sentencing and, in particular, to reduce the use of custody (where the government thought that this was inappropriate, or where continuing penal crises dictated that the prison population should be reduced) however, have been circumvented by sentencers. For example, when community service orders were introduced in 1972 (largely as an alternative to custody, though the aim was perhaps never entirely clear), research revealed a strong element of 'up-tariffing' (Pease, 1980); that is, their use replaced the use of penalties lower down on the scale rather than custodial penalties. As a second example, even though the introduction of partly suspended sentences in 1977 was intended to reduce the use of custody, in practice, offenders who would not normally have warranted a custodial sentence were given a 'taste of imprisonment' through the introduction of the partly suspended sentence (Bottoms, 1981; Harris, 1992). These examples show that new sentences, originally conceived as *alternatives* to imprisonment, were in practice used as *additions* and had little impact on the use of custody at all.

Not surprisingly, the English system has occasionally been ridiculed by scholars and other commentators, with sentencing practices described as a 'smorgasbord' or 'cafeteria' approach, where sentencers can 'pick and choose' or 'pick and mix' different sentences, with no apparent reason for their decisions. The very range of underlying theoretical precepts at play – deterrence and incapacitation, rehabilitation and just deserts for instance, as evidenced in the crime control and welfare models of criminal justice – underlines this (see von Hirsch and Ashworth, 1998; and Chapter 6 of this volume). In practice, the regional variations in sentencing (particularly in the resort to custody) are notable.

In 1990, the government finally responded to these and similar criticisms by publishing a White Paper, *Crime, Justice and Protecting the Public* (Home Office, 1990a). This formed the basis of an important step to limit the exercise of discretion and to institute clear principles and rules in sentencing that were eventually to be included in the Criminal Justice Act 1991.

Cavadino and Dignan (1997, pp.100–1) discerned four key themes in the White Paper:

1   A partnership between the legislature and the judiciary – with parliament establishing a framework consisting of general principles, and the courts (including the Appeal Courts) being left to decide how these principles should apply in any given instance.

2   A reinterpretation of the doctrine of judicial independence: this reasserted government responsibility for formulating sentencing policy while affirming the principle of government non-interference in individual cases.

3   The retention of a twin-track (or bifurcatory) approach to sentencing: at its crudest, this means that those who can be diverted from custody should be, and that those who have committed the most serious offences deserve the most severe punishment.

4   The theme of 'just deserts', which meant that the sentence imposed for a given offence must match, or be in proportion to, the seriousness of the offence.

The new framework also reflected an intention to place more focus on the *offence*, and less on the *offender* (Ashworth, 1992). By curtailing judicial discretion, the Criminal Justice Act 1991 gave primacy to some elements of 'due process', but in stressing the punitive nature of all sentences, it also reflected some 'crime control' concerns. The 1991 Act also encouraged sentencers directly to pass fewer custodial sentences by introducing statutory criteria to limit their use. In addition, it encouraged the use of community penalties, not least by changing the name from 'non-custodial penalties' to 'community penalties'. Other aspects of this shift included attempts to make pre-sentence reports more informative (with regard to the immediate reasons for the offending behaviour and how particular penalties might address the offending behaviour) and the content of community penalties more widely available; the increased involvement of the courts in enforcing community orders; the removal of the somewhat 'artificial' concept of alternatives to custody; and the bifurcation of crimes into those serious enough to justify imprisonment and those which can be dealt with by punishment in the community. Harris (1992) adds to this list by suggesting that private sector involvement in community punishment might be an inducement to sentencers to make more use of community penalties and less of imprisonment. (The use of electronic monitoring – promoted by private companies – can be seen as a way of buttressing community penalties in this respect by adding to the 'controlling' and 'punitive' content of community penalties so that they are not seen by sentencers nor, indeed, by the public, as a soft option.)

It was thought that private sector involvement with the Probation Service (who organize and enforce community penalties), through management inspection and through inter-agency work, could also improve the credibility of community penalties and operate as an incentive to sentencers to use them more. It might also be seen to increase or improve the accountability of the Probation Service. This reflects a government notion that private sector management expertise can be of benefit to 'public service' organizations; here the key concerns are more clearly bureaucratic or managerial in intent.

It was also hoped that the introduction of 'national standards', in the production of pre-sentence reports in a certain format and content and in the operation of community penalties (concerning the nature of work in community service orders for example), might increase respect for, and thus use of, community penalties (Ashworth *et al.*, 1992). Additionally, an attempt to make the system of fining fairer (and as a result increase confidence in the use of fines) was made by introducing a 'unit fine system', where the amount of a fine was based on calculations of disposable weekly income and ability to pay.

However, many of the Act's aims have been undermined since then as a consequence of magisterial, public and political pressure. Initial assessments of the impact of the Act suggested that community penalties were no more credible to magistrates than they were before the Act. The 'unit fine system' was met with resistance from sentencers from the outset because it was perceived that the system was capable of being exploited and because it proved unworkable – with notable cases catching the media's interest (the £1,000 fine for the man who dropped a crisp bag, for example) – and was repealed in the 1993 Criminal Justice Act by the then Home Secretary, Kenneth Clarke, in May 1993 (Rex, 1992; Gibson, 1990; Moxon *et al.*, 1990; Cavadino and Dignan, 1997). Amidst furore from political and professional groups about the future role of the Probation Service (and attempts to remove its rehabilitative or 'social work' orientations), the Home Secretary was adamant that community penalties did *not* work and that penalties had to be made even tougher – making it clear that elements of the welfare model were not to be countenanced. At the Conservative Party conference in October 1993, the new Home Secretary, Michael Howard, announced a 27-point plan of action on law and order and most famously stated that 'prison works'. Thus the attempt to implement a *rational* criminal justice system, formulated over the previous five years, was immediately subverted by political expediency and magisterial demands for more powers.

While there may have been some acceptance of the general pragmatic aims of the 1991 Act (to reduce the use of imprisonment, for instance), there appeared to be a limited recognition of its conceptual aims – proportionality, denunciation, retribution, public protection, reparation and reform (Crow *et al.*, 1993). However, it could be argued that even when *legislative* change fails to make an impact on practice, pressure on financial costs and resources may gradually constrain or erode judicial prerogative in sentencing (Home Office, 1992; Bottoms, 1995). Is this a case of managerial (cost-effectiveness) goals superseding all others?

An alternative to the Criminal Justice Act 1991 – and the philosophical and political changes that it signified – would have been the adoption of sentencing guidelines for the courts, as is done in Australia and some states in the USA. These guidelines prescribe in advance the appropriate penalty for a whole range of offender/offence combinations (Pease and Wasik, 1987). However, as Cavadino and Dignan (1997, p.5) point out, 'By providing sentencers with one set of criteria relating to the circumstances of the offence in question, and a different range of criteria taking into account relevant characteristics of the offender, the guidelines operate rather in the manner of a road mileage chart, enabling the appropriate, or "presumptive", penalty to be simply "read off" from the matrix supplied'. This suggests fixed and unchangeable sentencing, though closer reading of the guidelines indicates that they are intended as a starting-point only and sentencers are free to depart from the 'grid' if they can justify reasons for doing so. The most famous of these guidelines are those in Minnesota (Ashworth, 1992). 'The available data suggests that Minnesota sentencing guidelines were successful initially, and continue to be successful, in making sentences more uniform for offenders with similar conviction, offence and prior record, and have reduced disparities based on race and social class' (Frase, 1995, p.185). There are many variations, however, and it is doubtful that English sentencers would contemplate the use of such fixed guidelines.

Nevertheless, there have been concerted attempts in the Crime (Sentences) Act 1997 (with its mandatory sentences for certain offenders; see *A Guide to the Crime (Sentences) Act 1997*, Butterworths) and in the Crime and Disorder Act 1998 (with the concomitant establishment of a sentencing advisory panel; see *A Guide to the Crime and Disorder Act 1998*, Butterworths) to not only introduce clearer sentencing guidelines, but furthermore to impose more consistent sentencing across the courts in England and Wales. While special provisions to impose longer than commensurate sentences on special categories of offenders (violent and sex offenders) had been included in the 1991 Criminal Justice Act (section 2(2)b), Sections 1 and 2 of the 1997 Act required the courts to impose automatic life sentences on those who received second convictions for certain violent or sexual offences. These include:

- attempted murder; conspiracy to murder; incitement to murder; soliciting murder
- manslaughter
- wounding with intent to do grievous bodily harm
- rape or attempted rape; unlawful sexual intercourse with a girl under thirteen
- offences under sections 16, 17 and 18 of the Firearms Act 1968, and
- robbery where the offender had in his or her possession at some time during the commission of the offence a firearm or imitation firearm.

For the mandatory life sentence to apply, the previous and current offence need not necessarily be the same, provided that both are one of the offences on this list. A court may depart from the mandatory life sentence if it is of the opinion that there are 'exceptional circumstances' which justify this, in which case it must specify what these circumstances are. Section 3 of the same Act *prescribes* certain sentences for groups of drug offenders. Moreover, by 2000, New Labour Home Secretary, Jack Straw, had set his targets on burglars and was pressing ahead with plans for three-year mandatory minimum sentences for persistent three-time convicted burglars.

All of these measures reflected the 'three strikes and you're out', 'boot camp' and 'zero tolerance' mood of the times, but it is hardly surprising that their introduction has been accompanied by controversy and protest from liberal lawyers, academics and certain professional groups such as probation officers. As one group of academics put it, by far the most damaging effect of the 'prison works' approach has been its impact on the prison population and the associated crisis of resources. Following his chilly warning in 1993 that the government would no longer judge the success of the criminal justice by a fall in the prison population, both the home secretary and the prime minister appeared to go out of their way to encourage sentencers to adopt a more punitive approach in their dealings with offenders and suspects. ... Quite apart from the human misery which the resurgence of [the prison works approach] has inevitably inflicted on prison inmates and their families there has also been a considerable financial cost.

(Cavadino, Crow and Dignan, 2000, p.140)

If we were to try and characterize the mood of the 1990s and early twenty-first century we might mention the public, political and media response to the James Bulger case and to subsequent fears about persistent young offenders. Public consternation also followed the Stephen Lawrence affair, where London Metropolitan Police were shown to have displayed institutional racism in their investigation of the murder of the London teenager on 22 April 1993: this clearly dented public faith in the police and in the criminal justice system generally. Add to this a general politicization of crime and justice issues, and we can discern the reshaping of a criminal justice system to emphasize the following signal themes: *just deserts*; *managerialism*; *risk assessment* and *actuarial justice* (notions which involve an emphasis on the statistical probabilities of future crime based on offence seriousness, previous offending and offenders' social characteristics, and taking anticipatory action on the basis of these); incorporation of the *community* (participation based on consumerism and rights, especially the notion of victims' rights); *active citizenship* (encouragement for the shared responsibility for crime and crime prevention); *restorative justice* (involving a renewed emphasis on reparation – putting right the harm that has been done through the commission of offences); and *populist punitiveness* (an ideology which involves not just a reflection of public opinion, but also politicians tapping into, and using for their own purposes, what they believe to be the public's punitive stance) (Bottoms, 1995; and James and Raine, 1998).

The 1997 Crime (Sentences) Act, the 1998 Crime and Disorder Act, and the Youth Justice and Criminal Evidence Act 1999 all introduced by the Labour government since coming to power on 1 May 1997 appear to include elements of all these signal themes in legislative provision, albeit in varying degrees and with varying enthusiasm from the public. All three include measures to increase both the range of penalties available to the courts and their 'incursiveness'. The Crime (Sentences) Act of 1997, for example, with mandatory sentences for certain offences, emphasizes punishment as a deterrent (*populist punitiveness*), thus ensuring that both meanings of *just deserts* (proportionality and severity) can be achieved. The Crime and Disorder Act 1998 includes other key measures: for instance, the introduction of a national Youth Justice Board to give strategic direction to, set standards for, and measure the performance of the youth justice system as a whole, and local youth offending teams, in the process fulfilling the various *managerial* aspirations. There are also new measures in this Act to ensure that offenders address their offending behaviour and reduce *risk* to the community (through, for example, warnings, which trigger interventions from youth offending teams, action plan orders and drug treatment and testing orders), and measures to ensure protection of the community (through, for instance, anti-social behaviours orders) as well as those of individual victims (with the introduction of reparation orders) which serve to address *community interests* and *restorative justice* values. *Risk assessment* and *actuarial justice* positions, which encompass strong notions of taking anticipatory action on the basis of the probability of offending, are reflected in the 1998 Act's child safety orders for children under 10:

■ for what would be an offence if the child were aged 10 or over

■ for children who have acted in a manner that has caused, or is likely to cause, harrassment, alarm or distress

■ who have contravened a ban imposed by a curfew order (see below)

■ or where such an order is considered necessary to prevent offending.

The order, available in family proceedings courts – where the standard of proof required is lower than in the criminal courts – places the child under supervision for between three and twelve months. In the same Act, local curfew orders apply to all children under the age of 10 in a specific area and prevent them meeting in specified public places between 9 p.m. and 6 a.m. unless accompanied by a parent or responsible adult. Local authorities can impose these curfews on the grounds that such children are 'at risk' of committing offences. The theme of *active citizenship*, it can be argued, is reflected in a number of ways, most notably through the 1998 Act's parenting orders, which involve guidance or counselling sessions once a week for up to 12 weeks, and can be imposed on parents whose children are on a child safety order, an anti-social behaviour order or a sex offender order, and in particular where it is believed that a child under 16 may reoffend unless the parents are instructed in how to take greater responsibility for their offspring's behaviour. Sex offender orders are civil orders that allow the police to intervene before a further offence is committed by someone who has committed a sex offence in the past; these orders thus reflect *risk assessment* and *actuarial justice* approaches. Anti-social behaviour orders, which encourage neighbours to report on the perceived troublesomeness of local residents ('neighbours from hell'), also reflect the theme of *active citizenship*. Some of the signal themes, particularly *active citizenship* and *restorative justice*, are rehearsed in the 1999 Youth Justice and Criminal Evidence Act, which introduces a new primary sentencing disposal for all 10–17 year olds pleading guilty and convicted for the first time. The disposal involves automatic referral of most young offenders to the local youth offender panel – a forum seemingly away from the formality of the court – where a contract will be arranged with the young person to prevent further offending (Ball, 2000). Significantly, panel members may include Jill or Joe Bloggs as 'community panel members' and the contracts will include reparation to the victim or the wider community as well as a programme of activity designed to prevent further offending.

As for *populist punitiveness*, the New Labour agenda arguably involved a shift to the right in order to challenge the Conservative Party on its own ideological territory. Indeed, in early election promises it became clear that New Labour wanted to establish itself in the public's mind as the party best equipped to introduce tough and effective measures to deal with offenders – whatever their age. The Home Secretary himself argued that it is important to listen to 'ordinary' people in 'ordinary' communities. He claimed that for far too long 'the concerns of those who lived in areas undermined by crime and disorder were ignored or overlooked by people whose comfortable notions of human behaviour were matched only by their comfortable distance from its worst excesses. ...' (*The Times*, 8 April, 1998).

The Labour government's avowed attempt to 'talk tough' about crime and to say 'no more excuses' has clearly served it well in terms of assisting it to claim back 'law and order' issues from the Conservatives (Brownlee, 1998). Indeed, the main tenor of Labour criminal justice legislation between 1997 and 1999 mirrors not Labour's sympathetic thinking of the 1960s about 'children in trouble', but reflects an ideological shift in favour of punishment and crime control. This is reminiscent of Cohen's 'punitive city' (Cohen, 1985) in which more and more people, including children, are brought into the criminal justice system for an ever expanding range of 'criminal' or 'troublesome' behaviour (Muncie, 1999; Gelsthorpe and Morris, 1999). Continuous review and reflection are a necessity as the criminal justice system grapples with its own contradictions and is forced to meet changing circumstances, not least those posed by the European Convention on Human Rights and the Human Rights Act of 1998 (the Labour government's attempt to respond to the European Convention). Elements of the Labour Crime and Disorder Act 1998 appear to breach Article 8 of the European Convention concerning 'respect for private and family life': the waiving of consent for a community service order to be imposed, the imposition of electronic tagging, and the imposition of parenting orders and reparation orders are three instances. With regard to the 1997 Crime (Sentences) Act, it is possible that the mandatory life sentences imposed on certain categories of offenders may be seen as 'discretionary' and therefore in breach of Article 5, 'the right to liberty and security' (Cheney *et al.*, 1999).

Insofar as these signal themes are reflected in the sentencing framework and in the general erosion of judicial discretion, it is fair to say that we are left with a melting pot of contradictions, ideas and ideologies which may militate against each other rather than working together to ensure clear and consistent sentencing.

ACTIVITY 3.3

Consider the implications of curtailing or allowing sentencers too much discretion. What would count as 'too much' discretion? Does discretion provide a means to offer individualized justice or will it automatically lead to a series of injustices? Do you think that clearer sentencing guidelines or the Sentencing Advisory Panel will make any difference?

4.2   The neutrality of the judiciary and magistracy

impartiality

'The social service which the judge renders to the community is the removal of a sense of injustice', wrote Lord Devlin (1979). The concept of impartiality is arguably the foundation stone and guiding philosophy of the English legal system upon which the credibility and legitimacy of the criminal justice system depends; a judicial system which is partial cannot command universal consent or respect.

It is a common claim that judges are elderly, male and white and middle class. However, there is a maximum retiring age of 75 for the most senior judges (70 for others) and in the 1980s the average age for circuit and High Court judges was 60 years and nine months, which is perhaps approaching elderly but not indisputably so. It is true, however, that senior judges, though, still come from a social and educational elite. There is little doubt that most judges in the UK do share remarkably similar backgrounds: of the new appointments to the judiciary from 1989 to 1991, 84 per cent had attended public school and 77 per cent were graduates of either Oxford or Cambridge universities. On 1 April 1999 there were 35 lords justices, 98 High Court judges and 560 circuit judges (with 878 Recorders and 398 Assistant Recorders). Six per cent of the circuit judges, 9 per cent of Recorders and 17 per cent of Assistant Recorders were women. Five judges, 13 Recorders and 14 Assistant Recorders were known to be from ethnic minorities (Home Office, 1999). Nevertheless, Malleson (1999) argues that approximately 600 new appointments are made to the judiciary each year and the increasing professionalism of the appointments process because of its aim to eradicate bias amongst other things will lead to changes in the social composition of the judiciary in time.

Judges appointed in the High Court or above must have been former barristers. In 1995, solicitors were not eligible, though this was under review. Circuit judges, Recorders and assistant judges can be either solicitors or barristers – though a good proportion in each category are still barristers. It is sometimes alleged that most judges have been to public school and 'Oxbridge' (Griffith, 1991, pp.30–5); it could be argued that entrants to the legal profession in general, and barristers in particular, are largely middle class and university educated. A 1989 Law Society survey found that over a third of solicitors had come from fee-paying schools despite the fact that only 7 per cent of the population attend such schools (cited in Elliot and Quinn, 2000). Part of the reason for this bias concerns the lack of funding for legal training which has made it very difficult for students without well-off parents to qualify, especially as barristers. In recent years, the difficulties have worsened as shortage of funds has meant that Local Education Authorities (LEAs) have become reluctant to award discretionary grants even to cover fees. A survey by the Law Society in 1992 found that of the 102 LEAs who replied, only six would consider giving discretionary grants to the students in the Common Professional Examination (CPE) course (a basic qualifying course for those whose degree is not in law: almost all lawyers start with a degree), and only 57 on a similar Legal Practice Course (designed for law graduates and those who have passed the CPE) on practical skills, including advocacy.

It is worth highlighting that in 1999 the Lord Chancellor made clear his commitment to ensuring that appointments to judicial office should be made on the basis of merit only, irrespective of ethnic origin, gender, marital status, sexual orientation, political affiliation, religion or disability (Lord Chancellor's Department, 1999). While there may be no direct relationship between judges and politics, the social origins and political views of judges can, of course, have a subtler influence. According to Griffith (1991), judges interpret the 'public interest' from the point of view of their own class. Moreover, he argues that their main role is to be seen as upholders of law and order, of the established distribution of power and of the conventional view (see Extract 3.1 overleaf).

Although magistrates are no longer predominantly male, successive studies have shown them to be overwhelmingly white, middle aged and middle class. In 1999, there were a total of 25,974 lay magistrates in England and Wales (approximately 51 per cent men and 49 per cent women). A breakdown of the statistics by ethnicity is hard to find, but we do know that in 1999 just 1.6 per cent of magistrates were believed to be Black, and 2.1 per cent Asian (plus 0.7 per cent 'other'); 95.5 per cent were reported to be White (Home Office, 1999b). They also tend to be 'middle-minded', partly, but not exclusively, because of the selective (and until the 1990s highly secretive) 'puff of smoke' recruitment procedures by which they are appointed. This suggests that, in the main, magistrates are imbued with a particular self-perception about their role in a way that comes close to producing a consistent ideology. Indeed, Parker *et al.* (1989) show that the chief influence on sentencing practice in magistrates' courts is not the law or the advice received from other professionals in court, nor even the way in which similar cases have been decided by that particular court in the past. It is the 'sentencing culture' of a particular bench, into which new recruits are gradually socialized by watching their more experienced colleagues at work.

Extract 3.1 Griffith: 'The political role of the judiciary'

Many regard the values of the bench and Bar in Britain as wholly admirable and the spirit of the common law (as presently expressed) to be a national adornment. The incorruptibility of the English bench and its independence of the government are great virtues. All this is not in issue. When I argue that they regard the interests of the State or the public interest as pre-eminent and that they interpret those interests as meaning that, with very few exceptions, established authority must be upheld and that those exceptions are made only when a more conservative position can be adopted, this does not mean that the judges are acting with impropriety. It means that we live in a highly authoritarian society, fortunate only that we do not live in other societies which are even more authoritarian. We must expect judges, as part of that authority, to act in the interests, as they see them, of the social order.

The judges define the public interest, inevitably, from the viewpoint of their own class. And the public interest, so defined, is by a natural, not an artificial, coincidence, the interest of others in authority, whether in government, in the City or in the church. It includes the maintenance of order, the protection of private property, the promotion of certain general economic aims, the containment of the trade union movement, and the continuance of governments which conduct their business largely in private and on the advice of other members of what I have called the governing group. ...

Judges are concerned to preserve and to protect the existing order. This does not mean that no judges are capable of moving with the times, of adjusting to changed circumstances. But their function in our society is to do so belatedly. Law and order, the established distribution of power both public and private, the conventional and agreed view amongst those who exercise political and economic power, the fears and prejudices of the middle and upper classes, these are the forces which the judges are expected to uphold and do uphold.

In the societies of our world today judges do not stand out as protectors of liberty, of the rights of man, of the unprivileged, nor have they insisted that holders of great economic power, private or public, should use it with moderation. Their view of the public interest, when it has gone beyond the interest of governments, has not been wide enough to embrace the interests of political, ethnic, social or other minorities. Only occasionally has the power of the supreme judiciary been exercised in the positive assertion of fundamental values. In both democratic and totalitarian societies, the judiciary has naturally served the prevailing political and economic forces. Politically, judges are parasitic.

(Griffith, 1991, pp.327–8)

In Extract 3.2, we shall consider former Law Lord, Lord Devlin's objections to Griffith's argument. Lord Devlin contends that Griffith glosses over important differences between judges and their pronouncements (indeed, 'many of them refuse to toe the party line'), but what is interesting is Lord Devlin's response that 'the oligarchs who rise to the top in a democratic society are usually mature, safe and orthodox men [*sic*]' (Devlin, 1979). Devlin stresses both the real impartiality of judges and the importance of the 'appearance of impartiality': justice must be seen to be done. This is revealing, for it seems that just as it is important for judges to be impartial for justice to be done, the *appearance* of impartiality can perform the critical function of maintaining the consent of the governed to the rule of law, thereby underpinning the legitimacy and stability of the whole social order (see Extract 3.2).

Extract 3.2 Devlin: 'The appearance of impartiality'

In theory the judiciary is the neutral force between government and the governed. The judge interprets and applies the law without favour to either and its application in a particular case is embodied in an order which is passed to the executive to enforce. It is not the judge's personal order; it is substantially the product of the law and only marginally of the judicial mind. If its enforcement is resisted or evaded, the judge is no more concerned than if he were an arbitrator.

British judges have never practised such detachment. The reason may lie in their origin as servants of the Crown or perhaps in the fact that for a long time the law they administered was what they had made themselves. A mixture of the two has left the High Court with the power to enforce its order in civil cases by treating disobedience as contempt itself.

In the criminal law the judges regard themselves as at least as much concerned as the executive with the preservation of law and order. Then there is what can best be described as the expatiatory power. Whereas under most systems the judgement is formal, brief and to the legal point, the British judge may expatiate on what he is doing and why he is doing it and its consequences; and because of his prestige he is listened to.

These high powers make the British judiciary more than just a neutral arbitral force. On the whole their wise and cautious deployment has enabled the judiciary to use its reputation for impartiality and independence for the public good. But it is imperative that the high powers should not be used except in support of consensus law. If the judges are to do more than decide what the law means, if they are also to speak for it, their voice must be the voice of the community; it must never be taken for the voice of the government or the voice of the majority.

(Lord Devlin, 1972, quoted in Griffith, 1991, pp.272–3)

While this suggests an active process – where law is negotiated – Griffith argues that there is an underlying conservatism in all this and that the judges favour the Establishment. Comprehensive surveys of decisions, nonetheless, do not provide evidence of the strong claims by Griffith that *all* decisions reflect the fact that judges are biased against the common man (*sic*). Zander (1989, p.122) provides useful evidence that at least some legal decisions go in favour of the 'common man' (in cases involving disputes between workers and employers) and he reminds us that in a number of cases Conservative government ministers have been called to task.

What about impartiality in criminal cases when a politician is accused of a criminal offence? There is some evidence to suggest that the relationship between judicial authorities and senior politicians may be too close. An instance of this was when the cases of the Guildford Four and the Maguire family were put forward to the home secretary (alongside the predicament of the Birmingham Six) in an all-party delegation of MPs and peers in January 1987, the Home Secretary refused to intervene. However, the imprisonment of Jonathan Aitken, a Conservative MP defeated in the 1997 election, following conviction for perjury in 1998 serves as an example of disparity between the interests of politicians and the judiciary.

procedural justice

Another underlying issue in this debate is the question of whether judges should be involved in the formulation of justice or merely in its delivery. It could be argued that the function of the judge is simply to apply disinterestedly the known law (procedural justice), but there are arguments that the process of applying the law is inevitably political, and that judges act as a 'tool' of government, reflecting its most conservative policies in order to preserve the status quo. Griffith (1991) is persuasive in his argument that the judiciary serves as an 'essential part of the system of government in underpinning the stability of that system and as protecting the system from attack by resisting attempts to change it'. Devlin's (1979) position, as we have seen, is that judges should act according to what they perceive to be the consensus in order to give the appearance of impartiality. This position goes some way to recognizing that judges are not free from the pressures of society, whilst it preferences the role of judges as deliverers of justice rather than law-makers or formulators of justice.

Roshier and Teff (1980) have qualified Griffith's claims when, in response to Griffith's first edition (1977) of *The Politics of the Judiciary*, they suggest that we can describe the politics of the judiciary as reflecting a plurality of different factors. They argue that the outcomes, directions and tendencies of judicial policy do not appear to conform to any one pattern, and point to the tensions between the different courts (especially the Court of Appeal and the House of Lords). (We can also see in studies of magistrates' courts that there are clear differences in the way they operate: those involved in the legal process do not behave in a uniform way – see Parker *et*

Circuit court judges in procession ... the public believes the judiciary does not know what 'ordinary people think'.

al., 1989). But Roshier and Teff are equally prepared to admit that judges are attached to formal rules – a *formal legalism* – which is fundamentally conservative and which reflects the structure and strictures of a politically designed 'justice'.

It is arguable, however, that political interference in the so-called independent judiciary is sometimes necessary: the introduction of the Criminal Justice Act 1991, the Crime (Sentences) Act 1997 and the Crime and Disorder Act 1998 were all efforts to structure the discretion of sentencers in order to achieve a more equitable system of justice. Whilst some parts of the 1991 Act seem progressive, in particular the attempt to encourage sentencers to reflect before sentencing offenders to imprisonment and to reduce the scale of penal responses to crime, however, there have been suggestions that recent legislation (barring the introduction of the Sentencing Advisory Panel in the 1998 Act) is restrictive, punitive and expensive (Travis, 1999; Hutton, 1999; Penal Affairs Consortium, 1997).

4.3   Fair trial by jury?

Trial by jury has long been associated with the preservation of individual liberties and the distinctive spirit of English law. Trial by one's 'peers' (as ordinary lay citizens) is seen to impose justice in the context of a hierarchical, adversarial, confusing and often perplexing legal drama in which the defendant sometimes has only a 'walk-on part'. It is true also that trial by jury in the higher courts can lead to a higher rate of acquittal than in magistrates' courts (Vennard, 1985), though many defendants who elect for trial in the Crown Court are unaware of large differences in sentence severity between the Crown Court and the magistrates' courts (Hedderman and Moxon, 1992).

The basic rules governing juries are found in the Juries Act of 1974. These stipulate that the minimum age to serve on a jury is 18, although the maximum age of jury members was raised from 65 to 70 in the Criminal Justice Act of 1988 (jury service is voluntary after the age of 65). Initial selection of a jury is from names on the electoral roll though some people are not eligible to serve on a jury because of the jobs they do – for example, those involved in the administration of justice, like prison officers, police officers, solicitors, and so on – or because they are mentally disordered. Others are disqualified from jury service because they have been sentenced to more than five years' imprisonment (people who have served any period of imprisonment or who have been given a suspended sentence are also disqualified for specified periods). Those on bail are also disqualified from jury service.

The composition of juries has been a cause for concern. The Commission for Racial Equality has frequently raised questions about the selection of jurors and the need for juries to reflect a multicultural society. Contentiously, Zander and Henderson's Crown Court study (1993) suggested that neither women nor people from minority ethnic groups were badly under-represented. As Padfield (1995, p.280) has described, however, what is of chief concern is perhaps the *distribution* of jurors in individual cases. In 65 per cent of cases there were no people from minority ethnic groups on the jury and in one case, there were no white jurors. The Court of Appeal held, in *R* v. *Ford* [1989] QB 868, that there is no right to a multiracial jury. However, the Royal Commission on Criminal Justice (1993), prompted by the concerns of the Commission for Racial Equality, has indicated that, in some cases, 'race' should be taken into account. The commission suggested that, before trial, the prosecution or defence should be able to apply to the judge for a multiracial jury (including up to three members from minority ethnic groups), though the judge should grant this only if the applicant's case was reasonable because of some special feature. One important question is whether the background of jury members makes any difference to the verdict. Early research found that it was very difficult to predict verdicts on the basis of general characteristics such as age, sex, 'race' or social class (Sealy and Cornish, 1973). More recent research on the Crown Court, carried out by Zander and Henderson (1993), looked specifically at the influence of age and found that, if anything, older juries were more likely to acquit than the younger. This research was limited to the influence of age, however, and should not be taken as a guide to the influence of 'race', class and gender. In the absence of up-to-date detailed research, we simply do not know what the influence of such factors might be; and, in any case, bias may well intrude into the court room in more subtle ways than by overt discrimination (for example, through jury members' reaction to a defendant's demeanour).

We should also note criticisms of jury 'rigging' (i.e. partial selection) to favour the prosecution or, at the very least, that the random selection of jurors is avoided (Baldwin and McConville, 1979; Roshier and Teff, 1980). At the same time, they can be seen more positively by the public as a defence against the oppressive use of state power, as in the case of Clive Ponting, for example, the civil servant who was acquitted by a jury in relation to the allegation that he had disclosed 'official information' concerning the sinking of the Argentine warship *The Belgrano* during the Falklands War in May 1982 to an unauthorized person (in this case Tam Dalyell, MP). The jury – representing the public – accepted Ponting's defence that he had disclosed official information because he felt it to be 'in the interest of the state'. Former Assistant to Ministry of Defence (MoD), Clive Ponting, was acquitted after a high-profile trial in which he was accused of breaking the UK's Official Secrets Act. He was the civil servant who had responsibility for 'the policy and political aspects of the operational activities of the Royal Navy' during the time of the Thatcher government's 1982 war with the Malvinas. Ponting had the job of drafting answers on the sinking of *The Belgrano* by the Royal Navy. He felt that the government was being deliberately misleading and so acted out of professional conscience in sending documents to the MP. At the same time, there are plenty of cases in which the jury has initially given 'unsafe' verdicts – a well-known example is the case of the 'Guildford Four', where four men found guilty of pub bombings that killed five people in October 1974 were sentenced in 1975 to life imprisonment, only to have their sentences quashed in October 1989. Another instance was the case of the 'Birmingham Six', in which six men, found guilty of 21 murders arising from the bombing of two Birmingham pubs in 1974 and sentenced to life imprisonment, had their convictions overturned in 1991. Juries can and do make 'unsafe' and apparently 'unfounded' decisions.

Acquitted members of the Birmingham Six, sent to prison in 1975 for the IRA's bombing of two pubs, gather with their Member of Parliament (centre) after they walk from court as free men, 14 March 1991

Defendants do have some say in the matter of selection of jury members although it can be argued that their powers to 'choose' the jury members are extremely limited. Those summoned for jury service make up an initial 'jury panel'. From this panel of 20 the jury is selected randomly in open court by the clerk reading out the names. At this point, each juror can be challenged by the prosecution or the defence. The defence used to have the right of peremptory challenge – the right to challenge prospective jurors without having to give reasons – but this was reduced from seven to three challenges for each defendant in the Criminal Law Act of 1977 and abolished altogether in the Criminal Justice Act 1988. The government felt that peremptory challenges interfered with the random selection of the jury, were being abused by defence counsel (particularly in multi-defendant cases), and were leading to unmerited acquittals (a case here of 'due process' being subverted by 'crime control', perhaps?). Research provided no foundation for the government's move, however (Vennard and Riley, 1988).

What such challenges allowed for was the right of defendants or their counsel to exclude prospective jury members whom they perceived to be unlikely to reach a fair verdict, for instance where the juror is personally known by the defendant. In 1999 the defence can 'challenge for cause' only (that is, they have to give reasons); the prosecution has a similar right and in addition can, in very exceptional circumstances, require a juror to 'stand-by for the Crown' (which means standing down from the jury at the Prosecution's request and is rather like a pre-emptory challenge). Although there are specified grounds for this, in practice no reason need be given, and this is generally how the information supplied by jury vetting is used. Criminal records and other security records can be checked to see whether or not prospective jurors are 'dubious', but this practice remains controversial because it is seen by some critics as interference in the random selection of juries and thus in the administration and delivery of justice. Debates about the role of the jury have been given fresh impetus with the advent of cases involving serious fraud, which are notoriously long, difficult, expensive and arguably beyond the limits of the jurors' comprehension, and certainly beyond their powers of endurance.

Another concern is the exalted position of the 'plain common sense' of the jury over a panoply of legal and professional judgement. Former Metropolitan Police Chief Commissioner, Sir Robert Mark, once exclaimed that juries 'know little of the law, are occasionally stupid, prejudiced, barely literate, and are not applying the law as public opinion is led to suppose they do' (*The Observer*, 16 March 1975). Simulated jury exercises (McCabe and Purves, 1972; Baldwin and McConville, 1979), provide *some* reassurance that 'real' juries and 'mock' juries concord, but this does not mean that their decisions are appropriate or rational.

The centrality of the jury trial to the English criminal justice system is undeniably being eroded, not least because only a very small percentage of cases are dealt with in the Crown Court (about 5 per cent in 1998). In what could be seen as an increasingly technical, government and Treasury-led criminal justice system where the managerial model appears to dominate (Bottoms, 1995), their very validity is being questioned. In May 1999, Home Secretary, Jack Straw, announced plans to legislate for magistrates alone to decide on jury trials, arguing that 'It has long been a source of irritation to police officers and others, that defendants in many cases are "working the system" by demanding Crown Court trial for no good reason other than to delay proceedings' (Home Office, 1999 and see *The Guardian*, 19 May 1999, reproduced overleaf). The Home Secretary's proposals were rejected in the House of Lords early in 2000, but this is unlikely to be the last word on the situation.

Thousands will lose the right to trial by jury

By Alan Travis, Home Affairs Editor

More than 18,500 defendants a year are to be stripped of their time-honoured right to a jury trial, the home secretary will announce today.

The decision to end the right to elect trial by crown court jury represents a further blow to Britain's ancient jury system in the wake of plans to abolish jury trials for complex fraud cases.

Jack Straw, who in opposition said the reform was 'wrong, short sighted and likely to prove ineffective,' has now swung behind the move. It comes after pressure from the lord chancellor, Lord Irvine, who sees it as a measure which could save millions of pounds.

The announcement is expected to be made in a speech by Mr Straw to the Police Federation in Blackpool.

The home office says the right to choose a jury trial in its modern form dates back to 1855 and covers a wide range of middle ranking offences, including theft, handling stolen goods and some other crimes which are minor but also strike at the accused's reputation for personal honesty.

Defendants charged with these 'either way' offences can choose whether their case is heard in the magistrates' or crown court. The reform would affect about 20% of cases currently tried before a judge and jury in England and Wales – last year this amounted to 18,500 cases.

Mr Straw is to press ahead despite strong opposition from the Bar Council and the Law Society, which insist that the proposal would abolish a right which goes back to the 12th century.

Bruce Holder, of the Bar Council, said: 'This is the back door removal of jury trial and will be an unfortunate inroad into something which is being marginalised all the time.'

The Bar Council also warns that recent home office research showed that black defendants get a worse chance in magistrates' courts than they do before juries.

In theft cases, a higher proportion of black defendants are sent to prison by magistrates than white defendants. A much higher proportion of black defendants elect to jury trial than whites, believing there is a better chance of acquittal in the crown court.

The research says this is a major reason for defendants opting for jury trial, coupled with belief that magistrates are on 'on the side of the police.' But the research also shows they are mistaken if they go to the crown court in the hope of a lighter sentence.

Mr Straw is expected to say the change is designed to end abuse of the system which leads to delay, a waste of resources, and a prolonged wait for justice. It is estimated that the average cost of contested jury trial is £13,500, compared with £2,500 for a magistrates' court case.

(The Guardian, 19 May 1999)

5   Discriminatory practices

discrimination

A chief concern about sentencing since the 1990s has been the possibility of discrimination, particularly in terms of 'race' or gender. 'Discrimination' may be a legally defined concept, but its interpretation lies well beyond the law. There are a number of problems when it comes to defining and measuring discrimination. First, what is conceived of as 'racial' may vary according to its external determinants and other factors (Fitzgerald, 1993). In other words, the disadvantages experienced by minority ethnic groups – for instance, in housing, education, harassment – may also be experienced by others; therefore not all disadvantages can be attributed to racial discrimination, even if experienced disproportionately by minority ethnic groups. Second, it is important to recognize that there are variations in the experiences of minority ethnic groups, and that there may be no 'common' experience. What is racial may be multi-faceted; it may arise and manifest itself differently in different places at different times for different groups. *Moreover, it is extremely unlikely that any one research method can conclusively pin down the chimera of 'pure' discrimination which seems to be required to recognize that discrimination exists* (Reiner, 1993). While a key theme in debates about discrimination is that some people receive 'worse treatment' than others, this is far from easy to measure. For example, is cautioning 'better' or 'worse' than a recommendation for prosecution, which has some chance of resulting in an acquittal? Similarly, is a probation order 'better' or 'worse' than some other penalty?

The ideal of justice is abstract and it includes implicit assumptions that all are equal before the law. However, it is important to discuss what is meant by equal treatment. At one extreme, it means the impartial application of existing rules and principles, regardless of the outcome (procedural justice). At the other, there is the view that any policies or procedures that have the effect of punishing a higher proportion of one social group than another are unjust, and that law and policy should be adjusted so as to achieve equal outcomes (substantive justice).

Some rules or procedures may work to the disadvantage of a particular social group (for example, African-Caribbeanss may be remanded in custody rather than bailed because their family circumstances do not directly fit the criteria used in such decisions). Ensuring that equal proportions of different social groups are punished cannot be a valid aim of the criminal justice system, since it is assumed that the verdict in individual cases depends on the evidence and the punishment on the offence and previous record of the offender. These two extreme views parallel models of justice implied in anti-discrimination law. McCrudden *et al.* (1991) describe them as, respectively, the *individual justice model* and the *group justice model* of legislation against 'race' and sex discrimination. With regard to *individual justice*, the aim is to secure fairness by eliminating illegitimate considerations in the process of dealing with individuals. With regard to *group justice*, the aim is to improve the relative economic position of certain social groups (minority ethnic groups, for example). This becomes relevant when we learn that a high proportion of people in minority ethnic groups are unemployed and there may be links between this factor and crime rates.

The waiting room outside Highbury Magistrates' Court, London

Much of the research evidence on discrimination, in relation to both 'race' and gender issues, is statistical in nature, and this has limitations. First, it presupposes that discrimination can be proved (or not) through sophisticated statistical analysis (and perhaps even manipulation). Second, it ignores the more dynamic aspects of decision-making – the significance of the defendant's appearance and demeanour, people's prejudices revealed in attitude rather than in specific decisions, and the interaction between defendants and officials. Third, it assumes that discrimination is something that can be considered in an ahistorical, atheoretical and apolitical context (Jefferson, 1993; Modood, 1994; Brittan and Maynard, 1984). Fourth, it is myopic to take for granted that snapshot images of sentencing produced through research give a complete picture; it is more useful perhaps to consider discrimination in the light of the *cumulative* and *interactive* effects of disadvantage. Research often focuses on a single process or moment of decision-making, and on a single factor (for example, 'race' *or* gender *or* class), when a number of factors may be relevant *in combination*. Despite these limitations, it is worth considering some of the issues and evidence in more detail. (The terminology used in the following sub-sections tends to reflect that used in the research studies under discussion.)

5.1   'Race' issues in the criminal justice system

The starting-point for any discussion about the possibility of racial discrimination in sentencing has to be the over-representation of minority ethnic groups in prisons. According to the annual Labour Force Survey, the minority ethnic population of Great Britain is 6 per cent. The minority ethnic population of the national prison population, however, is significantly higher at about 18 per cent. This over-representation is greatest among prisoners classified as Black African and Caribbean and it is especially pronounced among remand prisoners and among women. Some of the disproportion may be accounted for by the imprisonment of foreign nationals on the grounds of drug-trafficking and 'muling' as it is sometimes known – but not all of it by any means. (A high number of women are used as 'mules' – carriers of drugs – since it is thought that they will not raise suspicion in the same way as men. The women are promised rich rewards for the task, clothes, education for their children for instance, but they are frequently caught and imprisoned and transported home.) African and Caribbean (and Other) British nationals provide some 10.2 per cent of the total male prison population and 11.8 per cent of the total female prison population – figures which grossly exceed black (African, Caribbean, and Other) presence in the general population (males 15–64 – 1.5 per cent of the British national population; females 15–54 – 2 per cent of the British national population). (Figures drawn from White (1999) and the Home Office (1999).)

5.1.1   Differential crime patterns

What is the involvement in crime of minority ethnic groups? Prison figures suggest that crime rates amongst African-Caribbeanss are much higher than those for whites. The gulf is larger for women than for men but this would appear primarily to be explained by the presence of a relatively large number of foreign nationals (mainly from West Africa) sentenced for drug smuggling and due for deportation at the end of their sentences. That is, African-Caribbean females who are normally resident in the UK may be over-represented in British prisons, but only to the same degree as their male counterparts.

Setting aside questions of the exact degree of over-representation, there are good reasons to expect that crime rates for whites and African-Caribbeans will differ. The African-Caribbean population is, on average, younger than the white and therefore a higher proportion of this group falls within the 'peak age' for offending, which is 18 for males and 17 for females (Home Office, 1997). In particular, African-Caribbean males are strongly characterized by socio-economic factors associated with known high offender rates (high levels of unemployment, low educational attainment and residence in areas of high recorded crime).

It is also important to note that there are few studies of self-reported offending (which involve surveys of people and their self-confessed or reported involvement in crime) that can demonstrate ethnic differences in *actual* offending levels. It is difficult to establish whether there is a higher rate of offending amongst ethnic minority groups or whether it is a matter of perception, but at least one self-report study found that Asian youth 'have significantly lower rates of offending than whites and African-Caribbeans who have very similar rates of offending than whites' (Graham and Bowling, 1995, p.2).

Whatever the differences in actual offending rates, research suggests that there are also important differences in the trajectory of whites and African-Caribbeans through the criminal justice system.

5.1.2   Pre-court decision-making

Whilst not strictly related to court room sentencing, it is at least worth acknowledging that a person's entry to the courts is determined by their treatment earlier in the criminal justice system. Early studies on police stop and search powers (for instance, Willis, 1993; Norris *et al.*, 1992) pointed to higher rates of blacks than whites being stopped by the police. Lord Dholakia (rehearsing Home Office research findings, Phillips and Brown, 1998) reports that black people were five times more likely to be stopped and searched than white people in 1997–98, and six times more likely in 1998–99 (Dholakia, 1999). Similarly, Marian Fitzgerald's study for the Metropolitan police, following in the wake of the Macpherson report into the Stephen Lawrence murder inquiry, highlights concern about undue targeting of young Asians by misusing stop and search powers (*The Guardian*, 16 December, 1999). The evidence is not straightforward since police decisions following the stops were similar in respect of black and white persons. But the claims are worrying (Brown, 1997 and see Chapter 2 of this volume).

While there is a clear need to acknowledge that positive moves through police training and changes in policy strategies are being made to reduce discrepancies in police stops and searches, the concerns do not stop here. A number of studies (for instance, Landau and Nathan, 1983; Commission for Racial Equality, 1992) have indicated discrepancies in cautioning rates. There is also some encouraging evidence in this regard: Phillips and Brown (1998), in their major study of police arrests and outcomes in ten police stations in seven forces (using information on about 4,250 suspects/detainees) for example, point to evidence which suggests that the key determinants of decisions whether to charge or caution are:

- seriousness of offence
- the perceived need for a court sentence
- the fact that the offender was an adult
- the presence of recent and/or serious previous convictions and
- the offender's degree of involvement in the offence.

However, it is worth noting that black juveniles were much less likely than their white or Asian counterparts to have their cases referred for inter-agency consultation and this may in itself lead to injustice. The lower cautioning rate for black people and Asians is strongly linked to the lower rate at which guilt is admitted among these two groups (although this in itself begs the question of why this might be so).

5.1.3   Court of trial and bail and remand decisions

Studies that touch on the issue of court of trial have found that African-Caribbeans are more likely than whites to be tried at Crown Court. Two broad explanations can be suggested for this: (a) African-Caribbeans are tried for more serious crimes; (b) a higher proportion of African-Caribbeans facing triable-either-way charges go to Crown Court (an offence which is triable-either-way can be dealt with either in the magistrates' court or in the Crown Court, depending on its severity).

There is some conflict in the studies over the extent to which this is due to defendants electing trial by jury or to magistrates declining jurisdiction in cases involving African-Caribbean defendants. Shallice and Gordon's study of four London magistrates' courts in 1985 indicates that it was defendants' choice to go to Crown Court (Shallice and Gordon, 1990), while Brown and Hullin (1992), in their study of magistrates' courts in Leeds in 1988, suggest that a much higher proportion of cases going to Crown Court result from committal by magistrates. Phillips and Brown (1998) confirm this finding.

Differences in plea may have important consequences for outcome in that they may be related to the court of trial. As a result, it appears that African-Caribbeans are more likely to plead not guilty and, partly for this reason, are more likely to be tried at Crown Court. Once tried, they are more likely to be acquitted (apparently vindicating their plea). But it is also the case that if they are found guilty, they may incur heavier penalties than Asians and whites. (Moreover, defendants who plead 'not guilty' cannot benefit from the 'discount' associated with a 'guilty' plea.)

The published statistics consistently show even greater over-representation of African-Caribbeans in the remand population than amongst sentenced prisoners. Hood, who constructed a 'custody remand score' to take account of legally relevant variables (that is, to determine risk of custody), found that whites in his sample were slightly less likely to be remanded than expected (taking into account such factors as the seriousness of the offence and previous offences, for example), but that African-Caribbeans were very significantly more likely to be remanded than released on bail (Hood, 1992).

5.1.4 Sentencing

Prior to the 1991 Criminal Justice Act, social inquiry reports by the probation service provided the courts with essential social background information on offenders. These included reference to education, family circumstances, remorse, employment status and likelihood of responding to a particular penalty in a positive way so as to avoid further offending. The change in name from 'social inquiry' to 'pre-sentence' reports, which took place in the 1991 Act, signified a new emphasis on the *current* offence and circumstances of the offender. In the Criminal Justice Act of 1991, the government decided that reports should be mandatory whenever sentencers were considering a custodial sentence but later, in the Criminal Justice and Public Order Act of 1994, it reverted to previous policy, which allowed sentencers to request reports where and when they think necessary. (Such controversies highlight the tensions between judicial discretion and procedural justice and between due process and managerial initiatives.)

pre-sentence reports

The lack of a report can disadvantage a person because it may weaken their chance of receiving a community penalty where they are found guilty after a trial. Studies by Moxon (1988) and Voakes and Fowler (1989) found that the relative absence of pre-sentence reports on African-Caribbean (compared with white) offenders could be linked to their greater likelihood of pleading not guilty. Reports are not usually prepared on those who plead not guilty. In cases where offenders do plead guilty, sentencers are more likely to call for pre-sentence reports on black offenders than on whites. Where this occurs, there are two key considerations: whether probation officers' recommendations are similar (taking all relevant factors into account) for different groups and whether the courts are equally disposed to follow probation officers' recommendations.

The research evidence with regard to bias in reports can be difficult to interpret. Some studies show that reports can be biased because of inappropriate language or assumptions. The example below bears this out:

> Since about the 2nd or 3rd of this month he has not shown any particular signs or symptoms of true mental illness. Admittedly there is about him a mild paranoid attitude which I believe to be part of cultural mores associated with his ethnic propensities ... as far as I am able to ascertain, his personality is that of a normally developed person considering his background and origins.
>
> (quoted in Whitehouse, 1983, p.44)

Other practitioners and academics argue that overt racism is no longer the issue and that, instead of simply analysing reports to detect racism, we should look at the *processes* of production – for example, how cases are allocated to officers to prepare reports, the home visits in order to prepare reports, gate-keeping and monitoring (which often involve peer groups or managers checking reports). There may be discrimination in these parts of the production process that are not captured in the 'polished' report presented to the court (Gelsthorpe, 1992).

There is clear evidence of differential sentencing between blacks and whites when it comes to non-custodial/community disposals, although there is no overall pattern to the types of non-custodial/community disposal given to those from minority ethnic groups. This tends to differ from one study to another (possibly reflecting general differences between courts in patterns of non-custodial disposal). There does tend to be agreement, however, that African-Caribbeans are less likely than whites to receive probation (Brown and Hullin, 1992; Moxon, 1988; Mair, 1986; Walker, 1989).

Nevertheless, commentators have usually come to diametrically opposite conclusions from the research data, suggesting on the one hand that they provide evidence of 'up-tariffing' of African-Caribbean offenders (where African-Caribbeans are given higher penalties than others) and, on the other, that there is no significant difference in the court disposal of offenders from minority ethnic groups once relevant variables are taken into account (for example, age of defendant, court of trial, charge, plea, previous convictions and pre-sentence report suggestions, see Reiner, 1993 and Smith, 1997).

5.1.5   A cumulation of factors

Few studies have attempted a comprehensive analysis of all the relevant variables. McConville and Baldwin (1982), in their analysis of four random samples of Crown Court trials in London and Birmingham in 1975 and 1979, and Mair (1986), in his analysis of cases in two magistrates' courts in Leeds and Bradford in 1983, attempted to match white offenders with those from minority ethnic groups on a range of variables before making comparisons. Both studies, however, are characterized by methodological problems: McConville and Baldwin grouped African-Caribbeans and Asians together and the size of Mair's sample was perhaps too small to draw any firm conclusions.

Hood (1992) has shed considerable light on the interaction of factors. His study, with a sample of 6,000 individuals sentenced at five Crown Courts in the West Midlands in 1989, found that black males had a 17 per cent greater chance of imprisonment than whites. Hood found a 5 per cent greater risk of custody for black males than for whites with the same characteristics. Moreover, he points out that the disparity would have been greater still if African-Caribbeans had not already been disproportionately remanded in custody. A remand in custody itself

Extract 3.3 Macpherson: Defining institutional racism

6.6 The phrase 'institutional racism' has been the subject of much debate. We accept that there are dangers in allowing the phrase to be used in order to try to express some overall criticism of the police, or any other organisation, without addressing its meaning. Books and articles on the subject proliferate. We must do our best to express what we mean by those words, although we stress that we will not produce a definition cast in stone, or a final answer to the question. What we hope to do is to set out our standpoint, so that at least our application of the term to the present case can be understood by those who are criticised.

6.7 In 1981, Lord Scarman's Report into The Brixton Disorders was presented to Parliament. In that seminal report Lord Scarman responded to the suggestion that '*Britain is an institutionally racist society,*' in this way:-

'*If, by* [institutionally racist] *it is meant that it* [Britain] *is a society which knowingly, as a matter of policy, discriminates against black people, I reject the*

allegation. If, however, the suggestion being made is tha[t] practices may be adopted by public bodies as well a[s] private individuals which are unwittingly discriminator[y] against black people, then this is an allegation whic[h] deserves serious consideration, and, where proved, swi[ft] remedy'. (Para. 2.22, p.11 – Scarman Report). ...

6.15 When Lord Scarman asserted in his final conclusio[n] that '*institutional racism does not exist in Britain: b[ut] racial disadvantage and its nasty associate raci[al] discrimination have not yet been eliminated*', (Para 9.[] p.135), many took this statement as the classic defenc[e] against all allegations that '*institutional racism*' exists i[n] British society. His earlier words '**knowingly**, *as a matte[r] of policy, discriminates*' and '*practices may be adopte[d] ... which are* **unwittingly** *discriminatory,*' were n[ot] separated and given equal weight. Whilst we must nev[er] lose sight of the importance of explicit racism and dire[ct] discrimination, in policing terms if the phras[e] 'institutional racism' had been used to describe not on[ly] is a strong predictor that a custodial sentence is likely to be imposed, so discrimination is often cumulative. In this case, a greater number of black than white males had been remanded in custody and at least part of the apparent discrimination can be attributed to this, rather than to discriminatory attitudes towards black males at the sentencing stage. On the other hand, Hood found that there were no significant differences for women; that the overall custody rate for Asians was rather lower than the score predicted, and that the differences seemed to be confined to men over 21. The study also confirmed Mair's finding that, relative to whites, black defendants with social inquiry reports were disadvantaged not by the recommendations of the reports (given their case characteristics), but by the greater extent to which the courts sentencing a higher proportion of black defendants to custody ignored these recommendations. The fault thus lay with the courts, not with the probation officers.

Hood's study provides evidence of both direct and indirect discrimination at the Crown Court and of the influence of social criteria in sentencing:

- Direct discrimination is implied by the findings of unexplained ethnic differences for men (when all relevant explanations were taken into account) in the bail/remand decision, in the rate at which black people were sentenced to custody, and in the length of the custodial sentences imposed on those who pleaded not guilty.

- Hood also points out that defendants from minority ethnic groups were inadvertently subjected to a form of *indirect discrimination* at the point of sentence, because they more often chose to contest the case than others (and were thus ineligible for the usual discount on guilty plea), and because there were therefore no reports from probation officers (probation officers tend not to prepare reports on those who contest cases). Hood maintains that black people put themselves at risk of custody and longer sentences in these ways.

licit manifestations of racism at direction and policy el, but also unwitting discrimination at the anisational level, then the reality of indirect racism in more subtle, hidden and potentially more pervasive ure would have been addressed. ...

7 Unwitting racism can arise because of lack of lerstanding, ignorance or mistaken beliefs. It can e from well intentioned but patronising words or ions. It can arise from unfamiliarity with the naviour or cultural traditions of people or families n minority ethnic communities. It can arise from st stereotyping of black people as potential criminals roublemakers. Often this arises out of uncritical self-lerstanding born out of an inflexible police ethos of 'traditional' way of doing things. Furthermore such tudes can thrive in a tightly knit community, so that re can be a collective failure to detect and to outlaw breed of racism. The police canteen can too easily its breeding ground. ...

6.34 Taking all that we have heard and read into account we grapple with the problem. For the purposes of our inquiry the concept of institutional racism which we apply consists of:

The collective failure of an organisation to provide an appropriate and professional service to people because of their colour, culture, or ethnic origin. It can be seen or detected in processes, attitudes and behaviour which amount to discrimination through unwitting prejudice, ignorance, thoughtlessness and racist stereotyping which disadvantage minority ethnic people.

It persists because of the failure of the organisation openly and adequately to recognise and address its existence and causes by policy, example and leadership. Without recognition and action to eliminate such racism it can prevail as part of the ethos or culture of the organisation. It is a corrosive disease.

(Macpherson, 1999, pp.20–3, 28)

Importantly, Hood suggests that the use of *social criteria* such as employment and family circumstances may put members of certain groups at a particular disadvantage. One obvious example concerns the effect of unemployment on the bail/remand decision since a very high number of black people are unemployed. Interestingly, whereas the probability of black offenders receiving a custodial sentence is between 5 and 8 per cent higher than for white offenders, the probability of their having been remanded in custody is at least double that (16 per cent higher). There are thus 'knock-on' or cumulative effects.

Hood's research is not without flaws: definitional problems can be found in his terminology regarding the categories of 'white', 'black' and 'Asian'; there are also problems with his sampling and problems of generalizability, given the exclusive focus on Crown Courts (Halevy, 1995). Nonetheless, von Hirsch and Roberts (1997) defend the research for its methodological sophistication and robustness, contending that it is significant in that it augments available evidence that racial discrimination can and does occur in the criminal justice system, while demonstrating the complexity of the problem. While the Phillips and Brown study (1998) does not carry the same weight as the Hood study in respect of sentencing due to its small sample sizes, it reiterates a number of key points regarding the cumulation and interaction of legal and social factors. Certainly, the statistical analyses in respect of key decisions affecting entry to the criminal justice system point to the fact that the ethnic origin of the suspect is a factor which, independently of others, can predict particular outcomes (for instance, in contrast to whites, a higher demand for legal advice, a lower rate of admitting to offences, a lower referral to juvenile justice consultancy teams, a higher case termination on the part of the Crown Prosecution Service (CPS)). Then again, interpretation is by no means simple, and we cannot read off discrimination from this in a straightforward fashion.

Leaving aside the thorny issue of whether or not the researchers had access to all the relevant variables and the fact that data analysis is particularly tricky when information on decision-making is provided by the decision-makers themselves, the first point to make is we still need to find out more about the respective offence patterns of whites and blacks, for this could help explain matters. Secondly, some differences between ethnic groups disappear when other factors – for example, the lower cautioning rate for blacks and Asians makes sense in the light of a lower rate of admitting to offences – are taken into account. Thirdly, it is possible that differences in the treatment of ethnic minority groups at one stage in the process may be countered or compounded by differences at other stages. The higher rate of Crown Prosecution Service termination cases involving ethnic minorities, for instance, may work to counteract a possible imbalance in charges by the police where the evidence is not sufficient for a successful prosecution. Importantly, none of this is to deny the possibility of discrimination; rather, it emphasizes that disentangling racial effects is an extremely complex affair. Discrimination cannot be said to be universal nor always methodically applied, which suggests that there is a need for more sophisticated understandings of how (and where) it occurs and how it can be dealt with. This point is emphasized in the Macpherson report that followed the Stephen Lawrence Inquiry where the notion of 'institutionalized racism' is referred to. This does not mean that all individuals in an organization are racist, but that decision-making processes, attitudes and behaviour, unwitting prejudice, ignorance, thoughtlessness, and racist stereotyping are all relevant to an understanding of collective failure to deliver an impartial and professional service (see Extract 3.3).

Above all, recognition should be given to the way in which the decisions of criminal justice agencies (and other relevant bodies, including the legal profession and forensic experts) interact with and compound each other. None can be viewed in isolation; even if there are small ethnic differences in the key decisions taken by each, their cumulative impact may be very large indeed (Reiner, 1993; NACRO, 2000).

5.2   Gender issues in the court room

ACTIVITY 3.4

How do you think women are treated in the courts compared with men? Do you think there are differences in the way they are treated? Justify your responses with examples, if possible.

A common assumption is that women are treated more leniently than men in the criminal justice system. They are thought to be less likely than men to be arrested, prosecuted, convicted or imprisoned. This is often referred to as the 'chivalry' hypothesis, since the majority of decision-makers are male (though magistrates number nearly as many women as men) and it is believed that they respond to female offenders in much the same way that they might respond to their wives, daughters and mothers (*sic*). Some writers, however, describe the process in quite a different way. They see the criminal justice system's treatment of women as discriminatory and sexist, and believe that women are punished for breaching not only the criminal law, but also traditional sex role expectations. **chivalry**

Criminal statistics seem at first glance to support the 'chivalry' hypothesis, since they have repeatedly shown that a far greater proportion of women than men are cautioned by the police, rather than prosecuted (Home Office, 1997). They also show that a smaller proportion of women than men (21 years and over) receive custodial penalties (the figures for 1997 were 13 per cent and 26 per cent respectively) and that a greater proportion of women than men receive probation or discharges (the figures for 1997 were 21 per cent and 27 per cent for women compared with 11 per cent and 14 per cent for men). This picture is similar for both Crown Courts and magistrates' courts and for offences for which women are commonly sentenced (for example, theft from shops) and for offences for which women are rarely sentenced (for example, assaults). Compared with men, women are also generally given shorter sentences of imprisonment for all offences (except drugs).

These statistics do not necessarily show that women are dealt with *more leniently* than men; they show that women are being dealt with *differently* from men, but they do not tell us why this occurs. Before accepting the 'chivalry' hypothesis, therefore, we need to know whether these differences arise simply because of the sex of the offender or for some other reason. We would perhaps expect those with either no or very few previous convictions to stand a greater chance of being cautioned (instead of being prosecuted) than those with many previous convictions. If they were prosecuted, we would perhaps expect them to be less likely to receive custodial penalties. We thus need to examine whether there is any evidence that women are 'less serious' offenders and less criminally sophisticated than men, which alone might account for the differences in cautioning and sentencing outcomes.

Overwhelmingly, recorded crime is a male activity. In 1997, about 82 per cent of those found guilty of, or cautioned for, indictable offences, were men, while only 17 per cent were women – with 1 per cent of offences committed by others, for example, companies (Home Office, 1997). Interestingly, while 34 per cent of males born in 1953 have been convicted before the age of 40, only 8 per cent of females fall into this category (Farrington, 1997).

Table 3.1 below shows that nearly two-thirds of women's offences are theft related (primarily theft from shops) compared with just over one-third of men's. The other main disparity in offending occurs in relation to burglary, with 2 per cent of women compared with 9 per cent of the men being found guilty or cautioned for this offence. Overall, it is accepted that women generally commit less serious offences than men. *Within* offence categories (since legal categories cover a multitude of sins), research also suggests that women again commit the less serious offences: for example, research into theft from shops suggests that women steal fewer items, and of less value, than men (Farrington and Buckle, 1984). This suggests that women are both less serious and less frequent offenders than men. It may be these *differential crime patterns* that explain the differing police cautioning and court sentencing patterns, not the mere sex difference.

Table 3.1 Percentage of offenders found guilty or cautioned by type of offence, age group and sex, England and Wales 1998

	All ages		18–20[1]		21 and over	
	Male	**Female**	**Male**	**Female**	**Male**	**Female**
Violence against the person	12	9	11	8	12	8
Sexual offences	1	0	1	0	2	0
Burglary	9	2	9	2	6	1
Robbery	1	1	2	1	1	0
Theft and handling stolen goods	35	59	31	56	32	53
Fraud and forgery	4	8	3	9	6	11
Criminal damage	3	1	3	1	3	1
Drug offences	22	12	28	15	24	15
Other (excluding motoring)	11	7	11	8	13	9
Motoring	2	0	1	0	3	1
TOTAL	100	100	100	100	100	100

1 Until Criminal Justice Act 1991, offenders aged 17 and under 21.
All figures have been rounded.
Home Office, 1998, Table 5.10

5.2.1 The sentencing of women in the court room

Evidence that women receive preferential treatment from the police, simply because they are women, is weak and complicated (Morris, 1987 and Gelsthorpe, 1989), and research with respect to sentencing has produced contradictory findings. Kapardis and Farrington (1981) adopted an experimental approach in which magistrates were presented with a description of a hypothetical theft offence and were asked to say which sentence they would regard as appropriate. Only the value of the goods and the sex of the offender were varied in order to test the effect of both sex and the seriousness of the offence on sentencing. They found that there was *no difference* in the sentencing of women and men involved in the *less serious* offences but that women were treated *more leniently* than men for the *more serious* offences.

Farrington and Morris (1983) abstracted information from court records on just over 100 women and almost 300 men and found that women appeared to be dealt with more leniently than men. However, when the nature of the offence and previous convictions were taken into account, they found that the two sexes were dealt with in the same way. Sex was not related to sentencing severity independently of other factors. Women only received more lenient sentences because they committed less serious offences and were less likely to have been previously convicted. Type of offence, current problems and previous convictions were the main influences in the sentencing decisions.

Mair and Brockington (1988), on the other hand, using a different methodology (matching male and female defendants on certain characteristics, such as offence) did not produce such clear-cut results. They collected data on 225 women and 950 men who appeared in two magistrates' courts and were sentenced for indictable or triable-either-way offences. On the basis of unmatched data, female defendants received fewer community service orders and more probation orders than male defendants. Though the situation changed when matched groups were compared, women, even when matched, were more likely to be conditionally discharged and less likely to be fined than men. Disparities in sentences of imprisonment, however, were reduced by matching. Overall, no firm conclusions were drawn.

Moxon (1988) suggested more conclusively that women were dealt with more leniently than men. He examined sentencing practice in the Crown Courts and found that women were significantly more likely than men to receive non-custodial sentences even after allowing for the nature of the offence and criminal record. Dominelli (1984), however, claimed that women were dealt with more harshly than men. From an examination of all community service orders made in one area between 1976 and 1981, she suggested that women given community service orders had often been convicted of less serious offences and had fewer previous convictions than their male counterparts. However, if sentencing is based on a clear 'just deserts' approach, it can be argued that it might be expected that women who are first and less serious offenders should be concentrated in the lower tariff options. Dominelli did not, however, examine sentencing practice *generally* in the areas she studied, and her claim that women were dealt with more harshly than men is thus of doubtful validity.

In contrast, in a study of women who kill their children (Wilczynski and Morris, 1993), which involved the analysis of 474 cases recorded between 1982 and 1989, there was evidence of lenient treatment towards women: mothers were less likely than fathers to be convicted of murder (they were convicted of lesser charges such as manslaughter – often on the grounds of diminished responsibility); they were also less likely to be sentenced to imprisonment and more likely to be given probation and psychiatric disposals (although psychiatric disposals are not always lenient and are open to different interpretation).

Research based on statistical analysis of sentencing on a sample of some 13,000 adult cases of offences against the person, drug offences, and theft from shops, drawn from the Offender Index in 1991, by Hedderman and Dowds (in Hedderman and Gelsthorpe, 1997) indicated certain differences in sentencing patterns of males and females. Do sentencers adopt a different approach when dealing with women and with men or can the difference in sentencing patterns be explained by the different features of the cases, i.e. seriousness of offence and culpability? Although based on small statistical samples in certain areas, the results of the first part of this study suggest that, overall, women

- receive less severe sentences – even when previous convictions are considered
- tend to be fined less regularly and
- receive either a discharge or a community sentence more frequently.

However, the more robust finding is that there is no consistently different pattern in the sentencing of women: there are merely tendencies, which might be explained by more detailed information about particular cases. The second part of this study (Gelsthorpe and Loucks, in Hedderman and Gelsthorpe, 1997) breaks new ground by exploring, through interviews with 189 lay magistrates and 8 stipendiaries, their approaches to sentencing. The interviews reveal the complexity of sentencing behaviour and also show that many of the most influential factors are related to gender. Family circumstances, appearance and demeanour, for instance, appeared to be dominant. Women were also more likely than men to be viewed as 'troubled' rather than 'troublesome'. Magistrates were more likely to view a woman's offence as a matter of survival, or as the result of provocation or coercion, or attributable to some mental disturbance, than a man's. One of the best-known studies that has succeeded in looking at gender and the severity of punishment is American research by Kathleen Daly (1994). Daly analyses women's and men's cases routinely processed in felony courts (dealing with offences of homicide, aggravated assault, robbery, larceny and drug offences). She first presents a statistical analysis of sentencing disparity from a wide sample of cases and then forms a 'deep sample' by comparing forty matched pairs of women and men convicted of similar offences, examining in each case the pre-sentence investigation reports and transcripts of the remarks made in court on the day of sentencing. By providing numerical and narrative descriptions of their crimes and punishments, Daly underlines the inadequacies of statistical analysis in isolation (as in other studies); although her statistics suggest leniency towards women in sentencing, her close comparison of the matched pairs and analysis of the narratives indicates that gender differences are negligible when the details of the cases are taken into consideration.

To help elucidate issues of discrimination, an examination of race, gender and social class factors in combination is necessary. Ruth Chigwada-Bailey (1997) attempts to focus on race and gender by examining what she calls a 'discourse of disadvantage' affecting black women in the criminal justice system. Her study is based on twenty interviews with women who had experience of the criminal justice system in England and Wales. Although she asks some searching questions about the interaction of race, class and gender, these themes are not pursued in a systematic and methodologically sound fashion and at times more general claims (from other research studies) obscure what we can learn from the women themselves. Similarly, Biko Agozino (1997) attempts to analyse the interactions of race, class and gender, but whilst his treatise is interesting, the claims lack substantial empirical grounding. A sophisticated study that is able to encompass race, class and gender issues is clearly imperative. Whilst research to date may be partial or incomplete, there is certainly sufficient impetus for such a study in order to fully understand and respond to discrimination.

ACTIVITY 3.5

In light of the preceding discussion, study the reports from *The Guardian*, 20 May 1994, and *The Sunday Times*, 9 April 1995, reproduced on the following pages. How can we make sense of such diverse research findings? Make a list of possible explanations and the factors involved in interpreting the data.

The very different findings may simply mean that different research methodologies (experimental, matching, multivariate analysis) tend to produce different results. Or it may be that different courts in different areas operate in quite different ways (the magistrates' courts covered in the projects mentioned above were in Cambridge and West Yorkshire). Or it might be that we need to consider the importance of *gender* rather than *sex* to explain the apparent disparities in sentencing.

Courts 'lenient toward women'

Alan Travis
Home Affairs Editor

HOME OFFICE research published yesterday challenges the widely held assumption that the courts and criminal justice discriminate against women.

Academics and pressure groups have long argued that women are treated much more severely by the courts than men, a claim based on statistics showing that 38 per cent of women in jail are there for their first offence compared with 10 per cent of men.

A Home Office research study, by Carol Hedderman and Mike Hough, now claims that when it comes to men and women with similar criminal backgrounds charged with similar crimes, women receive more lenient sentences.

The research into court treatment shows that girls are much less likely to commit the sort of crimes carried out by young boys, such as burglary or breaking into cars. 'Although there has been a rise in the proportion of females dealt with for violence and drug offences in the last 10 years, 71 per cent of their offences in 1992 were theft and handling – in contrast to only 43 per cent of males.'

Three-fifths of women convicted of offences were cautioned, compared with only a third of men. At court women were far less likely to receive a prison sentence, except in drug cases where there appeared little difference.

Women are also far less likely to go to crown court, and so receive on average 17 months for women over 21 – compared with 21 months for men.

(*The Guardian*, 20 May 1994)

Males

37% | 18% | 8% | 18% | 17%

Females

27% | 21% | 7% | 6% | 36%

- ☐ Absolute or conditional discharge
- ☐ Fine
- ☐ Probation or community service
- ☐ Suspended prison
- ☐ Immediate custody

Sentencing adults: Percentage of males and females sentenced for offences – 1992 (figures rounded to the nearest whole number)

Courts condemn women to tougher sentences than men

Liz Lightfoot and
Andrew Anderson

WOMEN are consistently receiving harsher sentences than men. Many are being jailed by courts that allow men who have committed virtually identical offences to walk free.

Probation officers, academics and prison support groups blame the discrimination on judges and magistrates, who they say are less tolerant of women who commit crimes, particularly if the offence is seen as 'setting a bad example' if they are also mothers.

Government policies to target persistent serious offenders are also penalising women, particularly those who return before courts because they are too poor to pay fines.

Last year the number of women imprisoned rose by nearly a quarter to almost 3,000, causing an overcrowding crisis in jails. The growing concern over the sentencing of women is to be addressed by the Magistrates' Association at a meeting next month.

The trend, which challenges the notion that women are treated more sympathetically by courts, is typified by Sheila Kent, 48, who gets out this week after a four-month sentence imposed by magistrates in Boston, Lincolnshire.

Kent, who has two children, was jailed after failing to keep up with her £10-a-month fine for motoring offences and not having a television licence. Although she had met her payments for 11 months, she was able to pay only part of the fine for two months because of a delay in receiving child benefit.

Yet the day after Kent was jailed in February, the same magistrate sitting at the same court gave Michael Hardstaff, 28, a 28-day suspended prison sentence after he admitted he had not made any payment of his £20-a-week fine, imposed for burglary and motoring offences, for 17 months.

Hardstaff, who had been told by Sheila Bannister, the magistrate, that the court took a 'very dim view' of his non-payment, admitted this weekend that he had been leniently treated compared with Kent. 'I was expecting to be sent down for a lot more than 28 days but they let me go,' he said.

Women offenders and their families are not alone in their concern about discrimination in sentencing. Prison support groups say a growing number of women inmates – including those on remand – are there unnecessarily and to the detriment of their families.

Although women make up less than 4 per cent of the total prison population, the number of women receiving 'immediate' custodial sentences in England and Wales (as opposed to fine defaulters) rose by 24 per cent last year to 2,952.

Many are in jail for 'minor' offences. Last year more than 300 women were imprisoned for non-payment of fines for not having a television licence, according to research by Leeds and York universities. 'The imprisonment of women for non-payment of television fees is one of the great scandals of our time,' said Professor Jonathan Bradshaw, of York.

The upsurge in the number of women jailed has led to crisis measures in women's prisons. Internal prison service documents reveal governors are being forced to find places in high-security jails for women whose offences mean they should serve their sentence in low-security prisons.

Even for women who escape jail, punishments are still tougher than for men. A *Sunday Times* survey of more than a third of the 54 probation areas in England, Wales and Northern Ireland has shown that women are twice as likely as men to receive probation for first offences.

Rosemary Thomson, chairman of the Magistrates' Association, said government changes to toughen up probation had reduced sentencing options. 'It appears probation is still being used for women who have not committed serious offences but need help with their lives. It is wrong, but it is understandable.'

Women are also being jailed because the alternative – community service orders – are not felt suitable. Magistrates and probation officers believe the work is too physical or is not suitable for mothers with family commitments.

For Rebecca Gillon, 26, the findings come as no surprise. She was seven months pregnant when she was jailed for 21 days last year for her first offence of 'borrowing' £380 from her bank employers. Gillon, from Lesbury, Northumberland, was jailed for stealing from Barclays, even though she paid the money back before an audit showed it was missing. She was given a conditional discharge after an appeal.

Lord Mackay, the lord chancellor, called yesterday for more women to apply for top jobs in the judiciary and promised 'affirmative action' to ensure all applicants were treated fairly on their merits. Fewer than a tenth of the applicants for the bar are women.

His concerns were echoed by Cherie Booth, the barrister wife of Tony Blair, the Labour leader. She said the lack of women high court judges – only six out of 95 – was a result of few women coming to the bar.

Additional reporting by Ciaran Byrne, Rajeev Syal and Michael Greenwood

(*The Sunday Times,* 9 April 1995)

Gender-related behaviour is that social behaviour we associate with each of the sexes; masculinity is a characteristic we normally associate with men, whilst femininity is a social characteristic we normally associate with women. Gender considerations denote the assumptions we have about appropriate and inappropriate sex-role behaviour which are socially and not biologically constructed. Thus, traditionally, women were expected to be passive, dependent, wives and mothers; men, on the other hand, were expected to be active, independent, breadwinners. These are, of course, stereotypical conceptions, but nonetheless they appear to remain influential today, and thus the woman who enters the court room is expected to behave in certain ways.

Broadly speaking, a large body of research has identified three main themes that are particularly relevant for the sentencing of women – pathology, domesticity and respectability. We can, however, add one further theme, sexuality, which is particularly relevant for girls.

First, a woman who enters the criminal justice system has been described as 'incongruous', 'out of place' or 'invisible' (Worrall, 1990). Explanations for her presence are sought within the discourse of the 'pathological' and the 'irrational': menstruation, mental illness, poor socialization, broken homes, for example. Men are not viewed as so out of place in the court room and so their offending is explained in different ways, within the discourse of 'normality' and 'rationality'. Their behaviour is more likely to be viewed as the product of such factors as boredom, greed and peer-group pressure. These different types of explanations for women's and men's behaviour may then influence their subsequent processing through the criminal justice system.

In addition, certain factors seem to influence the sentencing of women but not that of men. Farrington and Morris (1983) found that distinctions were made in court between women (see Table 3.2 below). The main distinguishing factors were: the involvement of other offenders, marital status, family background and the sexual composition of the bench. Women convicted with one or more

Table 3.2 Factors influencing sentence severity in order of importance

Total sample	Men	Women
Type of offence	Type of offence	Current problems
Current problems	Current problems	Convicted in the previous 2 years
Number of previous convictions	Number of previous convictions	Other offenders involved
Legal representation[1]	Legal representation	Number of Theft Act offences
Convicted in the previous 2 years	Number of Theft Act offences	Marital status[3]
Age	Age	Family background
Plea[2]	Plea	Sexual composition of the bench[4]

1 Those represented received the more severe sentences.
2 Pleading guilty led to more severe sentences.
3 Divorced and separated women were given more severe sentences.
4 Women appearing before a bench containing two female magistrates were sentenced more severely than those appearing before a bench containing two male magistrates.

Source: Farrington and Morris, 1983, p.244

other offenders were more likely to receive more severe sentences than those convicted on their own. Divorced and separated women received relatively more severe sentences than married women, as did women coming from a 'deviant' rather than a stable background. Women appearing before a bench made up of two women and a man were dealt with more severely than women appearing before benches of two men and a woman.

Simple statistical analyses such as these, however, are not able to answer the question of why differences in sentencing might occur; rather, they enable researchers only to speculate about why these differences might appear. Few of the researchers, for example, observed magistrates or judges at work, or interviewed them. Nor do they place much focus on those processes that might shape sentencing outcomes, for instance, pleas in mitigation or the provision of social inquiry or pre-sentence reports. A few researchers did do this, however, and it is to their research that we now turn.

Pearson (1976) conducted a small-scale observational study of the magistrates' court in Cardiff. She focused only on women (restricting the general applicability of her research), and argued that the sentencing of women was highly individualized and that women were not seen to be fully responsible for their offences: 'quasi-juvenile status' is how she describes it. Edwards (1984) also studied only female offenders. She observed cases in Manchester City magistrates' court and in some Crown Courts. Her conclusion was that women were 'on trial both for their legal infraction and for their inappropriate femininity and gender roles'. It was women's respectability that was at issue. This was particularly noticeable when women appeared before the Crown Court for violent offences. However, Edwards' conclusion is based on the observation of only a small number of cases and must be treated with caution.

The theme of punishment for the breach of traditional sex role expectations is reiterated in Carlen's (1983) interviews with male sheriffs in Scotland. The most significant finding was that the women who were sent to prison were those who, in the eyes of the sheriffs, had 'failed' as mothers. Thus, sheriffs wanted to know not only whether the woman was a mother but also whether or not she was, in their view, a 'good' mother:

> If she's a good mother, we don't want to take her away. If she's not a good mother, it doesn't matter. …

> If a woman has no children then it clears the way to send her to prison. If they are in care, I treat her as a single woman. …

> (Carlen, 1983, p.67)

Here, domesticity is the key issue. Worrall cites a prison governor who once echoed these sentiments: 'Women should come here for at least 6 months, then we can train them to be good mothers and they're grateful' (Worrall, 1990, p.61). Eaton, on the other hand, argued (on the basis of observation of over 100 cases involving women and over 200 involving men and interviews with magistrates) that family circumstances are considered important in deciding sentences for *both* sexes, along with the nature of the offence and the offender's previous record (Eaton, 1986). The family was central to pleas in mitigation offered by counsel and to social inquiry reports prepared on behalf of both women and men. Magistrates commented that they would be influenced by the presence of children if the defendant was responsible for child-care, whether that defendant was male or female. However, responsibility for children was more likely to arise in cases involving women and, because of this, women and men were presented differently to the court – 'women as dependent and domestic' and 'men as breadwinners'. Here, we see the reinforcement of 'traditional' gender roles. The result, according to Eaton, was that women who were negatively assessed *as women* were dealt with more severely.

Allen (1987) reached the opposite conclusion. She argued that the psychiatric and social inquiry reports that she examined (100 on women and 100 on men) drew on sex stereotypes that systematically placed women 'at a moral advantage and men at a moral disadvantage'. She found other striking differences. Reports on female offenders almost invariably addressed the woman's mental state. This was in sharp contrast to reports on male offenders: these tended to focus on the more external aspects of the offender's behaviour and life-style. According to Allen, such differences occurred independently of the material facts of their behaviour.

If report writers, advocates and decision-makers view women in a particular way, it is hardly surprising that certain dispositions (probation and hospital orders, for example) are 'naturally' recommended for and given to women whilst others (community service, for example) are not. The Probation Inspectorate (1991) found that all the community service schemes they visited during their inspection had at least some child-minding provision; but they also found, four years after research on the issue by Jackson and Smith (1991), that social inquiry reports on female prisoners continued to refer to the unsuitability of a mother for community service:

The ages of her children mean she is not suitable for community service. …

As a single woman with two small children she is not suitable for community service. …

Community service, regrettably, is not a viable option in view of her responsibilities as a mother. …
(Jackson and Smith, 1987, quoted in Probation Inspectorate, 1991, p.47)

Paradoxically, all of these women (and other women in the six prisons where the Inspectorate examined social inquiry reports) had been sent to prison and yet, as stated by the Inspectorate, at least some of the women came from probation areas known to have child-minding facilities (Barker, 1993). The Inspectorate's 1996 Report was no less gloomy in this regard with probation staff (including pre-sentence report writers) seemingly unaware of child-care facilities or considering work tasks unsuitable for women (Her Majesty's Inspectorate of Probation, 1996; see also The Howard League, 1999). It is also important to note that requests for a social inquiry report are more commonly asked for on women (Mair and Brockington, 1988) despite the increasing emphasis that probation is meant to be a high-tariff option. This confirms the suggestion that women in court are 'out of place' and hence their presence requires explanation. The content of the reports frequently focuses on the social and sexual behaviour of the women, suggesting that women are sentenced for who they are and not what they have done.

Mair and Brockington (1988) also argue that the mere existence of a social inquiry (pre-sentence) report tends to lead to a move up the tariff: towards probation and away from discharges and small fines. They also stress that it seems that probation is being used differently for women (low tariff and for welfare/need reasons) and for men (high tariff and for punitive/offence reasons) (see also Hedderman and Gelsthorpe, 1997).

ACTIVITY 3.6

What are the main lessons of this review of the research findings with regard to gender discrimination in the courts? Imagine that you have been asked by a newspaper editor to provide a very short statement about the sentencing of women in the courts. What would you say?

In summary, there is *some* evidence that *some* women are dealt with in a discriminatory way. It is argued that those who fit stereotypical conceptions of 'ladies' or 'nice girls' seem to receive different (and more lenient) sentences than those who breach these expectations. This issue is more complex, however, when we interact gender with both ethnicity and class. This makes it inappropriate to present women's experiences in the criminal justice system as a unitary experience. Black women, for example, are over-represented in UK prisons, and we need to be able to account for this. To assume that men are dealt with in non-sexist and non-discriminatory ways is patently also incorrect. Men and male defendants are socially 'constructed' (though in different ways from women and girls), and, clearly, certain men are punished more harshly than others. For example, black men are over-represented in prisons and, as suggested earlier, this is not fully accounted for by differences in offence gravity or previous record. Distinctions are drawn between different women. There is perhaps no crime other than women killing their own children in which there is such a direct confrontation with notions of 'femininity' and 'motherhood'. Wilczynski (1991) examined 22 infanticide cases in her research, 14 of whom were clearly identified as essentially 'good' women and mothers for whom something had gone tragically wrong. They were given probation or hospital orders. Eight women, however, were given prison sentences. These women tended to be viewed as having acted in ways inconsistent with traditional stereotypical conceptions of women's appropriate behaviour. That is to say, they were viewed as 'bad' women – selfish, cold, neglectful, uncaring and sexual. According to Wilczynski, these were not 'real' or 'objective' categorizations, but they are examples of the types of distinctions which can be drawn between women who have committed the same serious act.

5.2.2   A 'sex-neutral' criminal justice system?

Can there be a 'sex-neutral' criminal justice system? Taken overall, these research findings do raise the question of whether or not we could, or should, aim to have a sex- (and 'race'- and class-) neutral criminal justice system. The White Paper, *Crime, Justice and Protecting the Public* (Home Office, 1990a), stated that: 'there must be no discrimination because of a defendant's race, nationality, standing in the community or any other reason' (sex is implicitly rather than explicitly included). Discrimination is not always conscious, direct or overt, however; it may be argued that it is very often unconscious, indirect and covert. How can we ensure, then, that stereotypical conceptions of 'women' and 'men', of female and male offenders, or of defendants' 'needs' and 'responsibilities' do not affect assessments of, for example, a defendant's 'just deserts'?

There is also a much broader theoretical point relating to the concept of equality. MacKinnon (1987) has written that any approach that focuses on equality assumes that the sentencing of men is somehow 'right' and sets the standard against which women should be judged. This led Allen (1987) to argue that women should be dealt with more punitively in order to further women's equality. She described leniency as a 'tactic of patriarchal oppression' and argued that women should be 'exposed to the full rigour of penal sanctions'. An alternative approach would be to deal with men less punitively. Furthermore, this focus on equality assumes that the law operates in a gender- or sex-neutral way; but the law, in its construction and its practices, is already gendered (Kingdom, 1981), a point which Collier (1995) supports when he argues that there is an inherent masculine bias in legislation. To ask for one practice – discrimination – to cease to be gendered may be meaningless **(Smart, 1990)**.

A different approach may be to ask whether equal treatment is the correct objective. There may be differences between women and men which justify differential dispositions. Walker (1981) draws a distinction between paper and real justice. 'Paper justice' would involve giving like penalties to women and men for like offences; 'real justice', on the other hand, would involve taking the consequences of a penalty into account: for example, in the United Kingdom, child-rearing remains primarily the responsibility of women. Real justice would consider the likelihood that a child might suffer much more from a mother's imprisonment than a father's. This distinction once more highlights the fact that we cannot take the concept of justice for granted and that criminal justice is not necessarily synonymous with social justice.

paper justice/ real justice

Carlen (1990) has advocated what she calls 'a women-wise penology'. This has two fundamental aims: to ensure that penal policy for women does not further increase their oppression as women and that penal policy for men does not brutalize them to the extent that they become more oppressive to women. In practical terms, she identifies the danger that pre-sentence reports for women may push women further up the tariff in order to help them with their 'problems', rather than offer such help in a non-statutory context.

Heidensohn (1986) also raised the question of whether there is a 'female' or 'feminist' conception of justice which would be more appropriate for women than the current system of justice. In attempting to answer this, she distinguished two models which she called Portia and Persephone. Portia, the woman in Shakespeare's *The Merchant of Venice* who tricks money-lender, Shylock, out of his pound of flesh, represents what can broadly be called the due process model and stresses rights, fairness, formality and equality. Heidensohn considers this a model unresponsive to the needs of women and to be a 'masculine' approach. Persephone, the goddess of harvest exemplifying the cycle of fertility, represents what could be loosely termed the welfare and rehabilitation model, stressing reformation, co-operation, informality and reparation. Heidensohn argues that this second model is more appropriate for women since it represents 'feminine' values. It can be argued, however, that it does little more than replicate traditional welfare approaches that have been criticized for stereotyping women.

Notwithstanding this criticism and the fact that 'Persephone' may be of equal importance to men and women rather than just women, as Heidensohn seems to imply, Masters and Smith (1998) argue that criminal justice systems need to incorporate both elements of 'Portia' (the ethic of justice) and 'Persephone' (the ethic of care). Indeed, they suggest that there is far more scope for 'relational justice', 'reintegrative shaming', and 'restorative justice', which are conceptually closer to the Persephone and the 'ethic of care' model than has generally been realized. Relational justice proponents, Burnside and Baker (1994), are interested in repairing the breakdown in relationships caused by crime through informal mediation and reparation. Protagonists of 'reintegrative shaming' **(Braithwaite, 1989)** are concerned with repentance for and reparation for the harm done through crime. 'Restorative justice' (Bowen and Consedine, 1999) with its focus on restitution and reparation through family group conferences and the like outside but linked to the formal criminal justice system in New Zealand and Australia, in particular, are also compatible with the ethic of care. As Masters and Smith (1998) put it, 'Portia needs Persephone', but how much persuasion do politicians and policy makers need to accommodate such concerns remains in question. (We return to this point in the conclusion.) For the moment, let us return to the issue of possible discrimination of women in sentencing and how best to serve women's needs through the criminal justice system.

The difficulty is in finding ways to challenge stereotypical pictures of women (and men) and at the same time to meet women's (and men's) real needs and responsibilities. While these needs and responsibilities might in theory be best met outside of the criminal justice system, in practice it seems unlikely that this will happen. However, it can be argued that factors such as child-care and child-rearing responsibilities should be irrelevant at the sentencing stage (because otherwise discriminatory practices may be perpetuated), but should be relevant in the determination of penal policy: for example, providing crèches for women doing community service, changing the nature of mother and baby units in prisons and an increased contact for mothers with their children throughout a prison sentence.

5.3 Other forms of discrimination and 'injustice'

When focusing on 'race' and gender issues, it is important also not to lose sight of the notion of a class-based justice. Whilst Sanders (1985) confines his attention to differential rates of prosecution between different agencies, Messerschmidt (1986) focuses on the ideology of the law and suggests that it is a tool of the middle/upper class and that it reflects and protects their interests by criminalizing the behaviour of others. Criminal acts and anti-social behaviour may certainly be interpreted in different ways.

ACTIVITY 3.7

Consider the following cases:

■ the theft of goods from a shop (to the value of £500)
■ a solicitor embezzling £500 from clients' funds
■ a fight outside a pub
■ a doctor sexually touching a patient
■ a fight inside a pub
■ a factory owner not adequately fencing factory machinery, which leads to an injury to a worker.

What is likely to happen in each of these cases? Do you think that prosecution will result in each case?

In practice, it is likely that the shop theft will be prosecuted, but the embezzlement dealt with by the Law Society (which could involve severe sanctions but not necessarily prosecution). Those involved in the fight outside the pub may be prosecuted, but the offence inside the doctor's surgery may be dealt with by the General Medical Council (again, there may be severe sanctions, but sanctions that will fall short of prosecution). Those involved in the fight inside the pub may or may not be prosecuted (the managers of the pub could decide to take action themselves and simply throw the offenders out), whilst the factory offence might be dealt with by the Factory Inspectorate, or a private prosecution could be initiated.

We need to be aware that different anti-social acts can be seen as subject to the criminal law and/or other regulatory bodies and that there can be different methods of enforcement (Sanders, 1985; Cook, 1989; Lidstone *et al.*, 1980; McBarnet, 1981). We also need to be aware that differences in socio-economic circumstances can lead to or inhibit a 'criminal' lifestyle (Farrington *et al.*, 1986a, 1997). Traditional criminological texts provide some support for the links between social class, lifestyle and crime (Elliott and Huizinga, 1983; Cohen, 1955; Merton, 1968; Cloward and Ohlin, 1960). In a prison survey of known offenders in England, almost three-quarters were below the poverty line and showed very poor educational attainment (Home Office, 1990b; see also Cook, 1997). Some criminologists, however, would argue that any links between social class and crime result from systematic bias. Tittle *et al.* (1978) suggest that a 'lower-class' person is more likely to be observed and detected than those from other classes and that a lower-class person is more likely to be arrested if discovered.

The variable of social class is too crude to explore direct discrimination, and a consideration of a cluster of factors, which are themselves linked to low social class, can be of more use. Indeed, Farrington *et al.* (1986b; 1997) suggest that, although socio-economic deprivation is an important risk factor for known offending, low family income, poor housing and large family size are better measures and produce more reliable results than low occupational prestige. But does any of this affect decision-making in the court room? It is probably of more direct relevance to consider the possible influence of unemployment:

> One often has to think of the reasons why people commit offences. Often it's because they are basically criminal people, professional criminals, but in my experience of magistrates' courts, that tends to be only a small minority of people. The vast majority of defendants who come before the magistrates' court are the disadvantaged, the inarticulate, and almost by definition, therefore, the people with little or no income, often the unemployed. So I don't think it's tunnel vision at all to regard that as a prime feature of any research.
>
> (solicitor quoted in Crow and Simon, 1987)

Crow and Simon (1987) suggest that unemployment has a limited direct impact on sentencing. However, it is important to remember that sentencing is a *social* process that takes place within a *social* context. While they suggest that sentencers have some awareness of changing circumstances with regard to the prospects of long and continued employment in a harsh economic climate and recession, they also found evidence of more traditional attitudes, such as 'anyone who seriously wants a job will get a job,' and the belief that some unemployed people are lacking in motivation and self-discipline. An employment record is often seen as indicating stability and character, reinforcing traditional attitudes towards work, its meaning and the way in which these attitudes are reflected in the court room. It is possible that the courts need to develop a broader concept of the purpose of sentencing in so far as it relates to the circumstances of the offender, placing more emphasis on the merits of the individual as a whole and less on his or her employment status and history. To fail to do this would be to promote exclusionary policies for those who are already subject to contemporary experiences of social exclusion (Finer and Nellis, 1998; Young, 1999).

6   Conclusion

A general critique of the existing policies and practices of the criminal courts would no doubt include reference to it being too expensive and too slow (Audit Commission, 1998); there are problems of access; there is a legitimation crisis; it is too centralized and too coercive; it is too inflexible and too bureaucratic; and is reflective of an undue formalism (Harrington, 1985). Critics have also suggested that the system is anonymous and that neither defendants nor victims feel involved in the judicial process. There are further claims that the system can no longer ignore the fact that we live in a multicultural society and that it should adapt accordingly, or putting the matter bluntly, the system is imbued with racism.

There are, of course, a number of non-judicial settlement approaches that might provide solutions to such problems. Corporate and public agency regulatory practices often focus on the informal rather than the formal (Marshall, 1985), for instance, and there are also forms of non-judicial settlement in the community: for example, dispute settlement, community mediation and reparation, community courts and neighbourhood justice. The notions of 'relational justice', 'reintegrative shaming' and 'restorative justice' that we came across in section 5.2.2 might all come under the heading of non-judicial and 'informal approaches' to criminal justice. Whether or not these would be wholly better than the more formal judicial system that we have, however, is open to question. In many cases, informal mechanisms for delivering criminal justice have developed alongside formal systems, thus aggravating the very system they were intended to supplant (Abel, 1982). It is also suggested that some informal approaches to criminal justice lead to an expanded state control (Scull, 1977; Cohen, 1988). Furthermore, it remains unclear whether community justice – family group conferences for example – is always less coercive and oppressive than the state system (Maxwell and Morris, 1993). What is more, 'community-based' criminal justice systems in Mauri New Zealand or in Aboriginal Australia cannot simply be parachuted into a wholly different culture and be expected to work. The very notion of 'community', for example, may be so very different that it would be absurd to expect things to function in the same ways as in their originating jurisdiction and culture (Morris and Gelsthorpe, 2000 and see Chapter 6).

What then is to be done? The six models that we described in section 3 are certainly useful in helping us to imagine the different kinds of criminal justice system that we might wish to choose. These are tidy theoretical models, however; the reality of policy and practice in the courts is messier: it incorporates elements of each of the models rather than a single model and a single political choice. This invariably leads to criticisms of incoherency and inconsistency in sentencing.

The Labour government reforms of the second half of the 1990s arguably express a valiant attempt to address some of the critical issues regarding justice and thus critical issues and decisions in the courts. The Crime and Disorder Act 1998 was described as a 'comprehensive and wide-ranging reform programme' (Home Office, 1997b, p.1) and as 'the biggest shake-up for 50 years in tackling crime' (*The Guardian*, 26 September 1997, cited in Muncie, 1999). Disappointingly, however, as we saw in section 4.1, New Labour legislation seems more a melting-pot of contradictions, ideas and ideologies that could militate against each other rather than serving the notion of clear and consistent sentencing. Moreover, the policies inherent in New Labour's 'big three' Acts of 1997, 1998 and 1999 reflect political interest in the form of 'populist punitiveness', suggesting a singular short-sightedness in some respects and appearing to be riddled with practical problems in others. Ian Brownlee (1998) offers a searching critique of New Labour's 'new penology' reflected in the legislation by noting the continuing tendency to locate the causes of crime at the level of individual failure and a continuing punitive discourse. More significantly for students concerned with crime and criminal justice, he points to the dominance of managerial interests and to the tendency to 'identify, classify and manage unruly groups sorted by dangerousness' (1998, p.323) and then impose variable detention depending upon 'risk management' strategies rather than engaging in the diagnosis and then rehabilitation of individuals. Further, continuing this critical theme, and to give one or two examples of short-sightedness and other problems, is it likely that parenting orders will be effective in encouraging greater parental responsibility for children where these orders are *imposed* on parents, rather than there being a voluntary educational relationship between counsellors and parents? The evidence suggests not (Gelsthorpe, 1999). Is it likely that restorative justice principles will work when reparation orders can be *imposed* on offenders without their consent? Again, this is unlikely. Further, what does it mean when victim–offender mediation is a *possibility* as part of a reparation order, but not an integral part of it? This seems to be at odds with restorative values which see the offender as a key decision-maker in order for the processes to be fully 'restorative' (Maxwell and Morris, 1993). Despite the rhetoric of a 'radical shake-up of the system', the central messages of blame, coercion and punishment seem to echo earlier policies and practices. The reforms perhaps bring us no nearer to effective and principled 'criminal justice'. One way out of this gloom might be to think more about what could be effective in terms of reducing crime, whether that be social justice (including a redistribution of resources) or sentencing based on 'what works' according to research evidence without there being 'political interpretations' of that evidence. Certainly, the idea of basing sentencing policies on what seems to work in terms of reducing crime – taking into account the social conditions which are often related to its inception, often remains at the level of rhetoric – 'tough on crime, tough on the causes of crime', for example. Would that there were the political will to abandon the tough rhetoric and pursue effective criminal justice in reality and in a clear and consistent way in the court room.

Review questions

- On the basis of reading this chapter, what does the notion of 'justice' mean as it is currently construed and practised in the criminal courts?

- Why are criminal justice systems as capable of delivering 'injustices' as they are 'justice'?

- How can sentencers respond to the individual needs of offenders without sacrificing the potential benefits of a system that comes with formality and consistency?

- How can the theoretical models or perspectives described in section 3 illuminate different research findings?

- How far do you think the Labour criminal reforms of the late 1990s and beyond address some of the problems referred to at the beginning of the chapter?

Further reading

A useful introduction to criminal justice processes can be found in King (1981), not least because he is one of a few who attempts to give the debates and issues some theoretical underpinning. Bottoms (1995) and James and Raine (1998) discuss the philosophy and politics of sentencing in general. The impact of differential treatment in the courts is explored by Hood (1992), Fitzgerald (1993) Reiner (1993) and Smith (1997) in regard to 'race'; and by Eaton (1986), Worrall (1990), Kennedy (1992), Hedderman and Gelsthorpe (1997) and Heidensohn (1997) in regard to gender. Both Carlen (1976) and Parker *et al.* (1989) provide fascinating accounts of the ideologies and practices which govern the production of 'justice' in the court room. **Braithwaite (1989)**, Schluter (1994) and Marshall (1999) present stimulating accounts of how we can re-imagine the pursuit of justice without recourse to formal and inflexible systems.

References

Abel, R. (ed.) (1982) *The Politics of Informal Justice*, vols I and II, New York, Academic Press.

Agozino, B. (1997) *Black Women and the Criminal Justice System*, Aldershot, Ashgate.

Allen, H. (1987) *Justice Unbalanced: Gender, Psychiatry and Judicial Decisions*, Milton Keynes, Open University Press.

Ashworth, A. (1992) 'Sentencing reform structures', in Tonry, M. (ed.) *Crime and Justice: A Review of Research,* vol.16, Chicago, University of Chicago Press.

Ashworth, A., Cavadino, P., Gibson, B., Harding, J. and Rutherford, A. (1992) *Materials on the Criminal Justice Act 1991*, Winchester, Waterside.

Audit Commission (1998) *Misspent Youth '98: The Challenge for Youth Justice*, London, Audit Commission.

Baldwin, J. and McConville, M. (1979) *Jury Trials,* Oxford, Clarendon.

Ball, C. (2000) 'The Youth Justice and Criminal Evidence Act 1999: A significant move towards restorative justice, or a recipe for unintended consequences?', *Criminal Law Review*, April, pp.211–22.

Barker, M. (1993) *Community Service and Women Offenders*, London, Association of Chief Probation Officers.

Beccaria, C. (1963) *On Crimes and Punishments,* New York, Bobbs-Merrill (first published in 1764). (Extract reprinted in Muncie *et al.* 1996.)

Bottoms, A.E. (1981) 'The suspended sentence', *British Journal of Criminology*, vol.21, pp.1–26.

Bottoms, A.E. (1995) 'The philosophy and politics of sentencing', in Clarkson, C. and Morgan, R. (eds) *The Politics of Sentencing Reform*, Oxford, Clarendon.

Bowen, H. and Consedine, J. (eds) (1999) *Restorative Justice. Contemporary Themes and Practice*, New Zealand, Ploughshares Publications.

Braithwaite, J. (1989) *Crime, Shame and Reintegration*, Cambridge and New York, Cambridge University Press. (Extract reprinted as 'Reintegrative shaming' in Muncie *et al.*, 1996.)

Brittan, A. and Maynard, M. (1984) *Sexism, Racism and Oppression*, Oxford, Blackwell.

Brown, D. (1997) *PACE Ten Years on: A review of the Research*, Home Office research study no.155, London, HMSO.

Brown, I. and Hullin, R. (1992) 'A study of sentencing in the Leeds Magistrates' Courts: the treatment of ethnic minority and white offenders', *British Journal of Criminology*, vol.32, no.1, pp.41–53.

Brownlee, I. (1998) 'New Labour – new penology? Puritive rhetoric and the limits of managerialism in criminal justice policy', *Journal of Law and Society*, vol.25, pp.313–35.

Burnside, J. and Baker, N. (eds) (1994) *Relational Justice: Repairing the Breach*, Winchester, Waterside Press.

Carlen, P. (1976) *Magistrates' Justice*, London, Martin Robertson.

Carlen, P. (1983) *Women's Imprisonment: A Study in Social Control*, London, Routledge and Kegan Paul.

Carlen, P. (1990) *Alternatives to Women's Imprisonment*, Buckingham, Open University Press.

Cavadino, M. and Dignan, J. (1997) *The Penal System: An Introduction*, 2nd edn, London, Sage.

Cavadino, M., Crow, I. and Dignan, J, (2000) *Criminal Justice 2000 Strategies for a New Century*, Winchester, Waterside Press.

Cheney, D., Dickson, L., Fitzpatrick, J. and Uglow, S. (1999) *Criminal Justice and the Human Rights Act 1998*, Bristol, Jordan Publishing Limited.

Chigwada-Bailey, R. (1997) *Black Women's Experiences of Criminal Justice*, Winchester, Waterside Press.

Clarkson, C. and Morgan, R. (eds) (1995) *The Politics of Sentencing Reform*, Oxford, Clarendon.

Cloward, R. and Ohlin, L. (1960) *Delinquency and Opportunity: A Theory of Delinquent Gangs*, New York, The Free Press.

Cohen, A. (1955) *Delinquent Boys: The Culture of the Gang*, New York, The Free Press.

Cohen, S. (1985) *Visions of Social Control*, Cambridge, Polity Press.

Cohen, S. (1988) *Against Criminology*, New Brunswick, NJ, Transaction.

Collier, R. (1995) *Masculinity, Law and the Family*, London, Routledge.

Commission for Racial Equality (1992) *Cautions* v. *Prosecutions: Ethnic Monitoring of Juveniles by Seven Police Forces*, London, Commission for Racial Equality.

Cook, D. (1989) *Rich Law, Poor Law: Different Responses to Tax and Supplementary Benefit Fraud*, Buckingham, Open University Press.

Cook, D. (1997) *Poverty, Crime and Punishment*, London, Child Poverty Action Group.

Crow, I. and Simon, F. (1987) *Unemployment and Magistrates' Courts*, London, NACRO.

Crow, I., Cavadino, M., Dignan, J., Johnston, V. and Walker, M. (1996) *Changing Criminal Justice: the Impact of the Criminal Justice Act 1991 in Four Areas of the North of England*, Centre for Criminological and Legal Research, University of Sheffield.

Daly, K. (1994) *Gender, Crime and Punishment*, New Haven, Yale University Press.

Devlin, P.D., Baron (1979) *The Judge*, Oxford, Oxford University Press.

Dholakia, N. (1999) 'Criminal behaviour,' *The Guardian*, 16 December 1999.

Dominelli, L. (1984) 'Differential justice: domestic labour, community service and female offenders', *Probation Journal*, no.31, pp.100–3.

Dyer, C. and Travis, A. (1999) 'Boy killers denied fair trial', *The Guardian*, 17 December 1999.

Eaton, M. (1986) *Justice for Women? Family Court and Social Control*, Milton Keynes, Open University Press.

Edwards, S. (1984) *Women On Trial*, Manchester, Manchester University Press.

Elliott, D.S. and Huizinga, D. (1983) 'Social class and delinquent behaviour in a national youth panel', *Criminology*, no.21, pp.149–77.

Farrington, D. (1997) 'Human development and criminal careers', in Maguire, M., Morgan, R. and Reiner, R. (eds) *The Oxford Handbook of Criminology*, Oxford, Clarendon.

Farrington, D. and Buckle, A. (1984) 'An observational study of shoplifting', *British Journal of Criminology*, vol.24, no.1, pp.63–73.

Farrington, D. and Morris, A. (1983) 'Sex, sentencing and reconviction', *British Journal of Criminology*, vol.23, no.3, pp.229–48.

Farrington, D., Gallagher, B., Morley, L., St Ledger, R. and West, D. (1986a) 'Unemployment, school leaving and crime', *British Journal of Criminology*, vol.26, pp.335–56.

Farrington, D., Ohlin, L. and Wilson, J.Q. (1986b) *Understanding and Controlling Crime,* New York, Springer-Verlag.

Findlay, M. (1999) *The Globalisation of Crime,* Cambridge, Cambridge University Press.

Finer, C., Jones, and Nellis, M. (eds) (1998) *Crime and Social Exclusion,* Oxford, Blackwell Publishers.

Fitzgerald, M. (1993) *Ethnic Minorities and the Criminal Justice System,* Royal Commission on Criminal Justice Research Study No.20, London, HMSO.

Foucault, M. (1980) *Power/Knowledge,* Brighton, Harvester.

Frase, R. (1995) 'Sentencing guidelines: progress report', in Clarkson, C. and Morgan, R. (eds) *The Politics of Sentencing Reform,* Oxford, Clarendon Press, pp.169–98.

Gelsthorpe, L. (1989) *Sexism and the Female Offender,* Aldershot, Gower.

Gelsthorpe, L. (1992) *Social Inquiry Reports: Race and Gender Considerations,* Home Office Research Bulletin No.32, pp.17–22.

Gelsthorpe, L. (1999) 'Youth crime and parental responsibility', in Bainham, A., Sclater, S., Day, and Richards, M. (eds) *What is a Parent? A Sociological Analysis,* Oxford, Hart Publishing.

Gelsthorpe, L. and Loucks, N. (1997) 'Magistrates' explanations of sentencing decisions', in Hedderman, C. and Gelsthorpe, L. (eds) *Understanding the Sentencing of Women,* Home Office Research Study 170, London, Home Office Research and Statistics Directorate.

Gelsthorpe, L. and Morris, A. (1999), 'Much ado about nothing – a critical comment on key provisions relating to children in the Crime and Disorder Act 1998', *Child and Family Law Quarterly,* vol.11, no.3, pp. 209–21.

Gibson, B. (1990) *Unit Fines,* Winchester, Waterside.

Graham, J. and Bowling, B. (1995) *Young People and Crime,* Research Findings No.24, Home Office Research and Statistics Department, London, HMSO.

Griffith, J.A.G. (1991) *The Politics of the Judiciary,* 4th edn, London, Fontana, 1st edn, 1977.

Halevy, T. (1995) 'Racial discrimination in sentencing? A study into dubious conclusions', *Criminal Law Review,* April, pp.267–71.

Harrington, C. (1985) *Shadow Justice: The Ideology and Institutionalization of Alternatives to Court,* Westport, CT, Greenwood.

Harris, R. (1992) *Crime, Criminal Justice and the Probation Service,* London, Routledge.

Hay, D., Linebaugh, P., Rule, J.G., Thompson, E.P. and Winslow, C. (eds) (1975) *Albion's Fatal Tree: Crime and Society in Eighteenth-Century England,* London, Allen Lane.

Hedderman, C. and Gelsthorpe, L. (eds) (1997) *Understanding the Sentencing of Women,* Home Office Research Study 170, London, Home Office.

Heidensohn, F. (1986) 'Models of justice: Portia or Persephone?', *International Journal of the Sociology of Law,* vol.14, nos3–4, pp.287–98.

Heidensohn, F. (1997) 'Gender and crime', in Maguire, M., Morgan, R. and Rainer, R. (eds) *The Oxford Handbook of Criminology,* Oxford, Clarendon.

Her Majesty's Inspectorate of Probation (1991) *A Review of Probation Service Provision for Women Offenders*, London, Home Office.

Her Majesty's Inspectorate of Probation (1991) *Report on Women Offenders and Probation Service Provision*, London, Home Office.

Her Majesty's Inspectorate of Probation (1996) *A Review of Probation Service Provision for Women Offenders*, London, Home Office.

Home Office (1990a) *Crime, Justice and Protecting the Public* (White Paper), Cm 965, London, HMSO.

Home Office (1990b) *National Prison Survey,* London, HMSO.

Home Office (1992) *The Costs of Criminal Justice*, London, HMSO.

Home Office (1995) *Digest 3 Information on the criminal justice system in England and Wales*, London, Home Office.

Home Office (1997) *Criminal Statistics: England and Wales*, London, HMSO.

Home Office (1998) *Criminal Statistics: England and Wales,* London, HMSO.

Home Office (1999) *Digest 4 Information on the criminal justice system in England and Wales*, London, Home Office.

Home Office (1999a) Press Release 155/99 19 May. www.nds.coi.gov.uk/col/coipress.n, accessed May 2000.

Home Office (1999b) Section 95 Report, *Race and Criminal Justice*, London, Home Office Research, Development and Statistics Directorate.

Hood, R. (1992) *Race and Sentencing,* Oxford, Clarendon.

Hopkins, N. (1999) 'Met stop and search now hitting Asians', *The Guardian*, 16 December.

Howard League for Penal Reform (1999) *Do Women Paint Fences Too? Women's Experience of Community Service*, Briefing Paper, London, Howard League for Penal Reform.

Hutton, W. (1999) 'Throwing good money after bad lads', *The Observer*, 17 January.

James, A. and Raine, J. (1998) *The New Politics of Criminal Justice*, London, Longman.

Jefferson, T. (1993) 'The racism of criminalization: police and the reproduction of the criminal other', in Gelsthorpe, L. (ed.) *Minority Ethnic Groups in the Criminal Justice System*, Cropwood Conference Series, no.21, University of Cambridge, Institute of Criminology.

Jones, C. (1993) 'Auditing Criminal Justice', *British Journal of Criminology*, vol.33, no.3, pp.45–52.

Kant, I. (1796–97) *Rechtslere*, (trans. T.M. Knox, 1942, as *Philosophy of Right*, Oxford, Oxford University Press).

Kapardis, A. and Farrington, D. (1981) 'An experimental study of sentencing by magistrates', *Law and Human Behaviour*, no.5, pp.107–21.

Kennedy, H. (1992) *Eve Was Framed: Women and British Justice*, London, Chatto and Windus.

King, M. (1981) *The Framework of Criminal Justice*, London, Croom Helm.

Kingdom, E. (1981) 'Sexist bias and law', in *Politics and Power vol.3: Sexual Politics, Feminism and Socialism,* London, Routledge and Kegan Paul.

Landau, S. and Nathan, G. (1983) 'Selecting delinquents for cautioning in the London notification area', *British Journal of Criminology,* vol.23, no.2, pp.128–49.

Liberty (1992) *Unequal Before the Law,* London, Liberty.

Lidstone, K., Hogg, R. and Sutcliffe, F. (1980) *Prosecution by Private Individuals and Non-Police Agencies,* London, HMSO.

Lord Chancellor's Department (1999) *Press Release,* Judicial Appointments http://www.open.gov.uk/lcd/deprep/a/03judicialapp.htm, accessed May 2000.

Loveday, B. (1999) *The Impact of Performance Culture on Criminal Justice Agencies,* Occasional Paper No.9 (January), Institute of Criminal Justice Studies, University of Portsmouth.

MacKinnon, C. (1987) *Feminism Unmodified,* Cambridge, MA, Harvard University Press.

Macpherson, W. (1999) *The Stephen Lawrence Inquiry,* Report of An Inquiry By Sir William Macpherson of Cluny, Cm 4264, London, The Stationery Office.

Mair, G. (1986) 'Ethnic minorities, police and magistrates' courts', *British Journal of Criminology,* vol.26, no.2, pp.147–55.

Mair, G. and Brockington, N. (1988) 'Female offenders and the probation service', *Howard Journal of Criminal Justice,* vol.27, no.2, pp.117–26.

Malleson, K. (1999) *The New Judiciary. The Effects of Expansion and Activism,* Aldershot, Ashgate/Dartmouth.

Marshall, T. (1985) *Alternatives to Criminal Courts,* Aldershot, Gower.

Marshall, T. (1999) *Restorative Justice: An Overview,* London, Home Office.

Masters, G. and Smith, D. (1998) 'Portia and Persephone revisited: thinking about feeling in criminal justice', *Theoretical Criminology,* vol.2, no.1, pp.5–27.

Maxwell, G. and Morris, A. (1993) *Family, Victims and Culture: Youth Justice in New Zealand,* Social Policy Agency and Institute of Criminology, Victoria University of Wellington.

McBarnet, D. (1981) *Conviction,* London, Macmillan.

McCabe, S. and Purves, R. (1972) *The Jury At Work,* Oxford University Penal Research Unit Occasional Paper 3, Oxford, Blackwell.

McConville, M. and Baldwin, J. (1982) 'The influence of race on sentencing in England', *Criminal Law Review,* vol.29, pp.652–8.

McCrudden, C., Smith, D. and Brown, C. (1991) *Racial Justice at Work: The Enforcement of the 1976 Race Relations Act in Employment,* London, Policy Studies Institute.

McLaughlin, E. and Muncie, J. (1994) 'Managing the criminal justice system', in Clarke, J., Cochrane, A. and McLaughlin, E. (eds) *Managing Social Policy,* London, Sage.

McLaughlin, E. and Muncie. J. (2000) 'The criminal justice system: New Labour's new partnerships', in Clarke, J., Gewirtz, S. and McLaughlin, E. (eds), *New Managerialism, New Welfare?,* London, Sage.

Merton, R. (1968) *Social Theory and Social Structure,* New York, The Free Press. (First published in 1949.)

Messerschmidt, J. (1986) *Capitalism, Patriarchy, and Crime: Toward a Socialist Feminist Criminology*, Totowa, NJ, Rowman and Littlefield.

Mill, J.S. (1859) *On Liberty*, London, Parker.

Modood, T. (1994) *Racial Equality: Colour, Culture and Justice*, London, Institute for Public Policy Research, Commission on Social Justice.

Morris, A. (1987) *Women, Crime and Criminal Justice*, Oxford, Basil Blackwell.

Morris, A. and Gelsthorpe, L. (2000) 'Something Old, Something Borrowed, Something Blue, but Something New? A comment on the prospects for restorative justice under the Crime and Disorder Act 1998', *Criminal Law Review*, pp.18–30, January.

Moxon, D. (1988) *Sentencing Practice in the Crown Court*, Home Office Research Study No.103, London, HMSO.

Moxon, D., Sutton, M. and Hedderman, C. (1990) *Unit Fines – Experiments in Four Courts*, Home Office Research and Planning Unit Paper No.59, London, HMSO.

Muncie, J. (1999) 'Institutionalized intolerance: youth justice and the 1998 Crime and Disorder Act', *Critical Social Policy*, vol.19, no.2, pp.147–75.

Muncie, J., McLaughlin, E. and Langan, M. (eds) (1996) *Criminological Perspectives: A Reader*, London, Sage in association with The Open University.

NACRO (2000) *Let's Get it Right: Race and Justice 2000*, London, NACRO.

Norris, C., Fielding, N., Kemp C. and Fielding, J. (1992) 'Black and blue: an analysis of the influence of race on being stopped by the police', *British Journal of Sociology*, vol.43, no.3, pp.207–24.

Nozick, R. (1974) *Anarchy, State and Utopia*, New York, Basic Books.

Packer, H. (1969) *The Limits of the Criminal Sanction*, Stanford, CA, Stanford University Press.

Padfield, N. (1995) *Text and Materials on the Criminal Justice Process*, London, Butterworth.

Parker, H., Sumner, M. and Jarvis, G. (1989) *Unmasking The Magistrates*, Milton Keynes, Open University Press.

Pearson, R. (1976) 'Women defendants in magistrates' courts', *British Journal of Law and Society*, no.3, pp.265–73.

Pease, K. (1980) 'Community service and prison: are they alternatives?', in Pease, K. and McWilliams, W. (eds) *Community Service By Order*, Edinburgh, Scottish Academic Press.

Pease, K. and Wasik, M. (1987) *Sentencing Reform: Guidance Or Guidelines?* Manchester, Manchester University Press.

Penal Affairs Consortium (1997) 'Mandatory Sentences Will Damage Interests of Victims', Press Release, 13 February.

Phillips, C. and Brown, D. (1998) *Entry into the Criminal Justice System: a survey of police arrests and their outcomes*, Home Office Research Study 185, London, Home Office.

Quinney, R. (1974) *Critique of Legal Order*, Boston, MA, Little, Brown and Co.

Raine, J. and Willson, M. (1997) 'Beyond managerialism in criminal justice', *The Howard Journal*, vol.36, no.1, pp.80–95.

Rawls, J. (1971) *A Theory of Justice*, Cambridge, MA, The Belknap Press of Harvard University Press.

Reiner, R. (1993) 'Race, crime and justice: models of interpretation', in Gelsthorpe, L. (ed.) *Minority Ethnic Groups in the Criminal Justice System*, Cropwood Conference Series, No.21, University of Cambridge, Institute of Criminology.

Rex, S. (1992) 'Unit Fines – twenty questions', in Ashworth, A. *et al.* (eds).

Roshier, B. and Teff, H. (1980) *Law and Society in England*, London, Tavistock.

Royal Commission on Criminal Justice (1993) *Report,* Cm 2263, London, HMSO.

Rozenberg, J. (1994) *The Search For Justice*, London, Hodder and Stoughton.

Sanders, A. (1985) 'Class bias in prosecutions', *Howard Journal of Criminal Justice*, no.24, pp.176–99.

Schluter, M. (1994) 'What is relational justice?', in Burnside, J. and Baker, N. (eds) *Relational Justice: Repairing the Breach*, Winchester, Waterside.

Scull, A. (1977) *Decarceration: Community Treatment and the Deviant – A Radical View*, Englewood Cliffs, NJ, Prentice Hall.

Sealy, A. and Cornish, W. (1973) 'Jurors and their verdicts', *Modern Law Review*, no.36, pp.496–508.

Shallice, A. and Gordon, P. (1990) *Black People, White Justice? Race and the Criminal Justice System*, London, Runnymede Trust.

Smart, C. (1990) 'Feminist approaches to criminology or postmodern woman meets atavistic man', in Gelsthorpe, L. and Morris, A. (eds) *Feminist Perspectives in Criminology*, Buckingham, Open University Press. (Extract reprinted in Muncie *et al.*, 1996).

Smith, D. (1997) 'Ethnic origins, crime and criminal justice', in Maguire, M., Morgan, R. and Reiner, R. (eds) *The Oxford Handbook of Criminology*, Oxford, Clarendon.

Thomas, D. (1979) *Principles of Sentencing,* 2nd edn, London, Heinemann.

Thompson, E.P. (1975) *Whigs and Hunters*, London, Allen Lane.

Tittle, C., Villemez, W. and Smith, D. (1978) 'The myth of social class and criminality', *American Sociological Review*, no.43, pp.643–56.

Travis, A. (1999) 'Straw to target burglars', *The Guardian*, 13 January.

Tuck, M. (1991) 'Community and the criminal justice system', *Policy Studies*, vol.12, no.3, pp.22–37.

Vennard, J. (1985) 'The outcome of contested trials', in Moxon, D. (ed.) *Managing Criminal Justice*, London, HMSO.

Vennard, J. and Riley, D. (1988) 'The use of peremptory challenge and stand by jurors and their relationship to trial outcome', *Criminal Law Review*, pp.731–8.

Voakes, R. and Fowler, Q. (1989) *Sentencing, Race and Social Enquiry Reports*, West Yorkshire Probation Service.

von Hirsch, A. (1976) 'Giving criminals their just deserts', *Civil Liberties Review*, no.3, pp.23–35. (Extract reprinted in Muncie *et al.*, 1996.)

von Hirsch, A. and Ashworth, A. (eds) (1998) *Principled Sentencing, Readings On Theory And Policy*, Oxford, Hart Publishing.

von Hirsch, A. and Roberts, J. (1997) 'Racial disparity in sentencing: Reflections on the Hood study', *The Howard Journal*, vol.36, no.3, pp.227–36.

Walker, M. (1989) 'The court disposal and remands of White, African-Caribbean and Asian Men (London 1983)', *British Journal of Criminology*, vol.29, no.4, pp.353–67.

Walker, N. (1981) 'Feminists' extravaganzas', *Criminal Law Review*, pp.379–86.

Weber, M. (1954) *On Law in Economy and Society* (trans. E. Shils and M. Rheinstein), Cambridge, MA, Harvard University Press.

White, P. (1999) 'The Prison Population, 1998: a Statistical Review', *Research Findings*, no.94, London, Home Office Research, Development and Statistics Directorate.

Whitehouse, P. (1983) 'Race, bias and social enquiry reports', *Probation Journal*, vol.30, no.2, pp.30–2, 43–9.

Wilczynski, A. (1991) 'Images of women who kill their infants: the mad and the bad', *Women and Criminal Justice*, no.2, pp.71–88.

Wilczynski, A. and Morris, A. (1993) 'Parents who kill their children', *Criminal Law Review*, pp.31–6.

Willis, C. (1983) *The Use, Effectiveness and Impact of Police Stop and Search Powers*, Research and Planning Unit Paper 15, London, Home Office.

Worrall, A. (1990) *Offending Women: Female Law Breakers and the Criminal Justice System*, London, Routledge.

Young, J. (1999) *The Exclusive Society*, London, Sage.

Zander, M. (1989) *A Matter of Justice: The Legal System in Ferment*, Oxford, Oxford University Press.

Zander, M. and Henderson, P.F. (1993) *The Crown Court Study*, Royal Commission on Criminal Justice Study No.19, London, HMSO.

CHAPTER 4

Prison Histories: Reform, Repression and Rehabilitation

by John Muncie

Contents

1 Introduction

This chapter traces the origins and development of the prison in British society. In the main, it is structured around three key 'moments' and their associated discursive rationales: namely, the *reform* of prisons and prisoners towards the end of the eighteenth century; the *repressive* practices of the mid nineteenth century; and, at the beginning of the twentieth century, the emergence of notions of prisoner *rehabilitation*. Prior to this, a necessary contextualization is provided in section 2 by a brief discussion of the scale and role of incarceration in feudal or early modern societies. Throughout, the chapter recalls, and accounts for, the shifting role of, and the different claims made for, the imposition of imprisonment.

It is important to note from the outset that there is no *one* history of prisons and imprisonment. Neither can we claim that there is a linear history from reform, through repression to rehabilitation. All of these rationales are likely to co-exist in some form at any one time. As a result, whilst legislative and organizational landmarks can be placed quite accurately, the role and purpose of the prison is the subject of ongoing dispute and controversy. Following the lead taken in Chapter 1 (on the history of the police), section 3 of this chapter presents and analyses *competing* histories of penal transformation..

Broadly speaking, a basic distinction between Whig histories and revisionist histories can be made in order to illustrate the issue of alternative historical 'readings'. For example, until the 1970s historians relied more or less solely on documentary material that frequently provided a one dimensional vision of penal reform. Characteristically, such reform was viewed as the end result of the humanitarianism of powerful and/or key individuals. Reform was celebrated as progress and change as improvement. History was thus usually constructed 'from above'. The early exception to this was the pioneering work of Rusche and Kirchheimer (1939) who used a Marxist framework to contend that the driving force of penal reform lay, not in humanitarianism, but in the demand in early capitalist and mercantile societies for a disciplined labour force. Nevertheless, it was not until the 1970s, and in particular **Foucault's (1977)** location of the prison within a continuum of disciplinary institutions designed to regulate the minutiae of daily life, that critical or revisionist historical research began to flourish. Broadly speaking, revisionist historiographies marked a radical departure from traditional Whig accounts by retelling the story of 'reform' in the context of economic interests, power relations and the diversification and strengthening of state power. Reform was analysed not so much as humanist, benevolent progress, but as a more insidious extension of structures of centralized power and control. This dispute is used to provide a structuring device for the discussion of late 18th and early 19th century penal reform in section 3 of this chapter. However, by the late 1980s the limitations of such a polarized debate came increasingly to be recognized by many sociologists and historians alike, such that an integration of the two positions has been proposed (for example, Garland, 1990; Weiner, 1990). Sections 4 and 5 of this chapter, which analyse further modernizing developments in penal reform from the 1830s to the 20th century, adopt such an integrative approach by combining elements of the whiggish and revisionist approaches and by recognizing the existence of multiple revisionisms. Nevertheless, a basic distinction between Whig and revisionist historiographies remains important in alerting us to the issue of contested histories. It serves as a fruitful starting-point for any student of penal reform, and in section 6 of this chapter it is returned to as a means of summarizing the chapter's key themes.

The key point to stress about historical research is, as historians now increasingly acknowledge, that it is neither atheoretical nor untainted by ideological and political concerns. As Thomas remarks: 'History is a profoundly political subject and the way in which it is written deeply affects our perception of the present' (Thomas, 1988, p.2). Nevertheless, Pisciotta's conclusion that: 'historians would be more honest in their search for "truth" if they wrestled with their own assumptions and made them explicit in their writings' (Pisciotta, 1981, pp.122–3) retains a certain pertinence, particularly when we consider how privileged versions of penal history are continually reproduced in prison museums around the world. The unveiling of assumptions and the demystification of rhetoric in social history research are two of the key issues addressed by this chapter.

2   Gaols and houses of correction

Before beginning any exploration into the origins of the prison we would be well advised to heed Harding *et al.*'s (1985) warning that the task is doomed to failure if we look specifically for a precise statutory enactment. As they remark, some form of detention becomes necessary as soon as disputes are settled in any but the most brutal fashion, such as by mutilation, death and exile.

The holding of defendants prior to trial was probably the earliest use of imprisonment. According to Pugh (1968), in England this practice dates from the ninth century. At that time, the use of custody pending trial was reserved for the foreigner or for those who could not stand their own surety. Some of the gaols in which they were held were purpose-built (such as the Tower and the Fleet), but the majority were within existing castles or walled towns. Their use was rare and haphazard. An early attempt to establish a gaol in every English county was made by Henry II in 1166, and by the thirteenth century the first national network of prisons – the county gaols – was in place. Pugh argues that, in medieval England, imprisonment came to serve three main purposes:

1   Custodial – to provide for the custody of those awaiting trial or execution of sentence.

2   Coercive – to provide for the coercion of fine defaulters, debtors and those contemptuous of the court.

3   Punitive – as a punishment in its own right.

This threefold conceptual distinction clearly remains pertinent today. However, the main purposes of the medieval prison were custodial and coercive. Fox argues that the penal law of Europe at the time was dominated by the 'idea of the illegality of imprisonment as a punishment' (Fox, 1952, p.20). Imprisonment was not considered a proper punishment. The primary role of the prison was to detain rather than punish. A majority of inmates were indeed incarcerated for failure to pay fines and released only when such civil debt was met: it would thus be the poor who were the more likely to be subjected to such detention. As we will see, the punitive function of gaols – custody as punishment – whilst present in medieval society and on the increase from the thirteenth century, did not attain prominence until the late eighteenth century.

The county gaols of the thirteenth century were supplemented by 'franchise' and 'municipal' prisons, privately owned by local lords or ecclesiastics. It is likely that most private courts had access to a private prison. Although such prisons conflicted with the wish of successive monarchs to centralize justice, they survived until the end of the eighteenth century. They differed in vital respects from their modern counterparts in that they were small, of widely different design and were not always intended to be used solely as prisons. Their population was also generally small – each holding about 30 inmates at any one time. They were almost exclusively commercial undertakings: gaolers charged prisoners for accommodation, food and all other services (including the hammering on and the knocking off of leg-irons!). Prisoners were also hired out to local contractors. Thomas (1988, p.9) argues that these privatized, commercial and profit-making activities remained a part of penal organization until centralization in 1878 (only to re-emerge in the 1990s: see Chapter 5). Fortunately for the poor prisoner, the practice of alms-giving was regarded as a Christian duty, especially in Catholic England. Without such relief, survival in, or release from, prison would have been impossible for many (Peters, 1998, p.32).

A prison sentence for those without resources was virtually a death sentence. Unsanitary conditions, risk of disease and starvation were forever present. Prison conditions were generally regarded as deplorable, despite attempts to ensure regular inspections and to discipline prison staff who broke regulations. Expense, exposure to disease and bodily hardship were viewed as necessary corollaries of imprisonment. The success of a prison was measured not by the reform of offenders, but by its ability 'quite simply to prevent escapes; to hold suspects until the courts required them; to hold debtors until they paid up; and those under punishment until the sentence of the court expired' (McConville, 1981, p.5). To this end, the use of irons and stocks (being cheaper than the provision of secure buildings) was widespread.

During the fifteenth and sixteenth centuries the use of imprisonment, whatever its purpose, was to decline. Until then the death penalty and mutilation had been used only in extreme cases to supplement fines and imprisonment; now they were to become the most common measures. Draconian penal codes were developed throughout Europe to combat a perceived increase in crime from vagrants, 'vagabonds', beggars, robbers and the unemployed. Such groups were considered to pose a threat, not only in criminal terms, but as a danger to the social order. Execution, banishment, mutilation, branding and flogging became commonplace public spectacles. Practically every crime was punishable by death; judicial discretion remained only in deciding the manner in which death should be inflicted.

Towards the end of the sixteenth century, however, methods of punishment began to undergo a gradual change. The possibility of exploiting the labour of prisoners now received increasing attention. Galley slavery, transportation to the colonies and penal servitude with hard labour were introduced. By the middle of the seventeenth century transportation to America (and subsequently to Australia in the eighteenth century) became one of the principal ways of dealing with petty, serious and political offenders alike. Those escaping such measures found themselves facing a new philosophy of imprisonment in the county gaols and in houses of correction.

Houses of correction combined the principles of individual reformation and punishment. The key rationale behind their establishment was the counteraction of idleness (Spierenburg, 1991, p.12): their aim was to make the labour power of unwilling people socially useful. By being forced to work, it was hoped that prisoners would form industrious habits to facilitate their return to the labour market. It was through these means, outside the penal system, that the function of correction was to be introduced into penal philosophy. Initially, such **correction** institutions were created for the specific purpose of ridding the towns of beggars and vagrants. The earliest house of correction was probably the Bridewell in London, established in 1555. England thus led the way in the development of houses of correction, but it reached a peak in Holland at the end of the century. The reasons for this appear to be that, at the time, Holland was the most developed capitalist society in Europe, but did not have the reserve of labour power that existed in England after the breakdown of the manorial system and the onset of the first enclosure movement. In Holland, therefore, such innovations in reducing production costs and drawing on all available labour reserves were enthusiastically welcomed.

This use of imprisonment for 'correctional' purposes was a radical departure from existing practice, where custodial and coercive principles were paramount. As a result, Mannheim (1939) and McConville (1981) both cite the house of correction as the first example of modern imprisonment: a point underlined by Spierenburg's (1991) preference to call such institutions 'prison workhouses'. The usual inmates were able-bodied beggars, vagrants, prostitutes and thieves. However, as the reputation of the institutions became established, more serious offenders, as well as the poor, the needy and spendthrift dependants, were interned. Their labour power was utilized either for the economic advantage of the institution itself or for the benefit of external private employers. Men were usually engaged in rasping hardwoods to be used by dyers (the Rasp Huis first introduced in Amsterdam) and women prepared textiles. This example was studied and followed throughout Europe, particularly in the Hôpitaux Généraux in France and the Spinnhaus in Germany. The function of the houses of correction was, however, not only to enforce the discipline of labour, but also to encourage religious observance. Prisoner reformation was couched as much in moral as in economic terms.

Adopting a Whiggish perspective, Austin van der Slice (1937) attributes the rise of the houses of correction to the increasing numbers of 'vagabonds' and vagrants resulting from changes in land tenure and enclosure. He argues that their use was progressive in that they provided a more humane alternative to the county gaols and offered the possibility of reformation rather than simply detention. From a Marxist perspective, Rusche and Kirchheimer (1939), however, provide a rather different interpretation of their function. They argue that, far from being motivated by humanitarianism, the establishment of houses of correction reflected a growing demand for a regulated and disciplined labour force in the days of emerging agrarian capitalist and mercantile societies. In reviewing changes in forms of punishment from the late Middle Ages to the 1930s, they contend that:

transformation in penal systems cannot be explained only from changing needs of the war against crime. Every system of production tends to discover punishments which correspond to its productive relationships … the origin and fate of penal systems … are determined by social forces, above all by economic and then fiscal forces.

(Rusche and Kirchheimer, 1939, p.5)

The rationale for the houses of correction, it is argued, lies in the fact that they were primarily factories turning out commodities at a particularly low cost due to their cheap labour. Their use burgeoned in Holland because the relative labour shortage in the general population, as mentioned earlier, coincided with the development of mercantilism. In short, to secure the development of an emerging capitalism, the labour of prisoners was to be exploited. Thus, in summary, the thesis put forward by Rusche and Kirchheimer proposes that the shift from prisons as places of custody to places of punishment and labour exploitation was based on economic rather than humanitarian motives: the principal objective was not the reformation of inmates, as argued by van der Slice, but the rational exploitation of their labour power.

Whilst, in theory, there remained a distinction between houses of correction (institutions for sentenced thieves, pickpockets and the like) and the workhouse (institutions for the detention of beggars and vagrants), Rusche and Kirchheimer contend that it was the conditions of the local labour market which frequently determined whether this separation actually took place. Valuable, able-bodied workers tended to be confined in the houses of correction for as long as possible, their term of confinement arbitrarily fixed by the houses' administrators:

> Of all the forces which were responsible for the new emphasis upon imprisonment as a punishment, the most important was the profit motive, both in the narrower sense of making the establishment pay and in the wider sense of making the whole penal system a part of the state's mercantilist program.

(Rusche and Kirchheimer, 1939, p.67)

Despite the often-reported 'successes' of the system, the houses of correction had lost much of their distinctive identity by the end of the seventeenth century. In function and administration they largely became merged with the gaols. In the growing puritan moral climate of Stuart social policy, the able-bodied poor and minor offenders were increasingly treated as criminals, and their separation presented fewer and fewer conceptual problems for penal administration (McConville, 1981, p.46). Thus, by the eighteenth century, the prison had returned to its traditional roles of custody and coercion: that is, detaining the accused before trial and enforcing the payment of fines. Within a criminal justice system that extended the use of the death penalty to an ever-increasing range of offences, the prison and prison conditions were rarely a focus for attention. However squalid, disease-ridden, dangerous and expensive prisons were for their inmates, such conditions were tolerated because the primary response of policy-makers was to maintain the coercive function of imprisonment. Even by the end of the eighteenth century half of the average daily prison population comprised debtors (Morgan, 1977).

Penal reformer John Howard's description of prison regimes and prison conditions in the 1770s is indicative of the state of prisons at that time, as Extract 4.1 makes clear. As you will see, graphic descriptions, such as Howard's, provided part of the impetus for fundamental reform of the prison system in the late eighteenth century. It is through these reforms, that it is widely assumed, particularly by Whig historiographies, that the modern prison was to emerge.

Extract 4.1 Howard: 'Distress in prisons'

There are prisons, into which whoever looks will, at first sight of the people confined, be convinced, that there is some great error in the management of them: their sallow meagre countenances declare, without words, that they are very miserable. Many who went in healthy, are in a few months changed to emaciated dejected objects. Some are seen pining under diseases, 'sick, and in prison'; expiring on the floors, in loathsome cells, of pestilential fevers, and the confluent smallpox; victims, I must not say to the cruelty, but I will say to the inattention, of sheriffs, and gentlemen in the commission of the peace.

The cause of this distress is, that many prisons are scantily supplied, and some almost totally destitute of the necessaries of life.

There are several bridewells (to begin with them) in which prisoners have no allowance of food at all. In some, the keeper farms what little is allowed them: and where he engages to supply each prisoner with one or two pennyworth of bread a day, I have known this shrunk to half, sometimes less than half the quantity, cut or broken from his own loaf.

It will perhaps be asked, does not their work maintain them? for every one knows that those offenders are committed to hard labour. The answer to that question, though true, will hardly be believed. There are few bridewells in which any work is done, or can be done. The prisoners have neither tools, nor materials of any kind: but spend their time in sloth, profaneness and debauchery, to a degree which, in some of those houses that I have seen, is extremely shocking.

Some keepers of these houses, who have represented to the magistrates the wants of their prisoners, and desired for them necessary food, have been silenced with these inconsiderate words, Let them work or starve. When those gentlemen know the former is impossible, do they not by that thoughtless sentence, inevitably doom poor creatures to the latter? ...

Many prisons have no water. This defect is frequent in bridewells, and town gaols. In the felons' courts of some county gaols there is no water: in some places where there is water, prisoners are always locked up within doors, and have no more than the keeper or his servants think fit to bring them: in one place they were limited to three pints a day each: a scanty provision for drink and cleanliness!

And as to air, which is no less necessary than either of the two preceding articles, and given us by Providence quite gratis, without any care or labour of our own; yet, as if the bounteous goodness of Heaven excited our envy, methods are contrived to rob prisoners of this genuine cordial of life, as Dr. Hales very properly calls it: I mean by preventing that circulation and change of the salutiferous fluid, without which animals cannot live and thrive. It is well known that air which has performed its office in the lungs, is feculent and noxious. Writers upon the subject show, that a hogshead of air will last a man only an hour: but those who do not choose to consult philosophers; may judge from a notorious fact. In 1756, at Calcutta in Bengal, out of a hundred and seventy persons who were confined in a hole there one night, a hundred and fifty-four were taken out dead. The few survivors ascribed the mortality to their want of fresh air, and called the place Hell in miniature.

(Howard, 1929, pp.1, 3–4, originally published in 1777)

3 Theorizing penal reform and the rise of the penitentiary

The bare bones of penal reform in the late eighteenth century are uncontroversial. Throughout much of the eighteenth century, prison conditions were such that there was no segregation of men from women, no classification of offenders, and no separation of the tried from the untried. The sale of alcohol to prisoners was freely permitted. Extortion by prison staff went unchecked. Prisons, as Howard (1777/1929) recorded, were characterized by lack of light, air, sanitation, washing facilities and general cleanliness. Diseases, such as typhus, were rife. Many prisons were run as enterprises for private profit: tables of fees were drawn up, according to which the 'keeper' or 'gaoler' would provide such items as bedding, food and alcohol. Following his inspections, Howard recommended that secure, sanitary and cellular accommodation be provided; that prisoners be separated and classified according to offence; that useful labour be introduced; and the sale of liquor be prohibited. In 1774 the Discharged Prisoners Act had allowed for the payment of the fees of prisoners who were acquitted at their trials, and the Health of Prisoners Act required prisons to be ventilated, regularly cleaned and provided with baths and medical facilities; the use of underground cells (dungeons) was prohibited. In 1784, an Act of Parliament provided for the establishment of separate cells in all new prisons, but was generally ignored as at the time the principle of state management was virulently disputed (Forsythe, 1989). In 1779 the Penitentiary Act detailed proposals for the building and management of two 'ideal penitentiary houses'. This initiative, which marked central government's first direct involvement in prison administration, was made not simply as a result of widespread dissatisfaction with existing forms of punishment, but because the American War of Independence of 1776 had left the government with nowhere to send those sentenced to transportation. With the loss of the American colonies, transportation had ceased in the same year and prisoners were housed instead on prison ships, known as hulks, and employed on public works, such as dredging rivers.

penitentiary

Influenced by the work of Howard, the Penitentiary Act promoted a new view of the purpose of imprisonment. The prisons proposed by the Act were to have both a punitive and a reformative function. The term 'penitentiary' was significant in its implication that prisoners were to undergo a process of expiation and penance. They were to be put to work 'of the hardest and most servile kind, in which drudgery is chiefly required ... such as treading in a wheel ... sawing stone, rasping logwood, chopping rags' (quoted in Harding *et al.*, 1985, p.117). Prisoners were also to be classified into groups within a reward/ punishment hierarchy. Profits from work would pay for prison staff, uniforms were to be issued and prison governors appointed. From 1811, it became increasingly assumed that only the state was competent enough to prevent neglect and cruelty and to create reformatory systems of prison discipline (Forsythe, 1989). Because of the emphasis on hard (though unproductive) labour, the prison was envisaged not only as a morally and physically healthy place, but also as a positive means to reform the offender.

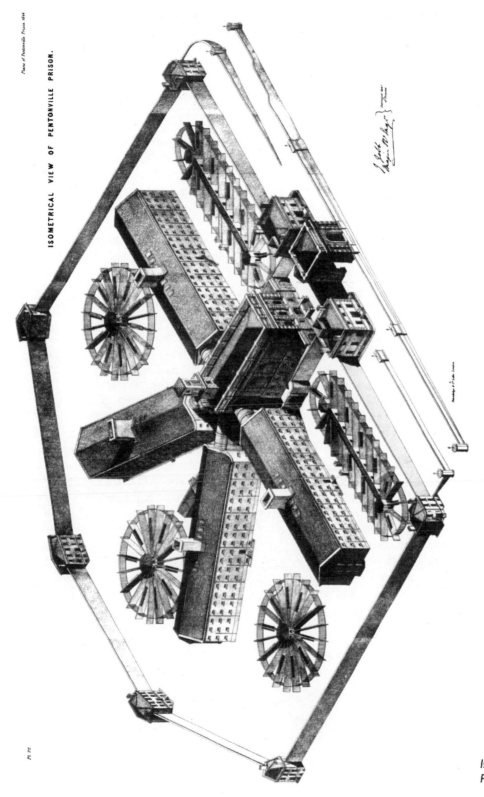

*Isometrical view of
Pentonville prison, 1844*

From 1785 there was a spate of local prison Acts which empowered local communities to build new prisons. Gloucester penitentiary was opened in 1789, 'a spacious and handsome' prison was opened in Manchester in 1790 and another at Ipswich in 1792 (Thomas, 1988, p.153). In 1816 the first *national* penitentiary at Millbank was opened and with it the 'separate' system of solitary confinement was introduced. Meanwhile, the discovery and colonization of Australia resulted in – indeed, was founded upon – the restarting of transportation. However, by the late 1830s the Australian governments had become extremely reluctant to accept any more convicts and over the next 20 years central government in England was forced to build or reopen several new prisons, notably Pentonville in which convicts were to be subjected to a term of penal servitude; Dartmoor, which had originally served as a prison for French and American prisoners of war; Parkhurst, designed specifically for juveniles; and Brixton, the first purpose-built prison for women. The initial response of the early Victorians to their 'unwanted' populations was, it seems, the building of institutions for their confinement. By 1853 transportation had been abolished for the great majority of the criminally convicted.

The 1823 Gaol Act was the first comprehensive statement of principle from central government to be applied to local prisons and attempted to impose uniformity in penal practice at the same time as imposing Howard's recommendations for health requirements, abolition of the sale and the use of alcohol and the promotion of regular prison inspections. In 1835 government inspectors were introduced to visit prisons and report to the Secretary of State. Pentonville penitentiary was finally opened in London in 1842 and its regime of silence and solitude quickly became a model for prison architecture and discipline, not only in England, but throughout Europe. This was the culmination of over 60 years of attempts to devise a totally rational and reformative mode of imprisonment.

penal transformation These legislative and institutional landmarks of prison reform are easy to establish. The precise reasons *why* such developments occurred, however, and with what effects, remain the subject of considerable debate. Cohen (1985) argues that, at the end of the eighteenth century, a major transformation in modes of penal and social control was inaugurated, of which the emergence of the modern prison was but one reflection. By the mid nineteenth century a number of key shifts had taken place: from an arbitrary and decentralized state involvement in penal practice to a rationalized and centralized state-organized system; from little or no differentiation between deviant groups to their increasing classification and categorization into separate groups, each with their own particular problems and requiring specialized forms of intervention from accredited professionals or experts; from forms of punishment aimed at the 'body' (physical pain) to forms of punishment aimed at the 'mind' (isolation, penitence); and from a punitive rationale of 'just-deserts' to one of neo-positivist individual reformation. Within these processes the prison emerged as 'the dominant instrument for changing undesirable behaviour and as the favoured form of punishment' (Cohen, 1985, p.13).

ACTIVITY 4.1

Now spend some time studying the correctional changes listed by Cohen in Table 4.1. Note in particular his argument that, from the end of the eighteenth century, the prison emerges as a key site in which the principles of *centralization, rationalization, classification, professional dominance* and a *state monopoly over control* came to be realized. Make some notes of your own, summarizing the nature of these shifts.

Table 4.1   Changes in deviancy control

		Phase one (pre-eighteenth century)	Phase two (from the nineteenth century)
1	State involvement	Weak, decentralized, arbitrary	Strong, centralized, rationalized
2	Place of control	'Open': community, primary institutions	Closed, segregated institution: victory of the asylum, 'Great Incarcerations'
3	Focus of control	Undifferentiated	Concentrated
4	Visibility of control	Public, 'spectacular'	Boundaries clear, but invisible inside – 'discreet'
5	Categorization and differentiation of deviance	Hardly developed at all	Established and strengthened
6	Hegemony of law and criminal justice system	Not yet established; criminal law only one form of control	Monopoly of criminal justice system established, but then supplemented by new systems
7	Professional dominance	Not at all present	Established and strengthened
8	Object of intervention	External behaviour: 'body'	Internal states: 'mind'
9	Theories of punishment	Moralistic, traditional, then classical, 'just deserts'	Influenced by positivism and treatment ideal: 'neo-positivist'
10	Mode of control	Inclusive	Exclusive and stigmatizing

Source: Cohen, 1985, pp.16–17, from Table 1

The remainder of section 3 will be devoted to examining competing theories and explanations of late eighteenth-century penal reform. Did the penitentiary symbolize the re-emergence of humanitarian ideals or did it trigger a more insidious and total regulation of 'deviant' populations? Did reform stem from the 'enlightened vision' of philanthropists or from the changing social and political needs of an emerging industrial capitalist economy? Or was it always a matter of the (often coincidental?) convergence of any number of determining factors? You will be invited to reflect on these issues through an analysis of competing explanations of this major correctional change.

3.1   The Whig tradition: humanitarian histories

The Whig tradition of historical research is characterized by Cohen (1985, p.18) as promoting an 'idealist' view of history in which change occurs through advances in knowledge. The ideals and visions of key individuals are seen as providing the motor for social change. All change constitutes reform and is motivated by benevolence, altruism, philanthropy and humanitarianism. In **humanitarianism** addition, the accumulation of successive changes reveals an underlying progress in penal reform: the refinement of legislation indicates success.

Writers in this tradition have dominated the field of social history research until quite recently. Historians have characteristically portrayed the origins, development and impact of prisons as humanitarian innovations that replaced more barbaric and repressive forms of social control. As Pisciotta argues: 'writers in this tradition are readily identifiable because of their tendency to lionize the founders of the system and selectively emphasize their successes' (Pisciotta, 1981, p.111).

The principal starting-point in the study of the reform of the penal codes of Europe in the eighteenth century is usually taken to be the publication in 1764 of Cesare Beccaria's *On Crimes and Punishments* (**Beccaria, 1963**). This contained a wholesale condemnation of the use of the death penalty and its tendency to corrupt people rather than to prevent crime. Located within an emergent classicist and utilitarian philosophy, Beccaria argued that punishment should be predictable, rational and proportionate to the offence. In Britain such ideals were promoted by William Eden in his work *Principles of Penal Law*, published in 1771, but reached their most practical application in the utilitarian philosopher Jeremy Bentham's 1778 plan for a prison to 'grind rogues honest' that he called the Panopticon. This architectural design would enable the constant surveillance of all prisoners from a central point while inmates were prevented from knowing when they were being watched. The prison was to be financed solely by the prisoners' labour and the best measurement of their reformation was to be the quantity of work they performed. This accorded with the modernizing principle of classicism that people behave in a rational fashion according to their calculation of the likely benefits or pains involved in their chosen course of action. The prison was conceived as a means of making the idle, industrious and the offender, conformist (Morrison, 1996). Bentham's scheme was initially welcomed and certainly influenced later penitentiary designs, but, in consideration of questions of expense and commercialism, it was eventually to be abandoned in its pure form by the Holford Committee of 1810.

panopticon

Bentham's design for a reformed prison: the Panopticon, 1791. As described in Melossi and Pavarini (1981, p.40): 'The formal principle upon which the Panopticon is based consisted of two multi-floored coaxial cylindrical containers, each having opposing and complementary functions: the circular crowns in correspondence to the floors of the outer cylinder, were placed between six radials in cellular units completely opened out towards the central space and lit by the outer perimeter; this section was allotted to those to be controlled. The inner coaxial cylinder, concealed by thin, opaque partitions placed along the length of the perimeter was for the warders — very few, it was specified — who, without any chance of being seen, could have exercised tight and constant control at every point of the outer cylinder by means of well placed peep-holes; nothing could have escaped their scrutiny'

Other figures who loom large in these traditional accounts are John Howard and Elizabeth Fry – not so much for their adherence to a classicist philosophy but because of their 'philanthropic vision'. As we have seen, philanthropy – the provision of practical benevolence – has a long history in alleviating the suffering of the poor and the incarcerated, dating back at least to the thirteenth-century Catholic practice of alms-giving.

Howard's own personal history lies in that of the wealthy country gentry. In 1775 he was appointed high sheriff for Bedfordshire, and from that time began to catalogue the conditions inside prisons and the abuses of power that the penal system appeared to encourage. In subsequent years he embarked on numerous self-financed travels in Britain and throughout Europe to witness and record prison conditions first-hand. His self-defined purpose was to 'attempt the relief of the miserable'. In this he was undoubtedly influenced by his own religious and spiritual enthusiasm: he 'confronted the horrors of the prison system as an angel of divine will grappling with evil' (Open University, 1987, p.52). Howard's work commanded attention not only for the shocking revelations it offered, but also for the novel conceptions of prison regimes that he developed on his travels. He was highly influential in designing an entirely new regime of punishment that eventually was given practical expression with the building of the penitentiary. Howard believed that prisons should be quiet and clean, and

John Howard, 1726–1790

The chapel at Pentonville where prisoners were screened from each other to prevent contact, c.1840

based on a strict routine of prayer and work, and that prisoners should be excluded from the rest of society, uniformed, treated impersonally and segregated into classes in order to avoid moral contamination of the novice by the experienced offender. He did not question the right to punish, but was concerned that such punishment should not degenerate into cruelty, abuse and injustice. Above all, as Harding *et al.* record:

> Howard gave the developing bourgeoisie a perfect hero. He stressed the bourgeois values of authoritarianism, self reliance, frugality, the rejection of luxury and an obsession with inquiry and measurement and through his quasi-saintly character, he gave these values a rightness and a righteousness ... for the bourgeoisie, the corrupt prison was a symbol of the corrupt nature of the old ruling class, and Howard a symbol of a new, caring, frugal, disciplined society of the bourgeois.
>
> (Harding *et al.*, 1985, p.113)

However, by the time of his death in 1790, few of Howard's recommendations for penal reform had been implemented. Two Acts of Parliament had been passed as a result of his work – abolishing gaolers' fees and improving prison conditions – but even by the early nineteenth century little improvement in prisons had been achieved.

Elizabeth Fry was another English philanthropist who, like Howard, became involved in issues of penal reform. Born to a Quaker family in 1780, she first

Elizabeth Fry,
1780–1845

visited Newgate Gaol in London in 1813 in order to distribute clothing, where she found conditions little changed from Howard's day. Though domestic matters prevented her from returning to Newgate for a further three years, from 1817 onwards she devoted herself to improving the moral and physical welfare of the women prisoners by tackling overcrowding (she had found, for example, that 300 women and their children had to share just two rooms and two cells in which they stayed night and day, in appalling conditions of 'riot, licentiousness and filth'), providing education and ensuring the segregation of the women and children from the men.

In 1817 Fry, together with other women who under her leadership had also become interested in the provision of education in Newgate, established the Association for the Improvement of the Female Prisoners in Newgate. This was the first of many Ladies' Societies for Promoting the Reformation of Female Prisoners to be formed, initially in other parts of England from 1821, subsequently in Scotland in 1828 and in Ireland in 1834. These Societies gradually drew public attention to the plight of women in prison. Their general aim was to:

> provide for the clothing, the instructions and the employment of these females, to introduce them to a knowledge of the holy scriptures and to form in them ... those habits of order, sobriety and industry which may render them docile and peaceable whilst in prison, and respectable when they leave it.
>
> (quoted in Dobash *et al.*, 1986, p.44)

As a result, a new daily routine for women was initiated in which Bible classes and employment (needlework, knitting) were central. Begging, swearing and gambling were prohibited, behaviour was monitored by orderlies and any infractions reported to an appointed matron. The approach was one of simultaneously improving conditions and promoting moral reform through a

Female convicts at work during the silent hour, Brixton prison, c.1850

combination of discipline and compassion. Above all, as Zedner records, Elizabeth Fry's 'insistence on the need for individualization became widely accepted as the most distinctive feature of the treatment of women' (Zedner, 1991, p.120). Indeed, the work of the Ladies' Societies was widely credited with improving not only conditions at Newgate and elsewhere, but also the 'manner and habits' of female prisoners, and with preventing recidivism.

The impact of people like Howard and Fry on penal reform has been lauded by many historians (for example, Gibson, 1971; Ramsay, 1977; Krebs, 1978; Radzinowicz, 1978) and their names are constantly evoked in any standard textbook on prison histories (for example, Fox, 1952; McConville, 1981; Harding *et al.*, 1985; Radzinowicz and Hood, 1990). As a consequence, the impression given is that the work of enlightened individuals was paramount in promoting the view that prisons were positive institutions and humane alternatives to the death penalty, corporal punishment and transportation. The tendency, as Cohen (1985, p.18) argues, is to view individual vision as the principal motor for change from a system of barbarity to one of humanitarianism.

ACTIVITY 4.2

To consolidate your study so far, consider the following questions:

1   What are the key characteristics of a Whig interpretation of history?

2   Was humanitarianism the only principle underlying penal reform?

Making notes on your responses will help you to compare Whig interpretations of history with those of the revisionists, which is discussed in section 3.2 below.

disillusioned liberalism

Some recent historians have argued that the humanitarianism of the late eighteenth century was more rhetoric than reality. Good intentions are seen as capable of being frustrated and overturned by subsequent events. Cohen (1985, p.19) characterizes such analysis as disillusioned liberalism. In Rothman's (1971) account of the asylum and penitentiary institutions in Jacksonian America, for example, we are warned that the harbingers of benevolence must themselves be distrusted:

> the most popular historiographical response to the invention of the asylum is to call it a 'reform' but the volumes that follow this tradition do not ask why the society adopted this particular measure, rather than another. By describing the innovation as a reform, they assume that the asylum was an inevitable and sure step in the progress of humanity. Ostensibly it was an obvious improvement not only over existing conditions but over *other possible alternatives*. But such perspective is bad logic and bad history. There was nothing inevitable about the asylum form, no self-evident reason why philanthropists should have chosen it … By what standard is it an improvement to relieve the poor within almshouses rather than in their own homes? By what criterion is a penitentiary an improvement over the stocks or a system of fines and whippings?
>
> (Rothman, 1971, pp.xiv–xv)

In this way Rothman questions the taken-for-granted meanings of reform, progress and philanthropy. Within the proliferation of institutions for the insane, the poor and the criminal, he witnesses not the dawning of a new humanitarianism, but an 'emphasis on authority, obedience and regularity turning all too predictably into a mechanical application of discipline. And by incarcerating the deviant and dependent and defending the step with hyperbolic rhetoric, they discouraged – really eliminated – the search for other solutions that might have been less susceptible to abuse' (Rothman, 1971, p.295).

Similarly, commenting on the development of prisons for women, Dobash *et al.* (1986) and Zedner (1991) note that Fry's faith in a policy of 'kind superintendence' was not universally shared. Opponents stressed that conditions should be deliberately made worse than those experienced outside; that prison should be made a hard and unpleasant place. With the creation of the penitentiaries (Millbank and Pentonville in London, Perth in Scotland) and the introduction of the 'separate system', the imposition of uniform regimes for men and women alike meant that Fry's vision of a network of reformative institutions for women was never realized. By the mid nineteenth century, women *were* separated from men in most prisons and women warders were appointed, but 'impersonal and more abstract approaches increasingly gained acceptance along with an emphasis on humiliation, degradation, human accounting, hard useful labour and religious exhortation' (Dobash *et al.*, 1986, p.61). Moreover, given their smaller numbers (a fifth of those convicted), the imprisonment of women frequently remained an afterthought to be fitted into a system designed for men with 'least effort and expense, with the result that they often suffered much worse conditions than men convicted of similar offences' (Zedner, 1991, p.136). Visions of protecting these more 'vulnerable' prisoners from corruption and restoring them to 'true femininity' created regimes that were generally more oppressive than those endured by men (Zedner, 1998, p.323). Likewise, Dobash *et al.* conclude that, whilst regimes became similar, 'patriarchal and paternalist conceptions played a crucial role' such that the surveillance and regulation of women was 'always closer and more omnipresent than that usually directed at men' (Dobash *et al.*, 1986, p.61).

These latter accounts thus note how reformist ideals and attempts to humanize the prison were either barely implemented or were diluted by opposing political interests or unintended consequences. The paradoxes of humanitarian reform are such that improvements in conditions are set against increases in regimented control; that the desire to 'rescue' individuals rests uneasily against concurrent demands to establish the prison as punishment; and that the implementation of reform is far more complex than that implied by terms such as 'progress', 'benevolence' and 'philanthropy'.

3.2   The radical tradition: revisionist histories

The radical tradition within prison history research offers a different interpretation of that history and challenges almost every detail of Whig historiographies. Radical historians have contended that the prison and other correctional institutions were repressive forms of social control, born out of class conflict and designed to protect the vested interests of a wealthy and governing class. Below, we consider two variants of this radical tradition: first, that of an 'orthodox Marxism', which has argued that systems of punishment are manipulated by the powerful in order to maintain a cheap and reliable supply of labour; and, second, that of a more complex and critical persuasion, which places more emphasis on ideological, political and legal transformations in the process of re-establishing order on a new foundation. Both diverge from Rothman's (1971) stance by insisting that the new punitive element in penal regimes did not represent a *failure* of reform, but actually succeeded in its unstated purpose of establishing acceptance of the 'need' for 'disciplinary regimes' in all walks of life.

orthodox Marxism

ACTIVITY 4.3

You should now read Extract 4.2 where Rusche and Kirchheimer, adopting an orthodox Marxist position, evaluate the social and penal consequences of the Industrial Revolution for prison labour. As you do so, consider the following questions:

- What in their view was the driving force behind penal reform?
- How and why did the role of prison labour change?

Extract 4.2 Rusche and Kirchheimer: 'Prison labour'

We have seen that the houses of correction used to spur the inmates to greater industry by paying them according to their work or by giving them a share of the profits. They were punished only if they failed to perform their task, whether from lack of skill or from laziness [Riedel, 1750, pp.78–9]. Now that it no longer paid to employ prisoners, however, they were frequently left with nothing to do. This raised the whole problem of the purpose of imprisonment, and brought its repressive, deterrent side to the fore. The way was open for the realization of the programs of reformers like Pearson and Mittelstädt, who sought to make the prisons rational and efficient means of deterring the lower classes from crime, means which would not allow the convict to perish, but which would impress him once and for all by fear and terror. England, with its large industrial reserve army, led the way. Work was introduced as a form of punishment, not as a source of profit, and moral arguments were brought forward as a justification. One experienced administrator explained in 1821 that work which was to produce profit would interfere with discipline and moral improvement, because, for purposes of manufacture, the taskmaster would seek to assemble prisoners who would otherwise not be permitted to associate with each other [Webb and Webb, 1922, p.85, quoting Holford].

Prison labour became a method of torture, and the authorities were expert enough in inventing new forms; occupations of a purely punitive character were made as fatiguing as possible and were dragged out for unbearable lengths of time

[Koch, 1928, p.389]. Prisoners carried huge stones from one place to another and then back again, they worked pumps from which the water flowed back to its source, or trod mills which did no useful work. A simple form of treadwheel, easily applicable to all prisons, was devised by William Cubitt about 1818 for use in the Suffolk County Gaol at Bury, and it was from this example that the practice spread. The cheapness and simplicity of the 'stepping-mill' or 'everlasting staircase,' as it was called, the severe physical exertion required, and the hatred engendered by 'wheel-stepping' commended the new device to Quarter Sessions, and models were set up in every reformed prison, grinding corn or grinding nothing, raising water, supplying power for hemp-beating, cork-cutting, or other machines [Webb and Webb, 1922, p.97]. Not only was the treadwheel regarded as a success because it afforded a cheap and easy method of forcing prisoners to work, but also because it deterred persons who might use the gaol as a place of ultimate refuge [Webb and Webb, 1922, pp.98–9].

References

Koch, C. (1928) 'Der soziale Gedanke im Strafvollzug', in Bummke, E. *Deutsches Gefängniswesen*, Berlin.

Riedel, A.C. (1750) *Beschreibung des im Fürstentum Bayreuth zu Sanct Georgen am See errichteten Zucht- und Arbeits-Hauses*, Bayreuth.

Webb, S. and Webb, B. (1922) *English Prisons under Local Government*, London.

(Rusche and Kirchheimer, 1939, p.112)

As we saw in section 2, in their analysis of the house of correction, Rusche and Kirchheimer contend that the driving force for reform lay not in humanitarian principles, but in the economic necessities of the time. They argue that the shift from corporal and capital punishment to systems of incarceration was rendered necessary by the underlying aim of capitalism to socialize production and create a submissive and regulated workforce. Similarly, the modern prison, they argued, was a part of a larger rationalization of social relations in nascent capitalism. Within this development, although humanitarianism loomed large in its justificatory rhetoric, it had little or no place in practice. Prison conditions remained deplorable, and the new regimes of prison labour (for example, the use of the treadmill) were meaningless, degrading and unproductive. The new prison was intent not on teaching particular skills, but on deterring disorder through *disciplined* routine and strict regimentation. Rusche and Kirchheimer's thesis maintains that there is a *direct relationship* between forms of punishment and wider labour-market conditions. So, for example, the origins of forced labour in the houses of correction lie in population decline and subsequent shortages of labour in the seventeenth century. Over-population in the eighteenth century coincided and combined with the emergence of industrial capitalism to create 'a roaming, landless, depressed class, competing for employment' (Piven and Cloward, 1972, p.33), together with the need for a compliant and disciplined labour force. The house of correction was the institutional result of the substitution of outdoor relief, as in poor law, by confinement and forced labour. The aim of the prison was to teach the discipline of labour and to make the poor accept any conditions imposed on them by an employer (Piven and Cloward, 1972, p.33).

rationalization

The treadmill at Brixton prison, 1821

Conditions in all institutions, from the workhouse to the prison, had to be made worse than the life of even the poorest of free workers. As a result, prisons developed as systems of intensified punishment epitomized by unproductive hard labour. They formed one part of a wider strategy to impose ubiquitous control and regulation. A modern reading of this orthodox Marxist position makes much the same point:

> The bourgeoisie state assigns to all of them [segregated institutions] a directing role in the various moments of the formation, production and reproduction of the factory proletariat: for society they are essential instruments of social control, the aim of which is to secure for capital a workforce which by virtue of its moral attitude, physical health, intellectual capacity, orderliness, discipline, obedience, etc., will readily adapt to the whole regime of factory life and produce the maximum possible of surplus labour.
>
> (Melossi, 1981, p.42)

According to this thesis, during the Industrial Revolution the rationale for imprisonment changed from being economic – and indirectly rehabilitative – to something more punitive and repressive. The creation of a reserve army of unemployed people throughout Europe made prison labour less of a sought-after commodity and the prison became more a means of inflicting control and intimidation for its own sake. It is in these terms that Rusche and Kirchheimer (1939) talk of a decline and decay in prisons: as the rationale for prison in the old mercantilist social regime was to provide cheap forced labour, it became obsolete in the days of high unemployment and pauperism that accompanied the Industrial Revolution.

However, commentators on this Marxist theorization have criticized it for its reductionist and essentialist stance: that is, for developing in advance a one-dimensional theory of penal relations and then imposing this upon history. Indeed, it is notable that Rusche and Kirchheimer's analysis of penal institutions and labour-market conditions appears applicable to the mercantilist period of the sixteenth and seventeenth centuries, but in their consideration of the rise of capitalism, the primacy of the economic gives way to the significance of a bourgeois *ideology* of deterrence. The changing role of prison labour in itself suggests that a major transformation occurred in penal purpose in the late eighteenth century, and that histories of productive penal labour and deterrent labour are analytically separate and discontinuous. In other words, the correlation between imprisonment and production conditions is imposed by theory rather than explained empirically. Similarly, it can be argued that prisons were a logical concomitant of prevailing political philosophy rather than *consciously* devised as a tool to develop and sustain the social relations of capitalism. If the penal system is to be understood as a fundamentally ideological and political apparatus within capitalism, then any relationship it has with labour-market conditions cannot be posed as direct, unaffected by the superstructure in which it is located. As Hogg concludes: 'an analysis which postulates some *a priori* relationship between imprisonment and the capitalist mode of production relieves itself of the necessity to look at the contradictions, the discontinuities, the whole process of change in its specificity' (Hogg, 1979, p.69).

Similarly, Garland's review of Rusche and Kirchheimer's work finds that:

> As might be expected when such a single-minded interpretation is imposed upon a broad historical canvas, historians have been quick to show the many points at which the thesis needs to be qualified in the light of more detailed evidence … Historians of the house of correction have argued that although commercial motives played a part … few of them could in fact sustain any financial benefits … [Similarly] the building of penitentiaries and model prisons was often a massive financial expenditure undertaken with little prospect of reimbursement … prisoners' labour and its profitability was frequently subordinated to other considerations such as prison discipline, general deterrence or individual reformation.
>
> (Garland, 1990, pp.106–7)

It was the task of refining the Rusche and Kirchheimer thesis (whilst acknowledging the whole new vista of understanding that it opened up) that was subsequently taken up by such writers as Michael Ignatieff (1978) in his attempt to realize the full complexity and contradictory nature of late eighteenth-century reform.

As Cohen (1985, p.23) notes, Ignatieff's history rejects 'economic determinism' and 'Marxist functionalism'. Instead, he developed a revisionist **revisionism** position which set out to explore what he refers to as the 'complex and autonomous structure of religious and philosophical beliefs' that informed the reformist vision of the penitentiary. In this respect he pays more attention to the stated intentions and complex motives of reformers. For Ignatieff, the new prison was not born from a functional necessity of the economic system, but from reformers' fears for social order, their political self-interest *and* their religious beliefs. Philanthropy, then, played a key role, but was mediated through the emergence of new sets of class relations brought about by the establishment of industrial capitalism. In Ignatieff's account the new control system succeeded because, despite its brutality, it convinced the offender and the rest of society of its humanity and justness, (in comparison to the Bloody Code), and was central to establishing the full legitimacy of the law and the legitimacy of the new class relations that it supported.

His analysis of the development of the penitentiary dwells not on its purported new humanism, but on its role in replacing punishment of the body (for example, flogging) with punishment directed at the mind (such as solitary confinement). These new types of pain – the treadmill, the crank, the straitjacket, the solitude – represented not so much a failure of reform, but a success. To view reform as a cycle of good intentions (like Howard's) subsequently overturned by unintended consequences (as in Rothman's analysis), misses its wider ideological and symbolic functions and its ultimate success in 're-establishing order on a new foundation'. Thus while the penitentiary was continually criticized during the early nineteenth century for its functional shortcomings, it continued to 'command support because it was seen as an element of a larger vision of order that by the 1840s commanded the reflexive assent of the propertied and powerful' (Ignatieff, 1978, p.210).

Ignatieff explores the different strands that helped to form the 'ideology' of the new prison. In particular, he reveals how close parallels are drawn between the language of disease and the language of punishment. Reform was multifaceted: improving physical conditions, but also improving moral habits, instigating the ethos of discipline and founding a new social stability by popular consent. As Figure 4.1 reveals, the offences of prisoners were as much moral as legal in nature. In an increasingly unequal and divided society, the new prison was one means of providing an image of humanity whilst simultaneously fortifying consent 'without compromising security'. In conclusion, Ignatieff contends that lauding the process of reform obscures its function as a 'legitimation for an intensification of carceral power' (Ignatieff, 1978, p.212); humanitarianism was inextricably linked to the practice of **disciplinary** domination and the establishment of disciplinary regimes throughout the social **regimes** order.

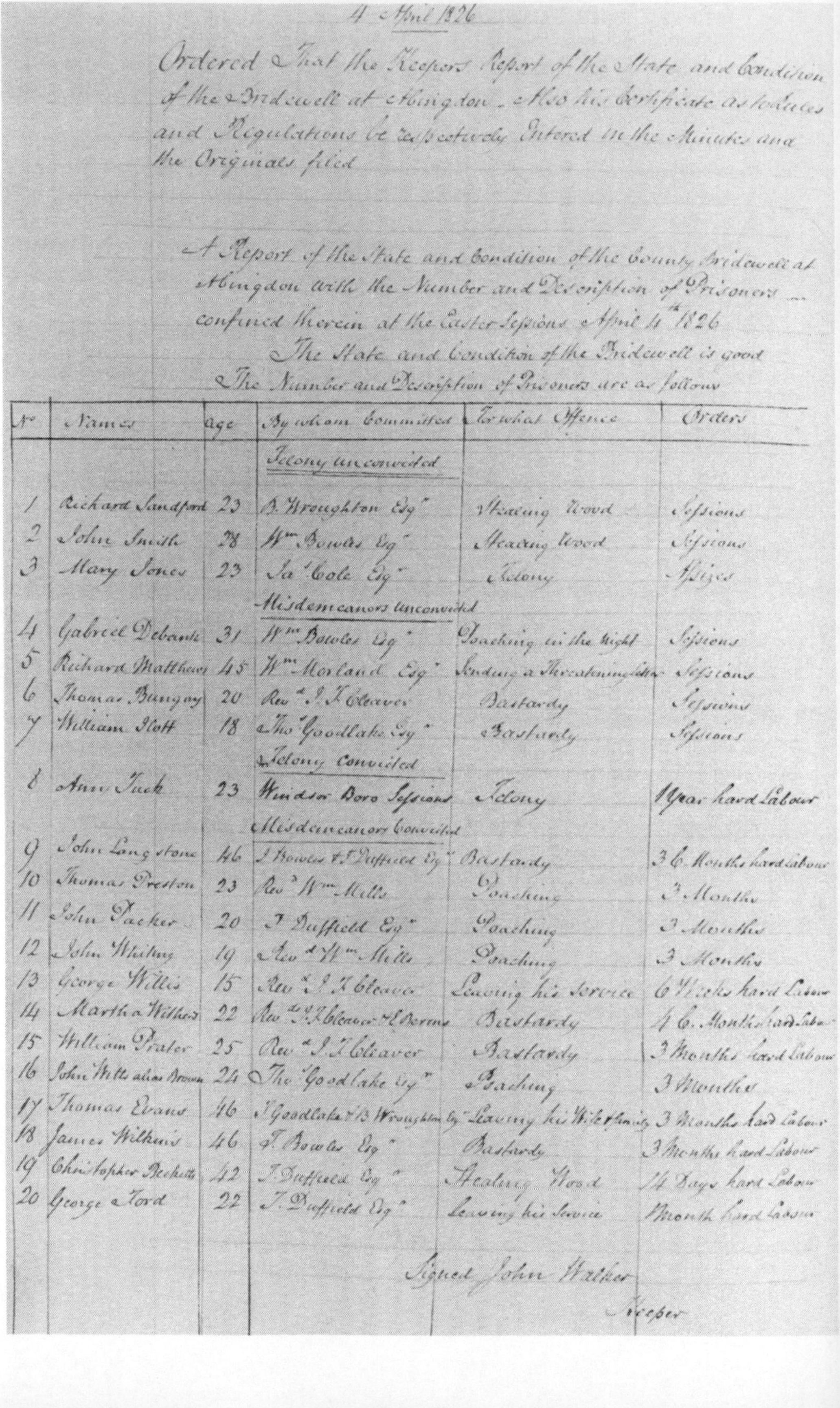

4 April 1826

Ordered That the Keepers Report of the State and Condition of the Bridewell at Abingdon – Also his Certificate as to Rules and Regulations be respectively Entered in the Minutes and the Originals filed

A Report of the State and Condition of the County Bridewell at Abingdon with the Number and Description of Prisoners confined therein at the Easter Sessions April 4th 1826

The State and Condition of the Bridewell is good

The Number and Description of Prisoners are as follows

No	Names	Age	By whom Committed	For what Offence	Orders
			Felony unconvicted		
1	Richard Sandford	23	B. Wroughton Esqr	Stealing Wood	Sessions
2	John Smith	28	Wm Bowles Esqr	Stealing Wood	Sessions
3	Mary Jones	23	Jas Cole Esqr	Felony	Assizes
			Misdemeanors unconvicted		
4	Gabriel Debank	31	Wm Bowles Esqr	Poaching in the Night	Sessions
5	Richard Matthews	45	Wm Morland Esqr	Sending a Threatening letter	Sessions
6	Thomas Bungay	20	Revd J. T. Cleaver	Bastardy	Sessions
7	William Flott	18	Thos Goodlake Esqr	Bastardy	Sessions
			Felony convicted		
8	Ann Tuck	23	Windsor Boro Sessions	Felony	1 Year hard Labour
			Misdemeanors convicted		
9	John Langstone	46	J. Bowles & T. Duffield Esqr	Bastardy	3 C. Months hard Labour
10	Thomas Preston	23	Revd Wm Mills	Poaching	3 Months
11	John Packer	20	T. Duffield Esqr	Poaching	3 Months
12	John Whiting	19	Revd Wm Mills	Poaching	3 Months
13	George Willis	15	Revd J. T. Cleaver	Leaving his Service	6 Weeks hard Labour
14	Martha Withers	22	Revd J. T. Cleaver & E. Berens	Bastardy	4 C. Months hard Labour
15	William Prater	25	Revd J. T. Cleaver	Bastardy	3 Months hard Labour
16	John Mills alias Brown	24	Thos Goodlake Esqr	Poaching	3 Months
17	Thomas Evans	46	T. Goodlake & B. Wroughton Esqr	Leaving his Wife & family	3 Months hard Labour
18	James Wilkins	46	J. Bowles Esqr	Bastardy	3 Months hard Labour
19	Christopher Beckett	42	T. Duffield Esqr	Stealing Wood	14 Days hard Labour
20	George Ford	22	T. Duffield Esqr	Leaving his Service	1 Month hard Labour

Signed John Walker
Keeper

Figure 4.1 Crime in the early nineteenth century: a moral and legal problem. Prisoners confined at the Bridewell at Abingdon at the Easter Sessions, 4 April 1826

This approach is to some degree shared by Foucault in his book *Discipline and Punish* (1977). However, Foucault gives less attention to any materialist connection between prison and industrial capitalism, and more to the power of ideas, knowledge and discourses. Foucault is less concerned with exploring the origins of the prison *per se* and more with identifying a continuous disciplinary discourse (without giving privileged attention to any one source) that informed and was thoroughly intertwined with all forms of social control in the late eighteenth century. Thus the reform of prisoners, education of children, confinement of the insane and supervision of industrial workers all form part of an emerging 'carceral society'. The discourse is **carceral** powerful enough ultimately to affect our very vision of the world: it enters the 'human **society** soul'. All social relations become relations of domination. The power of the prison, then, is less explicable in terms of penal philosophy 'than it is in a 'power of normalization' that operates in such non-penal institutions as the school, the hospital and the factory. Power emanates not just from the state, or indeed from any particular institutions, but from *forms of knowledge* that inform all social relations at all levels in the social hierarchy. The emergence of prison is but one reflection of the diffusion of new forms of knowledge, grounded in the human sciences, which surfaced in the eighteenth century (for a discussion of Foucauldian analysis see, for example, Smart, 1989; Garland, 1990, Chapters 6 and 7). The aim is to produce a new kind of 'individual subjected to habits, rules, orders, an authority that is exercised continually around him and upon him, and which he must allow to function automatically in him' (Foucault, 1977, pp.128–9). Foucault's investigation of the prison in the early nineteenth century thus becomes a means of exploring the wider theme of how domination is achieved and how individuals are socially constructed in the modern world.

The key to Foucault's thesis is that, because the prison has always been a failure – in reducing crime and in preventing recidivism – the question of its continuing existence has to be addressed in different ways. He argues that the prison is useful in a strategy of political domination because it works to divorce crime from politics, enhances fear and divides the labouring classes against themselves: 'The prison does not control the criminal, so much as control the working class by creating the criminal' (Garland, 1990, p.150). The prison is retained because of its failures rather than in spite of them. In this process, the prison stands at one end of a continuum in which regulation and surveillance become normalized throughout the social body. Indeed, Foucault coins the phrase 'carceral archipelago' to describe the chain of institutions that stretches out from the prison, conjuring up images of a totalitarianism not usually ascribed to Western liberal democracies. Foucault's work remains influential because it allows a greater sensitivity to the nuances of the disciplinary and normalizing aspects of the penal system in the context of wider issues of power, knowledge and governance (Open University, 1992; Foucault, 1977).

Nevertheless, such revisionist histories have been taken to task for oversimplifying complex socio-historical processes. For example, Forsythe (1991, p.241) argues that a concentration on the social control aspects of reform tends to deny the genuine (rather than merely rhetorical) aspirations and achievements of the reformers to improve the lot of prisoners and to ameliorate the more barbaric conditions of imprisonment. Delacy's (1986) study of prisons in Lancashire reveals that the process of rationalization was not uniformly adopted throughout the country. In particular, she questions whether the 'separate system' did in fact operate in many prisons outside London, thus casting doubt both on Foucault's vision of a universal 'carceral archipelago' and Cohen's mapping of a general penal transformation (as in Table 4.1). Similarly, Spierenburg (1991) is sceptical of the idea that the modern prison dramatically emerged in a moment of rapid transformation in and around 1800. He prefers to see a more protracted evolution in which old and new practices co-existed for much of the period from 1770 to 1870. Moreover this 're-establishment of order' was also grounded in much broader shifts in social and cultural life; including *privatization* and the gradual withdrawal of social relations from public to private space; *new attitudes to the body* and a growing aversion to physical suffering; and the *changing character of the family* such that prisoners were viewed in need of quasi-patriarchal forms of discipline (Spierenburg, 1998, p.47). Ignatieff (1983), in a review of his earlier work, also acknowledges that the process of reform is never one-dimensional and cannot always be' explained in terms of a disciplinary logic. Revisionism, he argues, was flawed by adopting a position which described all social relations in the language of domination and subordination. The challenge remains to:

> find a model of historical explanation which accounts for institutional change without imputing conspiratorial rationality to a ruling class, without reducing institutional development to a formless, ad hoc adjustment to contingent crisis and without assuming a hyper-idealist, all triumphant humanitarian crusade … the problem is to develop a model that avoids these while actually providing explanation.
>
> (Ignatieff, 1983, pp.77–8)

Garland (1990) makes much the same point by arguing that the *specific* agencies, apparatuses, rules, procedures, strategies, rhetorics and representations that make up the penal complex each have their own *specific* histories and *specific* effects. Any broad theoretical model, whether Whiggish or revisionist, will tend to lose sight of such nuances through the application of predetermined structuring patterns:

> In the shaping of any penal event … a large number of conflicting forces are at work. Broad ideological ambitions may run up against immediate financial constraints, political expediency may conflict with established sensibilities, the perceived requirements of security may differ from those of morality, the professional interests of one group may be in tension with those of another, and the pursuit of any one value will generally involve the violation of several others. These swarming circumstances are only ever resolved into particular outcomes by means of the struggles, negotiations, actions and decisions which are undertaken by those involved in the making and the implementation of policy, and can only be traced by detailed historical work. There is no settled hierarchy of purposes or causal priorities which prevails at every point allowing us to describe, once and for all, the sequence of forces and considerations which 'determine' the specific forms which penality displays … Theory should be a set of interpretative tools for guiding and analysing empirical enquiry – not a substitute for it.
>
> (Garland, 1990, pp.285–6)

revision of revisionism

In this form of analysis (sometimes referred to as a 'revision of revisionism') the insights of such theorists as Foucault, Rusche and Kirkhheimer are drawn on selectively as resources, rather than adopted wholesale. They provide some of the conceptual tools necessary for identifying the processes of penal reform, but further more nuanced research into specificities as well as long term trajectories is still called for (Matthews, 1999, p.24). However, we can still assume that the process of historical interpretation can never simply rely on eclecticism. Some informed choices need to be made if we are to develop any integrated and meaningful answer to why different forms of imprisonment achieved ascendancy at particular historical moments.

ACTIVITY 4.4

Given below are six statements from various analysts of penal reform. You should be able to locate each of these as either 'Whiggish', 'liberal', 'orthodox Marxist' or 'revisionist' approaches.

statement 1

Howard's work and abiding influence were not limited to the ascertainment and exposure of evil: he proposed remedies and influenced others to work for them … he wished to bring back the forgotten notion that Houses of Correction should correct. Prisons should be sanitary and secure, moral improvement should be sought through the influence of religion and prisoners should be provided with useful work. [Through] the personal prestige of Howard with Parliament a well intentioned group of Acts was passed in which most of these ideas were embodied. (Fox, 1952)

statement 2

In the Victorian philanthropic tradition, prisoners were not the only ones whose right to be treated as human beings was made conditional on their submission to moral improvement. No attempt to raise the housing, educational, or sanitary standard of the poor was made without an accompanying attempt to colonize their minds. In this tradition, humanitarianism was inextricably linked to the practice of domination. The extension of the state's obligation to its citizens was invariably justified in terms of recasting their characters into that caricature of ascetic rectitude that the rich adopted as their self-image. (Ignatieff, 1983)

statement 3

If there is an overall political issue around the prison, it is not whether it is to be corrective or not; whether the judges, the psychiatrists or the sociologists are to exercise more power in it than the administrators or supervisors; it is not even whether we should have prison or something other than prison. At present, the problem lies rather in the steep rise in the use of these mechanisms of normalization and the wide-ranging powers which, through the proliferation of new disciplines, they bring with them. (Foucault, 1977)

statement 4

The luminaries who invented liberty also invented discipline. (Foucault, 1977)

statement 5

The disciplinary moment of the work relation coincides with the institutional moment, that is with the entrance of the employee into the factory, namely into the place where the employer forcibly organizes the factors of production. It is the same in punitive relations: the condemned (free subject) becomes subordinated subject (prisoner) on entering the penitentiary … For the worker the factory is like a prison (loss of liberty and subordination); for the inmate the prison is like a factory (work and discipline). (Melossi and Pavarini, 1981)

statement 6

Proposals that promise the most grandiose consequences often legitimate the most unsatisfactory developments. One also grows wary about taking reform programs at face value; arrangements designed for the best of motives may have disastrous results. But the difficult problem is to review these events without falling into a deep cynicism. (Rothman, 1971)

The contrast between Whig and revisionist histories should now be clear. Of key importance is that, despite their internal differences, 'revisionist' histories stand against their 'Whig' counterparts in their argument that:

■ The motives of philanthropic reformers were more complicated than a simple desire to 'do good' and to improve the conditions of imprisonment – they also, for example, were a reflection of religious zeal, Calvinist discipline and fear of the labouring poor.

■ We should place the emergence of the prison in the social and historical context of the time.

■ The emergence of the prison is related to the emergence of similar institutions of the same period.

■ We need to move beyond stated intentions and reformist visions to theories that take cognizance of the power of discourse, class relations and the state.

■ Reform was a 'success' in terms of establishing a new social order functional to the requirements of industrial capital.

In the following sections an account of penal reform from the 1830s to the early twentieth century is presented which draws selectively on the conceptual tools and modes of analysis presented earlier. Our key concern is to illustrate the multi layered, mulit-faceted and often contradictory nature of successive attempts to modernise the prison.

4 From reform to repression?

During the nineteenth century the penal system was to undergo major reforms, but the rhetoric of prisoner reformation was to collapse. The death penalty diminished in importance as an imposed penalty, the use of corporal punishment declined, public whipping was abolished in 1862, transportation was abolished in 1868 and by the 1870s the prison was established as the normal punishment for both trivial and serious offences. For most of the century, prisons were controlled by local authorities, with subsequent wide variations in regimes, costs and conditions. The movement towards central government control of the whole prison system can be traced back to the early nineteenth century, and in particular **centralization** to the appointment of inspectors in 1835, but full centralization and nationalization did not occur until the passing of the Prison Act in 1877. The control of the prisons was then passed to a Prison Commission, whose main objective was to introduce a uniform and rational regime throughout the country, based firmly on the principle of deterrence by severity of punishment rigidly and efficiently applied. The most infrequently used prisons were closed down and those remaining were refurbished to conform to prescribed standards of architectural and sanitary design. Prison warders were appointed, trained and paid by central government, issued with uniforms and subject to disciplinary procedures. The general regime of local prisons was based on the 'separate system' in which prisoners worked, ate and slept in their cells, removed from any contact with their fellow inmates. Although different architectural designs were used, most prisons conformed to that of the cellular prison buildings in which each prisoner was held in a separate cell with standard dimensions and minimal furnishings, thus ensuring ease of surveillance and control. Prison work remained generally non-productive and of a harsh nature, designed to enforce obedience and discipline rather than to teach any particular industrial skills.

These developments, at one and the same time, marked a further rationalization of the prison system, and a shift in its justificatory rhetoric from one of prisoner reformation to one of deterrence and repression. As the prison evolved as the dominant form of punishment, the already existing debates between reformers and punishers, and between religious and secular approaches, focused on the specific form that prison discipline should take. Paramount was the felt need for *certainty* and *uniformity* in punishment. Discretion and individualization were successively removed from the system. As Weiner argues: 'power was now generally seen as most legitimate and most effective when least personal, most humane when least human' (Weiner, 1990, p.105). As a result, the prison became a highly regulated and impersonal instrument to contain and control. The governor of Leicester Gaol was the first to use the crank for overtly punitive purposes, declaring that: 'if a man will not work, neither shall he eat' (*Report of the Commissioners*, 1854, p.v). The imposition of a regime of 1,800 revolutions of the crank before breakfast, 4,500 before dinner, 5,400 before supper and 2,700 after supper, reflected the Victorian obsession not only with punishment, but also systematic regulation and classification. Throughout the penal system, regimes became more and more standardized in clothing, discipline, work and architectural design as well as in diet, yet such attempts to 'break the spirit' were also capable of being justified through appeals to prisoner reformation, For example, a notice on the cell walls at Leicester County Gaol in the 1850s stated that the purpose of prison labour (i.e. the crank) was to 'encourage habits of willing and steady industry and a cheerful obedience' *(Report of the Commissioners,* 1854, p.iv).

repression

Penal servitude: a prisoner at the 'crank' in Surrey House of Correction, c.1860. As described by Hawkings (1992, p.24): 'Together with the treadmill the crank was used for prisoners sentenced to hard labour. It had the additional advantage from the prison authorities viewpoint that the prisoner was shut up in his cell. The crank was made up of a narrow iron drum mounted horizontally in a frame with a handle on one side which, when turned, caused a series of cups or scoops in the interior to revolve. At the lower part of the inside was a thick layer of sand or gravel which the cups scooped up and carried to the top of the wheel where they emptied themselves rather like a dredging machine. A dial plate fixed in front of the crank showed how many revolutions the machine had made. A man could make about 20 revolutions in a minute moving a weight of up to 12 lbs per revolution, that is 1200 revolutions per hour. It was usual to stipulate that a prisoner completed 10,000 turns per day which would take him about 8 hours and 20 minutes. Some prisoners were able to turn the crank much faster than others and to retard their efforts the gaoler could turn a screw which tightened the mechanism and rendered the crank more difficult, and therefore slower, to rotate. Hence gaolers became known as "screws"'

The Victorian obsession with classification: prison diet ordered at Somerset Quarter Sessions, 1850

DIETARIES.

The following are the amended Dietaries ordered at the Somerset Epiphany Session, 1850.

Class 1.

Convicted Prisoners confined for any Term not exceeding Seven Days.

Males.		Females.	
Breakfast—Oatmeal Gruel	1 pint.	Oatmeal Gruel	1 pint.
Dinner——Bread	1 lb.	Bread	1 lb.
Supper——Oatmeal Gruel	1 pint.	Oatmeal Gruel	1 pint.

Class 2.

Convicted Prisoners for any Term exceeding Seven Days and not exceeding Twenty-one Days.

Males.		Females.	
Breakfast—Oatmeal Gruel	1 pint.	Oatmeal Gruel	1 pint.
„ Bread	6 oz.	Bread	6 oz.
Dinner——Bread	12 oz.	Bread	6 oz.
Supper——Oatmeal Gruel	1 pint.	Oatmeal Gruel	1 pint
„ Bread	6 oz.	Bread	6 oz.

Prisoners of this class employed at hard labour, to have, in addition, 1 pint of soup per week.

Class 3.

Convicted Prisoners employed at hard labour for Terms exceeding Twenty-one Days, but not more than Six Weeks; and convicted Prisoners not employed at hard labour for Terms exceeding Twenty-one days but not more than Four Months.

Males.		Females.	
Breakfast—Oatmeal Gruel	1 pint.	Oatmeal Gruel	1 pint.
„ Bread	6 oz.	Bread	6 oz.

SUNDAY AND THURSDAY.

Dinner——Soup	1 pint.	Soup	1 pint.
„ Bread	8 oz.	Bread	6 oz.

TUESDAY AND SATURDAY.

„ Cooked Meat without Bone	3 oz.	Cooked Meat without Bone	3 oz.
„ Bread	8 oz.	Bread	6 oz.
„ Potatoes	½ lb.	Potatoes	½ lb.

MONDAY, WEDNESDAY, AND FRIDAY.

„ Bread	8 oz.	Bread	6 oz.
„ Potatoes	1 lb.	Potatoes	1 lb.
Supper——Same as Breakfast		Same as Breakfast	

Class 4.

Convicted Prisoners employed at hard labour for Terms exceeding Six Weeks but not more than Four Months; and convicted Prisoners not employed at hard labour for Terms exceeding Four Months.

Males.		Females.	
Breakfast—Oatmeal Gruel	1 pint.	Oatmeal Gruel	1 pint.
„ Bread	8 oz.	Bread	6 oz.

SUNDAY, TUESDAY, THURSDAY, AND SATURDAY.

Dinner——Cooked Meat without Bone	3 oz.	Cooked Meat without Bone	3 oz.
„ Potatoes	½ lb.	Potatoes	½ lb.
„ Bread	8 oz.	Bread	6 oz.

MONDAY, WEDNESDAY, AND FRIDAY.

„ Soup	1 pint.	Soup	1 pint.
„ Bread	8 oz.	Bread	6 oz.
Supper——Same as Breakfast		Same as Breakfast	

The Victorian obsession with classification: prison diet ordered at Somerset Quarter Sessions, 1850

In such an environment, notions of reformation collapsed into notions of deterrence: 'That pain was required for reformation was rarely questioned ... whether they inclined to stress deterrence or reformation, almost all early and mid-Victorians thought the latter should be as painful as the former' (Weiner, 1990, p.111). As the Earl of Chichester, appointed to superintend Pentonville, put it in 1856:

> Human nature is so constituted that when a man had been long addicted to a life of crime or sensual indulgence it requires a severe affliction to force him to reflect – he must be providentially deprived of those sources of animal pleasure and excitement which have hitherto enabled him to silence his conscience and to shut out from his mind all thoughts of the future – there must be something external to afflict, to break down his spirit, some bodily suffering or distress of mind, before the still small voice will be heard and the man brought to himself.
>
> (Earl of Chichester, quoted in Ignatieff, 1978, p.199)

Class 5.

Convicted Prisoners employed at hard labour for Terms exceeding Four Months.

Males. Females.

SUNDAY, TUESDAY, THURSDAY, AND SATURDAY.

	Males		Females	
Breakfast—Oatmeal Gruel	1 pint.	Oatmeal Gruel	1 pint.
„ Bread	8 oz.	Bread	6 oz.
Dinner—Cooked Meat without Bone	4 oz.	Cooked Meat without Bone	3 oz.
„ Potatoes	1 lb.	Potatoes	½ lb.
„ Bread	6 oz.	Bread	6 oz.

MONDAY, WEDNESDAY, AND FRIDAY.

	Males		Females	
Breakfast—Cocoa	1 pint.	Cocoa	1 pint.
made of ⅜ oz. of Flaked Cocoa or Cocoa Nibs, sweetened with ⅜ oz. of Molasses or Sugar		made of ⅜ oz. of Flaked Cocoa or Cocoa Nibs, sweetened with ⅜ oz. of Molasses or Sugar	
„ Bread	8 oz.	Bread	6 oz.
Dinner—Soup	1 pint.	Soup	1 pint.
„ Potatoes	1 lb.	Potatoes	½ lb.
„ Bread	6 oz.	Bread	6 oz.
Supper—Oatmeal Gruel	1 pint.	Oatmeal Gruel	1 pint.
„ Bread	8 oz.	Bread	6 oz.

Class 6.

Prisoners sentenced by Court to Solitary Confinement.

Males. Females.

The ordinary Diet of their respective Classes. The ordinary Diet of their respective Classes.

Class 7.

Prisoners for examination, before Trial, and Misdemeanants of the first Division, who do not maintain themselves.

Males. Females.

The same as Class 4. The same as Class 4.

Class 8.

Destitute Debtors.

Males. Females.

The same as Class 4. The same as Class 4.

Class 9.

Prisoners under Punishment for Prison offences, for Terms not exceeding Three Days.

1 lb. of Bread per diem.

Prisoners in close confinement for Prison offences under the provision of the 42nd section of the Gaol Act.

	Males		Females	
Breakfast—Gruel	1 pint.	Gruel	1 pint.
„ Bread	8 oz.	Bread	6 oz.
Dinner—Bread	8 oz.	Bread	6 oz.
Supper—Gruel	1 pint.	Gruel	1 pint.
„ Bread	8 oz.	Bread	6 oz.

Note.—The Soup to contain, per pint, 3 ounces of cooked Meat without Bone, 3 ounces of Potatoes, 1 ounce of Barley, Rice, or Oatmeal, and 1 ounce of Onions or Leeks with pepper and salt. The Gruel to contain 2 ounces of Oatmeal per pint. The Gruel on alternate days to be sweetened with ⅜ oz. of molasses or sugar, and seasoned with salt. In seasons when the potato crop has failed, 4 ounces of split peas made into a pudding, may be occasionally substituted: but the change must not be made more than *twice* in each week.—Boys under 14 years of age to be placed on the same diet as females.

The foregoing Dietary having been submitted to me, I hereby certify the same as proper to be adopted in the Gaols for the County of Somerset.

(Signed)

Whitehall, 31st January, 1850. G. GREY.

From Wason's Albion Printing Office, Shepton Mallet.

The issue came to a head in the 1860s with the ending of transportation to Australia. For the first time the authorities were faced with the task of administering long-term sentences in the rapidly growing number of convict prisons. At the end of their sentence, convicts were released on a ticket of leave or parole. In 1853 the first of such prisoners were released amidst much public panic.

With the outbreak of a spate of robberies in London in 1862, in which a garrotte was used to immobilize the victim, it was the parole system in particular, and philosophies of reformation in general, that were subject to sustained critique (Davis, 1980; **Sharpe, 2001**). In 1863 the Carnarvon Committee, set up to consider the relative merits of deterrence and reformation, came down firmly in favour of the former, reporting that severe labour 'is the chief means of exercising a deterrent effect' and that this was to be achieved through increased use of the crank and treadmill rather than by 'industrial occupation' (Forsythe, 1987, p.158). Indeed, the

Committee heard that the Leicester system of 'no work, no food' based on crank labour in separate cells was a powerful deterrent and ought to be widely followed, despite the fact that prison inspectors in 1854 had condemned the practice as 'unwarranted by the Law of England' (*Report of the Commissioners*, 1854, p.v). The Earl of Carnarvon himself had argued in the House of Lords that: 'in a large proportion of the gaols and houses of correction in the kingdom there was an insufficiency of penal discipline' and that:

> it was perfectly idle to put into operation all the elaborate machinery provided in gaols for the instruction and reformation of prisoners, ideas which were fanciful theories likely to invite the criminal to commit crimes in the sure knowledge that there merely awaited him a good diet, warm bed and light, often voluntary, labour.
>
> (Eafl of Carnarvon, quoted in Forsythe, 1987, p.145)

Instead, Carnarvon was impressed by the view that:

> the large majority of criminals were low and brutish 'mainly swayed by self gratification and animal appetite'. It followed that such brutes must be managed physically: 'the enforcement of continuous labour, which the true criminal abhors, and … an uninviting diet, which is unquestionably the most odious penalty in his eyes'. Self gratifying instincts should be foiled by withholding all indulgences and diversions such as secular books, slates, hammocks and the like 'which are frequently awarded with too prodigal and indiscriminate a hand'. By taking a supposedly middle course between leniency and severity – 'a discipline which a low and sensual nature understands and dreads' – it would be possible to achieve individual deterrence of some kind by imparting 'a lively impression of the irksome and even painful discomfort which is an inseparable part of prison life'.
>
> (quoted phrases from Earl of Carnarvon, 1864, in McConville, 1995, p.55)

These views were subsequently embodied in the 1865 Prison Act which implemented by law the principle of deterrence throughout the penal system. The Act formally abolished the distinction between gaols and houses of correction and reinforced the 'separate system' in a 'new' institution to be known as a *prison*:

> In a prison where criminal prisoners are confined, such prisoners shall be prevented from holding any communication with each other, either by … being kept in a separate cell by day and by night except when at chapel or exercise, or by every prisoner being confined by night in his cell and being subjected to such superintendence during the day as will prevent his communicating with any other prisoner.
>
> (Prison Act, 1865: 28 & 29 Vict., c.126)

The uniform application of Carnarvon's principles of deterrence and austerity was also not confined to the prisons of England and Wales. Lowe and McLaughlin (1993) suggest that mid nineteenth-century colonial administrators came to believe that they could and should control, guide and determine colonial prison regimes – from the Far East to the West Indies – through the adoption of the same rules and regulations that now operated in England. Though as Salvatore and Aguirre (1996) warn in their Latin American analysis, such a hegemony was never complete. The adoption of the penitentiary was uneven and sometimes ambivalent. 'Scientific' classification and ordering of prisoner populations may have been adopted worldwide, but it was also adapted to local conditions and served different purposes. In Latin America, for example, prison reform was also part of a social imaginary of emergent nation states and their integration into global economic markets.

In England for the thirty years following the 1865 Prison Act penal regimes in local prisons (financed by local taxes) and convict prisons (financed by central government) were made as uniform and austere as possible (McConville, 1998, p.131). The twin practices of separate confinement and hard (unproductive) labour were their hallmarks. Significantly, and in stark contrast to the 1830s, religion and the 'benefits' of moral instruction were conspicuous absences in the new penal discourse. In order to increase the punitive possibilities of prison, the Carnarvon Committee also recommended that dietary scales be lowered, that hammocks be replaced by hard wooden planks and that the daily time allowed for sleep be reduced to 8 hours. Although these measures were not given the force of law, McConville (1981, p.360) notes that, in all likelihood, they were widely practised given that local magistrates now had a mandatory duty to ensure that centrally determined modes of discipline were maintained. As Sim (1990, p.39) records, breaches of discipline were met with a 'further round of disciplinary activity' involving the use of shackles, manacles, chains, flogging, straitjackets and, in some cases, further reductions in diet. Thus he argues that prison doctors and surgeons were also drawn into the disciplinary network, with one doctor quoted as arguing that low diet:

> though it always seemed to me a more or less barbarous and senseless proceeding to apply to human beings, was nevertheless very necessary with unruly prisoners. I know of nothing approaching a scientific excuse for its use, except the principle on which a horse has his oats reduced in order to tame his spirit.
>
> (quoted in Sim, 1990, p.42)

The decline of reformation as a primary penal purpose was underlined by the appointment of Edmund Du Cane as chairman of the Prison Commission from 1877 to 1895. Du Cane argued that the purpose of imprisonment was to provide a *general* deterrence, rather than the deterrence or reformation of particular individuals. Thus in the convict prisons: 'A sentence of penal servitude is ... applied on exactly the same system to every person subjected to it. The previous career and character of the prisoner makes no difference in the punishment to which he is subjected' (Du Cane, 1885, p.155). With this absence of individualization, the possibility of prisoner reformation was given a low, or no, priority. By the 1870s the reformatory vision and zeal of evangelists and philanthropists had been effectively excluded from the penal system (see Forsythe, 1987). As Fox laments: 'for death itself, the system had substituted a living death' (Fox, 1952, p.51). The Victorian prison did not entertain notions of treatment. Whilst prisoners were classified and categorized according to sex, age, conviction and sentence length, their individuality was not recognized:

> Based upon puritan assumptions about human motivation and personal responsibility, Victorian prison policy was inspired by a famous House of Lords Committee of 1863 which concluded that they, the members of the committee, did *not* consider: that the moral reformation of the offenders holds the primary place in the prison system; that mere industrial employment without wages is a sufficient punishment for many crimes; that punishment in itself is morally prejudicial to the criminal and useless to society, or that it is desirable to abolish both the crank and treadwheel as soon as possible.
>
> (Thomas and Pooley, 1980, pp.22–3)

Austin Bidwell, sentenced to life imprisonment for fraud, described his experience at Chatham Convict Prison:

An English prison is a vast machine in which a man counts for just nothing at all. He is to the establishment what a bale of merchandise is to a merchant's warehouse. The prison does not look on him as a man at all. He is merely an object which must move in a certain rut and occupy a certain niche provided for it. There is no room for the smallest sentiment. The vast machine of which he is an item keeps undisturbed on its course. Move with it and all is well. Resist and you will be crushed as inevitably as the man who plants himself on the railroad track when the express is coming. Without passion, without prejudice, but also without pity and without remorse the machine crushes and passes on. The dead man is carried to his grave and in ten minutes is as much forgotten as though he never existed.

(Bidwell, 1895, quoted in Priestley, 1985, p.229)

5   From repression to rehabilitation?

Between 1877 (when prison administration was centralized) and 1895 (the retirement of Du Cane as chairman of the Prison Commission) the Victorian obsession with certainty, severity and systematic uniformity reached its fullest expression. Yet even in these years it was becoming apparent that the aim of subjecting *all* prisoners to the same uniform discipline was self-defeating. Weiner argues that: 'the utilitarian drive toward rationalization ultimately worked against its own universalist principles' (Weiner, 1990, pp.308–9). This was particularly the case when the commitment to classifying prisoners continually threw up new and exceptional categories which did not seem to fit the criminal stereotype for which the regime of punitive deterrence had been designed.

Most notable was the case of the juvenile prisoner. As early as the 1820s prison inspectors were beginning to conclude that it was impractical to subject juveniles to the same penal regimes as those designed for adults. Uppermost in their minds was the belief that imprisonment with adults only served to strengthen the criminal habits of the young. As a result, a separate juvenile prison was established at Parkhurst in 1838 and by 1854 reformatory schools (previously developed on an *ad hoc* voluntary basis) were given legal recognition. As May (1973, p.12) argues, it was through such refinements in prisoner classification that the categories of *juvenile delinquent* and *young offender* were first established.

reformation

An influential body of opinion from lawyers, magistrates, ministers of religion and prison administrators argued that children could not be held fully responsible for their misconduct and that their criminality could be accounted for more by a lack of moral and religious education than by any innate evil or self-volition – they needed reformation rather than punishment. Mary Carpenter, the daughter of a Unitarian minister, was pivotal in the reformatory movement in which she sought to replace penal incarceration for the young with detention in educational schools and home-like reformatories. She was a staunch critic of the Parkhurst regime, arguing that its punitive control 'attempted to fashion children into machines through iron discipline instead of self acting beings' (Carpenter, 1851, p.321). The use of leg-irons, distinctive prison dress and inadequate diet were all condemned. Delinquent children, she claimed, needed to be returned to a family environment in which they could be 'gradually restored to the true position of childhood' (Carpenter, 1853, p.298). By 1858 over 50 reformatory schools had been established, mainly through voluntary effort, and Parkhurst was closed for juveniles in 1863.

However, state support for the schools was not won without opposition. A strong lobby persisted in arguing that all individuals, regardless of age, should be held responsible for their actions and that all should remain equal in the eyes of the law. Carpenter's vision was thus subject to legislative compromise. Before entering a reformatory, a prison sentence of at least 14 days had to be served. Moreover, the Youthful Offenders Act 1854 was only permissive and magistrates could continue to send juveniles to prison if they so decided. The reformatory system (which was to evolve first into the system of approved schools and subsequently into childrens homes in the twentieth century) was grafted on to existing penal institutions and did not replace them. For much of the century the presence of the reformatories did not preclude the committal of children to prison for the most petty of offences including stealing apples, trespassing in fields and vagrancy (Priestley, 1985, pp.55–6). In addition, the regimes in the reformatories were far from standardized on any domestic model. Whilst some schoolwork and religious instruction was usually present, the child's day consisted, in the main, of gruelling work: digging the land to convert the criminal through 'the sweat of his brow' (Radzinowicz and Hood, 1990, p.191). Court records from the 1880s show that reformatories were also used for the most trivial of offences:

> Patrick McGuiness, age 12, stealing one bottle of beer, no previous convictions, committed to one calendar month imprisonment and five years Reformatory.

> John Jones, age 12, stealing three pairs of boots, no previous convictions, committed to 21 days hard labour and four years Reformatory.

> William Folly, age 12, stealing 9d from the person, one previous conviction, committed to 14 days imprisonment and five years Reformatory.
> (quoted in Radzinowicz and Hood, 1990, pp.184–5)

Thus, whilst it would be misleading to view the reformatories as progressive institutions with liberal regimes, they nevertheless began the process of providing for 'exceptional' categories and in establishing alternative institutions to those of the 'Victorian orthodoxy'.

For most of the nineteenth century penal regimes for men and women were similar, even though women were gradually to be allocated to separate wings or to separate prisons (the first being Brixton in 1853). However, at the same time scores of reformatories and refuges were created expressly for the purpose of 'saving' girls and young women. Their work in these institutions was chiefly designed to train them to fill the 'enormous demand for household servants' (Dobash *et al.*, 1986, p.74). Women continued to be committed to prison at the same rate per conviction as men, but, due to reductions in their length of sentence, the female proportion of the local prison population fell from 22 per cent in 1870 to 16.5 per cent in 1895; in convict prisons from 14 per cent to 6.75 per cent (Weiner, 1990, p.309). Prison populations were thus also becoming more markedly male. Other groups which began to demand specific consideration were political prisoners (notably the Irish Nationalists), middle-class or 'gentleman' prisoners (usually imprisoned for embezzlement) and those with learning disabilities. All of these 'exceptions' put the case that they be considered as unfit for (and in some cases undeserving of) the full rigours of penal discipline.

By 1890 the efficacy of Du Cane's repressive regime was being increasingly called into question by influential modernizing elites. Debate centred on two issues: the question of short sentences and the problem of recidivism (Garland, 1985, p.61). In England the average duration of all prison sentences was 28 days; in Scotland it was 15 days. This practice of using prison as a first resort and for minor offences became increasingly criticized for its high financial costs, its overcrowding and the fear of 'needless' contamination of young offenders by older prisoners. Recidivism – reported as high as 78 per cent for simple larceny – pointed to the failure of imprisonment itself, in particular its much toted ability to deter offenders: 'Prison was seen to produce that which it should prevent, to manufacture delinquents instead of mending them' (Garland, 1985, p.62). These practical issues merged with a growing reassessment of the state's role in the disciplining and regulation of the working classes to stimulate the appointment of a Departmental Committee of Inquiry to review the principles of the whole penal realm.

The resulting recommendations contained in the 1895 Gladstone Report mark another key transformation in British penal policy. Criticizing existing regimes for 'crushing self-respect' and 'starving all moral instinct', the report **rehabilitation** argued that reformation should coexist with deterrence and that rehabilitation should be given priority (see Extract 4.3).

In place of inflexible and punitive methods of control, Gladstone proposed more scientific methods of *treatment*. First offenders, juveniles, habitual criminals, drunkards, the 'weak-minded', female prisoners with children and the unconvicted, it was argued, should be classified separately and treated according to their individual natures and needs. In 1898 the prison commissioners for the first time defined the purpose of imprisonment as 'the humanization of the individual' (Weiner, 1990, p.378). Such a policy clearly marked a radical break with the past. Sir Evelyn Ruggles-Brise, chairman of the Prison Commission from 1895 to 1921, put the position clearly enough when he insisted that: 'each man convicted of crime is to be regarded as an individual, as a separate entity of morality, who by the application of influences, of discipline, labour, education, moral and religious, backed up on discharge by a well-organized system of patronage is capable of reinstatement in civic life' (Ruggles-Brise, 1911, quoted in Garland, 1985, p.26). Similarly, the editor of the *Journal of Mental Science* argued that: 'it is now recognized that primitive measures alone are not corrective, and effective reformation of criminals can only be attained by making our prisons true schools and moral hospitals' (quoted in Weiner, 1990, p.378). The contrast with Du Cane's objective, some 25 years earlier, could not have been more stark. It resurrected the notion that confinement should do more than punish and once more set in train a series of debates concerning the proper purpose of imprisonment. The issue remains, though, of how far such policy was put into practice. Forsythe, for example, argues that often the new projects fell short of the claims made for them. In particular, the local and convict prisons 'clung tenaciously to the concepts of measured punishment, moral culpability, limited deterrence and uniformly administered discipline' (Forsythe, 1991, p.239). The process of reform was thus often slow and imperceptible.

Extract 4.3 Departmental Committee on Prisons: 'The Gladstone Report'

Character of Necessary Changes.

25. The next consideration is the general direction of any changes which the course of our examination into the facts make us think necessary or advisable. Sir Godfrey Lushington thus impressively summed up the influences under the present system unfavourable to reformation: " I regard as unfavourable to reformation the status " of a prisoner throughout his whole career; the crushing of self-respect, the starving " of all moral instinct he may possess, the absence of all opportunity to do or receive a " kindness, the continual association with none but criminals, and that only as a separate " item amongst other items also separate; the forced labour, and the denial of all " liberty. I believe the true mode of reforming a man or restoring him to society is " exactly in the opposite direction of all these ; but, of course, this is a mere idea. It " is quite impracticable in a prison. In fact the unfavourable features I have men- " tioned are inseparable from prison life." As a broad description of prison life we think this description is accurate; we do not agree that all of these unfavourable features are irremovable. Already in many respects and in individual cases they have been modified, and we believe that this modification can be carried much further in the direction of the treatment adopted and practised by the best of the existing reformatories. We think that the system should be made more elastic, more capable of being adopted to the special cases of individual prisoners; that prison discipline and treatment should be more effectually designed to maintain, stimulate, or awaken the higher susceptibilities of prisoners, to develop their moral instincts, to train them in orderly and industrial habits, and whenever possible to turn them out of prison better men and women, both physically and morally, than when they came in. Crime, its causes and treatment, has been the subject of much profound and scientific inquiry. Many of the problems it presents are practically at the present time insoluble. It may be true that some criminals are irreclaimable, just as some diseases are incurable, and in such cases it is not unreasonable to acquiesce in the theory that criminality is a disease, and the result of physical imperfection. But criminal anthropology as a science is in an embryo stage, and while scientific and more particularly medical observation and experience are of the most essential value in guiding opinion on the whole subject, it would be a loss of time to search for a perfect system in learned but conflicting theories, when so much can be done by the recognition of the plain fact that the great majority of prisoners are ordinary men and women amenable, more or less, to all those influences which affect persons outside.

26. From this point of view it is interesting to notice that the Royal Commission of 1879 acquiesced in the objection to the penal servitude system made on the ground that " it not only fails to reform offenders, but in the case of the less " hardened criminals, and especially of first offenders, produces a deteriorating effect " from the indiscriminate association of all classes of convicts in the public works." It is true that this referred to convict prisons only, and that in 1882 the star class of first offenders was instituted to meet the views of the Royal Commission. But we think for reasons which we shall subsequently proceed to state that the general prison system is still open to this reproach. Our inquiry has led us to think that the evils attributed to contamination have been exaggerated so far as male criminals are concerned. But grave evils are liable to occur from surreptitious communications among the women prisoners, and every care should be taken to keep them from being crowded together in chapel. Leaving this point aside for the present, we call attention to the finding of the Royal Commission in 1879, that the convict system not only failed to reform offenders, but on the less hardened, and especially the first offenders, it produced a deteriorating effect. The failure is yet to be found in local as well as convict prisons, but we are not inclined to attribute it to direct contamination by association as a primary cause of mischief.

Margin references: 11,482.
116, 8687, 9438.
Report, par. 72.

(Departmental Committee on Prisons, 1895, p.8)

Nevertheless, from 1900 onwards a number of radical changes were made to the standard prison regime. Unproductive labour was officially abandoned, to be replaced by prison industries and work considered 'useful'. The 'separate system' was gradually eroded, so that prisoners could work in association. Educational facilities were increased and improved. Internal discipline was maintained through a reward/punishment system related to the introduction of remission. 'Specialists', such as psychologists, were appointed and prisoner categorization was extended. For juveniles, the Borstal system, largely derived from American experience, was introduced. A commitment to reformation became enshrined in the Prison Rule that stipulated that the purpose of imprisonment was to encourage prisoners to 'lead a good and useful life' (this became Prison Rule 6 in 1949 and was elevated to Prison Rule 1 in 1964).

However, as Garland (1985) notes, the most radical reforms of this period took place outside the prison system. It is in the introduction of a probation service, alternatives to imprisonment and the construction of specialist institutions (such as the Borstal where principles of rehabilitation were initiated) where Garland sees the major transformations that mark the beginning of current practice. As a result, rather than limit discussion to prison reform, he refers to **penality** wider developments in a whole realm of penality. Thus he is able to claim that:

> the prison was decentred, shifted from its position as the central and predominant sanction to become one institution among many in an extended grid of penal sanctions. Of course it continued to be of major importance, but it was now deployed in a different manner, for a narrower section of the criminal population and often as a back up sanction for other institutions, rather than the place of first resort.
>
> (Garland, 1985, p.23)

These external changes led to corresponding changes in the internal prison population. The numbers of the inebriate, the 'weak-minded', first offenders and juveniles were reduced, whilst the number of routine recidivists (under the auspices of preventive detention) and more serious offenders increased. From a daily average of 17,000 prisoners in 1900, the prison and Borstal population fell to 11,000 by 1936.

In this sense the task of reforming the prison population grew more difficult, but it was a task that was addressed by a proliferation of welfare, treatment and rehabilitative programmes. Garland (1985) accounts for this shift with reference to the impact of a fundamental change in official discourses of penality which came to reflect a developing *positivist* notion of behaviour and social order. No longer were all inmates to be treated equally – they were to be differentiated according to the judgements of such non-judicial professionals as probation officers, welfare workers, doctors, psychiatrists and psychologists. They were to be pitied, cared for and reclaimed, rather than reviled. Their criminality was no longer considered a matter of self-volition, but thought to be instigated by a number of psychological, physiological and environmental conditions that were effectively out of each individual's control. There was a marked shift of attention away from simply punishing a criminal *act* to identifying the needs and inadequacies of the *offender* (Matthews, 1999, p.22). Within this new discourse it made no sense merely to punish; the offender should also be treated and society protected (McConville, 1998, p.140). Or as Salvatore and Aguirre (1996, p.21) rather more critically put it, a positivist. quasi-medical discourse turned 'the prison into a clinic or laboratory, inmates into patients and the working poor into the endangered population of a disease called crime'.

ACTIVITY 4.5

As a result of such developments, Garland (1985, p.31) has argued that the precise origins of the modern prison lie in the turn of this century and not with Howard's reforms of the late eighteenth century. How far would you agree?

6   Conclusion: competing histories

It is reasonably straightforward to catalogue key moments of reform and to be tempted into 'reading' this history as one of a developing (albeit faltering and gradual) humanitarian approach to those imprisoned (see Table 4.2 which would appear to support such a reading). At one level there appears to be some truth to this claim. For example, the use of capital punishment reduced from 33 per 1,000 offenders sentenced for indictable offences in 1836 to 0.4 per 1,000 in 1912 (Radzinowicz and Hood, 1990, p.777). The death penalty though was not repealed until 1965 and it remains an important, but often neglected, subtext in the analysis of systems of punishment throughout this period. The logic of a continually progressive linear improvement is also far from easy to sustain. The new prisons of the early nineteenth century may be viewed as preferential to the Bloody Code, but the solitary confinement and regimes of hard unproductive labour may also be viewed as less 'humanitarian' than the productive labour regimes of the houses of correction. Is punishment that is aimed at the mind any more rational or beneficial than punishment that is aimed at the body? Similarly, the repressive regimes of the mid nineteenth century can be viewed not as some historical anomaly, but as a logical extension of the earlier ideas of reformation. The treatment programmes of the early twentieth century appear to be a more clear-cut example of humanitarianism, but if we are to follow the arguments of Foucault, they *penetrated* rather than overturned the primary rationale of deterrence. They were simply added on to a system whose purpose remained primarily punitive. Indeed preventive detention directed at the 'habitual offender' significantly increased sentence length such that people were punished not simply for what they had done, but because of who they were. Notions of rehabilitation also acted to expand the 'carceral archipelago', extending the logic of disciplinary control out of the prisons and into the rest of society.

Table 4.2   Key dates in the history of imprisonment

1556	The first Bridewell opened in the City of London.
1717	The Transportation Act provided for transportation to the American Colonies.
1776	The hulks were introduced.
1779	The Penitentiary Act included proposals for improved diet and paid labour in prisons.
1783	Public hangings moved from Tyburn to Newgate prison.
1787	The first fleet of convicts set out for Botany Bay.
1823	The Gaol Act imposed new systems of classification involving the separation of male and female prisoners.
1835	The Penal Servitude Act was passed under which women were to be governed by the same rules and regulations as applied to male prisoners.
1838	A separate juvenile prison was established in Parkhurst.
1840	Transportation to New South Wales ended.
1842	Pentonville prison in London opened.
1853	A separate wing for women prisoners was established at Brixton.
1857	The last prison hulk taken out of service.
1861	The Whipping Act abolished whipping for virtually all offences.
1863	The Carnarvon Committee was appointed to re-examine discipline in local jails.
1865	The Prison Act formally amalgamated the jail and the house of correction.
1867	Transportation ended.
1868	Public ceremonies of execution ceased.
1877	The Prison Act transferred control of local jails to central government.
1895	The Gladstone Committee on Prisons reported.
1898	The Prison Act introduced new categories of imprisonment based on the characteristics of the offender.
1901	A Borstal scheme was established in Rochester prison.
1907	The Probation Officers Act created the professional probation officer.
1908	The Children's Act created a separate system of juvenile justice.

Source: Matthews, 1999, p.25

From Cohen (1985, pp.15–30) we can view the literature of penal reform as offering four competing versions of history:

1   *Uneven progress* – reform is generated by benevolence and philanthropy. Mistakes may be made, but in the course of time, with goodwill and sufficient resources, the system is capable of being improved through good intentions (the Whig version).

2   *Good (but complicated) intentions but with disastrous consequences* – reform is not a matter of good intentions occasionally going wrong, but of continual failure. None of the reformist visions turned out as intended; the rhetoric of benevolence served to support a long discredited system by deflecting criticism and justifying 'more of the same' (the disillusioned liberal version).

3   *Discipline* – the rhetoric of reform always masks its real intentions of constructing a repressed and compliant labour force for capitalist exploitation (the orthodox Marxist version).

4   *Mystification* – reform was not a failure for its true rationale of subjugating populations to coercive discipline was never formally stated. In this sense reform was and continues to be a success. More and more people are drawn into a carceral network, both within and outside of the prison walls (the revisionist version).

These four 'visions' invite us to 'read' the history of the prison in completely different ways. It is not a matter of which, if any, are 'correct'. All four open windows for a full appreciation of the contradictions, inconsistencies and complexities of the development of systems of punishment that are today so often taken for granted (but whose rationale remains far from clear: see Chapter 5). Above all, as our summary of these histories of the nineteenth century has shown, the prison (and other forms of punishment) can be made to do different things at different times or numerous things all at the same time. Expectations of its purpose shift between coercion, custody, punishment, deterrence, repression, reformation, therapeutic welfare, prevention and rehabilitation (and any combination of these), depending on socio-political circumstance and historical contingency. But the questions of 'why prison?' and 'what constitutes penal progress?' remain vexed. Notably, it is such questions that politicians and penal administrators in the late twentieth and early twenty-first centuries have become less willing to ask.

Review questions

■   To what extent were the houses of correction the first modern system of imprisonment?

■   How far can the discipline of the penitentiary and the post-1860 repressive practices throughout the prison system be considered a success or failure?

■   What are the dangers in accounting for the expansion of the prison as simply a response to increases in crime and disorder?

■   What advantages do revisionist histories hold over Whig histories in accounting for penal reform?

■   What is the purpose of the prison?

Further reading

The three most thorough empirical accounts of Victorian penal reform can be found in Radzinowicz and Hood (1990) and McConville (1981, 1995). The edited collection by Morris and Rothman (1998) explores many of the perennial debates about penal purpose in various jurisdictions. A reformist understanding of this history is provided by Forsythe (1987, 1991), while Ignatieff (1978) and **Foucault (1977)** offer (differing) revisionist interpretations. Weiner (1990) attempts some synthesis of the two positions, whilst Garland (1990) gives the debate a much needed theoretical underpinning, at the same time arguing for 'integrated and pluralistic interpretations'. Meanwhile, Priestley's (1985) 'collective biography' is invaluable in revealing how Victorian 'total institutions' were experienced by prisoners themselves.

This chapter draws unashamedly on the framework first developed by Cohen (1985, Chapter 1). Students coming afresh to this area will be well served by beginning their study here.

References

Beccaria, C. (1963) *On Crimes and Punishments*, **New York, Bobbs-Merrill. (First published in 1764.) (Extract reprinted in Muncie** *et al.*, **1996.)**

Carpenter, M. (1851) *Reformatory Schools for the Children of the Perishing and Dangerous Classes and for Juvenile Offenders*, London, Gilpin.

Carpenter, M. (1853) *Juvenile Delinquents: Their Condition and Treatment*, London, Cash.

Cohen, S. (1985) *Visions of Social Control: Crime, Punishment and Classification*, Cambridge, Polity.

Davis, J. (1980) 'The London garotting panic of 1862', in Gatrell, V., Lenman, B. and Parker, G. (eds) *Crime and the Law*, London, Europa.

Delacy, M. (1986) *Prison Reform in Lancashire 1700–1850*, Manchester, Manchester University Press.

Departmental Committee on Prisons (1895) *Report from the Departmental Committee on Prisons* (The Gladstone Report), in *Reports from the Commissioner, Inspectors and Others: 1895*, House of Commons Parliamentary Papers.

Dobash, R.P., Dobash, R.E. and Gutteridge, S. (1986) *The Imprisonment of Women*, Oxford, Blackwell.

Du Cane, E.F. (1885) *The Punishment and Prevention of Crime*, London, Macmillan.

Forsythe, W.J. (1987) *The Reform of Prisoners 1830–1900*, London, Croom Helm.

Forsythe, W.J. (1989) 'Privatisation and British prisons – past and future', *Prison Service Journal*, January, pp.35–7.

Forsythe, W.J. (1991) *Penal Discipline, Reformatory Projects and the English Prison Commission 1895–1939*, Exeter, University of Exeter.

Foucault, M. (1977) *Discipline and Punish: The Birth of the Prison* **(trans. Alan Sheridan), London, Allen Lane. (Extract reprinted as 'The carceral' in Muncie** *et al.***, 1996.)**

Fox, L. (1952) *The English Prison and Borstal Systems*, London, Routledge.

Garland, D. (1985) Punishment and Welfare: A History of Penal Strategies, Aldershot, Gower.

Garland, D. (1990) *Punishment and Modern Society: A Study in Social Theory*, Oxford, Oxford University Press.

Gibson, J. (1971) *John Howard and Elisabeth Fry*, London, Methuen.

Harding, C., Hines, B., Ireland, R. and Rawlings, P. (1985) *Imprisonment in England and Wales: A Concise History*, London, Croom Helm.

Hawkings, D.T. (1992) *Criminal Ancestors: A Guide to Historical Criminal Records in England and Wales*, Stroud, Alan Sutton.

Hogg, R. (1979) 'Imprisonment and society under early British capitalism', *Crime and Social Justice,* no.12, pp.4–17.

Howard, J. (1929) *The State of the Prisons*, London, Dent. (First published in 1777.)

Ignatieff, M. (1978) *A Just Measure of Pain: The Penitentiary in the Industrial Revolution*, London, Macmillan.

Ignatieff, M. (1983) 'State, civil society and total institutions: a critique of recent social histories of punishment', in Cohen, S. and Scull, A. (eds) *Social Control and the State*, London, Martin Robertson.

Krebs, A. (1978) 'John Howard's influence on the prison system in Europe', in Freeman, J. (ed.) *Prisons: Past and Future*, London, Heinemann.

Lowe, K. and McLaughlin, E. (1993) 'An Eldorado of riches and a place of unpunished crime: the politics of penal reform in Hong Kong 1877–1882', *Criminal Justice History: An International Annual Review*, vol.14, pp.57–91.

McConville, S. (1981) *A History of Prison Administration, Vol.1, 1750–1877*, London, Routledge.

McConville, S. (1995) *English Local Prisons 1860–1900: Next Only to Death*, London, Routledge.

McConville, S. (1998) 'The Victorian Prison: England, 1865–1965' in Morris and Rothman 1998 (eds).

Mannheim, H. (1939) *The Dilemma of Penal Reform*, London, Allen and Unwin.

Matthews, R. (1999) *Doing time: An Introduction to the Sociology of Imprisonment*, Basingstoke, Macmillan.

May, M. (1973) 'Innocence and experience: the evolution of the concept of juvenile delinquency in the mid-nineteenth century', *Victorian Studies*, vol.17, no.1, pp.7–29.

Melossi, D. (1981) 'Creation of the modern prison in England and Europe (1550–1850)', in Melossi and Pavarini (1981).

Melossi, D. and Pavarini, M. (1981) *The Prison and the Factory: Origins of the Penitentiary System,* London, Macmillan.

Morgan, R. (1977) 'Divine philanthropy: John Howard reconsidered', *History*, vol.62, pp.388–410.

Morris, N. and Rothman, D.J. (eds) (1998) *The Oxford History of the Prison*, Oxford, Oxford University Press.

Morrison, W. (1996) 'Modernity, Imprisonment and Social Solidarity' in Matthews, R. and Francis, P. (eds) *Prisons 2000*, London, Macmillan.

Muncie, J., McLaughlin, E. and Langan, M. (eds) (1996) *Criminological Perspectives: A Reader*, London, Sage in association with The Open University.

Open University (1987) *Law and Disorder: Histories of Crime and Justice*, in D310 *Crime, Justice and Society*, Block 2, Milton Keynes, The Open University.

Open University (1992) *Prisons and Penal Systems*, in D803 *Doing Prison Research*, Part 1, Milton Keynes, The Open University.

Peters, E.M. (1998) 'Prison before the Prison' in Morris and Rothman 1998 (eds).

Pisciotta, A.W. (1981) 'Corrections, society and social control in America', in *Criminal Justice History*, vol.2, pp.109–30.

Piven, F. and Cloward, R. (1972) *Regulating the Poor: The Functions of Public Welfare*, London, Tavistock.

Priestley, P. (1985) *Victorian Prison Lives*, London, Methuen.

Pugh, R.B. (1968) *Imprisonment in Mediaeval England*, Cambridge, Cambridge University Press.

Radzinowicz, L. (1978) 'John Howard', in Freeman, J. (ed.) *Prisons: Past and Future*, London, Heinemann.

Radzinowicz, L. and Hood, R. (1990) *The Emergence of Penal Policy*, vol.5 of *A History of English Criminal Law*, Oxford, Clarendon.

Ramsay, M. (1977) 'John Howard and the discovery of the prison', *Howard Journal*, vol.16, pp.1–16.

Report of the Commissioners into the Condition and Treatment of Prisoners in Leicester County Gaol and House of Correction (1854), P.P.xxxiv, 197.

Rothman, D.J. (1971) *Discovery of the Asylum*, Boston, MA, Little Brown.

Rusche, G. and Kirchheimer, O. (1939) *Punishment and Social Structure,* New York, Columbia University Press. (Reissued in 1968 by Russell and Russell.)

Salvatore, R.D. and Aguirre, C. (1996) 'The birth of the penitentiary in Latin America: toward an interpretative social history of prisons', in Salvatore, R.D. and Aguirre, C. (eds) *The Birth of the Penitentiary in Latin America: Essays on Criminology, Prison Reform and Social Control 1830–1940*, Austin, TX, University of Texas Press.

Sharpe, J. (2001) 'Crime, order and historical change' in Muncie, J. and McLaughlin, E. (eds) *The Problem of Crime*, 2nd edn. London, Sage in association with The Open University.

Sim, J. (1990) *Medical Power in Prisons*, Buckingham, Open University Press.

Smart, B. (1989) 'On discipline and social regulation', in Garland, D. and Young, P. (eds) *The Power to Punish: Contemporary Penality and Social Analysis*, Aldershot, Gower.

Spierenburg, P.C. (1991) *The Prison Experience: Disiplinary Institutions and Their Inmates in Early Modern Europe*, New Brunswick, NJ, Rutgers University Press.

Spierenburg, P.C. (1998) 'The Body and the State: Early Modern Europe' in Morris and Rothman (1998).

Thomas, J.E. (1988) *House of Care: Prison and Prisoners in England 1500–1800*, Nottingham, Department of Adult Education, Nottingham University.

Thomas, J.E. and Pooley, D. (1980) *Exploding Prison: Prison Riots and the Case of Hull*, London, Junction Books.

van der Slice, A. (1937) 'Elizabethan houses of correction', *Journal of Criminal Law and Criminology*, vol.27, pp.45–67.

Weiner, M.J. (1990) *Reconstructing the Criminal*, Cambridge, Cambridge University Press.

Zedner, L. (1991) *Women, Crime and Custody in Victorian England*, Oxford, Clarendon.

Zedner, L. (1998) 'Wayward sisters: the prison for women', in Morris and Rothman (1998).

CHAPTER 5

Prisons, Punishment and Penality

by Richard Sparks

Contents

1 Introduction

This chapter offers a critical introduction to the nature, purposes and scope of penal institutions in contemporary western societies. The discussion focuses principally on problems of imprisonment, but tries to place these in the context of other available forms of punishment. Prisons are the most controversial and politically sensitive institutions within modern penal systems. When questions of punishment arise in media coverage or political campaigns and speeches, they often centre on imprisonment to the exclusion of other penalties or kinds of intervention: are prison conditions too 'cushy' or too degrading? Should this or that individual have been sent to prison or not? Was this or that sentence too short (or, more rarely, too long) for the purposes of protecting the public or expressing their outrage? The prison's central position in public and political vocabularies of punishment persists despite the fact that in no modern penal system (including the most apparently 'punitive' such as that in the USA) are the majority of convicted offenders sent to prison. This chapter explores the practice of imprisonment, and the many debates and controversies that surround it. The use of imprisonment is an important question of public policy in its own right. Moreover, the passions that imprisonment evokes also crystallize a wider range of concerns about social responses to crime in modern societies. With this in view, this chapter:

- Discusses some of the many objectives which prisons may be called upon to achieve. What does it mean to say that prisons do or do not 'work'? Can we envisage a prisons policy that would be rational, effective and orderly – and in these senses legitimate – or are the disputes intrinsic and permanent?

- Considers the notion of a 'crisis' in penal policy and looks at some of the efforts that have been undertaken towards reorganization and reform (especially the intervention of Lord Woolf in England in 1991), exploring some of the dilemmas they pose for the future.

- Offers a comparative overview of prison populations in the UK, Europe and the USA and asks how the variations between these can best be explained. If different countries use imprisonment in different ways, can we say which, if any, of these is preferable to the others?

- Highlights one area of special controversy, namely the question of prison privatization, and queries what it can tell us about trends in the nature and scope of penal practice. Is privatization just another tactical means of reorganization, or does it betoken a more historically significant development in our conceptions of punishment?

The concluding section of the chapter returns to some of the issues of interpretation and principle raised throughout, in order to review what we can learn about our own and other societies from the ways in which each deploys its power to punish. In summary terms we hope that you will gain from this chapter:

- A sense of the variety of both the practical and symbolic functions that prisons and other forms of punishment may be called upon to accomplish.

- An understanding that modern penal systems are complex organizations, and that attempts to manage and change them confront difficult issues of both effectiveness and legitimacy.

- Through comparative analysis, an awareness that no one form or level of prison use is natural or inevitable, but that each raises its own problems of both justification and explanation.

- A number of important questions (though fewer answers) about what the future of Western penal systems might hold.

2   Prisons and the contested nature of punishment

Methods of punishment or correction have long been amongst the more vexed and contested aspects of public life. At different moments in their historical development, modern Western societies have conceived of the causes of crime and disorder in distinct ways and have formulated their philosophies and practices of punishment variably, according to the dominant explanatory models, religious and other value systems and crime-control priorities of the times. (If we were to extend this discussion to include non-Western or 'traditional' societies, the range of customs, practices and beliefs that could be termed 'punishments' would be seen to be even more bewilderingly wide.) Even within particular moments or periods, the historical record suggests sharp disagreement on matters of justification and of method, as the disputes between deterrence and reformation as aims of imprisonment in Victorian England indicate (see Chapter 4). Thus, although particular criteria for deciding on questions of appropriate punishment and particular institutional arrangements for delivering it may predominate at any given time, we cannot assume that they ever achieve a consensus of support nor that they will not be subject to change. On one level this is because real institutions of punishment have never been 'perfected' in the way that their more visionary advocates (such as John Howard's ideal images of penitentiary imprisonment) imagined they could be. On quite another level, it is because matters of penal policy always broach some of the most basic questions of justice, order and social control that any society confronts, and on which settled agreement always seems elusive. This is why Garland comments that:

> The punishment of offenders is a peculiarly unsettling and dismaying aspect of social life. As a social policy it is a continual disappointment, seeming always to fail in its ambitions and to be undercut by crises and contradictions of one sort or another. As a moral or political issue it provokes intemperate emotions, deeply conflicting interests, and intractable disagreements.
>
> (Garland, 1990, p.1)

It would appear that whenever we discuss questions of penal policy we find ourselves in the presence of uncertainty and controversy. Even defining punishment (given the range of practices and penalties which have claimed justification in its name) is no easy matter (as we shall see in section 2.1). Perhaps, then, we must give up the idea that we will one day discover a form of punishment which is undeniably just and self-evidently effective. Rather, we may have to accept that any social practice that is so much caught up with issues of authority, legitimacy and compulsion is inevitably subject to what philosophers call 'the conflict of interpretations'. The morality of punishment is, as Lacey (1988, p.14), puts it, 'incurably relative'.

2.1   Punishment as an 'essentially contested concept'

There is, of course, one overriding reason why punishment poses these sorts of problems in an especially acute way. By definition, punishing offenders is generally taken to imply the imposition of some form of 'hard treatment' (von Hirsch, 1993). It involves 'what are usually regarded as unpleasant consequences' (Lacey, 1988, p.9). Justifications for punishing may be offered on a number of grounds. Let us briefly outline some of the fundamental positions. For many philosophers, and perhaps most ordinary people, the justification for punishing resides simply in the view that the penalty is seen as *deserved* for the offence (in which case the punishment is described as *retributive*). For others, the key question lies in a *practical* or *instrumental* benefit that is intended to follow. Thus it may be held that the principal aim of imposing a penalty for an offence is in order to *deter* its repetition, or to incapacitate the offender (that is, in some way to prevent them from repeating an action either by locking them up, placing them under supervision or removing their means of doing it). Still others propose that we punish mainly in order to express social disapproval ('denunciation'). Indeed, there has been a major revival of interest in the use of 'shaming' procedures in recent years – often presented by their advocates as directly preferable to an over-reliance on more instrumental interventions such as imprisonment **(Braithwaite, 1989)**.

incapacitation

denunciation

The most ambiguous case is where the penalty is held also to do the offender good (to rehabilitate them through participation in a programme of counselling, education or training). Yet even in the mildest forms of rehabilitation, offenders will be placed under a degree of compulsion. They can be required to do things that may inconvenience them and which they would not do voluntarily (attend appointments with a probation officer, spend Saturday afternoons at an attendance centre), usually with the threat of more severe penalties if they do not comply. The tensions which inevitably arise within such mixtures of helping and compelling may be even more acute where attempts to bring about rehabilitation occur *within* prisons. In liberal democratic societies like our own, punishment generally equates to some form of *deprivation*, whether of liberty, time or money (and, we might add, social standing or reputation).

rehabilitation

It is because punishment usually implies compulsion, and often deliberately imposed hardship, that decisions to punish always pose problems of moral justification and call for the provision of reasons. When we punish we are using the legal authority of the state to do things which would otherwise (if we did them privately, or if they were done without a sufficient reason) be '*prima facie* morally wrongful' (Lacey, 1988, p.14). Yet it is very often unclear whether punishment does achieve the effects that are claimed for it. Moreover, the major justifications that are used do not always go easily together. Retribution looks back towards the original offence, and seeks to punish proportionately (it is generally *intuitionist* with regard to what is deserved). Deterrence looks forward to the prevention of future crimes (it is *consequentialist*; if it does not work it cannot claim justification). As one commentator puts it, these two principal justifications for punishing 'stand in open and flagrant contradiction' (Bean, 1981, p.1). The primary point is that we should never be complacent about our grounds for punishing. It is often far from self-evident in any given case just

retribution

deterrence

which objectives are being pursued, still less whether they will be successful, and debate is often further clouded by political contingencies (Prison Reform Trust, 1993). Moreover, if one accepts that there may be 'latent' or unacknowledged functions of punishment (Foucault, 1977; Mathiesen, 1990) then it becomes doubly difficult to assess what counts as 'success'.

In most criminal justice systems (and certainly in the famously 'eclectic' English case), the different rationales for punishing have often co-existed in various, more or less uneasy, combinations. Criminal sentencing is a complex intellectual and cultural phenomenon, capable of answering to a range of institutional and political demands. It tends, therefore, to resist codification; however, many academic theorists of different stripes (be they pure retributivists or advocates of classical deterrence) insist that they have discovered the one true rationale for state punishment. Punishment is *overdetermined*: its aims may be simultaneously *instrumental* (concerned with the suppression of crime and the control of behaviour) and *symbolic* or *ideological* (concerned with the vindication of the law and its claims to exercise justice in the defence of the authority and legitimacy of the state). Historically, it is more common than not for retributive and deterrent principles to stand side by side in the armoury of possible sentences, even when purist advocates of each insist that they are logically incompatible.

2.2 The penal range and the choice of punishments

With the notable exception of the USA (see Zimring and Hawkins, 1986), the Western liberal democracies have abandoned the use of capital punishment. Even in the USA, where it is a highly politically charged issue, the death penalty is actually carried out only in a relative handful of cases each year (there were 14 executions in 1991), although the numbers executed have increased (31 in 1994; 74 in 1997); the number of persons under sentence of death, however, is very much larger (2,500 in 1991; 2,870 in 1994; 3,565 in 1999) (figures for 1991 from United States Department of Justice, 1992; for 1994 from Amnesty International, 1995, p.302; for 1999, *The Guardian*, 30 September 1999). In other respects, the 'penal range' (the variety of available penalties) in all such societies is broadly comparable, albeit organized and applied in very different ways. It extends from various forms of token penalty or admonition (in the UK, absolute and conditional discharges, binding over) through financial penalties (fines, compensation orders) and varieties of non-custodial or 'community' supervision (probation, community service, in some cases 'curfew orders') to imprisonment. In most systems, and certainly in the UK, financial penalties are by some margin the most commonly used. This has led some commentators (notably Young, 1989; see also Bottoms, 1983) to argue that in fact it is the 'cash nexus' of the fine that is the most characteristic form of contemporary punishment rather than the more drastic but more rarely used sanction of imprisonment.

Nevertheless, it is imprisonment which has probably received the lion's share of media debate, academic attention and political controversy. The reasons for this preoccupation are perhaps not too difficult to detect. The scale of punishment is organized hierarchically in the form of a 'tariff'. In most contemporary systems the prison is at the apex of this ordinal series of values. Although it is by no means the case that everyone who goes to prison has been convicted of grave offences, ordinary language (and judicial reasoning) generally sees a powerful connection between the severity of an offence and the likelihood or appropriateness of imprisonment. (This expectation was formalized in England and Wales in the sentencing structure of the 1991 Criminal Justice Act – see Chapters 3 and 6.) Moreover, imprisonment involves the deprivation of something on which most societies, and certainly ones in which liberalism is a dominant ideology, set a special value – liberty, freedom of movement and association. For this reason the general problems of justifying punishments are seen to apply in especially acute ways to imprisonment (witness the widespread public concern over 'miscarriage of justice' cases in England – most famously those of the Guildford Four and Birmingham Six; to be wrongfully imprisoned is acknowledged to be a very severe injustice: it is the wrongful application of the state's most draconian power over its citizens).

Plainly, other sanctions (such as community service orders and probation) also restrict liberty, but not in so obvious or readily understood a fashion. This leads to a number of ambiguities in the interpretation of such penalties. In much 'common-sense' discussion and in popular press imagery, non-custodial penalties are not regarded as 'proper' punishments at all. The equation between punishment and imprisonment for many people is so strong that for the offender to remain 'in the community' is for them to be 'let off'. Moreover, it is common for such measures to be described as 'alternatives to' imprisonment, implying that incarceration remains the central, perhaps the only 'real', sort of punishment (see Chapter 6).

We can therefore only really understand the uses of imprisonment within any particular criminal justice system in the context of the range of other measures that that system also applies. In recent times most Western penal systems have **bifurcation** moved increasingly towards a stance of bifurcation (or 'twin tracking') in an explicit attempt to reserve imprisonment for the more serious offences, whilst providing an 'adequate' range of 'community penalties' for the rest. Certainly, this philosophy underlay the British government's thinking in the formulation of the 1991 Criminal Justice Act which introduced the concept of a specific 'threshold' between custody and other penalties (see Wasik and Taylor, 1991, p.17). This meant that for the first time the court had to state explicitly that the offence was 'so serious that' no other penalty would suffice. Whilst this strategy has an obvious plausibility, its actual effects can be uncertain or even counter-productive. It presents itself as a **diversion** diversionary measure. Yet sentence lengths for the 'hard core' who continue to receive imprisonment may increase, as average prison terms in the UK did during the 1990s (Home Office, 1999; Morgan, 1997). Moreover, during periods of heightened controversy or anxiety about crime, the proportion of those sentenced who go to prison may also increase; and even slight swings in this direction can have sudden and substantial effects on the prison population. This tendency was also apparent in Britain in the later 1990s.

At the same time, non-custodial penalties may also be made consciously more severe in order to be made 'credible' to sentencers. In addition, such penalties may not always be strictly or appropriately applied: that is, they may move *down-tariff,* supplanting other 'lesser' penalties. This is now widely held to have been the fate of the suspended sentence in the UK since its introduction in 1967 (Bottoms, 1987). It may also be reflected in the increasing popularity amongst sentencers in the UK of community service orders which have tended to displace the longer established penalty of probation since about 1980 (Cavadino and Dignan, 1997, p.171). Such measures can serve to increase prison populations, either because imprisonment may follow when their conditions are breached (and the more demanding those conditions become the more likely this seems to be), or because courts treat subsequent offences in a more serious light. In either case the result is not so much 'twin tracking' as *punitive bifurcation*, in which both 'tracks' become more stringent (Cavadino and Dignan,1997, pp.108–9). The relation between imprisonment and its 'alternatives' is thus a complicated one. The history of attempts to introduce additional sentencing options, especially where these are meant to divert offenders from prison, is littered with unintended (and sometimes actively 'perverse') consequences.

Two considerations may be paramount in explaining why non-custodial sanctions have not had a profound effect in displacing the use of imprisonment. The first concerns, once again, the prison's symbolic position at the summit of the ascending scale of penalties. There would appear to be a widely held view amongst some sentencers, in press discourse and, perhaps by extension, in 'public opinion', that no other penalty adequately conveys the degree of reproof or censure necessary in responding to offences regarded as highly morally culpable (Bishop, 1988; Zimring and Hawkins, 1991). (One alternative conception is that espoused by Braithwaite who argues that sanctions should embody the ritual expression of both 'shaming' and 'reintegration' (**Braithwaite, 1989**; Braithwaite and Mugford, 1994; see also Cragg, 1992).

The second obstacle to decarceration includes a more practical dimension. A sanction is only likely to displace imprisonment to any marked degree if it is consistently used in cases where the offender *actually would otherwise* go to prison, and it has often proved difficult in practice to ensure that 'alternative' penalties are used in just this way. For any reductionist policy, the key offences are those which fall close to the 'in/out' boundary. When courts perceive such offences as containing elements of both harmfulness and persistence (as has often been the case, for example, with some drug-related offences and certain property crimes, such as burglary), then encouraging the more parsimonious use of imprisonment becomes difficult and frequently controversial. Meanwhile, sentencers and members of the public tend to focus on one of the most obvious and salient features of imprisonment: self-evidently it does confine people and set them apart from the general community for the duration of their sentence. Despite many efforts and no little evidence to the contrary, it seems inherently difficult to persuade people *either* that prisons generally do not prevent crime through incapacitation as effectively as is sometimes claimed for them (Greenberg, 1991; Zimring and Hawkins, 1991; Mathiesen, 1990), *or*, conversely, that other means of supervision, support or remedial assistance 'in the community' can do so (see Chapter 6).

As we have seen in Chapter 4, the activity of punishment is deeply involved in processes of social regulation and social change. It reflects changes in the distribution of power, in conceptions of individuals and their motivation, and in ideas of what is permissible or desirable in the defence of social order and legality. The reasons given by a judge when passing sentence are a 'vocabulary of motive' (Melossi, 1985). But as social scientists we may also wish to ask: Why does one such vocabulary, say deterrence or 'just deserts', come to predominate in one country or at one time rather than another? So, for instance, we might want to know why two neighbouring countries with very similar rates of recorded crime, such as England and Wales and The Netherlands, can come to differ markedly in their use of imprisonment (a real example, explored below in section 4.3). What might this reveal about differences in their political climates or intellectual culture? In posing such questions we move from the traditional concerns of penology (Whom should we punish? How much? By what means?) towards what Garland and Young (1983b) have termed the 'social analysis of penality'. When we do this we will tend no longer to talk of 'punishment' in the singular (as an 'it'), but to think instead about the varied ideologies, knowledges, professional specialisms and decisions involved in the field of penal practices and about the relations between that 'penal realm' and other spheres of economic and political life. The resulting differences in the 'scale of imprisonment' (Zimring and Hawkins, 1991) may tell us something of importance about the 'sensibilities' towards punishment (Garland, 1990) that prevail in each country. More specifically, they may reveal both constant and variable aspects of the ways in which prisons are used. Such comparative knowledge can be useful in helping us to decide what level of imprisonment we are prepared to accept as necessary or legitimate.

penality

2.3 Prisons and the problem of legitimacy

Prisons have a number of features that mark them out as unique amongst contemporary social institutions. Some of these are obvious but their implications are nonetheless important. Prisons confine people under conditions not of their own choosing, in close proximity with others whose company they may not desire, attended by custodians who are formally empowered to regulate their lives in intimate detail. It is true that prisons share some of these characteristics with other 'total institutions', if by 'total' we mean institutions that 'tend to encompass the whole of the lives of their inmates' (Goffman, 1961). Examples often cited of total institutions include barracks, boarding schools, children's homes and hospitals (see Cohen and Taylor, 1981); but the only really close analogy is probably with compulsory psychiatric confinement under mental health legislation. It is largely because of their 'total' character that prisons pose issues of *legitimacy* that are in some degree special. Why is this so? And why is it important? What is legitimacy anyway?

legitimacy

It has long been argued that prison administrators hold 'a grant of power without equal' (Sykes, 1958, p.42) in liberal democratic societies. Many political theorists argue that questions of legitimacy arise whenever states claim the right to exercise power over their citizens, especially when they support these claims with reference to the necessity of upholding the law or other aspects of the 'general good' (such as the maintenance of public safety through the suppression of crime). Legitimacy can thus be defined as a claim to justified authority in the use of power. It would seem to follow that the greater the power in question

Wakefield Prison, 1995:
a 'total institution'

the more urgently it stands in need of legitimation. Consider the following definition, taken from David Beetham's book *The Legitimation of Power* (1991):

Power can be said to be legitimate to the extent that:

(i) it conforms to established rules

(ii) the rules can be justified by reference to beliefs shared by both the dominant and subordinate

(iii) there is evidence of consent by the subordinate to the particular power relation.
(Beetham, 1991, p.16)

Beetham argues that all systems of power relations seek legitimation. Such criteria are almost never perfectly fulfilled and each dimension of legitimacy has a corresponding form of non-legitimate power. Where power fails to conform to its own rules of legal validity it is illegitimate. Where it lacks justification in shared beliefs it experiences a legitimacy deficit. Where it fails to find legitimation through expressed consent it may finally experience a crisis of delegitimation (withdrawal of consent) (Beetham, 1991, p.20). Most pointedly for the present discussion of prisons: 'the form of power which is distinctive to [the political domain] – organized physical coercion – is one that both supremely stands in need of legitimation, yet is also uniquely able to breach all legitimacy. The legitimation of the state's power is thus both specially urgent and fateful in its consequences' (Beetham, 1991, p.40).

Prisons, like other forms of punishment but in a particularly acute way, confront questions of legitimacy because they assume an especially high degree of power over the lives of their inmates, and that power is in the last instance buttressed by the right to use sanctions, including physical force, to secure prisoners' compliance. The question of legitimacy is also complicated by two further considerations.

First, to confine an individual is also to place them in a position of dependency. As Mathiesen (1965) puts it, prisoners are reliant on prison staff for the 'distribution of benefits and burdens' in both formal and discretionary ways. In this respect, in claiming the authority to imprison one of its citizens, a state is undertaking a responsibility for the prisoner's health, safety and physical and psychological well-being which is qualitatively greater than that which it owes to the free citizen. Questions thus arise concerning the scope of prisoners' rights or entitlements (Richardson, 1985; Livingstone and Owen, 1993) and of the mechanisms of legal accountability (Gearty, 1991), inspection (Morgan and Evans, 1994) and standards (Woolf, 1991) that govern the operation of prisons in complex modern societies (see section 3.3 and section 5).

Second, the question of legitimacy also arises in relation to the internal order and organization of the prison. It is notoriously true that prisons sometimes erupt in violent upheavals, protest and riots (most famously in the USA at Attica in 1971 and in England at Strangeways in 1990 – see Adams, 1992). Some would argue that this is a risk inherent in the process of confinement. King puts the matter succinctly:

> It is best to acknowledge at the outset that there is no solution to the control problem in prisons, nor can there be. The control problem – of how to maintain 'good order and discipline' – is inherent and endemic. For as long as we have prisons – and an institution that has become so entrenched in our thinking shows no sign whatever of becoming disestablished – then we will continue to hold prisoners against their will. At bottom that is what it is about.
>
> (King, 1985, p.187)

Yet, we also know that such endemic problems do not always and everywhere result in riots and major crises. It is intriguing and important to ask what marks the transition between a chronic background issue (in Beetham's terms, a 'legitimacy deficit') and a serious breakdown of order (a 'crisis of delegitimation'). Answers to this question encompass a complex range of factors, including levels of material provision in prison regimes (crowding, sanitation, food, work, education and so on – see King and McDermott, 1989) and procedural fairness (such as disciplinary and grievance procedures – see Woolf, 1991), as well as less readily quantifiable issues concerning the nature of social relationships between staff and prisoners (Sparks and Bottoms, 1995).

Since at least the late 1970s it has become commonplace to find references to the prison systems of a number of countries (the UK and the USA perhaps in particular, but latterly also countries such as Italy – see Pavarini, 1994) as being 'in crisis'. Increasingly, commentators on penal affairs have begun to think about such 'crises' – especially where they include serious problems of order or control – as being in the first instance problems of legitimation (Woolf, 1991; Sim, 1992; Cavadino and Dignan, 1992; Sparks, 1994; Sparks and Bottoms, 1995). We can thus regard legitimacy as a linking idea which runs throughout the apparently disparate questions of penal politics discussed in this chapter. Let us for the time being pose these issues as a series of open questions:

■ Is the allocation of punishments in any given society justified by coherent principles? Is it consistent and procedurally fair? Do sentences in the main achieve their stated objectives? Is punishment legitimate in Beetham's first sense (conformity with established rules)?

■ Do the system's present practices find widespread acceptance and support in the wider society or are they the subject of disagreement and ideological dispute? Are they therefore legitimate in Beetham's second and more 'external' sense (justification in terms of shared belief)?

■ Can the system sustain itself over time in a relatively stable and orderly way or is it subject to repeated challenge and resistance? Can it secure the consent (or even simply compliance) of its own subordinate members – in this case prisoners and to some extent lower level staff? Or has it entered a period marked by a 'crisis of delegitimation' (withdrawal of consent)?

In our view, these questions provide the framework for understanding what is meant by the term 'penal crisis' and for evaluating policy changes introduced with the aim of resolving or averting the most pressing problems. We turn now to a consideration of how these issues have been experienced in England and Wales in recent times. We then go on to ask more generally (in section 4): What can differences between countries in rates of imprisonment tell us about the extent to which each has elected to emphasize prisons or other options in addressing their crime problems? And how can we best explain the resulting variations in prison use?

3   Crises, change and modernization in penal policy

It became commonplace during the latter decades of the twentieth century to use the term 'crisis' to describe the state of the prisons. It is a standard term of journalism. But just what does this notion of 'crisis' involve? What *are* the main problems of the English and Welsh and Scottish prison systems? And why have they proved so resistant to change? Is 'crisis' perhaps an inappropriate term? Why might this be so? In common parlance, the term 'crisis' denotes something severe but usually of short duration: sterling crisis, Suez crisis and so forth. At the same time it includes an implication of change – if an illness reaches its crisis, the patient either dies or begins to recover. It is a term that in its ordinary usage now refers us to the visible symptoms of a problem (in this case overcrowding, insanitary conditions, brutality, riots) rather than the structural properties of the system that generates them. When the word is used in this

crisis

way a government can announce certain measures (end 'slopping out', improve visiting arrangements, install some telephones, build some more prisons or sack somebody) and claim, for all relevant purposes, to have averted the crisis, at least for the time being. Yet, as King and McDermott (1989) document, the English penal 'crisis', in particular, was never of this short-lived kind; rather, it has been a durable state of affairs but one which reached a deepening severity throughout the 1970s and 1980s. It seems necessary, therefore, to try to get behind this 'headline' language in order to explore just what the principal problems of the system have been and the responses that they have evoked. It may be helpful to think of the 'crisis' as the conjunction of four main sets of issues, namely:

1   the rising prison population;

2   costs, crowding and conditions;

3   purpose;

4   order.

3.1   The prison population

In the period between the end of the Second World War and the century's end, the prison population in England and Wales quadrupled from around 15,000 in 1946 to 60,000 in 1999. Much of this increase results from demographic factors and the six-fold increase in recorded crime during those post-war decades. However, although the absolute numbers in prison rose inexorably, the use of imprisonment *as a proportion* of all sentences actually declined markedly for much of this period (Bottoms, 1983). The prison population began to rise particularly steeply from 1974 onwards, rising every year from 1974 to 1988. Moreover, after 1974 the earlier proportionate trend away from imprisonment was reversed. Whereas in 1974, imprisonment accounted for 15 per cent of all sentences imposed, by 1986 it represented 21 per cent (Hale, 1989, pp.334–5). Towards the end of the 1980s, this proportionate usage again declined towards earlier levels and the prison population fell back somewhat for a time. However, the proportionate use of custody increased throughout the 1990s. In 1997, 25 per cent of all adults convicted of indictable offences received immediate custody. The prison population rose commensurately, attaining a new post-war record of 66,500 in 1998 (Home Office, 1999; Morgan, 1999).

The long-term trend in the prison population of England and Wales has thus been to increase in absolute numbers, but to fluctuate in proportionate terms. But it is also important to remember that such trends can contain (indeed conceal) some very abrupt changes in sentencing and 'surges' in prison numbers. Consider the strange case of 1993. By the end of 1993 the prison population of England and Wales stood at 47,200. This represented a rise of 4,600 in that year alone – an increase of some 16 per cent over the previous year's end. In the second half of the year the numbers in prison rose at the rate of 600 per month (Home Office, 1994). For many commentators this increase was regarded as particularly disappointing in that it followed some sharp falls (in the second half of 1992 the prison population fell by around 6,000, largely as a result of changes to sentencing and parole decisions introduced in the Criminal Justice

Act 1991) (Ashworth, 1993). These increases were particularly marked amongst young prisoners (those under 21) whose numbers rose by 22 per cent, despite the fact that this was one group whose representation within the prison population had fallen consistently during the 1980s. The numbers of prisoners on remand rose by an especially sharp 44 per cent during 1993. The number of women in prison also rose abruptly in this period, by around 16 per cent in 1993–94. There are some curious features to note here which have a bearing on how we are to explain changes in prison numbers. Whilst it is clear that the long-term structural trend in the prison population cannot be wholly divorced from the volume of recorded crime, it is also readily apparent that they have a degree of independence from one another. Indeed, the number of notifiable offences recorded by the police in 1993 *fell* by 1 per cent and continued to fall throughout the remainder of the 1990s, just as the prison population continued to rise. Such fluctuations may have 'local' and primarily political origins. However, prison population trends are also quite 'path-dependent' – they may be difficult to reverse once they are established, even if (as this example itself also demonstrates) they are not *in principle* irreversible.

3.2   Costs, crowding and conditions

It is not easy to see how the rates of increase in the adult prison population experienced throughout the 1980s and again in 1993–98 could be indefinitely sustained. The prison estate enlarged substantially (indeed by a total of some 25,000 places) after the inception of the government's building programme in the early 1980s (McLaughlin and Muncie, 1994; Prison Reform Trust, 1999 and see Figure 5.1 overleaf). By 1999, there were 135 Prison Service establishments in England and Wales, a further 22 in Scotland and 6 in Northern Ireland.

Overall capacity and population came more or less into balance in the early 1990s for the first time in many years, although overcrowding remained an obdurate problem in the city centre local prisons. Following the sustained increase in the prison population after 1993, overcrowding again became a serious systemic problem. At its most rapid (for example in 1993–4), the rate of increase in the prison population would have necessitated opening a new prison every month. At the century's end, roughly 80 per cent of local prisons

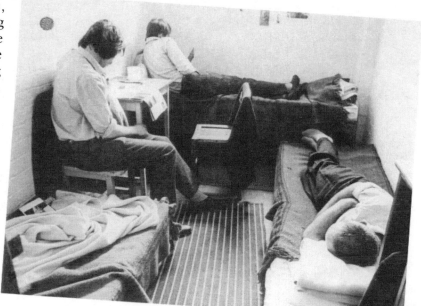

A cell housing three people

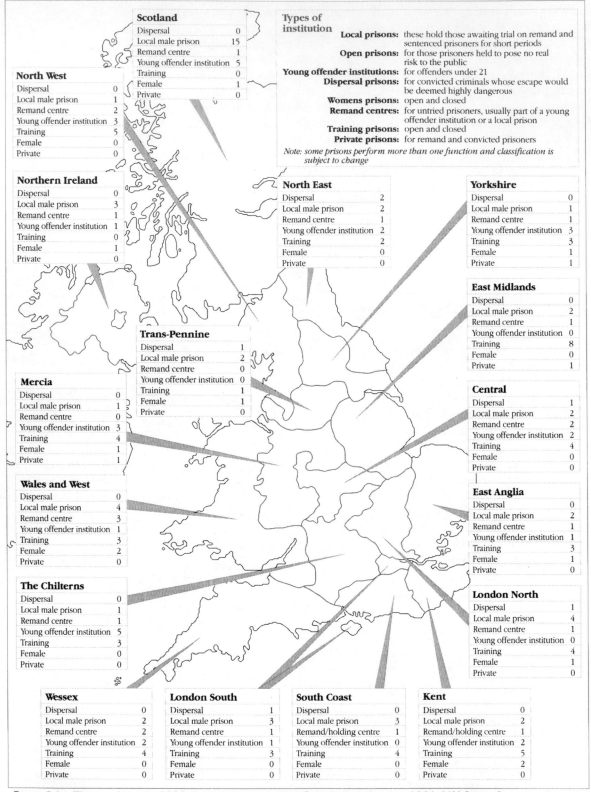

Figure 5.1   The penal estate, 1995 (Source: based on The Guardian, *8 October 1991; HM Prison Service, n.d.; Scottish Prison Service, 1995; Northern Ireland Prison Service, personal communication, November 1995)*

and around one-third of all prisons were overcrowded by more than 20 per cent (with the worst handful being of the order of 70 per cent overcrowded (Prison Reform Trust, 1999)).

Home Office projections suggested a continued increase – perhaps to as many as 75–80,000 by 2007 (Home Office, 2000b) – but, as Zimring and Hawkins (1994) have suggested for California, such projections are least useful when they are most anxiously sought, namely during sudden upsurges in population. For this reason, Home Office projections began to present various alternative scenarios depending on variations in custody roles and sentence lengths. The prospect of routinely resorting to the use of police cells, old army camps and prison ships (all of which arose during the 1980s) recurred.

Imprisonment is very costly. The average cost of a prison sentence in 1997–98 was about £2,000 per month (substantially more in maximum security 'dispersal' prisons). This is in the order of 20 times more than for the same period of a probation or community service order (NACRO, 1994b). In that year, the prisons cost the taxpayer about £1.8 billion (Home Office, 1999).

The persistence of overcrowding (partly engendered, albeit temporarily, by the system's very effort of modernization given the need to take accommodation out of use during refurbishment) has been routinely regretted by senior managers and condemned by a variety of interested commentators, such as successive Chief Inspectors of Prisons, representatives of the Prison Governors' Association and Prison Officers' Association and Lord Woolf. These factors have a major effect on conditions for prisoners and staff. Imagine the practical difficulties that arise in such workaday matters as bathing, clothing, visiting, education, ferrying prisoners to court, and so on (see King and McDermott, 1989). The Prison Officers' Association (1990) has argued strongly that such material strain on space and human resources has severely inhibited efforts to engender greater professionalism and creativity in working practices (see Hay and Sparks, 1991; Prison Reform Trust, 1999).

In addition to these obvious strains, the Prison Service is a complex organization in many less readily apparent respects. Prisons differ in their functions. For adult men (the largest group), these range from 'dispersal prisons' (highly secure long-term 'training' prisons for sentenced prisoners) through somewhat less secure training prisons and open prisons to local prisons and remand centres. Because of these distinctions, prison space is a relatively inflexible resource and has long been unevenly distributed regionally. The very much smaller number of women in prison encounter the special problem that the dozen or so women's establishments are especially geographically far-flung, imposing uniquely serious difficulties in sustaining familial and other social relationships, though the pivot of the women's system in England remains one large multi-purpose institution at Holloway in north London and in Scotland at Cornton Vale near Stirling. Young Offender Institutions are similarly scattered, a fact that has been widely taken as exacerbating the problems of suicide, self-injury and bullying that historically afflict custodial institutions for young people (Liebling, 1992; Howard League, 1999). Imprisonment remains numerically dominated by young adult men (though for various reasons, principally a trend towards greater average sentence lengths, the modal age of the prison population has tended to increase) and many would argue that the organization and culture of the prison system reflects this predominance. In general terms, prisoners in the UK (in common with those elsewhere) are disproportionately likely to be poor, to be members of minority ethnic groups, to have few occupational skills or academic attainments, to have been in local authority care, to have no permanent address and to have received (or be reckoned eligible for) a psychiatric diagnosis of some kind (Prison Reform Trust, 1991; Gunn *et al.*, 1991; Morgan, 1997). Table 5.1 and Figure 5.2 respectively provide information on the offences for which prisoners in England have been convicted and on the gender and ethnic origin of prisoners.

Table 5.1   Sentenced population in Prison Service establishments by offence group, England and Wales

Offence Group	30 June 1999	%	Number of persons 30 June 1998	% change 1998–99
Males total*	**48,956**	**100**	**49,902**	**-2**
Violence against the person	10,429	21	10,524	-1
Sexual offences	4,929	10	4,779	+3
Burglary	8,622	18	8,538	+1
Robbery	6,174	13	6,449	-4
Theft and handling	4,021	8	4,097	-2
Fraud and forgery	993	2	1,080	-8
Drug offences	7,294	15	7,099	+3
Other offences	5,178	11	5,208	-1
Females total*	**2,436**	**100**	**2,367**	**+3**
Violence against the person	429	18	420	+2
Sexual offences	17	1	16	+6
Burglary	158	6	118	+34
Robbery	157	6	177	-11
Theft and handling	390	16	395	-1
Fraud and forgery	111	5	119	-7
Drug offences	875	36	794	+10
Other offences	220	9	217	+1

* Offences do not sum to totals as totals include those for whom offence was not recorded centrally and those serving sentences in default of a fine.

Source: Home Office, 2000a, p.2.

It is, moreover, important to consider how the dimensions of the 'crisis' that we

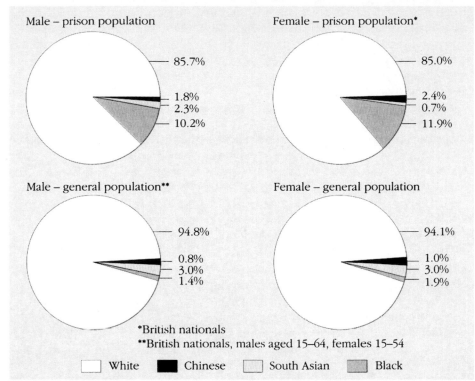

*British nationals
**British nationals, males aged 15–64, females 15–54

☐ White   ■ Chinese   ☐ South Asian   ☐ Black

Figure 5.2 Percentage of prisoners from ethnic groups in the prison population on 30 June, 1999, compared with those in the general population during 1999 (Source: Home Office, 1999)

have identified interact. The often strained and overburdened nature of the prison system has at times adversely affected both industrial relations and staff–prisoner relations. It has thereby inhibited the developments of attempts to move beyond reactive 'crisis management' postures towards any more proactive redefinition of the *aims and purposes* of imprisonment. Taken together, these matters have rather drastically undermined the *legitimacy* of the system, certainly in the eyes of many amongst its captive population. This in turn is intimately connected with the problem of *order*.

3.3 The problem of penal purpose

As we saw in Chapter 4, section 5, since 1895 an officially espoused aim of the English prison system has been to 'encourage and assist [prisoners] to lead a good and useful life'. Whilst doubt and scepticism has always attended this formulation, it was elevated in 1964 to the symbolically central position of Prison Rule 1. By the late 1970s, however, the combination of theoretical and practical doubts over the efficacy and coherence of such rehabilitative ideals (Martinson, 1974; Brody, 1976; Allen, 1981), with endemic industrial relations problems and the pressures of a rising population, meant that for many Rule 1 was considered a dead letter. In 1979 the May Committee concluded that 'the rhetoric of treatment and training has had its day and should be replaced' (Home Office, 1979, para 4.9). On the other hand, the Committee were anxious (perhaps

positive custody

presciently) that to abandon such ambitions altogether would 'lead to the cynicism of human warehousing' (Home Office, 1979, para 4.24). They therefore proposed a notion of 'positive custody', which they hoped would provide an acceptably realistic compromise formulation. The May Committee spoke hopefully of custody as 'severe and yet positive' and envisaged that it could 'preserve and promote prisoners' self-respect' and 'prepare them for and assist them on discharge' (Home Office, 1979, para 4.26). 'Positive custody' has found few defenders. Its most articulate critics (King and Morgan, 1980) regarded it as a hybrid notion, lacking in content, yet still giving too much ground to the notion that people might be sent to prison in their own best interests, hence failing to inhibit the growth of the prison population. (In 1968 Wheeler had discovered that in the USA 'progressive' judges – that is, those most convinced of rehabilitative ideals – had in fact been passing longer sentences than their more classicist colleagues, presumably on precisely this premise.) King and Morgan proposed the alternative objective of 'humane containment' on the grounds that the expectations placed upon imprisonment should be scaled down to those which it could reasonably be called upon to achieve (the minimum necessary use of custody, the minimum necessary level of security, humane conditions of confinement under circumstances of as great a 'normalization' as compatible with the fact of custody). Of course, such 'minimum' levels beg the question of defining 'necessity' within a given set of rationales for imprisonment. Implicitly, 'humane containment' allies itself with a 'just deserts' position, perhaps in conjunction with a degree of 'selective incapacitation' for those adjudged most dangerous. (This was almost precisely the position subsequently adopted by the 1991 Criminal Justice Act – see Chapters 3 and 6.)

humane containment

Neither 'positive custody' nor 'humane containment' have been regarded as wholly satisfactory by prison administrators. Ever since 1979 there has been a succession of attempts to revise and reformulate a coherent set of aims of imprisonment in the face of the demise of rehabilitation and 'treatment and training'. The less ambitious of these – for example, that of the Control Review Committee (Home Office, 1984) – accords closely with King and Morgan in emphasizing the prevention of 'further avoidable hardship' and the importance of respecting 'prisoners' lawful rights'. Yet such a 'humane containment plus' position (Bottoms, 1990) never looked likely to succeed in its primary purposes of providing *any* substantive principle which would legitimate the practice of imprisonment and which would offer prison staff 'something to believe in and some hope' (Dunbar, 1985) that might help motivate and co-ordinate their activity. Eventually in 1988 the Home Office issued a 'mission statement', a notice of which is now prominently displayed on entry to every prison in England and Wales.

HM PRISON SERVICE

PURPOSE VISION GOALS VALUES

Her Majesty's Prison Service serves the public by keeping in custody those committed by the courts.

Our duty is to look after them with humanity and help them lead law-abiding and useful lives in custody and after release.

HM Prison Service mission statement

218

Bottoms comments that this statement 'must be considered something of a disappointment' (Bottoms, 1990, p.15). He continues: 'It is difficult to quarrel with anything that is actually contained in the statement, except to doubt quite strongly the extent to which the last phrase is effectively translatable into practice'. Lord Woolf is rather more critical, pointing out that the notion of 'humanity' commits one to rather less than other more stringent possible principles such as 'justice' (Woolf, 1991, para 10.20). Nonetheless, this remains the official position. The greater part of subsequent activity has gone instead into formulating rather more managerially concrete 'tasks' and 'performance indicators', including identifiable targets for particular features of regimes (such as time spent in work or education and time out of cells). Such activity received a further stimulus from Woolf, whose intervention in 1991 was widely heralded by penal professionals as lending weight to efforts at modernization. The signal preoccupation of the prison system in England and Wales since the 1980s, therefore, has been with the efficiency of management practices, the distribution of resources and the cost-effective delivery of services. This trend in policy has produced reviews of management structure both within prisons themselves (under the Fresh Start initiative of 1987) and of more senior levels of decision-making. In 1993 the Prison Service, formerly a Department of State within the Home Office, became a semi-autonomous Executive Agency under a new Director General recruited from industry and with no civil service (let alone prison) background. In 1994 it published its first Business Plan and Corporate Plan, each with a strong emphasis on quantifiable measures of improvement in performance, backed for the first time by a published code of 'operating standards' for prison establishments.

The period of the later 1980s and 1990s must thus be viewed as a rather paradoxical one within the contentious history of the English prison. It was marked on the one hand by sharp fluctuations in population (latterly by effectively uncontrolled and probably unassimilable expansion), and by great disparities in levels of crowding and regime provision; and punctuated especially in the late 1980s and early 1990s by frequent, widespread and destructive disorders. At the same time, the period saw some of the first novel, strategic official thinking on imprisonment in modern times. One can interpret these developments as being in part a pragmatic response to some demonstrably great problems of poor and uneven provision and conditions, in part the outcome of externally imposed demands for change (notably from Lord Woolf), and in part the result of a very general governmental pressure for 'value for money' that has affected all public services since the early 1980s (McLaughlin and Muncie, 1994). The latter point may itself merely express a longer-term development towards 'managerialism' in criminal justice throughout the advanced societies (we take up this issue in section 5 below in discussion of one of its principal manifestations, namely privatization). Whether any of this is sufficient to fend away the underlying legitimacy deficit (Beetham, 1991) left by the decline of the rehabilitative ideal, the renewed politicization of penal issues since the 1990s and the resumption of expansionism, is another question.

3.4   The problem of order

Almost since the very inception of penitentiary imprisonment, riots and disturbances have occurred (Adams, 1992). It is more or less self-evident that prisoners do not necessarily respond compliantly either to the fact or to the conditions of their confinement. Between the end of the Second World War and the early 1980s, serious collective disorder in English prisons remained largely confined to the long-term adult male 'training' prisons, and in particular the maximum security 'dispersal' system (Woolf, 1991, paras 9.8–9.18; Home Office, 1984, Annex D). In Scotland, similarly, the main focus of unrest during that period remained the lonely fortress of Peterhead (Scraton *et al.*, 1991). Official responses (commonly unpublished) concentrated in large measure on improvements in the hardware and technique of riot control and on the identification of ringleaders. The long-term prisons proved amenable to being depicted as congregations of dangerous and violent men with nothing to lose.

However, the 1980s saw a marked widening of the incidence and extent of prison disorders. In 1986 there was a series of disturbances in prisons affected by prison officers' industrial action. In 1988 there were riots in lower security Category C prisons. In 1989, *unconvicted* prisoners occupied the roof at Risley Remand Centre. In April 1990 the single most significant event in modern English penal history, the 25-day rebellion and siege at Strangeways prison in Manchester, took place, followed by a wave of disturbances across England and Wales. The allegation that participation in active protest was the prerogative of the desperate few could no longer be sustained. Lord Woolf was invited by the Home Office to conduct an inquiry.

Woolf concluded that the scale and intensity of the 1990 protests at Manchester, Dartmoor, Bristol, Cardiff and elsewhere could only be attributed to a widely shared sense of injustice:

> A recurring theme in the evidence from prisoners who may have instigated, and who were involved in, the riots was that their actions were a response to the manner in which they were treated by the prison system. Although they did not always use these terms, they felt a lack of justice. If what they say is true, the failure of the Prison Service to fulfil its responsibilities to act with justice created in April 1990 serious difficulties in maintaining security and control in prisons.
>
> (Woolf, 1991, para 9.24)

Elsewhere, Woolf went on to argue against the historically received view that prisoners' goods and services should be regarded as 'privileges', awarded or removed by discretion (for example, Woolf, 1991, para 14.32 ff.). He referred instead to the 'threshold quality of life' of all prisoners and to the 'legitimate expectations' that prisoners have of their treatment (for example, para 12.129). For him, serious attention to justice in prisons required the Prison Service to make available to prisoners at least (i) a humane regime (for example, 'a dry cell, integral sanitation, … exercise, activities, association and food': para 10.20); and (ii) a reasoned explanation for all decisions adversely affecting individual prisoners, and fair procedures for dealing with prisoners' grievances and alleged indiscipline (para 10.20). Throughout his report, including the final paragraphs of the main text, Woolf emphasized his belief that such issues are fundamental to the stability of the system (see Extract 5.1).

Disturbances at Risley Remand Centre in 1989: at any one time about 25 per cent of the total prison population is made up of those unconvicted or untried

Disturbances at Strangeways Prison in 1990: the single most significant event in modern English penal history

Extract 5.1 Woolf: 'Justice in prisons'

9.19   The evidence from Part 1 of this Inquiry shows that there are three requirements which must be met if the prison system is to be stable: they are security, control and justice.

9.20   For present purposes, 'security' refers to the obligation of the Prison Service to prevent prisoners escaping. 'Control' deals with the obligation of the Prison Service to prevent prisoners being disruptive. 'Justice' refers to the obligation of the Prison Service to treat prisoners with humanity and fairness and to prepare them for their return to the community in a way which makes it less likely that they will reoffend. ...

9.37   The evidence of prisoners is that they will not join in disturbances in any numbers if they feel conditions are reasonable and relationships are satisfactory. These are matters of justice which the Prison Service must address more closely. They are fundamental to maintaining a stable prison system which is able to withstand and reject the depredations of disruptive and violent individuals. These are matters which must be resolved if we are to have peace in our prisons. ...

10.18   The Courts send prisoners to prison because in their judgement justice requires that the prisoner should receive a sentence of imprisonment. Imprisonment is the gravest punishment which it is open to the Courts to impose. The Courts do not, as they did at one time for some types of sentence, specify what form that punishment should take. They do not sentence someone to hard labour, or corrective training. They leave it to the Prison Service to decide how to provide the conditions of containment which are appropriate for that individual, having regard to all the relevant factors, including the length of sentence which he has to serve.

10.19   If the Prison Service contains that prisoner in conditions which are inhumane or degrading, or which are otherwise wholly inappropriate, then a punishment of imprisonment which was justly imposed, will result in injustice. It is no doubt for this reason, as well as because any other approach would offend the values of our society, that the Statement of Purpose acknowledges that it is the Prison Service's duty to look after prisoners with humanity. If it fulfils this duty, the Prison Service is partly achieving what the Court must be taken to have intended when it passed a sentence of imprisonment. This must be that, while the prisoner should be subjected to the stigma of imprisonment and should be confined in a prison, the prisoner is not to be subjected to inhumane or degrading treatment.

10.20   ... It is entirely acceptable to argue that the requirement to treat prisoners with humanity includes an obligation to treat them with justice. ...

14.437   Our suggestions are directed to one of the themes which has run through this report, the theme of justice in prisons secured through the exercise of responsibility and respect. The achievement of justice will itself enhance security and control. ...

14.438   ... Were these proposals to be followed, then we believe that they would substantially influence the way prisoners come to view the prison system. While not preventing all disruptions, they would marginalise those who claim they must resort to deeply damaging and costly disturbances on the grounds that there is no other way to have their voices heard.

(Woolf, 1991, pp.225–6; 228; 241; 431–2)

What Woolf is outlining here (albeit at times only implicitly) is something akin to a theory of *legitimacy*, of a kind that sociologists and political theorists would recognize. He believes, that is to say, that there are variable conditions which render it more or less likely that prisoners will accept, however conditionally, the authority of their custodians. What is novel here is not so much the insight itself (which, in a more or less developed form, is frequently affirmed on prison wings and landings by prisoners and prison staff), but rather the insistence that official discourse should articulate and act upon it (for fuller accounts of the relationship between order and legitimacy in prisons see Cavadino and Dignan, 1997; Sparks and Bottoms, 1995).

Just how radically innovative or successful Woolf's diagnosis proved to be remains disputed. For example, Sim (1994) draws attention to the fact that the Home Office response was ambivalent. Formally, much of Woolf's reform agenda was accepted, albeit over a very lengthy timescale of implementation. Yet simultaneously a new criminal offence of 'prison mutiny' was created, carrying a maximum sentence of 10 years. Furthermore, some of the most controversial aspects of penal control methods, namely governors' discretionary powers to segregate prisoners either for their own protection or 'in the interests of good order and discipline' (under Prison Rule 43) and to transfer them under the terms of Circular Instruction 37/1990 (subsequently Circular Instruction 29/1993), were left substantially unaltered by Woolf. Moreover, critics drew attention to those aspects of the 'institutional climates' of prisons which were much less determined by matters of procedure than by the informal cultures and working practices of prison staff (PROP, 1990; Sim, 1994; Sparks and Bottoms, 1995).

However much prison managers and reformers may have hoped for a period of quiet consolidation during which the Woolf agenda was to be implemented, the prison system did not remain free of damaging controversy for very long.

The prison population resumed its upward path at an accelerating rate after 1993 (see sections 4 and 6). In 1994 two high-profile escapes (from the Special Security Unit at Whitemoor and from Parkhurst) brought media allegations of laxity and collusion. Following much ill-tempered dispute (during which the governors of both prisons left their posts), the Director General of the prison service was sacked in 1995. Reports into these incidents by Sir John Woodcock and General Sir John Learmont struck a very different note from Woolf. Whereas Woolf had articulated a concern over justice and relationships, attention now returned to the traditional problem of stopping certain resourceful people from getting out. The key issues once again became those of patrolling, surveillance, searching and the provision of very secure accommodation. Moreover, in the climate of the time, their impact soon extended far beyond the Category A prisoners and Special Security Units which were their starting points. Woodcock in particular threw his full weight behind the 'volumetric control' of prisoners' property (meaning that henceforward prisoners would only be allowed to keep such property as would fit in a box of a certain, standard size) and the development of 'incentives-based regimes'. Departing from Woolf's conception of justice (which Woodcock casually and inaccurately termed 'a care ideology'), Woodcock sought a 'firm but fair regime where the dog wags the tail'.

The emphasis here falls on surveillance, intelligence and the individualized control of problematic behaviour. Whereas in Woolf there is some sense that trouble in prisons can intelligibly result from shared grievances, here the problem of penal order has returned to its historically more common characterization – the failure to adequately control individual miscreants. An extension of these concerns comes in June 1995 with the circulation of an Instruction to Governors (IG 74/1995) on 'Incentives and Earned Privileges'. This document states that the systematic introduction of 'earnable and losable privileges' will encourage 'responsible behaviour', 'hard work' and 'progress through the system' and will serve to create 'a more disciplined, better controlled and safer environment' for prisoners and staff. The instruction requires establishments to introduce incentive systems with 'basic', 'standard' and 'enhanced' privilege levels, each reflecting the individual's 'pattern of behaviour' over a certain period of time. To qualify for privilege levels above the 'basic' (roughly equivalent to Woolf's 'threshold quality of life'), prisoners are required to demonstrate 'good and responsible' behaviour. The precise details of such incentives schemes are not our main concern here. What is at issue is the model of penal order which they presuppose (and by extension the kinds of motivation and response that they envisage in the prisoner). It is also noteworthy that, in line with the new concern with the punitive sensibilities attributed to public opinion, IG 74/1995 insists that all privileges must be 'acceptable to reasonable public opinion' and 'justifiable in the face of informed criticism' and '*Above all* ... not bring the Prison Service into disrepute' (Annex A, para 17, emphasis added).

Finally, towards the end of the 1990s, allegations of oppressive, sometimes physically abusive and on occasion flagrantly racist behaviour by prison staff began to resurface – not least in a series of highly critical reports by the Chief Inspector of Prisons. The main (though not exclusive) focus of these controversies fell – not for the first time – on the London local prisons, especially Wormwood Scrubs, Wandsworth and Brixton, and at least one young offenders' institution, Feltham. The level of suicide and self-harm in prisons remained an acute cause for concern. Two points are worth noting: first, that despite many modernizing interventions, the quality of penal regimes remained highly variable; second, that a decade after Woolf, the questions of discretionary power and the potentiality for force and violence in the maintenance of control in prisons remained unresolved.

ACTIVITY 5.1

To ensure that you have understood the discussion so far, make some notes that address the following questions:

1   What do you understand by the terms 'penal crisis' and 'legitimation crisis'?
2   Why has the British penal system so often been seen as 'in crisis'?
3   How have the aims of imprisonment shifted in response to such 'crises'?

To differentiate the constituent elements within the 'crisis' of the penal system is to clarify the contribution made by each, not merely to an aggregation of discrete 'problems', but to its overall defensibility *as a system*. One somewhat optimistic aspect of this is the apparently greater preparedness not only of external critics, but also of some versions of official discourse (most particularly Woolf), to accept that the penal system confronts endemic problems of legitimacy, on the levels of its provision of appropriate conditions, its historical incapacity to provide a coherent statement of aims, and its long-standing inattention to problems of justice and procedural fairness in respect of discipline, grievances and other aspects of internal organization. However, by no means all the problems of the prison system are of its own creation. The numbers of people whom it must accommodate, and the adequacy of the reasons for which they are imprisoned in the first place, lie outside its control. In its responses to its entrenched legitimation problems, the English system would appear to have adopted a dual strategy. First, under the promptings provided by Lord Woolf, it has moved to introduce an increased measure of procedural fairness and explicitness in its dealings with prisoners, particularly as regards disciplinary and grievance mechanisms and more generally in relation to the provision of reasons for decisions. Second, and in the longer term this is the more structurally significant outcome, it has in many respects rather decisively opted for the 'managerialist' road towards 'modernizing' its organization, its delivery of 'services' and its standards of 'performance'.

4 Contemporary penal systems in comparative perspective

The rising prison numbers after 1993 reinforced the long-standing position of the three UK prison systems (England and Wales, Scotland, Northern Ireland) as lying at or very near the top of any 'league table' of comparisons with their European neighbours, albeit well behind such global 'leaders' as the United States, Russia and South Africa. In 1997, England and Wales stood second to Portugal amongst Western European states in proportion to its population, with a rate of detention of 120 per 100,000 inhabitants (see Figure 5.3 below).

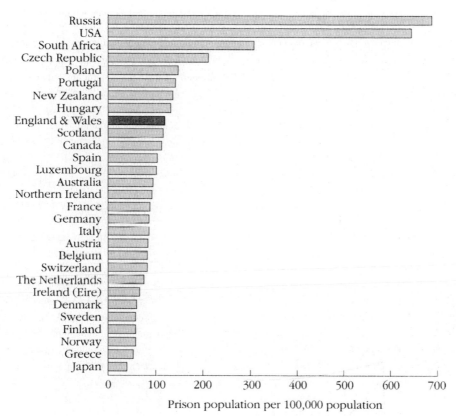

Prison population per 100,000 population

Figure 5.3 Prison population per 100,000 population for selected countries on 1 September 1997 (or nearest available date) (Source: Home Office, 1999, p.56)

The picture here is complex, and all such raw statistics must be treated with caution. They mask many differences in counting procedures, for example in such matters as the inclusion or exclusion of young offenders or those offenders confined following a diagnosis of mental disorder. Neither do these blunt comparisons include any indication of the proportionate relationship between imprisonment and recorded crime; and this often tends to moderate some of the very large disparities shown here. Many of the highest rates of imprisonment, and the most violent fluctuations, are in the countries of the former Soviet Bloc. These would require separate and detailed analysis in terms of the social and political transitions and instabilities of those societies (Russia in particular remains an outlier by any standard): but this exceeds our scope here. Yet even if we confine our attention to the countries of Western Europe, certain distinctions stand out. First, in many but not all of those countries, prison populations have risen, in some cases (the Netherlands, the Czech Republic, Portugal) sharply. Second, the gap between the lower and higher groups of countries (Ireland, the Scandinavian countries and Greece versus the three United Kingdom jurisdictions and Portugal) nevertheless remains wide.

'stock' and 'flow' data

There are a number of other aspects of the issue which this simple list tends to conceal. The 'rate of detention' as recorded in Figure 5.3 is a measure of the 'stock' of prisoners on a given day. It gives no indication of the 'flow' of prisoners through the system. Such 'flow' data include the numbers of committals to prison. This is known as the 'rate of imprisonments' (that is, how many individuals are received into prison in the course of a year). We also need to consider the lengths of time spent in prison. It is only when we know all these things (rate of detention, rate of imprisonments, duration of imprisonment) that we can really claim to describe how each system behaves. Such more detailed comparisons reveal some surprising discoveries. For example, Portugal has a strikingly high rate of detention, yet its rate of imprisonments is traditionally very much lower than, say, England and Wales. This indicates that the average duration of imprisonment in Portugal is unusually long. The 'flow' is slow, so the 'stock' is high. In Norway the reverse is the case. Norway actually has a somewhat greater rate of imprisonments than England and Wales. However, the average duration of imprisonment there is rather short. The 'flow' is quick, so the 'stock' remains comparatively low (see Muncie and Sparks, 1991a; Fitzmaurice and Pease, 1982; Young, 1986). In general terms a number of southern European countries (Portugal, Italy, Greece) have in common that they send fewer individuals to prison but for quite long periods. The Scandinavian countries do quite otherwise. There, rather large numbers of individuals go to prison, but often quite briefly.

All of this complicates quite sharply our understanding of which countries are 'lenient' and which are 'punitive' (Pease, 1994), although it does suggest that restricting average sentence lengths is one of the most efficacious ways of keeping overall prison populations in check. The 'exceptional' nature of the British prison populations now appears in clearer relief. The high rate of detention in England and Wales, for example, results from the combination of a rather high (though not the highest) rate of imprisonments with a rather long (though not the longest) average duration (though this discovery still begs the question as to why the system in England and Wales acts in this particular fashion). Its 'flow' is both strong and slow, so its 'stock' is high. Of these, it is probably the duration of imprisonment in England and Wales that is the key factor. In some countries, the smaller size of the prison population reflects greater parsimony in the decision to prosecute in the first instance. This holds for experience in Germany in the late 1980s (Graham, 1990; Feest, 1991) where it was the exercise of prosecutorial discretion rather than changes in legislation or sentencing that was credited with having reduced the prison population. Since additional restrictions were imposed on the use of cautioning as an alternative to prosecution in England and Wales in 1994, and since the average lengths of prison sentences increased from 8.1 months in 1981 to 15.8 months in 1997 (Home Office, 1999), the prospects for restraining the growth in the English and Welsh prison populations do not look very bright.

4.1 The prison population in the USA

There is, however, one Western society that makes the British prison populations look positively minute. In Europe only a few countries (such as the Czech Republic, Poland, Hungary and Portugal, as well as England and Wales and Scotland) have in recent years exceeded 100 prisoners per 100,000 inhabitants. In the USA the numbers of persons incarcerated has increased at an unprecedented rate since 1980 from around 500,000 in 1980 to 2 million in 2000: a rate approaching 700 per 100,000 inhabitants (Home Office, 2000c). To calibrate these trends against European comparisons, as Figure 5.4 below does for the years 1970–85, is to invite incredulity.

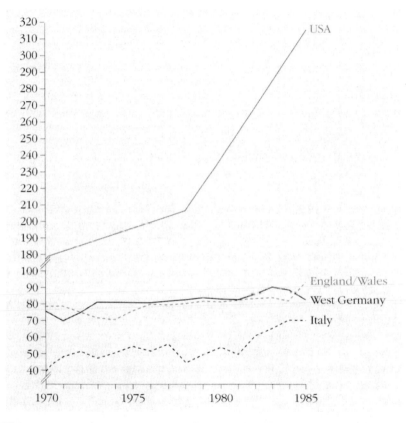

Figure 5.4   Average number of prisoners per 100,000 inhabitants for the USA, England and Wales, West Germany and Italy, 1970– 85 (Source: Mathiesen, 1990, p.2, Figure 1.1)

This picture is by no means uniform within the USA. Some states (for example, Minnesota) continue to imprison on 'European' levels. But this merely underlines the fact that certain other states have behaved in an even more discrepant fashion. Of these, the District of Columbia (an entirely urban area with a disproportionately poor black population) stands out as exceptional. There the imprisoned population in 1998 was 1,329 per 100,000 (Tonry, 1999)

Such figures have no parallel in the modern history of liberal democratic societies. They cry out for explanation. Yet some of the most temptingly obvious 'explanations' fail to hold water. Principal among these is that the USA must have an exceptionally high and ever-spiralling crime rate. This is certainly a commonly held view both within the USA itself and elsewhere. Many US citizens and policy-makers have at times shared the perception that the country's crime problem is out of control (Beckett, 1997; Tonry, 1999).

It is true that rates of many crimes in the USA (both officially recorded and as measured by victimization surveys) are high in international terms, but not to anything like the exceptional degree that is often asserted (United Nations, 1993). It is probably only in the crucially important but numerically quite small category of firearms-related violence that the USA is truly in a class of its own amongst the leading industrial nations (Zimring and Hawkins, 1997). Moreover, the USA is unusual amongst Western countries in that its recorded crime-rates remained rather static during the 1980s and fell for most of the 1990s. This confirms what we have already seen for England and Wales in 1993, namely that overall crime and imprisonment rates show no simple correspondence. The same is true over longer time-scales for the USA in the 1960s (crime rose, imprisonment fell – Zimring and Hawkins, 1991, p.122) and for Australia in the 1970s (where also crime rose and imprisonment fell – Biles, 1983, p.168). As Zimring and Hawkins report for California (a state whose incarcerated population tripled during the 1980s):

> Most of the increased imprisonment in California was not directly related to either increases in crime or changes in population. Most crime levels in 1990 were close to their 1980 rates. And the kinds of crime associated with the largest share in California's prison expansion – drug offences, housebreaking and theft – are precisely the offences that flood the criminal justice systems of every major Western democracy. We think that the sorts of policy shifts observed in California could double the prison population of any country in Western Europe experiencing no change in the volume or character of crime.
>
> (Zimring and Hawkins, 1994, p.92)

The 'policy shifts' that Zimring and Hawkins have in mind here are changes in discretionary law enforcement and sentencing rather than being centrally directed or statutorily required. They are, as Zimring and Hawkins put it, 'more a matter of sentiment than legislation'. The shifts in question include a disproportionate increase in the numbers imprisoned for lesser property offences (they report a 565 per cent increase in the number of persons imprisoned for the various categories of theft – Zimring and Hawkins, 1994, p.88). Meanwhile, although there is some evidence from survey data of a *decline* in illicit drug use in the USA throughout the 1980s, the numbers of persons arrested for drugs offences increased sharply, as did the proportion of those imprisoned following conviction. In fact, the numbers of males in Californian prisons for drugs offences increased by *15 times* during the 1980s (Zimring and Hawkins, 1994, pp.88–90). This followed the national shift in the mid 1980s towards a widely publicized, symbolically powerful and punitively oriented 'War on Drugs' as a primary way in which the USA was to address its problems of addiction.

4.2   'Getting tough'

As Zimring and Hawkins comment, it would appear that, given sufficiently great changes in the 'penal climate' or political culture of a society, its prison population may have an 'open ended capacity for change' (Zimring and Hawkins, 1994, p.92). That is, marked changes in penal practice can occur without corresponding changes in crime-rates, nor even radical changes in the statutory basis of sentencing. They seem to result rather from external pressures in the crime-control culture more broadly conceived and the priorities that emerge there for the stringent suppression of certain kinds of activity in particular, in this case especially drugs offences. Thus, whilst it is true that recent US penal developments have no precedent *in peace time*, perhaps the USA is, strictly speaking, not 'at peace' but rather has 'declared war': the 'war on crime'.

ACTIVITY 5.2

Read through Extract 5.2. As you do so, keep the following question in mind and make a note of your response: If Christie is correct to challenge the common-sense link between crime and punishment, what other sorts of explanations for levels of prison use do you think may be more plausible?

Extract 5.2 Christie: 'The crime explanation'

The conventional explanation of growth in prison rates is to see it as a reflection of growth in crime. The criminal starts it all, and society has to react. This is the re-active thinking … [which does] not hold up for Europe. And it fares no better in the USA:

The prison population has doubled during the last ten years. But here is what the Bureau of Justice Statistics tells (*National Update January 1992*, p.5) about the number of victims in that period:

Victimization rates continue a downward trend that began a decade ago.

There were approximately 34.4 million personal and household crimes in 1990, compared with 41.4 million in 1981.

From 1973 to 1990, the rate of personal crimes (rape, robbery, assault, personal theft) fell by 24.5% and the rate for household crimes (burglary, household theft, motor vehicle theft) fell by 26.1%.

Because the NCVS (The National Crime Victimization Survey) counts only crimes for which the victim can be interviewed, homicides are not counted. Their exclusion does not substantially alter the overall estimates.

The number of victims has gone down. Furthermore, and again in sharp contrast to folk-beliefs on crime in the USA, the number of serious offences reported to the police also shows a slight decrease. The FBI [Federal Bureau of Investigation] statistics on serious offences started at 5.1 million in 1980 and ended at 4.8 million in 1989. But the severity of the sanctions for these crimes has increased. In 1980, 196 offenders were sentenced to prison for every 1,000 arrests for serious crimes. In 1990 the number of imprisonments for such crimes had increased to 332, according to the Bureau of Justice Statistics on Prisoners in 1990.

Mauer (1991, p.7) has these comments:

While there is little question that the United States has a high rate of crime, there is much evidence that the increase in number of people behind bars in recent years is a consequence of harsher criminal justice policies of the past decade, rather than a direct consequence of rising crime.

Austin and Irvin (1990, p.1) say:

National statistics show that the majority (65 per cent) of offenders are sentenced to prison for property, drug and public disorder crimes. A significant number (15 per cent) of all admissions have not been convicted of any crime but are returned to prison for violating their parole 'conditions' (e.g. curfew violations, failure to participate in a program, evidence of drug use, etc.)

From their own research – a study based on a random intake to prisons in three states – they also conclude that the vast majority of inmates are sentenced for petty crimes that involve little danger to public safety, or significant economic loss to victims.

The explosion in the number of prisoners in the USA cannot be explained as 'Caused by crime'. We have to look for other explanations.

References

Austin, J. and Irvin, J. (1990) *Who Goes to Prison?*, The National Council on Crime and Delinquency, USA.
Mauer, M. (1991) *Americans Behind Bars: A Comparison of International Rates of Incarceration*, Washington, DC, The Sentencing Project.

(Christie, 1993, pp.90–2)

Christie denies that there is *any* necessary connection between changes in crime-rates and prison populations. He sees no 'natural limits' on either the upper or lower margins of possibility. For Christie, societies must be regarded as *choosing* to have a prison population of a certain size. What seems apparent from Zimring and Hawkins's (1994) discussion, and from Christie's, is that where changes in penal practice are sudden and drastic they are likely to stem from priorities that are political and ideological in origin rather than being simply pragmatic reactions to the demands of crime reduction. Moreover, the situation outlined by Zimring and Hawkins, in which very large numbers of people are indeed being arrested and imprisoned for certain offences, is itself likely to sustain a public perception of those crimes as a pressing problem, thereby reinforcing the pressure on elected politicians and public officials to show that something is being done. It is this sense of being seen to take firm measures that Mathiesen (1990, pp.138–9) calls the 'action function' of punishment.

It is for these reasons that Christie has consistently emphasized that the punishment levels that characterize different countries at particular times must be seen as *choices* (Christie, 1980, 1989, 1993). The volume of recorded and unrecorded crime in contemporary industrial societies is indeed very large – there is plenty of 'raw material' over which punishment choices may be exercised. Moreover, the scale of the problem, and especially its more shocking and dramatic aspects, is insistently emphasized in media coverage (Chibnall, 1977; Hall *et al.*, 1978; Ericson *et al.*, 1991; Schlesinger and Tumber, 1994; **Muncie, 2001**). It is therefore always possible for politicians to invoke 'public opinion' and social defence in the decision to 'get tough' (see *The Sunday Times*, 12 March 1995, reproduced opposite).

Inmates in leg chains at South Florida Reception Centre, Miami, from The Guardian, *15 February 2000*

Jails to become hell on earth

by Geordie Greig, New York

WHEN she thinks of the man who raped and murdered her seven-year-old daughter more than 21 years ago, Rosemarie d'Alessandro becomes angry. She pictures Joseph McGowan living a pampered life in prison, watching television, studying to become a lawyer and being kept warm, clothed and fed for free. She wants him to suffer.

Politicians across America could not agree more with this New Jersey woman: criminals have it too easy. But perhaps not for much longer. Legislation is being introduced in dozens of states to make punishments harsher.

Twenty years ago the central belief was that criminals should be rehabilitated and given the opportunity to start a new life. Prison was not simply punishment but a way to help offenders go straight.

This liberal approach has lost support from a public clamouring for swift and harsh retribution. Kirk Fordice, the Republican governor of Mississippi, wants life in prison to be so hellish that criminals will think twice before they offend. Already televisions and radios have been banned from the state's jails. Sports facilities have been dismantled and soon prisoners will be wearing striped uniforms.

Several jails in California are also doing away with weight-lifting equipment. In New Jersey there is a campaign to make prison life miserable, with almost no privileges. 'I don't think people would look forward to a life without television, basketball, weights, cigarettes and other amenities. It would make them think again,' said Gerald Cardinale, a state senator from New Jersey. There is even a move to charge prisoners rent.

Fed up with the rise in violent crime, Americans are in a dark mood. The biggest problem is young offenders: the number of children arrested for murder has doubled in 10 years. In the past fortnight three couples were killed by their children. Last week two seven-year-old twins were arrested in New Jersey for a string of burglaries. To public disgust they were released, too young to be charged.

But the get-tough agenda is spreading fast. Singapore, where Michael Fay, an American teenager, was caned last year for vandalism, is attracting admiration – and a school headmaster in Saint Louis, Missouri, has ordered unruly pupils to be handcuffed.

President Bill Clinton has tried to lead the get-tough campaign with his 'three strikes and you're out' law, which gives life sentences to criminals found guilty three times of certain federal offences. Some southern states want to replace this with execution.

Military-style boot camps are increasingly popular. Their method is to bash sense into criminals with a short, sharp shock. Inmates at Rikers Island jail in New York call their military unit the house of pain.

Some states have opted for even tougher sentences than those handed out by courts. Under Washington's 'predator law', officials can extend a rapist's sentence if they believe he is still a danger.

Special prisons known as 'maximaxis', where the tough nuts are kept away from the other inmates, are becoming more prevalent.

Prisoners are kept in cells 23 hours a day.

In fact nothing is being ruled out in the renewed campaign. In Alabama 300 sets of leg irons will be clamped on convicts next month and they will be marched in a chain gang along public roads.

The death penalty, meanwhile, has never had stronger support from politicians despite statistical evidence that executions are not a deterrent. 'America is angry and wants blood,' said one criminal lawyer. 'It is as simple as that'.

Criminologists are alarmed, arguing that harsher punishment may win votes but will not eradicate crime. Worse conditions in prison, they say, will make inmates nastier, more violent and an even greater threat when they are released.

Todd Clear, professor at the department of criminal justice of Rutgers College, said: 'This get-tough attitude is laughably irrelevant to the crime problem. Just turning up the heat does not bring solutions.'

He may have a point. In California the 'three strikes' law has already run into trouble with far fewer guilty pleas because criminals, knowing they could face life for a third offence, refuse to plea bargain. As a result, courts are clogged up. The Los Angeles district attorney expects a 144 per cent increase in jury trials this year and believes more than half the increase is caused by the three strikes rule.

The new law has also produced disturbing anomalies. Earlier this month a man being judged for his third offence was sentenced to 25 years in prison. His crime was stealing a slice of pizza from some children.

(*The Sunday Times*, 12 March 1995)

The relationship between punishment and public opinion is no less complex than that between punishment and crime. As Zimring and Hawkins point out, evidence from US opinion polls since the early 1970s suggests that a substantial majority of those polled reliably express the view that the courts are too lenient. Moreover, this settled perception has shown no sign of responding to the actual increases in penal severity that took place during the 1980s (Zimring and Hawkins, 1991, p.129). Rather, a state of public dissatisfaction with the perceived leniency of the courts appears to be a 'chronic condition': it expresses public concern and anxiety rather than a detailed knowledge of real penal practice. If this strand in public sentiment really is a constant feature of contemporary social life it follows that *any* increase in penal severity could *always* be legitimated in terms of 'public opinion'. In this respect, 'public opinion' is a sort of 'pool' – a resource that can be called upon in opportunist and episodic ways to legitimate political decisions: 'The *ad hoc* reference to punitive public attitudes when the prison population increases is analogous to the attribution of rainfall to the performance of a rain dance while conveniently overlooking all the occasions when the ceremony was not followed by rain but by prolonged periods of drought' (Zimring and Hawkins, 1991, p.130). Moreover, Katherine Beckett has shown that expressions of public concern (for example those nominating crime and/or drugs as 'the most important issue' in opinion polls) are episodic and that surges in such expressions tend to *follow* politicians' campaigns on these issues (Beckett, 1997; Beckett and Sasson, 2000).

This is why both Christie and Zimring and Hawkins stress the open-ended nature of prison expansion. This is perhaps particularly evident when one possible function of imprisonment for crime control is touted with special vigour. In the USA that function has been incapacitation (**Wilson, 1983**; van den Haag, 1975; Zedlewski, 1987). It is a function especially suited to provide the motor of penal growth since:

> As long as levels of crime are high enough to generate substantial anxiety, those who view increased imprisonment as a solution will continue to demand more prisons and will do so in terms that do not change markedly at any level of incarceration. Indeed the more attenuated the relationship between the malady and the proposed remedy, the more insatiable will be the demand for more of the remedial measure.
>
> (Zimring and Hawkins, 1991, p.104)

4.2.1 The 'war on crime' and the question of 'race'

It seems true by definition that times characterized as 'wars' are exceptional. At least some of the conventions and proprieties that govern the normal conduct of affairs may be suspended in favour of a more forceful range of emergency measures. Wars also assume a definable 'enemy', in this case one 'within' one's own society. And the prevailing depictions of such enemies (as seen by 'us') will tend to emphasize their alien and threatening nature. Viewed from the perspective of those who experience such a sense of threat and who have something to protect (tradition, property, safety), the priority is that such 'dangerous others' should be vigorously controlled or removed. George Herbert Mead recognized something similar as long ago as 1917 in his essay on 'The psychology of punitive justice', when he observed that to see oneself as being in a battle is to call for 'the destruction, or defeat, or subjection, or reduction of the enemy' (Mead, 1968). This is also one possible inference from Hall *et al.*'s (1978) analysis of the 'mugging panic' in the UK during the 1970s; a sufficient level of social anxiety about crime, especially one focused against particular groups, can engender an 'exceptional moment' in the way that authority is organized and deployed (see **Muncie, 2001**).

One problematic feature of recent US (and to some extent British) crime control rhetoric is its concentration on the idea of a distinct and separate 'underclass', defined not just by poverty but also by deviant lifestyles and criminogenic sub-cultures (see Murray, 1985, on the USA; **Murray, 1990**, and Anderson, 1993, on the UK). In many such appraisals, an equation is drawn between 'underclass', 'race', illegitimacy and crime. A possible outcome of such ways of thinking, therefore, is the polarization of much of social life, but especially of crime control, along 'racial' lines. There are diverse views on whether the disproportionate numbers of black and Hispanic prisoners in the USA actually result from discriminatory practices of policing and sentencing (Blumstein, 1988; Tonry, 1994). Nonetheless, in blunt empirical terms that disproportion is indeed stark. Tonry shows that by 1990 very nearly half of all prisoners and jail inmates in the USA were black, and their representation still increasing (at the end of the 1980s more black than white inmates were admitted annually to federal and state prisons) (Tonry, 1994, p.101). More alarmingly still, if one looks at these numbers as a rate of incarceration per 100,000 within each group, one discovers that black people were imprisoned at a rate of 1,860 to white people's 289 (Tonry, 1994, p.103), a ratio of 6.4:1. Tonry is careful to point out that most of this disproportion appears due to the over-representation of black people (especially young black men) in the kinds of crimes that most often come to the attention of law-enforcement agencies, rather than to overt racism at the point of sentence. He takes this over-representation to be a 'diagnostic marker of group social distress' (Tonry, 1994, p.112). However, he also argues that certain stances on crime control, most especially the US 'War on Drugs', have had 'foreseeably discriminatory effects' (Tonry, 1994, p.98) and that in social policy (as in criminal law itself) foreknowledge and intention should be regarded as morally equivalent: 'The decision heavily to favour law enforcement over prevention and treatment strategies in the American War on Drugs … was preordained to affect young black males especially severely and for that reason alone (there are others) the "war" should never have been launched' (Tonry, 1994, p.112).

The implications of the frequency of imprisonment of young black men for their life chances and for the reproduction of disadvantage are indeed stark, even in the eyes of the most 'moderate' commentators:

> if you focus on the highest risk group – black males in their twenties – the incarceration rate is about 4,200, or about 4.2 per cent of the group. That means that almost one in twenty black males in his twenties is in a state or federal prison today. Adding the local jails … we are up to 6.3 per cent … When you recognize that prison represents about one sixth of the number of people who are under the control of the criminal justice system (including probation and parole), you can then multiply the prior number by six and that comes to about twenty five per cent.
>
> (Blumstein, 1991, p.53, quoted in Christie, 1993, p.120)

Tonry argues that this way of thinking about prison numbers can show that the level of 'racial' disproportion in US prisons is *more serious* even than the 'headline' figures of the overall prison population at first suggest. Yet the US situation is at the same time *less exceptional* in international terms than at first appears. For example, Tonry shows that the overall incarceration rate of 89 per 100,000 in England and Wales in 1990 (of whom about 14 per cent were black) conceals a rate of 547 per 100,000 black people (Tonry, 1994, p.98; see also Chapter 3 of this volume). This should certainly provide pause for thought. The particular combinations of racial inequality, urban social problems, high crime-rates and 'get tough' political responses in the USA have produced a prison population which is exceptional on any measure (Beckett and Sasson, 2000). But this comparison offers no grounds for complacency. It should alert us to the unintended but 'foreseeably discriminatory' consequences that may follow in any country when politicians choose to speak to an anxious electorate in the language of 'going to war' against crime.

4.3 Explaining imprisonment

We have seen that broadly comparable societies differ markedly in their use of imprisonment and that amongst these the USA currently constitutes something of an exceptional case. Young (1986) identifies two major possible kinds of explanation for such differences. He terms these the 'deterministic' and the 'policy choice' models or schools of thought. By deterministic, Young means those views which attribute the variations to social influences external to the criminal justice system itself, such as economic conditions. Policy choice explanations, on the other hand, emphasize the values, attitudes and beliefs of criminal justice decision-makers themselves.

deterministic model

The most influential style of 'deterministic' theory is probably that deriving from the work of Rusche and Kirchheimer (1939) (as outlined in Chapter 4). Rusche and Kirchheimer argued that the level of imprisonment was primarily a function of labour market conditions. In their view, periods of economic hardship reduced the value of labour and hence the value placed on the life and capacities of the unemployed. Such periods also tended to give rise to fears of popular disturbance and crime amongst more affluent strata of society. Thus, they claimed, prisons would be used to deter members of the lower orders, whose temptations to resort to crime would be especially great during periods of economic upheaval (Melossi, 1985, 1993).

Few contemporary commentators argue for such a direct and apparently automatic relationship between economic conditions and punishment as Rusche and Kirchheimer did. However, their views have been revised and developed by a number of authors, notably Box and Hale (1982, 1985; Box, 1987; Hale, 1989). Box and Hale argue that there is indeed an association between increases in the prison population and recessionary periods in the economy, but that it is of a more complex and indirect nature than Rusche and Kirchheimer believed. Box and Hale use sophisticated statistical measures to argue that there is an independent relationship between unemployment and imprisonment. It is probably for this reason, they suggest, that the English prison population began

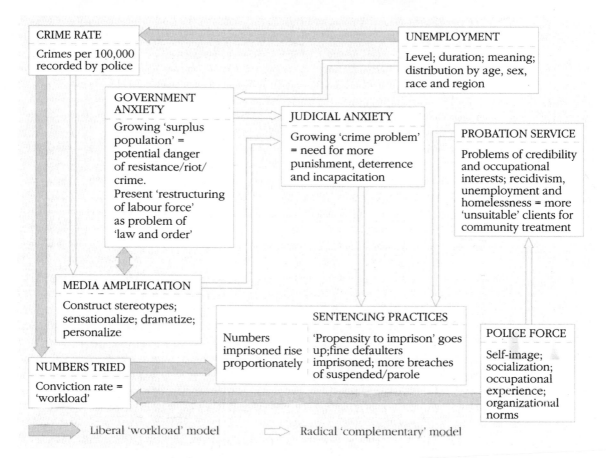

Figure 5.5 Two models of unemployment–crime–punishment (Source: Box, 1987, p.160, Figure 5.1)

its steep upward trend in 1974 with the onset of the oil crisis and the recession of the mid 1970s. But any such relationship is not automatic and direct; it is mediated by the beliefs and perceptions of sentencers. Box and Hale contend that judges and magistrates may well themselves believe that unemployment and idleness lead to crime, or at any rate see the unemployed as potentially a problem population. Whether or not judges and magistrates are correct in this view, their anxieties may lead to an increasing severity in their sentencing decisions. Thus, Box and Hale contend, prison populations increase in times of recession, not simply because the criminal justice system encounters an increased 'workload', but rather because of a range of intermediate factors. Indeed, Box has attempted to express these relationships between unemployment, crime and punishment diagrammatically (see Figure 5.5).

ACTIVITY 5.3

Consider the two models of unemployment–crime–punishment proposed by Box in Figure 5.5. What kind of 'argument' does each line represent, and how do their implications for understanding the relationship between punishment and the economy differ?

In this diagram the two sets of lines represent alternative ways of thinking about the unemployment – crime – imprisonment connection. The solid line depicts the assumptions that Box attributes to a 'workload' model of this relationship. It suggests that imprisonment increases because crime increases, without any differential intervention by the criminal justice system itself. The pale line, on the other hand, encapsulates Box's own view that there is a more complex and more worrying process at work. On this view, the increased level of unemployment stimulates social anxiety amongst politicians, judges and the media. Moreover, the employment status of individuals arrested, tried and convicted makes them vulnerable to more severe treatment on a discretionary basis. Box claims support for this hypothesis from his own work with Hale and from other studies conducted in the USA (Jankovic, 1977), Canada (Greenberg, 1977) and Australia (Grabosky, 1979). His argument is that, whilst each of these discretionary effects may be marginal in itself, 'they do, when aggregated, produce a macro-relationship between one effect of recession – unemployment – and one type of social control – imprisonment' (Box, 1987, p.190).

A somewhat different approach to such economy–punishment connections is suggested by Wilkins (1984) and Pease (1990) in the form of a 'tolerance of inequality' thesis. Wilkins and Pease focus not on unemployment as such, but rather on income distribution more generally. For Wilkins and Pease, punishment and reward in liberal societies can be thought of most simply as the two ends of a single polarity. Those Western societies with the widest ranges of income distribution (the USA, the UK) tend also to have the widest spread of penal values. That is, the concept of proportionate punishments is translated on to a more 'stretched out' tariff of penalties than in other comparable societies. It tends to follow that prison populations will be larger in part because a higher proportion of very long sentences will be imposed than in, say, Scandinavia or Japan where income distributions and penal ranges are both more compressed. This notion certainly has an intuitive plausibility when considering the exceptional nature of the US prison population. The USA stands out amongst liberal societies for the range of its income differentials and life chances (see Currie, 1990). It is also a country in which, conventionally, the American Dream holds out great admiration and rich rewards for self-made success. Perhaps, then, the notion that one 'makes one's own luck' applies in reverse ways to offenders. In such societies people may be held more radically responsible, and hence more severely culpable, for their offending.

policy choice model

Perhaps the best example of Young's 'policy choice' style of analysis is provided by Downes's comparison between post-war penal policy in The Netherlands and the UK (Downes, 1982, 1988). Downes points out that at the end of the Second World War the Dutch prison population was substantially higher than the British. Over the next four decades the positions entirely reversed, despite the broad similarities in crime-rates and associated social problems between the two countries. To summarize briefly, Downes argues that Dutch attitudes to crime and penal policy have been distinctive in a number of respects. First, there appears to have been a fairly conscious decision to limit penal capacity and to respond to pressure on the criminal justice and penal systems by channelling less serious cases out altogether rather than by expanding. Second, Dutch society seems to have developed a 'culture of tolerance' based on an assumption of pluralism and mutual accommodation between diverse social groups. Perhaps for this reason crime has been less politicized as a social issue than in either the UK or the USA. Third, it tends to follow that liberal criminal justice policy-makers have been less constrained by 'public opinion' and have felt freer to develop pragmatic crime-control policies, and that exchanges between academics, judges, prosecutors and social welfare agencies have developed to a quite high degree. There has therefore been less insulation and fewer boundary disputes between welfare-oriented and justice-oriented agents within the system. In particular, the 'Utrecht school' influentially advocated rehabilitative measures, and denied forcefully that prison was an appropriate environment in which to rehabilitate. This anti-penal emphasis was registered within the culture and training of the legal profession (from whom the judiciary are drawn) in ways never paralleled in British legal education. As Downes summarizes:

> Some of these trends can be accounted for by 'policy' considerations. The 'principle of opportunity', whereby the prosecutor may waive prosecutions for reasons of public interest, provides the constitutional imprimatur for considerable flexibility. The progressive waiving of prosecutions may thus be linked with the shortening of prison terms by judges. Explanations in terms of a generalised 'culture of tolerance' within the context of a 'politics of accommodation', help to explain how the elites concerned were enabled to carry their policies through without eliciting fierce opposition or public hostility. The context of an unusually generous welfare state which gave high priority to the assimilation of minority groups would also ease the task of justifying such measures. But the main burden of accounting for the trends seems to fall ultimately on variables closely connected with the actual accomplishment of sentencing by the prosecutors and judges themselves; and here the manner of judicial training and socialisation, and the character and timing of the brief ascendancy of rehabilitative policies, seem to be crucial.
>
> (Downes, 1982, pp.349–50)

Other examples of policy choice perspectives include the closure by Jerome Miller of the Massachussetts reform school system in 1970 (Rutherford, 1986) and the case of changes in the exercise of prosecutorial discretion which led to a reduction in the prison population in Germany in the mid 1980s (Feest, 1991). In each case the emphasis of such analyses falls on the innovative work of key criminal justice decision-makers themselves. No such effects are guaranteed to continue indefinitely, however. During the 1990s the Dutch practice of penal moderation (so admired by Downes) underwent great change. For much of that decade the Dutch prison population rose even more quickly than the English one. In Downes's more recent account (1998) some of the 'shields' that formerly protected Dutch 'tolerance' and moderation have begun to 'buckle' under the pressure of persistently rising crime-rates and an awareness that the borders cannot be sealed against transnational trends, for example in relation to drugs and other illegal enterprises. Insofar as these are 'globalizing' tendencies, the question arises as to how far any contemporary western society can insulate itself against the 'penal temptation' (Wacquant, 1999).

ACTIVITY 5.4

In your view, how useful is the distinction that Young (1986) makes between 'deterministic' and 'policy choice' models of imprisonment levels? Making some notes on your response will enable you to summarize and clarify the discussion in this section.

Young's differentiation appears to capture a difference of theoretical emphasis between those explanations which focus mainly on aspects of political economy (Box and Hale, 1982) and those which emphasize the differing nature of criminal justice systems themselves (Downes, 1982). However, the distinction cannot be a sharp one. Box and Hale's views stress that changes in sentencing practice are mediated by judicial attitudes; they do not just 'happen'. Conversely, Downes's more 'culturalist' interpretation of the Dutch case nevertheless places the 'culture of tolerance' within an understanding of its surrounding political and economic environment. And it has not been lost on a number of commentators that, as the Dutch economy has encountered its own problems of low growth and increased unemployment since 1980, so its prison population too has tended to rise (Box, 1987; De Haan, 1990). Perhaps the sharpest differences lie in the political implications that each approach supposes. Box and Hale's views tend to suggest that criminal justice is a 'second order' phenomenon; if you wish to change its operation, this may have to go hand in hand with other kinds of economic and social development. 'Policy choice' views (Rutherford, 1986; Christie, 1989) tend to be more optimistic. Education, political will and local innovation can all make significant impacts. In particular, it follows from Christie's claim that there are no 'natural limits' on the level of punishment (or 'pain delivery' as he terms it) and that: 'We are free to decide what level of pain we find acceptable' (Christie, 1989, p.9).

5 A case study of penal managerialism: the privatization debate

What do we mean when we speak of developments in criminal justice policy as having a 'managerialist' dimension? In essence, this term means that practices that have traditionally been thought of as being in the first instance about moral questions in the state's legitimate use of authority come to be reconsidered primarily in terms of the most efficient methods of organizing the functions and processes within the system. As an outlook, managerialism is less concerned with debating problems of purpose than with streamlining and modernizing systems that already exist. Amongst the numerous themes implicit in the 'managerialization' of public services (see Newman and Clarke, 1994), two stand out as having special relevance to prison systems. First, there is the prevalent view that in order to become efficient the organization must conform as fully as possible to 'good business practices' as these are held to exist in dynamic private companies. Second, there is the view that management itself is neutral with regard to the substantive goals of the system: these are defined elsewhere, in the political and judicial systems. The challenge of management is the effective superintendence of complex processes, in both their financial and their 'human resource' aspects. If these are indeed developmental tendencies of contemporary criminal justice management, one point at which they come together in a uniquely clear and important way is in the debate on the privatization (or contracting out) of prison management.

managerialism

privatization

Amongst the most striking features of the prison privatization debate in the UK is the rapidity with which the contracting out of prison management emerged as a favoured official stance. As late as 1987 it was possible for the then Home

Secretary, Douglas Hurd, speaking in the House of Commons, to deny, in good faith as far as we know, that there was 'any prospect' of the delegation of prison management to private agencies on the horizon (quoted in Shaw, 1989, p.47). At that time serious intellectual advocacy of prison privatization in the UK was in its infancy (Young, 1987; House of Commons, 1987) and advocates were at pains to explain that they were calling only for 'experimental' initiatives and only in the context of the remand system (Fulton, 1989; Gardiner, 1989). Their hopes for a sympathetic hearing by the Home Office were to this extent realized in the publication in 1988 of the Green Paper, *Private Sector Involvement in the Remand System* (Home Office, 1988).

During 1992 the Wolds Remand Prison near Hull (managed by Group 4 Securitas) opened, 'experimentally', and shortly afterwards tenders for other prisons, holding sentenced as well as remand prisoners, were invited. These included the new facility at Blakenhurst, near Redditch (the contract for which was awarded to UK Detention Services – a partly owned subsidiary of Corrections Corporation of America) and, symbolically, the newly refurbished Strangeways (where the incumbent management won the contract). Home Office ministers began to speak increasingly of a 'mixed economy' of penal provision. The Prison Service was to be accorded a more autonomous 'Agency Status' – in line with Woolf's (1991) views – in advance of which all senior managers were to have their positions 'market tested'. By the end of the 1990s the language of 'market testing', 'tendering' and 'best value' had become embedded features of the penal landscape, and increasingly detailed reporting of costs and other measures of 'performance' were commonplace. In 1999 there were eight privately run prisons in England and Wales, and private-sector involvement in immigration detention and latterly in Secure Training Centres for 12–14 year olds was well established.

The rapidity of these developments may mask just how radically they overturn certain previous orthodoxies, principally the view that the delivery of punishment is an activity that can only be undertaken by directly employed state agents. In order to gain a clear sight of the issues, it is therefore important that we review the arguments for and against prison privatization from first principles.

Back to the eighteenth century? The privatized prison at the Wolds, Humberside

5.1   Intellectual advocacy of privatization

It is as well to begin by acknowledging that there is a moral and ideological dispute at stake in arguments over prison privatization. Most of those who argue most eloquently in favour of privatization are also strongly convinced of the virtues of liberal, 'free market', economic and political theory more generally. Thus, Charles Logan (the most persuasive and disinterested of the US proponents) asserts quite clearly: 'The privatization of corrections, or punishment, is an especially significant part of the broader privatization movement. By challenging the government's monopoly over one of its ostensible "core" functions, this idea directly threatens the assumption that certain activities are essentially and necessarily governmental' (Logan, 1990, p.4).

On this basis, Logan presents a shrewd and beguiling case. He never denies that private prisons generate and encounter moral and practical problems, only that these are not directly to do with their private or 'contractual' character:

> It is primarily because they are prisons, not because they are contractual, that private operations face challenges of authority, legitimacy, procedural justice, accountability, liability, cost, security, safety, corruptibility and so on. Because they raise no problems that are both unique and insurmountable, private prisons should be allowed to compete (and co-operate) with government agencies so that we can discover how best to run prisons that are safe, secure, humane, efficient and just.
>
> (Logan, 1990, p.5)

Thus, provided we accept (i) a certain definition of the responsibilities of the state (broadly that it is there to see that certain tasks are carried out), and (ii) that imprisonment is such a 'function', then the delivery of that task by certain delegated agents becomes unproblematic, in theory if not in practice. In essence, privatization (like the privatization of telephones or electricity) is simply a strategy of social policy. It is to be judged primarily on its quantifiable effects. This is **consequentialism** therefore a consequentialist outlook. The consequentialist view in favour of prison privatization has three main strands:

1   *Purchasers and providers:* it is an axiom of classical economics that wherever possible the purchasers and providers of services should be distinct. Where the state divests itself of the role of provider it ceases to find itself in the embarrassment of having both to justify and to inspect its own performance and frees itself from the claims of the 'vested interests' of its own employees. It becomes instead a rational consumer in an undistorted market, purposively seeking out the best services at the cheapest price.

2   *The stimulus of competition:* it follows, on this view, that efficiency is inherently advanced by the resulting competition. Instead of allocating its budget to itself, the state has in its gift a valuable contract for which others must compete, on terms which the state is free to specify. This breaks down the inertia and restrictive practices of managers and unions. The state shops around, thereby stimulating innovation. Contracts are time-limited. On termination, tendering is repeated, and contracts are again allocated to whomever makes the best bid at the time.

3   *Accountability and the destruction of the public sector monolith:* in the view of privatization proponents, the above processes necessarily enhance the public accountability of the system in question. It is no longer defensive. The state loses the propensity to conceal or gloss over its own failures. Instead, it ruthlessly polices its contractors for signs of inefficiency or abuse. Rather than find him or herself in the dock on the basis of occasional civil litigation by individual prisoners, the Home Secretary becomes, in effect, their ally and advocate, free to prosecute the contracting company for any breach of contract or legality. Moreover, contractual arrangements are inherently explicit whereas governmental administrative procedures are commonly permissive and discretionary. Oversight and monitoring are thereby facilitated and accountability increased.

Taken together, these views present an attractive case. Clearly, they convinced Kenneth Clarke who, when Home Secretary, argued that:

> To me this is the final answer to the moral question. It cannot be more moral to lock up prisoners for long hours a day with little chance to associate, limited opportunity for visits and little access to work, education or PE, than to see them unlocked all day with access to a full programme of useful activities, simply because the poor programme is provided by staff directly employed by the state and the better programme by staff employed by a contractor of the state.
>
> (Clarke, 1992, p.17)

In Mr Clarke's view, this is the kernel of the argument – the prison which provides the better material conditions just *is* the better prison. It is argued strongly that the private sector is inherently better able to provide such conditions – indeed, the terms on which their contracts are awarded will ensure that they do so. In the unlikely event that they do not, then the mechanisms of competition will weed them out. The primary questions are costs and quantitative regime conditions.

ACTIVITY 5.5

How persuasive do you find these arguments? Try to consider them dispassionately and on a 'best case' interpretation. Moreover, consider what your own position would be if you were Home Secretary, charged with overall responsibility for managing the prison system. In the face of rising prison populations, scarce resources, repeated scandalous revelations about decaying Victorian buildings and spartan regimes and many other problems, would you not wish to explore any innovation that might seem to offer possibilities of modernization? Does not privatization offer an opportunity to experiment and to develop new standards of accommodation and services? And might you not thereby change the way things are done in the state-run prisons too, by showing new examples of good practice and efficiency savings? You should seek to develop in your own mind the most convincing possible case for one side of the argument before going on to consider opposing views.

5.2 Objections to privatization

intuitionism

Many objections to privatization are intuitionist. They begin and end with the feeling that 'it is wrong to profit from punishment'. For those who hold this position strongly no further argument is possible or necessary. However, this leads at least one commentator (McConville, 1990) to observe (rather dismissively) that proponents and opponents of privatization are talking incommensurable languages, so that the argument between them can never be settled. It would seem that this intuition in itself is a rather slight basis for a critical perspective. Are there then further arguments which would rebut the weight of the privatization case more convincingly? Such a view might contend that the pro-privatization position may be correct in points of detail but still not touch the main concerns in the arguments about the nature of state punishment and the justifications for imprisonment. If this is correct, privatization misconceives what is really at stake politically, ideologically and economically in the operation of penal systems. Let us outline three specific sets of objections to privatization initiatives.

1   *Sentencing practices and prison populations*:
    (a) Is privatization wedded to growth in the prison population? Privatization moves have to date primarily occurred in earnest in Western industrial states in those jurisdictions which have experienced the most prolonged and severe problems of high prison populations and high overcrowding – principally the USA and the UK. If privatization generally gains momentum and plausibility under the pressure of such contingencies, does this compromise its general claims to offer a preferable model for the future of prison systems as such? Thus privatization offers itself as a policy solution in those situations where prison populations are regarded as escaping willed political control.

    This contrasts sharply with the much slower growth in interest in privatization in most of those countries which had more deliberately and successfully chosen to limit penal expansion (Downes, 1988; McConville, 1990). For these reasons, privatization may be seen as making most sense where one means to accept a prison estate at or above its present size. Or as the promotional literatures for the private prison contractors more eloquently have it: 'As a nation we have an unprecedented need to acquire new prisons and jails' (E.F. Hutton); 'The Fastest Way to Put Offenders Behind Bars' (Kellman Industries); 'Gelco Space Solves Overcrowding' (Gelco Space) (all quoted in Lilly and Knepper, 1992b, p.51; see also Christie, 1993; Shichor, 1993).

    (b) Is privatization wedded to 'warehousing'? More speculatively, one might argue that there is an elective affinity between the provision of privately managed prisons and particular philosophies of sentencing. The sentencing principle most commonly espoused to date by private interests in the USA in their advertising is that of incapacitation. Its focus is on the provision of adequate space in which to contain humanely: 'We help separate the outside world from the inside world' (Electronic Control Security Inc, quoted in Lilly and Knepper, 1992b, p.51). Is it the case that privatization is intrinsically tied to what a number of radical critics have identified as a key function of contemporary penality: namely the containment of 'surplus' or dangerous populations (Box and Hale, 1985; Mathiesen, 1990)?

2   *The economics of private prisons and the problem of accountability:*

(a) Is there a 'corrections-commercial complex'? Lilly and Knepper (1992b) use this term by analogy with Eisenhower's prescient warning of the influence of the 'military-industrial complex'. Indeed, they point out that the similarity between the political economy of defence and of imprisonment is more than passing in that a number of the key corporate players in the private prisons industry are literally defence contractors looking to diversify in the aftermath of the end of the Cold War (Lilly and Knepper, 1992a, p.184). The two positions are strikingly comparable. In each territory there is only one domestic customer (the state – or in the USA the individual states and the federal government) and obvious export markets (other states). The state contracts for what it regards as a vital function. It thus develops close relations of mutual dependency with its contractors (see Shichor, 1993). Far from Logan's (1990) optimistic vision of a state free to hire and fire contractors at will in the event of unsatisfactory performance or a reduction in demand, the more likely outcome is one of a high level of dependency on a small number of near-monopoly providers.

(b) Is this a 'sub-governmental system'? What results in such market conditions is a routine exchange of expertise and personnel between government agencies and corporate contractors. In Lilly and Knepper's view this exchange can be characterized as constituting a 'sub-governmental system' (Lilly and Knepper, 1992b, p.45). Governmental and private experts interact regularly and in private, and identify the outcomes of the mutual deliberations as constituting the public interest. All of this raises issues of the most basic kind for accountability and political control (not to mention ethical propriety and financial management).

3   *Compulsion, order and control:*

(a) Can the state delegate coercive powers? The simple, descriptive answer to this question would now appear to be 'yes, it can and does'. As we have seen, the logic of the privatization case rests on a distinction between the allocation of punishment and the oversight of its administration (the state's responsibilities) and the practical provision of services (the private sector's role). Thus Hutto (vice-president of Corrections Corporation of America) contends that 'the administration of justice is the exclusive prerogative of the state but not of state employees' (quoted in Weiss, 1989, p.34). Prisoners enter prisons by compulsion and during their confinement the responsibilities which authorities undertake for their well-being are very extensive. As such, they involve practical and symbolic issues of authority (Weiss, 1989, p.39).

(b) What are the issues of legality and liability? There are a number of immediately practical ways in which issues of accountability become more complicated under a delegated arrangement. There arises potentially a problem of 'dispersed liability' (McConville, 1990; Weiss, 1989). Weiss shows that the complexity of private prisons creates a vast new legal terra incognita and that government agencies have specifically sought to argue in court that they are not liable in cases of complaint brought by detainees held by private contractors. There are a number of issues to do with, for example, the segregation or transfer of 'difficult' prisoners, or where the duty of care resides in cases of suicide, in which problems of dispersed liability seem very probable. (See further Shichor, 1998.)

ACTIVITY 5.6

How persuasive do you find this side of the argument? Make some notes on how the two sides of this debate differ in their basic assumptions about prisons and punishment.

It is not for us to make up your mind for you. However, it does now seem possible to identify some key issues. Perhaps the decisive question is whether you accept the distinction implicit in the privatization case between the *allocation* of punishment (by the courts) and its *delivery* (by a contractor). In other words, must punishment be *public* in order to be legitimate? If you think the answer is yes, what is it about the practice of punishment that makes this so? For those who are sympathetic to the privatization case (such as Logan, 1990), the contracting out of prison management is practically important (it improves standards), but has no theoretical bearing on the problem of punishment – that continues to be deliberated elsewhere. For those who oppose privatization (or who simply feel uneasy about it) there may be much more at stake – to redefine imprisonment entirely in terms of its constituent 'tasks' is to attempt to break a direct connection with the legitimacy of state punishment. One could therefore argue that privatization (and perhaps managerialism more generally) has a double-edged relation with questions of legitimacy. Prison administrators seek managerial solutions in part because poor management and inconsistent provision are implicated in legitimacy deficits and system failures. On the other hand, to focus principally on management as such (on means rather than ends) may do little to reassure people that the prison achieves a substantive penological goal which they can grasp as legitimate in terms of their beliefs. By the close of the twentieth century such scruples and reservations had however become a distinctly minority concern in many countries. Private-sector involvement had become a familiar feature of the penal systems not only of the US and UK but also Australia, South Africa and numerous European (especially eastern and central European) and African states.

5.3   A 'new penality'?: alternative futures of the prison

Privatization is an important substantive issue. Yet it is at least as important (as our use of the term 'case-study' suggests) for what it indicates about changing concepts of imprisonment, and beyond that about the changing position of penality, vis-à-vis the state, as for any of its practical consequences. There are those on both sides of the privatization debate who argue that these changes are profound. Nor is this the first time that the penal realm has undergone change of comparable magnitude, as we might usefully remind ourselves.

As we saw in Chapter 4, **Foucault (1977)** held that the late eighteenth century saw a 'great transformation' in the social nature of punishment. It ceased to be the ritualized vengeance of the sovereign, he argues, and became concerned instead with working upon 'the soul' of the offender through a variety of disciplinary and therapeutic techniques. Some observers of the contemporary scene believe that, almost unnoticed, our own era may be witnessing changes in the nature of punishment that could turn out to be of similar historical significance. In this view, managerialism is not just a question of method; it introduces profound changes in the nature and purposes of the penal realm (**Feeley and Simon, 1992**; Peters, 1986). Feeley and Simon (1992) argue that, whereas until very recently modern penology was centred on views of the individual and their moral or clinical defects, 'In contrast the new penology is markedly less concerned with responsibility, fault, moral sensibility, diagnosis, or intervention and treatment of the individual offender. Rather it is concerned with techniques to identify, classify and manage groupings sorted by dangerousness. The task is managerial, not transformative' (Feeley and Simon, 1992, p.452).

This is not an argument about what you or I as citizens believe. It is a view of the behaviour and practices of experts within the criminal justice and social control agencies. Feeley and Simon are suggesting that traditional and readily understood terms (such as guilt, recidivism, rehabilitation) are becoming of less significance to those systems than other more internal and specialized languages of prediction and risk management. The underlying logic of these developments, they believe, is incapacitative. Thus:

> The new penology is neither about punishing nor about rehabilitating individuals. It is about identifying and managing unruly groups. It is concerned with the rationality, not of individual behavior nor even of community organization, but of managerial processes. Its goal is not to eliminate crime but to make it tolerable through systemic coordination.
>
> (Feeley and Simon, 1992, p.455)

It is for such reasons, in Feeley and Simon's view, that an era of disappointment and reduced expectations about the effectiveness of criminal sanctions can nevertheless coincide with a qualitative expansion both of imprisonment and of other crime management techniques (such as electronic monitoring and the random drug testing of parolees in the USA), targeted especially at the 'underclass': 'understood as a permanently marginal population, without literacy, without skills and without hope' (Feeley and Simon, 1992, p.467).

Whether or not Feeley and Simon are wholly correct in this view, it does provide a possible perspective on prison privatization. The consequentialism implicit in privatization, its focus on cost-effectiveness and performance indicators (but not recidivism) and the incapacitative focus of much of its promotional literature, accord rather well with Feeley and Simon's argument. The danger (and Feeley and Simon's argument can be read as much as prophecy or awful warning as analysis) would be that punishment comes to be seen increasingly as a set of spheres of expertise rather than as a focus for informed public deliberation and discussion. Such a consequence, Feeley and Simon suggest (1992, p.470), would be 'fatal to a democratic civil order'.

At the same time, it is clear that however important the 'actuarial' and 'managerial' aspects of contemporary penality that Feeley and Simon emphasize may be, they are far from all that is going on. The episodic but at times intense politicization of penal questions is also independently significant in any attempt to assess the expansive scope of the penal enterprise in contemporary western societies. In a later essay, Simon and Feeley acknowledge that the new penology has by no means displaced other older and more emotively potent vocabularies (such as the 'war on crime' (Simon and Feeley, 1995; see also Beckett, 1997)). Pursuing a similar theme, David Garland (1996) argues that there are two distinct tendencies at work in contemporary penality. The first is a series of pragmatic 'adaptations' to the 'normality' of high crime-rates in late modern societies. The second is what Garland terms a 'punitive counter-tendency' (1996, p.13). In Garland's view, there is an increasing ambivalence on the part of contemporary states: the limited capacities recognized by the 'adaptation' strategies are implicitly denied by the 'punitive counter-tendency'. Thus:

> A show of punitive force against individuals is used to repress any acknowledgement of the state's inability to control crime to acceptable levels. A willingness to deliver harsh punishments to convicted offenders magically compensates a failure to deliver security to the population at large.
>
> (Garland, 1996, p.16)

In sum we might suggest that some of the more novel formations of penality that characterize our times, such as the spread of private sector involvement in imprisonment and indeed the growth of incarcerated populations in many western countries in recent years, are best understood as the hybrid product of both of these contrary tendencies. If this is indeed the case then it may follow that Garland's sharp contrast between 'adaptation' and 'counter-tendency' is overdrawn. If some of the key penological developments of our time are in fact hybrids that contain elements of each, then they will turn out to be more complex and less predictable than they at first appear.

6   Conclusion

This chapter has consciously 'painted with a broad brush'. It has focused on questions of the scale of imprisonment in contemporary societies, the tenuous relationship between crime-rates and imprisonment and the vulnerability of prison populations to political and economic circumstances. It has introduced the nature of penal 'crises'. Lastly, it has looked at some of the emergent trends towards managerialism and privatization which seem likely to characterize the penality of the first decades of this century. We have approached the topic in this way in the hope of providing as wide a context of understanding as is possible in the space available, so that you can use this as a basis for your own further exploration into more specific policy questions and as a platform for the evaluation of particular debates and political campaigns as they occur.

One such campaign was launched in October 1993 when the then Home Secretary, Michael Howard, announced to the rapture of his audience at the Conservative Party conference that 'Prison Works'. This claim rested on an amalgam of deterrent and (to a degree previously unfamiliar in British penal politics) incapacitative principles. Howard thus shifted the ground of discussion to a position much closer to the American experience where 'truth in sentencing' (that is, hostility to early release mechanisms) and 'three strikes and you're out' (that is, indefinite detention for persistent offenders) provisions have provided much of the motor of growth behind sustained (indeed 'open-ended') prison expansion. How are we to understand this development? It may well be (see section 2) that there are grounds for thinking that incapacitation is a more dubious enterprise in strictly penological terms than Mr Howard's slogan admits: yet it is also an intrinsic dimension of imprisonment and its intuitive appeal is strong. On another level (that of securing electoral advantage), we might argue that Mr Howard was acting very much as Melossi (1985) or Box (1987) might have predicted (see section 4). During periods of marked public anxiety about crime, of economic stringency and of considerable unpopularity for the governing party, the appeal to severity in punishment speaks powerfully to popular 'sensibilities' (Garland, 1990) and discontents (Hall *et al.*, 1978). On a third level (the emergent 'new penality' which **Feeley and Simon (1992)**, claim to identify), Howard's comments might be seen as part of a longer-run development, namely the shift towards the incapacitative 'management' of a crime problem regarded as in all other respects intractable'. If Mr Howard's gambit combined elements of old-fashioned populism with new-fangled managerialism, so too did his political opponents' main alternative propositions. Tony Blair's sound-bite (also first heard in 1993) that henceforward New Labour would be 'tough on crime, tough on the causes of crime' placed a somewhat different 'spin' on the merger between the punitive and the pragmatic in penal affairs. The flexibility which the 'tough on … tough on …' mantra provided has allowed New Labour in government to pursue yet another version of a 'new' penology.

On the one hand, there is an evident determination not to retreat in any way from 'toughness'. The acceleration in the prison population did not slacken throughout the first three years under the New Labour administration, and the incoming Home Secretary Jack Straw marked his departure from the stances of his (presumably 'old') Labour predecessors by declining to make the control of prison numbers a policy objective. Neither Straw nor Blair refrained from identifying categories of disreputable and marginal persons whom they considered worthy of condemnation, ineligible for public sympathy and ripe for stringent action by police and prosecuting authorities.

At the same time the New Labour dispensation is less flagrantly concerned with 'punitiveness' *tout court* than the Conservatives became after 1993, and the prison is to this extent dethroned from its position of solitary pre-eminence in penal politics. Rather, the signature notion of the post-1997 period became that of 'community safety', and the primary category of activity constituted under that heading has been 'anti-social behaviour'. These terms assumed statutory form under the Crime and Disorder Act 1998, one of the new administration's first pieces of 'flagship' legislation and one energetically promoted as indicative of its novel approach to governance. Whilst this legislation has been discussed already (see Chapter 3) and numerous concise summaries of its main provisions exist (for example, Brownlee, 1998), certain of its distinctive features merit brief mention here.

The Crime and Disorder Act 1998 imposes new statutory duties on local authorities to form 'community safety partnerships' and 'youth offending teams' (YOTs). Partnerships are required to carry out 'community safety audits' and to develop strategies based upon their findings. Amongst the more significant and controversial of the measures at the disposal of local authorities are Anti-Social Behaviour Orders (ASBOs) – civil orders designed to constrain the conduct of any person whose behaviour is deemed likely to cause 'alarm, harassment or distress' to any person outside their own household. YOTs, meanwhile, are to have at their disposal a significant array of new powers and orders to intervene in the lives of young persons in trouble or 'at risk', including (in the case of the Child Safety Order) those under ten. They may also impose Parenting Orders on the adult guardians of persistent young offenders. Amongst the more salient features of the new arrangements include: an evidence-based 'audit' component; the devolution of substantial centrally defined obligations upon localities; giving the responsible local bodies significant discretionary powers; a preference for civil rather than criminal measures, but backed up by penal sanctions (Burney, 1999); and a conscious targeting of high-risk populations, defined both by location and age. The result is intended to be a more pro-active and more stringently managed system. Government ministers and officials make much of the proposition that these policy shifts are 'evidence-based'. Certain forms of academic research – principally those directed towards risk-assessment and the evaluation of targeted initiatives, such as anti-burglary projects and other 'problem-solving' interventions – have received substantial new funding as part of a wide-ranging 'Crime Reduction Programme' (see Chapter 7).

Whereas Michael Howard's attention fell primarily on prolific offenders eligible for stringent deterrent and incapacitative punishment, New Labour penology also concerns itself with social and moral risks, especially to the young. It focuses on 'risk-factors' in young people's lives, including risks to their moral welfare (and law-abidingness) resulting from 'social exclusion'. Whereas Howard's instrumental utilitarianism largely precluded discussion of social causes of offending, New Labour knows no such inhibition. In this sense, it recovers and 'modernizes' a series of erstwhile 'welfarist' concerns but in a way that stipulates much firmer and more controlling interventions than the 'excuse culture' purportedly associated with youth justice was wont to undertake. What is intriguing here is the fusion effected between a technical (indeed often technocratic) language (the discourses associated with the diagnosis, measurement and reduction of risk) and a highly moralized one (the expression of tough love for society's wayward children). Ruth Levitas (1998) suggests that in New Labour discourse the notion of 'social exclusion' has shifted its sense. Having once been a term bearing some connection to social justice and redistribution it is increasingly one stressing normative integration in a *morally* inclusive 'community'.

It would thus appear that the clear distinction drawn by Garland (1996; see section 5.3 above) between pragmatic 'adaptation' and an 'hysterical' 'punitive counter-tendency' (or, put slightly differently between prevention and punishment) has tended over time to become somewhat clouded. There is no shortage of populist gestures, and the language of 'toughness' continues to predominate; but some of these themes also feed into more programmatic and preventively orientated policies. At the same time, there is a quite complicated relationship between 'new' innovations and the reinvention (or re-cycling?) of older and more durable motifs. We should probably expect politicians, of whatever party, to continue talking tough on crime for the foreseeable future. At the same time, we should also continue to track the many and varied shifts of emphasis that characterize contemporary penal politics. The point of these brief vignettes is not simply to dispute Howard's claim that 'Prison Works', though any such assertion is plainly a gross simplification of penological knowledge.

Neither have we set out to endorse New Labour's counter-claims. Rather, our aim is to show that any such rhetorical intervention is open to examination simultaneously on several levels – as a truth claim, as a political tactic and as part of an underlying systemic rationale. These are the forms of analysis which this chapter advocates and seeks to make available to you.

Review questions

- Consider the various arguments about the aims of punishment. In your view, can the major competing positions ever coherently be reconciled at the level of practical policy? If not, which considerations do you think should be primary?

- What are the main issues summarized under the term 'penal crisis'? Is the 'crisis' at least as much a moral and philosophical matter as it is a practical or material one?

- What, in your view, are the principal factors that we need to take into account in explaining changes in the prison population (a) in Europe and (b) in the United States in recent years?

- What is really at stake in the debates over prison privatization, and why can it be regarded as a key indicative issue for students of penal policy?

- Is it inevitable that the prison population in England and Wales will continue to increase over the first two decades of the twenty-first century much as it did during the 1990s?

Further reading

On theories of punishment, see Walker (1991) or Bean (1981) for accessible overviews; for more sophisticated (but still readable) treatments, see Lacey (1988) and Cragg (1992). Garland's (1990) informative overview of sociological accounts gives further insight into why the conflict of interpretations over the problem of punishment is unresolvable. On the British prison system generally see Morgan (1997) or Cavadino and Dignan (1997) for well-informed introductions, or Player and Jenkins (1994) for a survey of more particular issues. For the many questions regarding especially the imprisonment of women see Carlen (1998). For information on prisoners' families see Shaw (1992). On suicide and self-injury see Liebling (1992). On Scotland see Scraton *et al.* (1991) (with special reference to prison disorders) or (for an intelligent view by a thoughtful system 'insider') Coyle (1991). On prison rules, prisoners' rights and prison discipline see Maguire *et al.* (1985) and Livingstone and Owen (1993). On privatization see James *et al.*, (1997) for a judicious overview. The most convenient source of up-to-date information on many of these matters is the 'Penal Lexicon' website (http://www.penlex.org.uk). This is a subscription service.

References

Adams, R. (1992) *Prison Riots in Britain and the USA*, London, Macmillan.

Allen, F. (1981) *The Decline of the Rehabilitative Ideal*, New Haven, CT, Yale University Press.

Amnesty International (1995) *Amnesty International Report 1995*, London, Amnesty International.

Anderson, D. (ed.) (1993) *The Loss of Virtue*, London, Social Affairs Unit.

Ashworth, A. (1993) 'Sentencing by numbers', *Criminal Justice Matters*, no.14, pp.6–7.

Bean, P. (1981) *Punishment: A Philosophical and Criminological Inquiry*, Oxford, Martin Robertson.

Beckett, K. (1997) *Making Crime Pay*, Oxford, Oxford University Press.

Beckett, K. and Sasson, T. (2000) *The Politics of Injustice*, Thousand Oaks, CA, Pineforge Press.

Beetham, D. (1991) *The Legitimation of Power*, London, Macmillan.

Biles, D. (1983) 'Crime and imprisonment: a two decade comparison between England and Wales and Australia', *British Journal of Criminology*, vol.23, no.2, pp.166–72.

Bishop, N. (1988) *Non-custodial Alternatives in Europe*, Helsinki, Institute for Crime Prevention and Control.

Blumstein, A. (1988) 'Prison populations: a system out of control?', in Tonry, M. and Morris, N. (eds) *Crime and Justice: An Annual Review of Research*, Chicago, IL, University of Chicago Press.

Bottoms, A. (1983) 'Neglected features of contemporary penal systems', in Garland and Young (1983a).

Bottoms, A. (1987) 'Limiting prison use', *Howard Journal of Criminal Justice*, vol.26, no.3, pp.177–202.

Bottoms, A. (1990) 'The aims of imprisonment', in Garland, D. (ed.) *Justice, Guilt and Forgiveness in the Penal System*, Edinburgh, University of Edinburgh.

Box, S. (1987) *Recession, Crime and Punishment*, London, Macmillan.

Box, S. and Hale, C. (1982) 'Economic crisis and the rising prisoner population in England and Wales', *Crime and Social Justice*, vol.17, pp.20–35.

Box, S. and Hale, C. (1985) 'Unemployment, imprisonment and prison overcrowding', *Contemporary Crises*, vol.9, pp.208–29.

Braithwaite, J. (1989) *Crime, Shame and Reintegration*, Cambridge and New York, Cambridge University Press. (Extract reprinted as 'Reintegrative shaming' in Muncie *et al.*, 1996.)

Braithwaite, J. and Mugford, S. (1994) 'Conditions of successful reintegration ceremonies', *British Journal of Criminology*, vol.34, no.2, pp.139–71.

Brody, S. (1976) *The Effectiveness of Sentencing*, London, HMSO.

Brownlee, I. (1998) 'New Labour – New Penology? Punitive rhetoric and the limits of managerialism in criminal justice policy', *Journal of Law and Society*, vol.25, no.3, pp.313–35.

Burney, E. (1999) *Crime and Banishment: Nuisance and Exclusion in Social Housing*, Winchester, Waterside Press.

Carlen, P. (1998) *Sledgehammer: Women's Imprisonment at the Millennium*, Basingstoke, Macmillan.

Cavadino, M. and Dignan, J. (1997) *The Penal System: An Introduction*, 2nd edn, London, Sage.

Chibnall, S. (1977) *Law and Order News*, London, Tavistock.

Christie, N. (1980) *Limits to Pain*, Oxford, Martin Robertson.

Christie, N. (1989) Address to the conference on 'The Meaning of Imprisonment', Lincoln, July.

Christie, N. (1993) *Crime Control as Industry: Towards GULAGS, Western Style?*, London, Routledge.

Clarke, J., Cochrane, A. and McLaughlin, E. (eds) (1994) *Managing Social Policy*, London, Sage.

Clarke, K. (1992) 'Prisoners with private means', *The Independent*, 22 December, p.17.

Cohen, S. and Taylor, L. (1981) *Psychological Survival*, 2nd edn, Harmondsworth, Penguin.

Cragg, W. (1992) *The Practice of Punishment*, London, Routledge.

Currie, E. (1990) 'Heavy with human tears', in Taylor, I. (ed.) *The Social Effects of Free Market Policies*, Hemel Hempstead, Harvester Wheatsheaf.

De Haan, W. (1990) *The Politics of Redress*, London, Unwin Hyman.

Downes, D. (1982) 'The origins and consequences of Dutch penal policy since 1945', *British Journal of Criminology*, vol.22, no.4, pp.325–50.

Downes, D. (1988) *Contrasts in Tolerance*, London, Macmillan.

Downes, D. (1998) 'The buckling of the shields: Dutch penal policy 1985–95', in Weiss, R.P. and South, N. (eds) (1998) *Comparing Prison Systems*, Amsterdam, Gordon and Breach.

Dunbar, I. (1985) *A Sense of Direction*, London, HM Prison Service.

Ericson, R.V., Baranek, P. and Chan, J. (1991) *Representing Order*, Buckingham, Open University Press.

Farrell, M. (ed.) (1989) *Punishment for Profit?*, London, Institute for the Study and Treatment of Delinquency.

Feeley, S. and Simon, J. (1992) 'The new penology: notes on the emerging strategy of corrections and its implications', *Criminology*, vol.30, no.4, pp.452–74. (Extract reprinted as 'The new penology' in Muncie *et al.*, 1996.)

Feest, J. (1991) 'Reducing the prison population: lessons from the West German experience', in Muncie and Sparks (1991b).

Fitzmaurice, C. and Pease, K. (1982) 'Prison sentences and populations: a comparison of some European countries', *Justice of the Peace*, vol.146, pp.575–9.

Foucault, M. (1977) *Discipline and Punish: The Birth of the Prison* (trans. Alan Sheridan), London, Allen Lane. (Extract reprinted as 'The carceral' in Muncie *et al.*, 1996.)

Fulton, R. (1989) 'Private sector involvement in the remand system', in Farrell (1989).

Gardiner, E. (1989) 'Prisons – an alternative approach', in Farrell (1989).

Garland, D. (1990) *Punishment and Modern Society*, Oxford, Oxford University Press.

Garland, D. (1996) 'The limits of the sovereign state', *British Journal of Criminology*, vol.36, no.4, pp.445–71.

Garland, D. and Young, P.J. (eds) (1983a) *The Power to Punish*, Aldershot, Gower.

Garland, D. and Young, P.J. (1983b) 'Towards a social analysis of penality', in Garland and Young (1983a).

Gearty, C. (1991) 'The prisons and the courts', in Muncie and Sparks (1991b).

Goffman, E. (1961) 'On the characteristics of total institutions', in Cressey, D. (ed.) *The Prison: Studies in Institutional Organization and Change*, New York, Holt, Rinehart and Winston.

Grabosky, P. (1979) 'Economic conditions and penal severity: testing a neo-marxian hypothesis' (unpublished MS).

Graham, J. (1990) 'Decarceration in the Federal Republic of Germany', *British Journal of Criminology*, vol.30, no.2, pp.150–70.

Greenberg, D. (1977) 'The dynamics of oscillatory punishment processes', *Journal of Criminal Law and Criminology*, vol.68, pp.643–51.

Greenberg, D. (1991) 'The cost–benefit analysis of imprisonment', *Social Justice*, vol.17, no.4, pp.49–75.

Gunn, J., Maden, A. and Swinton, M. (1991) *Mentally Disordered Prisoners*, London, HMSO.

Hale, C. (1989) 'Economy, punishment and imprisonment', *Contemporary Crises*, vol.13, pp.327–49.

Hall, S., Critcher, C., Jefferson, T., Clarke, J. and Roberts, B. (1978) *Policing the Crisis*, London, Macmillan.

Hay, W. and Sparks, R. (1991) 'What is a prison officer?', *Prison Service Journal*, no.83, pp.2–7.

HM Prison Service (n.d.) Map of 'Prison establishments in England and Wales', London, HMSO.

Home Office (1979) *Committee of Inquiry into the United Kingdom Prison Services* (May Committee), London, HMSO.

Home Office (1984) *Managing the Long-Term Prison System: The Report of the Control Review Committee*, London, HMSO.

Home Office (1988) *Private Sector Involvement in the Remand System*, London, HMSO.

Home Office (1999) *Digest 4: Information on the Criminal Justice System in England and Wales*, Home Office Research Development and Statistics Directorate, London, HMSO.

Home Office (2000a) 'The prison population in 1999: A statistical review', Research Findings No.118, Home Office Research, Development and Statistics Directorate.

Home Office (2000b) *Projections of Long-term Trends in the Prison Population to 2007*, Home Office Statistical Bulletin, Issue 2/00, London, Government Statistical Service.

Home Office (2000c) *International Comparisons of Criminal Justice Statistics 1998*, Home Office Statistical Bulletin, Issue 4/00, London, Government Statistical Service.

House of Commons (1987) Fourth Report from the Home Affairs Committee: Contract Provision of Prisons, London, HMSO.

Howard League (1999) *Child Jails: The Case against Secure Training Centres*, London, Howard League.

James, A., Bottomley, A.K., Liebling, A. and Clare, E. (1997) *Privatizing Prisons: Rhetoric and Reality*, London, Sage.

Jankovic, I. (1977) 'Labor market and imprisonment', *Crime and Social Justice*, no.8, pp.17–31.

King, R.D. (1985) 'Control in prisons', in Maguire *et al.* (1985).

King, R.D. and McDermott, K. (1989) 'British prisons, 1970–1987: the ever-deepening crisis', *British Journal of Criminology*, vol.29, pp.107–28.

King, R.D. and Morgan, R. (1980) *The Future of the Prison System*, Farnborough, Gower.

Lacey, N. (1988) *State Punishment*, London, Routledge.

Levitas, R. (1998) *The Inclusive Society?: Social Exclusion and New Labour*, Basingstoke, Macmillan.

Liebling, A. (1992) *Suicides in Prison*, London, Routledge.

Lilly, J.R. and Knepper, P. (1992a) 'An international perspective on the privatization of corrections', *The Howard Journal*, vol.31, no.3, pp.174–91.

Lilly, J.R. and Knepper, P. (1992b) 'The corrections–commercial complex', *Prison Service Journal*, no.87, pp.43–52.

Livingstone, S. and Owen, T. (1993) *Prison Law*, Oxford, Oxford University Press.

Logan, C. (1990) *Private Prisons: Cons and Pros*, Oxford, Oxford University Press.

Maguire, M., Vagg, J. and Morgan, R. (eds) (1985) *Accountability and Prisons*, London, Tavistock.

Martinson, R. (1974) 'What works? Questions and answers about prison reform', *The Public Interest*, no.35, pp.22–54.

Mathiesen, T. (1965) *The Defences of the Weak*, London, Tavistock.

Mathiesen, T. (1990) *Prison on Trial*, London, Sage.

McConville, S. (1990) 'The privatization of penal services', in Council of Europe, *Privatization of Crime Control*, Strasbourg, Council of Europe.

McLaughlin, E. and Muncie, J. (1994) 'Managing the criminal justice system', in Clarke *et al.* (1994).

Mead, G.H. (1968) 'The psychology of punitive justice' (first published in 1917), in Petras, J.W. (ed.) *G.H. Mead: Essays in Social Philosophy*, New York, Teachers' College Press.

Melossi, D. (1985) 'Punishment and social action: changing vocabularies of motive within a political business cycle', *Current Perspectives in Social Theory*, vol.6, pp.169–97.

Melossi, D. (1993) 'Gazette of morality and social whip: punishment, hegemony and the case of the USA, 1970–92', *Social and Legal Studies*, vol.2, pp.259–79.

Morgan, R. (1997) 'Imprisonment', in Maguire, M., Morgan, R. and Reiner, R. (eds) *The Oxford Handbook of Criminology*, 2nd edn, Oxford, Oxford University Press.

Morgan, R. (1999) 'New Labour "law and order" politics and the House of Commons Home Affairs Committee Report on Alternatives to Prison Sentences', *Punishment and Society*, vol.1, no.1, pp.109–14.

Morgan, R. and Evans, M. (1994) 'Inspecting prisons – the view from Strasbourg', *British Journal of Criminology*, vol.34, no.1, pp.144–59.

Muncie, J. (2001) 'The construction and deconstruction of crime', in Muncie, J. and McLaughlin, E. (eds) *The Problem of Crime*, 2nd edn, London, Sage in association with The Open University.

Muncie, J. and Sparks, R. (1991a) 'Expansion and contraction in European penal systems', in Muncie and Sparks (1991b).

Muncie, J. and Sparks, R. (eds) (1991b) *Imprisonment: European Perspectives*, Hemel Hempstead, Harvester Wheatsheaf.

Muncie, J., McLaughlin, E. and Langan, M. (eds) (1996) *Criminological Perspectives: A Reader*, London, Sage in association with The Open University.

Murray, C. (1985) *Losing Ground*, New York, Basic Books.

Murray, C. (1990) *The Emerging Underclass*, London, Institute of Economic Affairs. (Extract reprinted as 'The underclass' in Muncie *et al.*, 1996.)

NACRO (1994a) *Criminal Justice Digest*, April, London, National Association for the Care and Resettlement of Offenders.

NACRO (1994b) *Prison Overcrowding – Recent Developments*, NACRO Briefing, 28, July, London, National Association for the Care and Resettlement of Offenders.

Newman, J. and Clarke, J. (1994) 'The managerialization of public services', in Clarke *et al.* (1994).

Pavarini, M. (1994) 'The new penology and politics in crisis: the Italian case', *British Journal of Criminology*, vol.34, no.1, pp.49–61.

Pease, K. (1990) 'Punishment demand and punishment numbers', in Gottfredson, D. and Clarke, R. (eds) *Policy and Theory in Criminal Justice*, Aldershot, Avebury.

Pease, K. (1994) 'Cross-national imprisonment rates: limitations of method and possible conclusions', *British Journal of Criminology*, vol.34, no.1, pp.116–30.

Peters, A. (1986) 'Main currents in criminal law theory', in van Dijk, J. *et al.* (eds) *Criminal Law in Action*, Arnhem, Gouda Quint.

Player, E. and Jenkins, M. (eds) (1994) *Prisons After Woolf*, London, Routledge.

Prison Officers' Association (1990) 'Evidence submitted to Lord Justice Woolf's Inquiry' (unpublished MS).

Prison Reform Trust (1991) *The Identikit Prisoner*, London, Prison Reform Trust.

Prison Reform Trust (1993) *Does Prison Work?*, London, Prison Reform Trust.

Prison Reform Trust (1999) *A System Under Pressure: The Effects of Prison Overcrowding*, London, Prison Reform Trust.

PROP (Preservation of the Rights of Prisoners) (1990) 'Evidence submitted to Lord Justice Woolf's Inquiry' (unpublished MS).

Richardson, G. (1985) 'The case for prisoners' rights', in Maguire *et al.* (1985).

Rusche, G. and Kirchheimer, O. (1939) *Punishment and Social Structure*, New York, Columbia University Press. (Reissued in 1968 by Russell and Russell.)

Rutherford, A. (1986) Prisons and the Process of Justice, Oxford, Oxford University Press.

Ryan, M. and Ward, T. (1989) Privatization and the Penal System, Buckingham, Open University Press.

Schlesinger, P. and Tumber, H. (1994) *Reporting Crime: The Media Politics of Criminal Justice*, Oxford, Clarendon Press.

Scottish Prison Service (1995) *Annual Report for 1994–95*, Edinburgh, HMSO.

Scraton, P., Sim, J. and Skidmore, P. (1991) *Prisons Under Protest*, Buckingham, Open University Press.

Shaw, R. (1992) *Prisoners' Children: What are the Issues?*, London, Routledge.

Shaw, S. (1989) 'Penal sanctions: private affluence or public squalor?', in Farrell (1989).

Shichor, D. (1993) 'The corporate context of private prisons', *Crime, Law and Social Change*, vol.20, pp.113–38.

Shichor, D. (1998) 'Private prisons in perspective: some conceptual issues', *The Howard Journal*, vol.37, no.1, pp.82–100.

Sim, J. (1992) '"When you ain't got nothing you got nothing to lose": the Peterhead rebellion, the state and the case for prison abolition', in Bottomley, A.K., Fowles, A.J. and Reiner, R. (eds) *Criminal Justice: Theory and Practice*, London, British Society of Criminology.

Sim, J. (1994) 'Reforming the penal wasteland: a critical reading of the Woolf report', in Player and Jenkins (1994).

Simon, J. and Feeley, M. (1995) 'True crime: the new penology and public discourse on crime', in Blomberg, T. and Cohen, S. (eds) *Punishment and Social Control*, New York, Aldine de Gruyter.

Sparks, J.R. (1994) 'Can prisons be legitimate?', *British Journal of Criminology*, vol.34, no.1, pp.14–28.

Sparks, J.R. and Bottoms, A.E. (1995) 'Legitimacy and order in prisons', *British Journal of Sociology*, vol.46, no.1, pp.45–62.

Sykes, G. (1958) *The Society of Captives*, Princeton, NJ, Princeton University Press.

Tonry, M. (1994) 'Racial disproportion in US prisons', *British Journal of Criminology*, vol.34, no.1, pp.97–115.

Tonry, M. (1999) 'Why are US incarceration rates so high?', *Overcrowded Times*, June.

United Nations (1993) *Understanding Crime: Experiences of Crime and Crime Control*, Rome, United Nations.

United States Department of Justice (1992) *Capital Punishment 1991*, Bureau of Justice Statistics Bulletin, Washington, DC, Department of Justice.

van den Haag, E. (1975) *Punishing Criminals*, New York, Basic Books.

von Hirsch, A. (1993) *Censure and Sanction*, Oxford, Oxford University Press.

Wacquant, L. (1999) *Les Prisons de la Misère*, Paris, Editions Raisons d'Agir.

Walker, N. (1991) *Why Punish?*, Oxford, Oxford University Press.

Wasik, M. and Taylor, R. (1991) *Blackstone's Guide to the Criminal Justice Act 1991*, London, Blackstone Press.

Weiss, R.P. (1989) 'Private prisons and the state', in Matthews, R. (ed.) *Privatizing Criminal Justice*, London, Sage.

Wheeler, S. (1968) 'Agents of delinquency control: a comparative analysis', in Wheeler, S. (ed.) *Controlling Delinquents*, New York, Wiley.

Wilkins, L. (1984) *Consumerist Criminology*, Aldershot, Gower.

Wilson, J.Q. (1983) *Thinking About Crime*, 2nd revised edn, New York, Basic Books. (Extract reprinted as 'On deterrence' in Muncie *et al.*, 1996.)

Woolf, Lord Justice (1991) *Prison Disturbances*, April 1990, London, HMSO.

Young, P. (1987) *The Prison Cell*, London, Adam Smith Institute Research.

Young, P.J. (1989) 'Punishment, money and a sense of justice', in Carlen, P. and Cook, D. (eds) *Paying for Crime*, Milton Keynes, Open University Press.

Young, W. (1986) 'Influences on the use of imprisonment', *The Howard Journal*, vol.25, no.2, pp.125–36.

Zedlewski, E. (1987) 'Making confinement decisions', *Research in Brief*, Washington, DC, National Institute of Justice.

Zimring, F. and Hawkins, G. (1986) *Capital Punishment and the American Agenda*, Cambridge, Cambridge University Press.

Zimring, F. and Hawkins, G. (1991) *The Scale of Imprisonment*, Chicago, IL, University of Chicago Press.

Zimring, F. and Hawkins, G. (1994) 'The growth of imprisonment in California', *British Journal of Criminology*, vol.34, no.1, pp.83–95.

Zimring, F. and Hawkins, G. (1997) *Crime is not the Problem*, Oxford, Oxford University Press.

CHAPTER 6

The Competing Logics of Community Sanctions: Welfare, Rehabilitation and Restorative Justice

by Gordon Hughes

Contents

1   Introduction

In the previous chapter, you were introduced to the central place occupied by imprisonment – both symbolically and institutionally – in the punishment of serious or persistent offenders in the contemporary UK. Indeed, the rhetoric of 'prison works' remains a crucial feature of strategies of crime control and of populist politics of law and order across most modern states. At the same time, the history of punishment has never been just a story of the prison. We know from Chapter 4 that using imprisonment as the preferred mode of punishment of the 'serious' offender by the sovereign state is a recent and very much modern invention. It is only in the last two centuries that it replaced the public spectacle of the punishment of the body and even older community-based sanctions of pre-modern 'traditional' societies. There is also the widespread view, especially among academic commentators, pressure groups and practitioners in the criminal justice system, that there are major failures associated both with the prison as an answer to the problem of controlling crimes and criminals and with the formal criminal justice's response to dealing with offenders more generally. (These themes run throughout previous chapters of this book.) Many social scientists have noted that a profound and long-term crisis in penal custody can be identified on a number of inter-related fronts, including the economic costs, waste of human lives and the persistent failure to rehabilitate associated with mass incarceration. This has led to heightened calls for alternative disposals to be developed in place of penal custody within the criminal justice system and – more radically – for alternative forms of conflict resolution to be developed outside the 'system' and within the 'community'. Indeed, at the beginning of the twenty-first century, it is difficult to avoid appeals to 'community' in policy debates and political pronouncements across a wide range of areas of public concern: from housing, health, and social care to policing, crime prevention and, of course, justice and punishment.

Much of this chapter focuses on the histories of community-based strategies of punishment and treatment of offenders and also surveys the key ideas that have informed such 'alternatives to custody'. Sanctions in the 'community' represent the middle ground between those for which a fine is viewed as sufficient punishment and those for which custody is viewed by sentencers as both just and necessary. Like the most popular contemporary punishment, the fine, community sanctions outnumber custodial punishments as forms of sentences in most modern penal systems. Despite this, community penalties, together with the fine, have not received the degree of criminological interest that has been accorded to the study of custodial penalties.

ACTIVITY 6.1

Why do you think there has been less criminological interest in 'middle order' punishments and rehabilitative strategies?

Since its origins in the late nineteenth century, mainstream criminology has been driven predominantly by a concern with finding the causes and the 'cure' of *homo criminalis*, most likely to be identified as the imprisoned recidivist. It is also probable that more criminological attention has been accorded to the study of the prison and its incarcerated subjects because of the greater public concern over, and interest in, the punishment of the most serious offences and offenders. In the UK, penal custody is popularly regarded as the 'real thing' in terms of punishing crimes and criminals while community disposals are widely viewed as 'soft' in the eyes of the mass media, most politicians as well as many magistrates, judges and police officers. This 'prison-centred' criminology is reflected in the widespread use of the term 'non-custodial' sanctions in criminological literature; sanctions tend to be understood almost exclusively in terms of their relationship to the prison and the 'custodial'. This chapter questions this dominant discourse in 'establishment' criminology, in particular by using the replacement concept of 'community sanction' rather than the more orthodox term, 'non-custodial sanction'. As John Muncie points out in Chapter 4, by the early twentieth century, prison was only one institution among many in the extended grid of sanctions termed 'penality'. Community sanctions and disposals, alongside the fine, represent a key part of this welfare, penal, judicial and administrative network of social control.

The criminal justice system, as Loraine Gelsthorpe notes in Chapter 3, is always in some degree of flux. This has been especially true in any discussion of the often-changing fortunes of community-based sanctions and initiatives in the twentieth century. There is a long and troubled history of attempts to reform and rehabilitate both young offenders and less serious adult offenders by means of a 'mix' of justice and welfare-based initiatives located outside the walls of the prison. It is not the aim of this chapter to chronicle the complex story of such developments in depth nor to offer detailed descriptions of the particular processes and procedures of these aspects of criminal justice. Instead, our concern is to develop an understanding of the key issues affecting the ways in which community-based sanctions are practised and delivered, contested and subject to major transformations and continuities in their practices and outcomes.

Many community sanctions have been located at the boundary of the welfare and criminal justice systems. Among the plethora of such initiatives over the last century, those linked to the youth justice and probation services have been most clearly associated with community-based penalties and rehabilitative and diversionary initiatives. The most significant debates surrounding the work of these two, closely related, but distinct, agencies of the 'penal-welfare complex' (Garland, 1985) of the modern state provide a key focus for the discussion that follows. Nonetheless, it is also important to recognize the increasing significance of more informal processes of restorative justice, which have come to the fore in a growing critique of formal, criminal justice system-based mechanisms of conflict resolution. This chapter will therefore also look at a case study of 'community-based' restorative justice.

Throughout this book, it has been argued that the changing policies and practices of crime control in contemporary society – from policing to the courts and prisons – cannot be understood adequately unless attention is paid to the broader political and ideological context in which they are located. This claim remains equally important in our analysis of the key developments at work in the realm of community sanctions. It is therefore important to note that there have been crucial shifts in the power arrangements between the major rationales or what we call here *logics* in this part of the penal-welfare complex of the modern state. In the discussion that follows, specific attention is given to the ebb and flow of three specific logics that have informed policy, practice and the politics of community-based strategies of crime control: 1) the logic of welfare, 2) the logic of rehabilitation, and 3) the logic of restorative justice.

You will recall from the discussion in Chapter 3 that the criminal justice system is an uneasy compromise of the adoption of contradictory elements. Although we will use one of the three logics in each of the sections below through which to view the 'rise and fall' and transformations of community sanctions, we should not expect that any one logic is implemented fully or operates in isolation from that of other competing logics and rationales. Nor should we assume that there is any linear or progressive history at play. Rather, the chapter will point to the complex ways in which different and competing rationales or logics often co-exist, at times seeming to 'die' only to be resurrected at another historical moment. It is also important to note that whilst legislative and organizational landmarks can be charted quite accurately, the role and purpose of community sanctions remains necessarily subject to ongoing dispute and controversy.

This chapter is organized in the following sections. Section 2 offers an introduction to the defining features of community disposals and sanctions. In section 3, we examine the *logic of welfare* in terms of its varying historical influence on the workings of youth justice. The focus in section 4 is on the rise and fall of the *logic of rehabilitation* in the history of the probation service. Section 5 explores the *logic of restorative justice* and its role in the development of alternative dispute-resolution approaches to those associated with formal criminal justice. Finally, section 6 draws together the key issues raised by these for wider developments in criminal justice and social control.

2   Defining the terrain of community sanctions

community sanctions Community sanctions is the catch-all term describing the range of strategies and programmes dealing with the punishment, rehabilitation, treatment or supervision of offenders without recourse to incarceration; sanctions which in turn claim to take place in the 'community'.

ACTIVITY 6.2

You will have noticed that we have tended to put the word 'community' in inverted commas. Stop and consider what images the notion of community conjures up. Why do you think social scientists often use inverted commas when discussing the wide range of policies and practices in both criminal justice and other areas of social policy that employ this label (e.g. 'community care', 'community policing', 'community development', 'community safety' and so on)?

'Community' remains a deeply contested concept in the social sciences – not least because it has both sociological and normative connotations that frequently stand in uneasy tension with each other. Most sociological definitions of community point to its basis in the close social relations associated with a specific place and particular shared beliefs and ways of behaving and belonging. At the same time, the modern world is viewed by most sociologists as having profoundly undermined such close communities, in particular through the growth of more individualized and atomized lifestyles associated with urbanization. We could argue that the normative appeal to community rests on its emotional 'pull' of an idealized past of social harmony and order and points to some imagined idyllic future (Hughes and Mooney, 1998, p.58). In Raymond Williams's (1988) expression, it is 'a warmly persuasive word' which never seems to be used unfavourably. However, such misgivings over the empirical reality of community in modern societies have failed to diminish the 'seductions' of the notion for politicians and policy-makers. The term continues to have a powerful rhetorical and legitimating quality, found especially in the local strategies of crime prevention (this is discussed further in Chapter 7). Communities may be composed or defined in many different ways: in terms of spatiality, culture, political characteristics, common values, or a combination of these characteristics. Both central and local governments have often used the word as a means of giving particular programmes and policies a more progressive and sympathetic cachet. For example, community is constantly invoked as a *cure* rather than a *cause* of crime, despite the welter of social scientific evidence over the years that many crimes often have their roots in the impoverished socio-economic conditions of the very communities to which the appeal is made. It remains a feel-good word, but can nevertheless have a sharper edge: 'community' can be used at times to 'shame' its offending members before their acceptance back into the 'fold'. Whatever the misgivings of sociologists with regard to the possibility of genuine community-based initiatives at the very time when the decline of traditional, close-knit and cohesive communities seems to be the historical reality of late modern societies, it is unlikely that appeals to 'community' will disappear from the policy agenda of welfare and criminal justice. Social historian Jeffrey Weeks (1996, p.74) asks whether 'community' is a necessary fiction in contemporary societies, the meaning of which remains fraught with both progressive and regressive potentialities.

With regard to the dominant official invocation and endorsement of 'community'-based sanctions, the idea of community deployed is predominantly territorial or spatial in character: in other words disposals that are implemented 'somewhere' outside the walls of the prison or related custodial institution. We have already noted that community-based penalties are generally viewed as being synonymous with 'alternatives to custody', and there is a marked diversity of programmatic activities having a community-based tag. This can range from the use of supervisory probation orders, community service orders, rehabilitation and treatment programmes, Intensive Intermediate Treatment (IT), half-way houses to electronic tagging and home curfews, restitutive schemes and even more draconian, shaming corrections and Detention and Training Orders (which combine custody and community).

Electronic tagging: alternatives to custody or the new custodialism in home?

Across the world, such strategies and programmes still generally exist on the 'borderlands' of criminal justice and social welfare, in which a mix of the principles of punishment, containment, rehabilitation, treatment, and restoration is evident to varying degrees. These programmes are particularly associated with the work of youth justice and the probation or corrections services in most western jurisdictions (Hamai *et al.*, 1995). Furthermore, the last decades of the twentieth century also saw an increased use of privatized correctional companies in the organization and delivery of such services (Johnston, 1995) and greater non-professional, voluntary participation (see also Chapter 5).

Since the 1970s, community corrections and rehabilitative programmes have been popularly perceived as 'soft options' when compared with custodial sentences, and widespread controversy continues over their 'effectiveness' – however defined. As we noted, they have also been widely viewed as marginal to the 'real work' of the sentencing processes of criminal justice, namely custody, despite the fact that the use of community penalties outnumbers those sentenced to custody in most countries (see Brownlee, 1998). In the USA, for example, there were 1.5 million adults sentenced to penal custody as against 3 million on community corrections in 1994 (Mair, 1997, p.1197). Meanwhile, in the UK at the end of the 1990s, 50 per cent of all youth sentences were community-based ones and over 150,000 adults were sentenced to community penalties and orders in comparison to the 70,000+ sentenced to immediate custody, as we see in Figures 6.1 and 6.2 below:

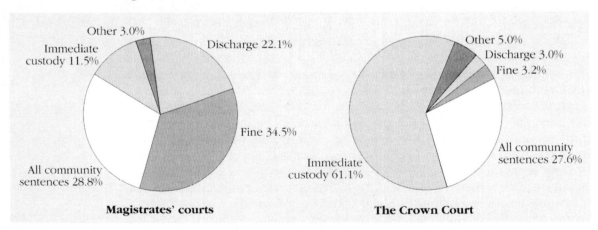

Magistrates' courts — Other 3.0%, Immediate custody 11.5%, Discharge 22.1%, Fine 34.5%, All community sentences 28.8%

The Crown Court — Other 5.0%, Discharge 3.0%, Fine 3.2%, All community sentences 27.6%, Immediate custody 61.1%

Figure 6.1: Offenders sentenced at magistrates' courts and the Crown Court for indictable offences by type of sentence or order, 1998

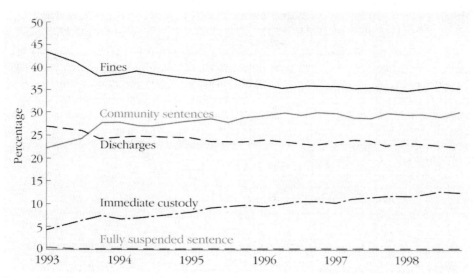

Figure 6.2: Offenders sentenced for indictable offences at magistrates' courts, by type of sentence and quarter, 1993–98

Source: Home Office, 1999

Community-based sentences and disposals tend to remain low-profile features of the criminal justice system. Until something goes 'wrong' – such as an incident involving someone on parole or probation committing some act of violence or repeat offending – or when media publicity is given to a seemingly inappropriate rehabilitative programme for young offenders (associated with headline tales of 'foreign holidays' for delinquents during the 1990s). That noted, community-based sanctions remain a central feature of the modern state's attempts to control or at best manage the problem of crime and disorder, not least due to the well-established critique of custody in terms of its expense and effectiveness. The rationale behind such disposals is by no means clear-cut and is subject to often contradictory demands as well as criticisms from both within and outside the criminal justice system. In the following sections, we explore in greater depth the community-based logics that have been influential at certain key moments in the history of this realm where 'care and control' meet criminal justice. We begin by looking at the logic of welfare and explore its place in the history of youth justice.

3   The logic of welfare

This section examines some of the key developments in youth justice in the UK in the twentieth century; we pay particular attention to the impact of welfarism on the regulation and treatment of young offenders. However, it is also crucial to note that the history of youth justice, since the point from the early nineteenth century when troubled and troublesome youth were first viewed as deserving a different response to that afforded adults, has been marked by what Muncie

Table 6.1: A comparison of welfare- and justice-based models of juvenile offending

Welfare	Justice
(a) delinquent, dependent and neglected children are all products of an adverse environment which at its worse is characterized by multiple deprivation. Social, economic and physical disadvantage, including poor parental care, are all relevant considerations;	(a) delinquency is a matter of opportunity and choice – other factors may combine to bring a child to the point of delinquency, but unless there is evidence to the contrary, the act is a manifestation of the rational decision to that effect;
(b) delinquency is a pathological condition; a symptom of some deeper maladjustment out of the control of the individual concerned;	(b) insofar as a person is responsible for his/her action, he/she should also be accountable. This is qualified in respect of children by the doctrine of criminal responsibility endorsed by statute;
(c) since people have no control over causal factors dictating their delinquency, they cannot be considered responsible for their actions or held accountable for them. Considerations of guilt or innocence are, therefore, irrelevant and punishment is inappropriate;	(c) proof of commission of an offence should be the sole justification for intervention and the sole basis of punishment;
(d) all children in trouble (both offenders and non-offenders) are basically the same and can be effectively dealt with through a single unified system designed to identify and meet the needs of children;	(d) sanctions and controls are valid responses to deviant behaviour both as an expressions of society's disapproval and as an individual and general deterrent to future similar behaviour;
(e) the needs or underlying disorders, of which delinquency is symptomatic, are capable of identification, and hence treatment and control are possible;	(e) behaviour attracting legal intervention and associated sanctions available under the law should be specifically defined to avoid uncertainty;
(f) informality is necessary if children's needs are to accurately determined and their best interests served. Strict rules of procedure or standards of proof not only hinder the identification of need but are unnecessary in proceedings conducted in the child's best interests;	(f) the power to interfere with a person's freedom and in particular that of a child should be subject to the most rigorous standard of proof which traditionally is found in a court of law;
(g) inasmuch as need is highly individualized, flexibility of response is vital. Discretion is necessary in the determination and variation of treatment measures;	(g) there should be equality before the law; like cases should be treated alike;
(h) the child and his/her welfare are paramount though considerations of public protection cannot be ignored. Prevention of neglect and alleviation of disadvantage will lead to prevention of delinquency.	(h) there should be proportionality between the seriousness of the delinquent or criminal behaviour warranting intervention and the community's response between the offence and the sentence given.

Source: adapted from the Northern Ireland Review Group (1979) (Black Report), pp.33–4

(1999, p.253) terms as 'confusion, ambiguity and unintended consequences'. Much of this complex history may be understood in terms of the ambivalence and tension between the contradictory appeals of punishment/justice for the wrong-doer and treatment/welfare for those in need of help. (Table 6.1 opposite compares welfare- and justice-based models of juvenile offending).

3.1   Key features and rationale

The logic of welfare is predicated on the assumption that interventions with **welfare** offenders (or rather people in trouble and in need of treatment) should be designed to help them and secure their reintegration into mainstream society. Welfare interventions may be located in specialized institutional regimes or in the community. The notion of welfarism assumes that offending behaviour is the result of specific pathological conditions, the causes of which may be located in the individual or in the wider social environment in which she or he is located. Criminality is thus a sickness or weakness that requires treatment, protection and care rather than punishment. Welfare interventions have accordingly focused on the social and psychological needs (as against deeds) of the offender. The intellectual perspective guiding the logic of welfare is positivism. Welfarism's key personnel are social workers, related welfare professionals and therapeutic experts employed and commissioned by the state.

3.2   Case study: a moment of welfare in the history of youth justice

The logic of welfare first emerged in the early nineteenth century when concern was voiced over the fate of troublesome and 'troubled' young people who were subject to the same retributive punishments as those given to adult offenders. From the mid nineteenth century, we can plot the development of separate institutions – for example, reformatories – for the care and containment of children and young people. The emergent assumptions were that young people needed to be treated differently, were less culpable, and were more amenable to rehabilitation than adults; there was also a concern to avoid 'contamination' with adult offenders. From its nineteenth-century origins, the youth justice system **youth justice** has been driven by the impulse not just to control young offenders but to also care for offenders and those considered 'at risk'. (For instance, age and neglect by parents were to be taken into account when dealing with juveniles.) An unintended consequence of this welfarist logic has been the tendency to draw in both offenders and the neglected, the deprived and the depraved. The development of separate institutions for delinquents based on welfarist assumptions then gained pace throughout the twentieth century. As a result, there is an underlying confusion in the youth justice system's fundamental rationale and purpose between the impulses to both control and to care for young people (Muncie, 1999, p.257). It is worth examining briefly a key moment in the operation of welfare in youth justice in the UK, by looking at developments in the 1960s.

From the outset, it is important to note that the welfarist reforms of the 1960s did not of course appear out of an ideological or policy vacuum. For example, the Children and Young Persons Act 1933 was a watershed in establishing the formal principle that work with young offenders should be linked to ensuring their general welfare. In particular, this legislation established that all courts should have primary regard to the 'welfare of the child' in which the personal influence of professionals was viewed as crucial to the delivery of this welfare-inspired form of justice. By the 1960s, the welfare approach underwent a major sea-change when custodial institutions began to be increasingly criticized for being dehumanizing, expensive, brutalizing, and criminogenic rather than welfare oriented. 'Justice' for juveniles was now also to be offered through the reduced use of custody and the establishment of a range of treatment units located in the community. In turn, the care and control of young offenders was handed over more and more to treatment-oriented experts from the social services and the psycho-social, therapeutic professions. The increasingly influential discourse was that of welfare and treatment rather than correction and punishment, and intervention was expanded to include less or non-delinquent populations 'at risk' or in need of help. What is vital to note, however, is that traditional notions of punitive justice were at no time undermined completely in the youth justice system but rather that the balance of power between the logics of punishment and welfare shifted at least rhetorically in favour of the latter during the mid-twentieth century.

In post-Second World War UK society, the development of welfare interventions towards delinquent and deprived youth was only one element in the wider social democratic solidarity project. At the height of the welfare state settlement in the first three decades of this post-war period, there was confidence in the state's capacity to deal with any social problems (of which crime and delinquency were crucial examples). Such social problems were to be analysed by social scientists commissioned by the government and solved by the 'bureau-professions' of the welfare state (Pitts, 1996, p.252; Clarke and Newman, 1997). Experts were to be trusted, whether they were medical doctors, engineers, probation officers, social workers or child and family therapists. At the same time, the new professionals of the social democratic state – such as social workers – were given responsibility to intervene proactively in the 'problem families' where delinquents were ostensibly congregated. By the 1960s in the UK, with a well-established welfare state and full (male) employment, it was argued that deprivation or lack of opportunity could no longer be considered to be at the heart of the social problem of juvenile delinquency and youth crime. Instead, the source of the problem was viewed as residing within the pathological characteristics and dynamics of certain 'problem families' and in the transmission of 'inadequacies' from one generation to the next.

ACTIVITY 6.3

Read the following extract 6.1 from *Crime–A Challenge to Us All* (1964) which was a highly influential report of a Labour Party Study Group. When reading this extract, think about what would be the policy implications of its views on the *causes* and *nature* of 'chronic or serious delinquency'.

Extract 6.1 *Crime – A Challenge to Us All*

Chronic or serious delinquency in a child is, in the main, we believe, evidence of the lack of care, the guidance and the opportunities to which every child is entitled. There are very few children who do not behave badly at times, but the children of parents with ample means rarely appear before juvenile courts. The machinery of the law is reserved mainly for working-class children who, more often than not, are also handicapped by being taught in too big classes in unsatisfactory school buildings with few amenities or opportunities for out-of-school activities. ...

We believe that in justice to our children, and for the health and well-being of society, no child in early adolescence should have to face criminal proceedings: these children should receive the kind of treatment they need, without any stigma or any association with the penal system.

Obviously the stage of development and the needs of children of any particular physical age vary widely, but there must be some dividing line. We believe that this line should be drawn at the statutory school-leaving age, and that no child under this age should be subjected to criminal proceedings. If society requires the child to remain at school, society may fairly be expected to ensure that he [sic] receives not only formal education but also training in social responsibility. ...

Opportunities for young people to develop and use to the full all their latent talents and frustrated energies – mental as well as physical – are not only their right but also the community's greatest safeguard against hooliganism, vandalism, and anti-social behaviour generally. Penal measures alone can never succeed. They must be supplemented (and eventually, we hope, made largely unnecessary) by the provision of a wide variety of things to do which will catch the imagination and engage the energies of boys and girls. ...

What is needed, therefore, is a mobilization of the whole community in a new drive for the *positive* prevention of crime, and an understanding by the whole community that the enlightened treatment of offenders is essential both for this limited but important end and for social progress in its widest sense.

(Labour Party Study Group, 1964, pp.21, 24–5, 29, 70)

The ideas embedded in such reports as *Crime–A Challenge to Us All* were part of a powerful movement in the 1960s inspired by the logic of welfare to decriminalize delinquency and to transform juvenile courts effectively into family therapy clinics. Accordingly, the 1960s may be viewed as representing *a moment* of triumph for the logic of welfare in the youth justice system. As a result, the traditional neo-classical concepts of crime control – 'criminal', 'responsibility', 'guilt and innocence', 'punishment', 'criminal offence', 'due process' – were being questioned by a discourse mobilized around alternative notions like 'welfare', 'treatment', 'disease susceptibility' and 'positive prevention'. Furthermore, the dominant view among policy and political élites was that young offending was both largely trivial and transient in nature and was also so commonplace that the full weight of the criminal law was unproductive and unnecessary. More serious or persistent juvenile offending was seen as an indication of maladjustment or damaged personality: conditions to be 'treated' rather than 'punished'. Alternatives to custody by way of treatment, non-criminal care proceedings and care orders together with a rise in the age of criminal responsibility (from 10 to 14) were advocated. The 1969 Children and Young Persons Act in England and Wales embodied many of these principles in tandem with the 1968 Social Work Act in Scotland. However, the realization of these welfarist aspirations went much further in Scotland than in England and Wales for several reasons that we will explore below.

The range of welfare interventions advocated in such 1960s' legislation was intended to deal with young offenders by means of systems of treatment, supervision and social welfare in the community rather than by means of custodial punishment. Here, the logic of welfare was in apparent ascendancy in youth justice. Embedded in such legislation was the assumption that there would be a dramatic reduction in the number of young people appearing before the courts. Most offenders would be dealt with either under care and protection proceedings or through more informal means. As a result, young offenders were to be dealt with by 'care' rather than 'criminal' proceedings. In turn, attendance centres and borstals were to be eventually abolished and replaced by community-based, intermediate treatment (IT) schemes that would offer guidance, counselling, supervised activities or residential care in local authority community homes with education. There was to be increased involvement of local authority social workers whose key role was to prevent delinquency by proactive intervention in the family life of the 'pre-delinquent', to provide expert assessment of the child's needs and to promote non-custodial disposals. Moreover, magistrates were to be removed from any involvement in the detailed decisions about appropriate treatment programmes and disposals. These proposals represent the high point of the welfare impulse towards young offenders in the UK in the twentieth century: 'Traditional concepts of criminal justice were overturned' (Muncie, 1999, p.259).

However, in the case of the 1969 Children and Young Persons Act in England and Wales, the distinction between what was proposed in the legislation and what was put into practice is intrinsic to the unfolding story of this welfare-inspired legislation. In fact, due to an 'unholy' coalition of forces including magistrates, the police, the legal profession, the probation service and conservative politicians (Bottoms, 1974), the Act's attempt to decriminalize the youth justice system was undercut from the start and vital elements of the Act were never implemented. Critics pointed to its excessively welfarist and permissive features. When the new Conservative government came into office in 1970, it rejected implementing key sections of the Act, including raising the age of criminal responsibility from 10 to 14 and replacing criminal with care proceedings. As a consequence of such developments and the continuing hostility of the police and magistrates to many of its remaining welfarist aims, the new principles were grafted onto the old structures of juvenile justice rather than replacing them. Punishment and treatment continued to coexist: intermediate treatment, for example, was implemented but attendance and detention centres were never abolished. Critics (Thorpe *et al.*, 1980) have also noted that in practice the welfare elements of the reformed system were most frequently employed with both a younger age group and less 'serious' categories, such as young women on the grounds of 'moral danger', low school achievers and truants. This was the domain of influence of social workers. Meanwhile, courts and thus magistrates continued to use the justice-based 'old' policy of punishing young offenders.

In Scotland, the 1960s' debate between punishment and welfare for young offenders saw a different outcome. The Kilbrandon Report (Scottish Home and Health Department and Scottish Education Department, 1964) argued that social work intervention in youth crime was most likely to be effective if it concentrated on the social and emotional problems and needs of children and young people in trouble rather than their offences and 'deeds' (Pitts, 1996, p.256). The subsequent Social Work (Scotland) Act 1968 drew fully on the recommendations of this report. As a result, new social work departments were set up to promote social welfare for children in need and the children's hearings system replaced courts for young offenders. As McAra and Young (1997) note, the 1968 Act abolished a separate probation service, established the unique Scottish children's hearings system and handed over administrative responsibility for both to local authority social work departments. 'In this one move, areas of criminal justice which are the province of criminal justice agencies in most other jurisdictions, became in Scotland the "property" of social work' (McAra and Young, 1997, p.8). This system of children's hearings has survived into the twenty-first century. According to its supporters, it has managed to both resist the politics of punitive populism of the Conservative governments of the 1980s and 1990s and to hold on to the 'Kilbrandon idea' that crime and delinquency ought not to be seen narrowly as violations of the criminal law but in the broader context of the psychological and social problems that are a part of growing up. It remains a 'brave experiment in decriminalization, it appears to have widespread support amongst practitioners and the public and there is no evidence that it fails to work' (McAra and Young, 1997, p.10 but see McGhee *et al.*, 1996).

These hearings are welfare tribunals serviced by lay people. Cases are first referred to a Reporter from a range of agencies and it is the role of the Reporter to sift referrals and decide on future courses of action. Reporters have considerable discretionary power. The main grounds for referring cases to hearings is a mix of both offence and non-offence factors. When a case reaches a hearing, it is deliberated upon by three lay members of a panel, the parents or guardians of the child, social worker representatives and the child. Legal representation is not encouraged. The hearing does not determine guilt or innocence and is only concerned with deciding future courses of action. Before any decision is reached, reports on the child from the social work department are heard.

ACTIVITY 6.4

The Scottish children's hearing system is often viewed as a model for the reform of justice-based systems. What are its main attractions when viewed from a welfare-oriented perspective and what are its disadvantages when viewed from a 'just deserts' viewpoint?

It is important to note at this point that the logic of welfare remains at least formally the cornerstone of all work with young offenders, both in the UK and internationally. Indeed, the United Nations Convention on the Rights of the Child requires that in all legal actions against people aged under 18 the 'best interests of the child' shall prevail. However, since the 1970s in England and Wales (if not Scotland), the welfarist logic has become increasingly contested and undermined in the politics and practices of youth justice.

3.3 The collapse of welfare and the resurgence of justice

Whilst it is crucial to remember that the logic of welfare always co-existed with custodial and justice-based rationales of intervention in the post-war youth justice system, it is clear that the welfarist settlement unravelled during the 1970s in England and Wales, if not Scotland. The post-war welfarist settlement around youth justice came under increasing attack throughout the 1970s from a number of different constituencies. These critical voices ranged from the liberal justice lobby, traditional conservative groups such as magistrates, both radical and administrative Home Office-based criminologists and others: children's rights pressure groups, radical practitioners and lawyers. The character of the contestations to the dominant logic of welfare ranged from the political, philosophical and moral to the pragmatic. Much of the impetus behind the critique of welfare was that welfarist interventions were too 'soft on crime'. However, radical voices also contended that the treatment model and rationale resulted in considerable and pernicious restrictions and controls over the lives and liberties of young people, particularly young women, which were out of proportion to the realities of being 'at risk' or the seriousness of the offence. Welfarism had proven to be just as capable of drawing more young people into the net of juvenile justice as it was of providing care and protection to its vulnerable 'charges'. Indeed, it may be argued that identifying needs effectively amounts to identifying reasons for intervention in the lives of more and younger rather than less young people. According to critics, behind the rhetoric of benevolence and humanitarianism lies the reality of discretionary and non-accountable processes, the denial of legal rights and due process and the capacity for the system to impose much greater interventions than would be justified on the basis of conduct alone.

ACTIVITY 6.5

It has been argued that welfarism appears to encourage greater intervention into the lives of young women relative to young men (Hudson, 1988). How might a feminist criminologist explain the fact that young women may find themselves committed into residential care of the local authority and are thus stigmatized, without having committed an offence at all?

Feminist criminologists (see Eaton, 1986) might point to the 'double standard' at work in the treatment of young women as against young men. There are stronger constraints on the social and sexual behaviour of females, transgressions of which may result in proactive interventions. For example, status offences such as running away from home, staying out late at night which are not punishable by law if committed by an adult, and rarely considered as 'serious' if committed by boys, may result in the 'pathologization' of young females, not least because they have deviated against social codes which prescribe what is appropriate and 'natural' for women (Hudson, 1988).

Alongside these criticisms of discretionary and discriminatory outcomes were the arguments that the interests of children and young people would be better served by restoring the principles of legality and due process to the youth justice system. This heralded the resurgence of a 'back to justice' movement. The key principles associated with this justice model of youth justice were those of equity and protection of rights, an end to indeterminacy and disparities in sentencing, and proportionality of punishment to the crime.

More pragmatic criticisms of welfare-based interventions were also voiced, most famously captured by the phrase 'nothing works'. Influential researchers in both the USA and the UK throughout the 1970s pointed to the lack of evidence that treatment-based interventions were successful in preventing re-offending and reconviction. The most famous and influential academic critique of welfare was Martinson's (1974) analysis of 231 research studies of treatment programmes in the USA. On the basis of his analysis, Martinson (1974, p.25) concluded that 'with few and isolated exceptions the rehabilitative efforts that have been reported so far have had no appreciable effect on recidivism'. Martinson's conclusion was widely viewed as the definitive confirmation from the academic research community that 'nothing works' in terms of welfare-inspired attempts to rehabilitate (young) offenders (although in fact he argued that nothing works better than anything else).

By the 1980s, alongside the re-emergence of a justice-based philosophy, a more pragmatic approach to managing the problem of youth offending by means of diversion came to the fore in much of the local routine processing of young offenders. Diversionary strategies tend to involve one or more of the following intentions and outcomes:

diversion

1   Diversion from prosecution, particularly through a police-driven system of cautioning minor offenders through informal and formal warnings.

2   Diversion from custody by means of various crime-prevention initiatives and through community-based programmes.

Community-based programmes to divert young offenders from crime: vehicle projects and photography classes

According to some critics (Pratt, 1989; Cohen, 1985), these efforts at diversion both further eroded the rights to due process of young offenders and widened the reach and intensity of state control. This critique may be accurate in terms of the lack of attention paid to the legal rights of the offender. (We will explore this further in section 5.)

Throughout the 1980s, cases were increasingly dealt with by multi-agency teams who bureaucratically decided on outcomes without recourse to questions of due process. However, the evidence from the numbers of young people being prosecuted and receiving custodial sentences during the 1980s appears to cast some doubt on the claim that the reach and intensity of state control increased in England and Wales during this period of diversion. By the mid-1980s there was a dramatic reduction in numbers sent to custody, and the custodial mode of disposal was increasingly replaced by informal cautioning and use of intensive supervision for more serious and repeat offenders. Between 1983 and 1993, the number of young offenders sentenced to immediate custody fell from 13,500 to 3,300 (Home Office, 1996). The period 1985–93 also saw a 39 per cent drop in 'known young offenders', which was partly due to demographic factors but mostly due to the 'increasing dominance of a diversionary paradigm among juvenile justice practitioners' (Newburn, 1998, p.200). A strategy of diversion had emerged which was designed to prevent young offending and keep them out of the 'systems' of court and custodial institutions. Newburn (1998) has noted that there is some cause for pride in the movement during the 1980s toward the virtual abolition of juvenile imprisonment.

Much of the impetus for this shift towards diversionary strategies was pragmatic and driven by cost-effective and efficiency impulses. Claims were made that such strategies would produce a better managed system and would also save on the excessive costs of both welfare and justice approaches. According to critical commentators such as Pratt (1989) and Crawford (1997), there is little point in considering these developments in youth justice in terms of either justice or welfare. Rather, it is argued that a new 'corporatist' strategy had emerged, which was characterized by administrative decision-making and the centralization of authority and co-ordination of policy. The new aim was to manage the 'at risk' population of young offenders in the most economic and efficient ways. In the 1990s, this managerialist, diversionary impulse received strong support from the influential reports of the Audit Commission (1996) and was embedded in aspects of the reforms brought to the youth justice system by the 1998 Crime and Disorder Act, with the new aim of 'preventing offending'. It is likely that goals of welfare or justice will continue in the future to be joined, challenged and possibly distorted and subverted by the more pragmatic managerial calculus of auditing 'what works' in terms of cost-effectiveness and efficiency.

It would be premature to assume, however, that a managerialist, multi-agency co-ordinated strategy of diversion achieved an unchallenged ascendancy in youth justice

Villains or victims? The moral panic over children as repeat offenders – eleven-year-old boy nicknamed 'Balaclava boy' was arrested numerous times for joy-riding in 1993. He came to represent the supposed pinnacle of children out of control. In 2000, he died of a drug overdose whilst in police custody

in the 1990s. Instead, we need to note the significance of yet another simultaneous and contradictory development in the 1990s – a return to dealing punitively with young offenders. This retributive turn involved the appropriation of a 'just deserts' philosophy and is associated with the renewal of the claim that custody should be promoted as the desired option versus last resort for offenders. This changing climate of opinion towards youth justice was doubtless influenced by the moral panic over youth crime and disorder associated with a number of 'riots' and disturbances, the media coverage of infamous repeat offenders and the key moment of the murder of two-year-old James Bulger in 1993 (and the subsequent public debate). It was also the early 1990s that saw the emergence of the 'prisons work' credo of then Home Secretary, Michael Howard. A dominant impulse was increasingly that of punishing all young offenders, whether in institutional or community settings. This in turn was associated with calls for the most efficient ways of delivering 'punishment in the community', epitomized by the 1991 Criminal Justice Act (discussed further in section 4 below). Bottoms (1995) has noted that the mid-1990s in the UK witnessed a heightened climate of populist punitiveness across the major British political parties. Indicative of this was the Labour party's recognition in 1996 that punishment took precedence over the welfare needs of the offender and that 'the welfare needs of the individual young offender cannot outweigh the needs of the community to be protected from the adverse consequences of his or her behaviour' (Labour Party, 1996, p.9).

populist punitiveness

Most commentators agree that youth justice is an uneasy coexistence of competing strategies of welfare-based, justice-based diversionary interventions and punitive deterrence through use of custodial interventions. As Muncie (1999, p.254) notes, the history of youth justice policy is 'predominantly a history of political and professional debate, in which the diverse and competing discourses of welfare, justice, diversion and custody have come to do battle over their respective places in the management of the "delinquent body"'.

4 The logic of rehabilitation

4.1 Key features and rationale

The logic of rehabilitation underlies the range of correctional strategies and techniques aimed at the reform of offenders. This logic is institutionalized in various treatment and reformative regimes which aim to retrain and re-socialize offenders. The logic is closely linked to the broader impulse of welfarism given its concern to *treat* rather than *punish* the offender but, as a correctional ideology, it is targeted more on the offender population in particular than broad-based welfarist strategies targeted at multi-faceted social problems (**Cullen and Gilbert, 1982**). The logic of rehabilitation has both 'moral' and 'scientific' roots in the criminal justice system. As Chapter 4 notes, it entered the workings of the prison system at the end of the nineteenth century by means of both moral humanitarian arguments ('saving souls') and scientific justifications in terms of treatment ('curing the sick'). The effect of this shift of strategy was not restricted to events inside the prison but reverberated throughout the merging correctional and preventive regimes in the penal-welfare complex in subsequent decades in the twentieth century. Indeed, by the mid-twentieth century the strategies of

rehabilitation

treatment-oriented rehabilitation gained ascendancy as the means of crime prevention *par excellence* (Hughes, 1998). According to its supporters, such as Cullen and Gilbert, rehabilitation as a correctional ideology is the only rational justification for criminal sanctions.

4.2 Case study: a moment of rehabilitation in the history of probation

probation The rehabilitative roots of the modern probation service lie in the late nineteenth century when religiously driven volunteers attended courts and sought to 'advise, assist and befriend' adult offenders in an effort to 'rescue' them and their souls from a life of sin, drunkenness and crime. Such missionaries realized their work by means of appeals to the magistrates to bind over to their charge those offenders for whom moral 'restoration and reclamation' through 'grace' was considered possible (McWilliams, 1983). This original moralizing and missionary impulse behind probation – moral rehabilitation – held sway into the early decades of the twentieth century and continued to play an important, if increasingly contested, role in probation work in the post-Second World War period. By the mid-twentieth century the probation service had been gradually transformed into a self-consciously therapeutic profession aimed at treating and rehabilitating offenders. Indeed, from the 1950s onwards, probation experts sponsored, wherever possible, non-custodial disposals in the name of rehabilitative therapy and against the impulse of retributive punishments (McWilliams, 1985).

The status of the probation service as the key bearer of genuine alternatives to custodial sentences was first established in the 1907 Probation of Offenders Act. In this Act and subsequent Criminal Justice Acts of 1925 and 1948, Bill Jordan (1971) has observed that probation was defined as a 'species of liberty (rather) than a species of imprisonment'. And although the probation service throughout the period continued to sit uneasily between the two competing impulses of control and care, it was its function as a social service designed to prevent further offending that impressed contemporary criminological commentators and members of the 'penal-welfare' complex alike (Radzinowicz, 1958; McWilliams, 1987). Eugene McLaughlin (1998, p.164) has observed that this opposition between the two roles – care or control – did not prevent the probation service being the 'jewel in the crown' of the social democratic criminal justice settlement. Indeed, the service was lionized for its provision of the first genuinely constructive alternative to custodial sentences for adult offenders and also for its commitment to ensuring that the rehabilitation of offenders was a legitimate goal of criminal justice. In the period of the post-war social democratic criminal justice settlement, it is thus possible to decipher a *moment* when the logic of rehabilitation largely defined the work and ethos of the probation service.

The probation order is arguably the most potent example of the long-standing association between punishment in the community and the reduction of future levels of offending through reform and rehabilitation. The formal goal of most community sanctions is the reduction of offending or re-offending. Traditionally, they have been justified on consequentialist grounds: namely that the imposition of the sanction is justified by pointing to some future 'good' which will follow as a consequence of the act. This justification is both forward looking and focused on ends. From its inception, the probation order held out the positive prospect of bringing about some positive changes in an offender's attitudes and behaviour (Brownlee, 1998, p.50). More generally, the consolidation of criminology as a positivist scientific discipline, promoting the development of 'normalizing' regimes based on the diagnosis and treatment of the causes of criminality, further reinforced the reformative zeal and mission of the probation service (McWilliams, 1987).

Throughout the first half of the twentieth century, the probation service entered what many commentators refer to as the 'second age of probation' (following the 'first age' of a moral and religiously driven mission), guided by the concept of *scientific diagnosis*. The emphasis then moved from saving lost souls to treating the pathologies of the sick (May, 1994, p.863). McWilliams (1986, p.257) has noted that this shift towards scientific diagnosis and therapy was strengthened further in the post-war social democratic welfare state. The mission of scientific diagnosis was to alter the relationship between probation officers and the courts so that the former were elevated from the subordinate position of supplicants for mercy to that of 'experts', present in court to both educate and guide magistrates into arriving at the correct disposal based on scientifically objective criteria. It is worth noting that the claim that the technical application of knowledge and expertise would be able to solve the 'ills' and problems of society, including that of crime and offending, would impose a burden of optimistic and grandiose expectations on rehabilitative regimes and the probation service that would prove to far outweigh any of their tangible successes.

By the 1960s, probation officers, whilst organized in 103 local services throughout England and Wales and formally under the direction of magistrates' committees, nonetheless had the hallmarks of an independent profession, particularly in their freedom to exercise discretion in their work. The only major limitation to their professional autonomy was the fact that officers had to accept the court's decision over the selection of their cases. Apart from this significant constraint, once the probation order was made, the officer of the (overwhelmingly male) probation service was able to supervise the client as 'he' chose and this freedom was further consolidated by the officer being personally responsible to the court for the conduct of each case. Officers thus enjoyed a considerable degree of professional autonomy and were able to use their discretion to determine the nature of the rehabilitative treatment 'programme' that they controlled.

Throughout the 1960s, the professional status and authority of probation officers was consolidated further. They became professional case workers with diagnostic skills in a specialized field organized around the logic of rehabilitation and epitomized by the social enquiry report. This report was delivered to the court as an objective, diagnostic appraisal of the offender and his or her 'needs' (McWilliams, 1985). In such reports as *The Morrison Committee of Inquiry into Probation* (Home Office, 1962), it was re-affirmed that the focus of the profession's work should continue to be on the offender's psychological needs and social responsibilities. The vocational purpose of the service in the 1960s appears to have been that associated with its origins, namely to 'advise, assist and befriend' offenders, to speak for them and to persuade the judiciary not to impose custodial sentences. In some ways, probation stood in opposition to both prison and punishment. However, even the Morrison report, which promoted the rehabilitative ethos of the service, noted the tension between the dual purposes of probation:

> It must be added that while, as a caseworker, the probation officer's prime concern is with the well-being of an individual, he is also the agent of a system concerned with the protection of society and as such must, to a degree which varies from case to case, and during the course of supervision, seek to regulate the probationer's behaviour. He must also be prepared, when necessary, to assert the interests of society by initiating proceedings for breach of the requirements of the probation order. This dichotomy of duties ... 'is one of which the probation officer cannot cease to be conscious, and the recognition of him as a representative of 'authority' will affect the casework technique that the officer employs.
>
> (Home Office, 1962, p.23)

By the end of the 1960s, the probation service underwent further expansion in its care and control responsibilities as a result of assuming responsibility for all prison, borstal and detention centre after-care. This development transformed the nature of the profession's role with an increasing proportion of its clients (from one-tenth in 1951 to one-quarter in 1971) supervised as a result of having been imprisoned rather than diverted from imprisonment (Brownlee, 1998, pp.71–2). As a consequence of this expanded role, the service came into increasingly close contact with the custodial parts of the penal system.

These potentially conflicting responsibilities (between care and control) would come to a head in the Labour government's attempt to construct a decriminalizing and rehabilitative settlement with regard to young offenders as we saw in section 3.2.

ACTIVITY 6.6

Look back to the discussion in section 3.2 and note the main threats which the proposed 'decriminalization' of juvenile justice in both England and Wales and Scotland may have held for the professional power and status of the probation service.

As we noted, government proposals for the reform of juvenile justice in both Scotland and England and Wales pointed to social workers taking over responsibility for young people in need of care, protection and control. According to Jordan (1971), almost overnight, the probation service was transformed into a conservative correctionalist force in the field of delinquency. In particular, the service fought to maintain its independent professional status by emphasizing its role as a court-based service for offenders (Bottoms, 1974). From this point, we can plot the unsettling of the formerly dominant logic of rehabilitation in probation.

The history of the probation service demonstrates quite clearly that this service, like those associated with youth justice, has always operated with a range of contradictory aspirations – both care and control, liberation and restraint, calling offenders to account and demanding social reform (Harris, 1992, p.154;

Brownlee, 1998, p.67). In section 4.3, we show how the balance in recent decades has shifted dramatically away from a logic of rehabilitation towards a rationale of supervision of community punishments and risk-management.

4.3 The emergence of community punishments and risk-management

From the 1970s to the mid-1990s, there was a broad political consensus and widespread acceptance among members of influential policy networks in the criminal justice system of the need to reduce the pressure of over-crowding in prisons, in particular as a result of the costs and failures of incarceration. This may seem counter-intuitive to those familiar with the law-and-order rhetoric of first the Heath government and then those associated with Thatcherism. However, given the likelihood that crime would continue to rise, policy makers were faced with the choice of financing an ever-increasing prison population or developing new initiatives to reduce the use of custody. As late as 1990, the White Paper, *Crime, Justice and Protecting the Public*, stated that 'for most offenders, imprisonment has to be justified in terms of public protection, denunciation and retribution. Otherwise it can be an expensive way of making bad people worse' (Home Office, 1990, para. 2.7).

The probation service was one of the major beneficiaries of this policy dilemma and the pragmatic responses that followed. It is hardly coincidental that this period witnessed a proliferation of community-based sanctions. Two main strands were evident in the 'reductive' policy, which emerged from the mid-1960s onwards. The first strand involved the introduction in 1967 of parole and its extension over the next two decades. The second was the attempt to encourage sentencers not to send people to prison at all through the creation of new 'alternatives to custody' (Brownlee, 1998, p.9). These measures included:

- the suspended sentence (1967)

- the community service order (1972)

- probation with special conditions (1972).

In terms of the reductive effects of such measures, there was little evidence that they worked to replace custodial measures and the prison population continued to rise. It was noted in Chapter 3 that attempts to reduce the use of custody by sentencers has often been circumvented by the sentencers themselves. For instance, sentencers may refuse to use such alternatives at all for offenders who may have received custodial penalties or may only use these forms of penalties for offenders who would previously have received other penalties lower down the scale (such as the fine). This 'up-tariffing' was the fate of community service orders introduced in the 1970s (Pease, 1980). As a consequence, new community sanctions often became 'additions' rather than alternatives to custody.

By the 1980s, given the increasing official recorded crime rate and the perceived failures of rehabilitation, punishment was increasingly emphasized as a core component of 'alternatives to custody' (May, 1991, p.221). More and more, the logic of rehabilitation was called into question in the work of probation officers with offenders as well as more generally in the criminal justice system.

Not surprisingly, throughout the 1980s and 1990s, the rationale and practice of probation was under increasing critical scrutiny. The social democratic settlement around the logic of rehabilitation – with the probation officer as its expert missionary – appeared exhausted. A new logic was under production and a new settlement awaited.

The 1991 Criminal Justice Act is widely recognized as a crucial watershed in the shift from a predominantly rehabilitative logic to a more punitive rationale for community-based sanctions. We saw in Chapter 3 that the 1991 Act was based explicitly on a just deserts model of punishment, with the focus on the offence rather than the offender. It was also predicated on a rationale of bifurcation (or twin-track approach) for the punishment of offenders, dependent on the classification of seriousness. It is important to recognize that the Act had the potential to reduce the use of custody for those defined as 'less serious' or 'non-dangerous' offenders. That noted, the Act was also particularly significant in the realm of community sanctions and disposals for its explicit use of the notion of 'community penalties' to replace what was viewed as the 'soft' and politically unacceptable term of 'non-custodial penalties'. In turn, the Act was designed to 'toughen up' the image and work of the probation service, a key task of which would be the organization and management of community punishment in its many guises. A community sentence was defined in section 6 of the Act as one which consists of one or more of the following:

bifurcation

- probation order
- community service order
- combination order
- curfew order (with the possible use of electronic tagging) for offenders over 16, which may be used on its own or in tandem
- supervision order (10–17 year olds only)
- attendance centre order (10–20 year olds only).

It is worth noting that the probation order was now a sentence of the court rather than a disposal in lieu of sentencing. Chapters 3 and 5 have already explored the ways in which much of the Act was largely undermined from the mid-1990s onwards, not least by the government's espousal of a rampantly punitive and populist 'prison works' agenda. Cavadino and Dignan (1997) describe this agenda as inaugurating a 'Law and Order Counter Reformation' of criminal justice policy, noting that it was driven by a populist, retributive ideological rationale rather than anything approximating a rational, evidence-based one. Following in the footsteps of developments in the USA, what Schichor and Sechrest (1998) term 'vengeance as public policy' emerged .

We noted at the beginning of this chapter that no one logic is all powerful in the work of agencies involved in community disposals and sanctions. We find instead an admixture of at times contradictory impulses in the work of both youth justice and probation services. What is worth emphasizing about these developments in the 1990s is the consolidation of the shift of direction towards a more explicitly punitive rationale for probation work rather than a complete change of direction from what went before (Broad, 1991, p.19). Despite some key reversals of the 1991 Act's potentially reductive, bifurcatory rationale for distinguishing serious and less serious offenders, what remained of its powers with regard to the ethos, practice and management of 'tough' punishment in the community dramatically affected the work of the probation service throughout the 1990s and into the twenty-first century. The 1991 Act converted the probation order into a punishment in its own right rather than the alternative to punishment that it had been previously. Probation was increasingly driven by an offence-focused regime of punishments in which retribution was the overriding principle (Brownlee, 1998, p.91). As a result, probation workers were identified more explicitly as agents of formal social control. They were now to be regarded as chiefly officers of the court whose primary responsibility was that of helping the court to assess the risk of re-offending.

Throughout the 1990s, the imposition of national standards on the probation service was indicative both of the sustained assault on the previous professional autonomy of the occupation and of the wish to transform probation from a service chiefly concerned with client rehabilitation to that of offender control. The expanded versions of the National Standards for the Supervision of Offenders in the Community (first published in 1992 and revised in 1995) were particularly significant in these toughening, centralizing and de-professionalizing developments. The latter underlined the remit of community sentences in both restricting the liberty of offenders and making very real mental and physical demands upon them. As a result of these National Standards, probation officers were now required to prepare pre-sentence reports for the courts that prioritized the seriousness of the offence(s) involved, and which addressed the possible reductive effects of a community sentence only where such a disposal was not rendered unlikely by retributive considerations (Brownlee, 1998, pp.20–1). As a result, pre-sentence reports throughout the 1990s became less focused on the diagnosis of offender needs and more on the sentencing requirements of the court. In Worrall's (1997, p.78) words, we saw a 'taking of the social out of inquiry reports'. The assault on the traditional rehabilitative and social work-oriented ethos of 'advise, assist and befriend' was further consolidated in the Green Paper, *Strengthening Punishment in the Community* (Home Office, 1995a), in which the reputation of probation as a 'soft option' was criticized. In that same year, the Home Secretary, Michael Howard, in an address to the National Probation Conference, rejected the 'approach which equated punishment in the community with social work with offenders' (*The Guardian*, 17 March 1995). Later that same year the legal requirement that probation officers hold a diploma in social work on entry to the service was dropped. Opposition was expressed towards the more draconian features of this assault on probation specifically, and the rehabilitative ethos more generally from, amongst others, previous Tory Home Secretaries and the vast majority of academics. However, in the run-up to the election of 1997 the major opposition party, Labour, refused to ally itself with opponents of law-and-order measures and instead sought to persuade the electorate of its own 'tough' on crime and 'law-and-order' credentials. A 'Dutch auction' thus ensued, with each party outbidding the other in terms of its punitiveness towards the increasingly demonized 'other', the supposed hard core of serious and persistent criminals.

A new political and ideological settlement around the punitive rationale of community-based sentences was thus firmly established by the mid-to-late-1990s. The period following the election of the Labour government in 1997 has witnessed the further hardening of a culture of severity with regard to toughening up both community punishments and the work of probation. Among the proposals made by ministers in the Blair government were uniforms for all those undertaking community service, new weekend or weekday 'part-time' custodial sentences (including sessions where people would be obliged to address their offending), and removal of income support for non-compliers. Meanwhile, towards the end of the 1990s, lengthy discussions were taking place in the Home Office regarding the re-naming of the probation service in England and Wales in an effort to highlight the new enforcement culture which would underpin its work. The title of 'Community, Rehabilitation And Punishment Service' was suggested until its unfortunate acronym was realized! The more prosaic 'Probation Service of England and Wales' was adopted: a re-branding that also signalled the growing centralization of the service. It is worth noting that much of the debate in the UK in the 1990s on custodial and community punishments and their management – in common with other aspects of crime control – drew on lessons from United States policy agenda and its 'war on crime', despite the extreme nature of the latter's preferred 'solution'. As Jock Young has observed, 'To attempt to learn crime control from the US is rather like travelling to Saudi Arabia to learn about women's rights' (cited in James and Raine, 1998, p.16).

In tandem with the shift towards a more clearly defined punitive enforcement role for probation services, there has also been an increased centralization of the administration, purpose and role of the probation service. The assumed commonality between the interests and experience of officers and those who managed them was also challenged by the ideas of the new public management in the 1980s and 1990s. In other words, there was an attack on the professional

'Shackled to mother': the American nightmare?

autonomy of the probation officer and an intensification of the managerialization of this criminal justice agency. This has clear parallels with the criminal justice system as a whole in this period (McLaughlin and Muncie, 2000). The influential public watchdog of economy, effectiveness and efficiency of public services, the Audit Commission (1996), has given strong support for community sentences on cost-efficiency and effectiveness grounds. More generally, the local autonomy of the service and its officers has been further constrained and undermined by the increasingly influential interventions of managerialist bodies of the 'new public management', such as the Audit Commission (again), the probation inspectorate as well as the more explicit promotion of 'leadership' and 'direction' from senior management within the service. As with other agencies of the criminal justice system, greater emphasis has been placed on external regulation and monitoring of the service. According to Tim May, probation has entered a 'punishment/administrative phase' (in contrast to the professional/therapeutic ethic) in which community rather than just prison becomes the place for punishment (May, 1994, p.870). Clearly, there is no single task for probation; according to James and Raine (1998, pp.9–10), contemporary probation involves three main tasks:

1 managing the non-custodial penalties passed by the court;

2 managing the process of reintegration of the offender into the community and the promotion of law-abiding behaviour after punishment;

3 protecting the public.

ACTIVITY 6.7

Compare the key concerns of a probation officer during the earlier period in which the logic of rehabilitation held sway with those of the probation officer at the end of the twentieth century.

The role and responsibilities of community-based criminal justice agencies were shaped in the 1990s by means of a series of key policy developments, all under the banner of 'public protection'. This has become a key rationale for the police, prison and probation services. While the emphasis on protecting the public rather than helping/rehabilitating the offender is hardly new to the criminal justice system, what is new is its unchallenged and seemingly unchallengeable primacy (Nash, 1998). As part of this rationale, probation work is increasingly focused on the assessment, prediction and management of dangerousness and risk of re-offending. Indeed, the attempt to produce risk-assessment guidelines was more and more common to a variety of criminal justice agencies, such as the police. The increasing significance and centrality to probation work of dealing with dangerous people was clearly embedded in the HMI report (Home Office, 1995b), *Dealing with Dangerous People: The Probation Service and Public Protection*. This report established the key principle that the protection of the public always takes priority over the right of confidentiality of those with whom the service is involved. It also established other new principles: all clients were now to be assessed for 'risk'. In addition, the supervision of dangerous offenders was to take priority over that of all other offenders. The new principles also emphasized the necessity of constant monitoring and supervision of the work of probation officers. Furthermore, there was a shift from the one-to-one confidential 'client'-based work to that of 'public partnership' work with other agencies, especially the police. As a result of such developments and revised guidelines and principles, the overriding responsibility of the reformed service at the beginning of the millennium was to identify potentially dangerous offenders and to manage and supervise the risk they could pose to the community. The 'effective' assessment and management of risk had become the key to the work of the service.

As the 1990s unfolded, the probation officer was 're-designed' from being a court 'social worker' (balancing the responsibilities of care and control) to a crime prevention officer charged with assessing and managing risk in order to protect the public. The core task of probation officers had less to do with the application of social work and rehabilitative skills and much more to do with 'system involvement and offender management' (Harris, 1994, p.34). Given the increasingly punitive and privatized climate at the end of the twentieth century, this new role has been embraced – albeit reluctantly and with little choice – by the probation service. It could be argued that this may be the only means through which the profession can remain in the public criminal justice system.

5   The logic of restorative justice

5.1   Key features and rationale

Sections 3 and 4 explored the rise to prominence and subsequent unsettling of the closely inter-related logics of welfare and rehabilitation, which have crucially informed the workings of community sanctions. Both were in part undermined by the apparent lack of a punitive impulse behind their rationales for dealing with offenders. Out of the crisis and unsettling of these two distinctive narratives of community sanctions has emerged a third logic, that of *restorative justice*, whose political cachet may lie in its appearing to offer a 'tougher' reworking of the concerns with welfare-based reform and rehabilitation of the offender alongside those of justice and rights for the victim and punishment for wrong-doing. It could be argued that the logic of restorative justice offers the means to both maintain some of the ambitions of the earlier logics of welfare and rehabilitation and also address the main criticisms to which they were subjected.

restorative justice

Restorative justice initiatives are one element in a much wider destructuring strategy of crime control, where the shared rationale is to transcend criminal justice and legal formalism by means of alternative informal and communal means of conflict resolution. Morris and Gelsthorpe (2000, pp.18–19) note that restorative justice means different things to different people. It is often equated with compensation, community service and victim–offender mediation. However, in Morris and Gelsthorpe's view, restorative justice is about more than a particular forum for decision-making or a set of outcomes. Rather, it is concerned with a particular set of values that underpin and influence processes and outcomes, and which should take priority over competing values. The

abolitionism

theoretical base of this broad strategy is influenced by abolitionism but is also made up of various, at times conflicting, perspectives ranging from critical criminology, labelling theory to communitarianism and neo-conservatism. Abolitionists in particular are keen to remind us that the events and behaviours that are criminalized make up only a minute part of the events and behaviour that can be defined as criminal. They suggest that crime is not the object but the product of crime-control philosophies and institutions. More particularly, social problems, conflicts and troubles are viewed as an inevitable part of everyday life and therefore cannot, or rather should not, be delegated to professionals and specialists claiming to provide 'solutions'. When professionals and state agencies intervene, the essence of social problems and conflicts are 'stolen' and represented in forms that only perpetuate the problems and conflicts (Christie, 1977; **de Haan, 1991**). Traditional state-based, adversarial justice makes the victim and offender passive spectators (if not victims) at formal and legalistic court proceedings. Christie (1993) suggests that the abolition of the 'crime control industry' would revitalize the social fabric by allowing other forms of conflict resolution, peace-making and community safety to be envisaged. The main tenet of the abolitionist critique of traditional formal criminal justice is founded on the criminalizing consequences of shaming and stigmatization and retributive punishment, and on the failures of contemporary criminal justice policies that rely, to an alarming degree, on imprisonment.

There is a revived interest in the notion that communities, rather than formal agencies of the criminal justice system, should take greater responsibility for dealing with both the causes of offending and disorder generally and the settlement of disputes between members of a community or neighbourhood. The rise of the logic of restorative justice also relates to a trend towards punishment practices designed to allow for emotional release, and covering the full spectrum of human sentiment – from forgiveness and reconciliation to debasement and humiliation and which are also intended to give out clear signs and messages to local communities and the public at large about the way to view offenders on whom these are inflicted, ranging from reintegration and re-acceptance to shaming and degradation. Appeals based on this moralizing communitarianism are arguably of greater influence on the largely state-sponsored moves to establish restitutive-, reparative- and meditation-based initiatives in the first decade of the twenty-first century rather than the decriminalizing and destructuring impulse of abolitionist calls for restorative justice. Communitarians of different varieties share the abolitionist bias towards informal, reintegrative and educational solutions (Hughes, 1996). However, they also openly accept that punishment is the inevitable concomitant of law enforcement and see censure as a mostly legitimate response to wrong-doing, with denunciation in the name of the victim and the common good as morally appropriate. The advent of the multi-agency approach to community-based crime prevention and justice has helped foster a communitarian rhetoric of direct community involvement in crime control; as a result, there has been the growth of involvement of non-statutory bodies in the provision and management of such sanctions. However, this should not be read as constituting any dramatic transfer of responsibility from statist, formally structured organizations towards the 'civil' and the 'informal'. The shift appears to be more about the relocation of some sanctions from segregative institutions into certain geographically defined localities. Punishments are increasingly *in* the community but not *of* the community (Brownlee, 1998, p.57).

communitarianism

restitution

reparation

mediation

ACTIVITY 6.8

What are the likely dangers of promoting punishments 'of' the community rather than 'in' the community? Try to think of some examples where direct community action against perceived dangerous others may threaten the rule of law and individual liberties.

The dangers of active and direct involvement of the community in the punishment and sanctioning of offenders are most clearly apparent in vigilante-style processes where members of the community 'take the law into their own hands' and use coercive power or violence over the wrong-doer. There are clear expressions of this in medieval law enforcement such as the blood feud in which reprisal by the victim is recognized as natural and seen also as a moral obligation. Contemporary instances which approximate this form of direct and informal 'community justice' could include the public hounding and shaming of paedophile sex offenders in the wake of certain notorious releases of known offenders from prison, and the punishment beatings by para-military groups of 'anti-social' individuals such as drug dealers in parts of Northern Ireland. Communities can be vicious and exclusionary and it is vital to bear in mind that at times the formal apparatus of the criminal justice system can help to protect offenders and others who deviate from the majoritarian mores of their neighbours and local communities. We also need to be wary of opening up criminal justice issues to direct 'democratic' participation when relations of trust between groups of citizens and between citizens and the state are by no means certain (Jordan and Arnold, 1995).

'Community vigilante justice' versus paedophiles: neighbourhood watch on Manchester's Varley Estate, 1997

4.2 Case study: a moment of restorative justice with family group conferencing

The contemporary appeal to community-based restorative justice for policy makers and practitioners has been based on less extreme criticisms of, and organizational departures from, adversarial justice and bureaucratic and professional institutional practices than that associated with either abolitionist or communitarian proposals. In reality, the practices of restorative justice and related forms of 'informalism' have been aimed for the most part at organizational reform of parts of the justice system which are viewed as failing due to the high costs, poor co-ordination and lack of participation and involvement of lay actors in the process. Here, we can observe clear parallels with the emergence of strategies of community safety in the last decades of the twentieth century (see Chapter 7).

Proponents of restorative justice argue that there is an alternative to both the passive and limited role of the community in formal state-run 'non-custodial' sanctions and the vicious and exclusivist impulse associated with 'direct action' vigilante community justice discussed above. In particular, the restorative justice movement invokes a wider and more inclusive conception of community. In this conception, the individual is not an isolated actor of liberalism but rather a member of a group of significant others whose responses count. The causes of crime are seen to lie primarily in the breakdown of social, familial and communal

Public shaming and naming reached a new level with the police decision to place advertisements for wanted suspects on city centre billboards in Birmingham in November 2000

ties and relationships. The logic of restorative justice asserts that the key task of justice is to 'heal wounds' rather than punish offences. It is argued that this is more likely to succeed if the offender remains 'in' and 'of' the community with the emphasis being placed on reintegration rather than expulsion of the wrong-doer. The Australian criminologist John **Braithwaite (1989)** has had a major influence on theory and practice in developing the conditions under which specific communities can be encouraged to become more actively involved in censuring and ameliorating offending and anti-social behaviour.

Braithwaite's (1989, 1993) theoretical work and research has made a major contribution to our understanding of the importance of the concept of shaming to modern criminology and its possible role in the contemporary workings of social control. Braithwaite has noted that shaming may take both 'disintegrative' and 'reintegrative' forms. Disintegrative shaming stigmatizes people and turns them into outcasts; it is the dominant norm across modern western societies and results in degrees of social exclusion for those defined as criminal. By way of contrast, reintegrative shaming promotes re-acceptance and re-integration into the social 'fold'. According to Braithwaite, reintegrative shaming is a type of disapproval dispensed within an ongoing relationship with the offender based on respect. This form of shaming focuses on the deed rather than the person who has committed the deed. In communities where this form of shaming is used, forgiveness, apology, and repentance are culturally important, and ceremonies, like the degradation ceremonies, are held along with other ceremonies, for instance, those that 'decertify' deviance. Reintegrative shaming allows expression of a society's disapproval of the act by bringing the wrong-doer, the victim and their close associates together in a group setting. It is suggested that much of its preventive success lies in its impact on the offender's conscience. Nonetheless, processes like these will only work in situations where loss of respect counts heavily. Braithwaite acknowledges that it is the presence of a communitarian culture that makes shaming possible. Unlike modern western systems of justice and punishment which isolate and stigmatize the guilty through exclusionary disposal (such as custody), reintegrative shaming aims to accept the guilty back into the community and so help prevent future offending through a process of active reintegration and the healing of wounds by members of the community

reintegrative shaming

themselves. Braithwaite (1989, p.434) points to the Maori restorative justice tradition in New Zealand and shaming processes in Japan as examples of this process:

> Punishment erects barriers between the offender and punisher through transforming the relationship into one of power assertion and injury; shaming produces a greater interconnectedness between the parties, albeit a painful one, an interconnectedness which can produce the repulsion of stigmatization or the establishment of a potentially more positive relationship following reintegration.

Despite the claims that shaming is unlikely to work in the complex, anonymous societies of the late modern era, Braithwaite has made a strong argument for reintegrative shaming's continuing salience as a restorative justice and crime prevention approach today. Braithwaite and other proponents of reintegrative shaming also view it as a crucial communitarian resource in mobilizing against those offenders who brutalize (such as abusers) and exploit (such as corporations) as well as restraining those who would trample on the rights of others who wish to be harmlessly deviant.

Restorative justice initiatives based on reintegrative shaming have taken root in a number of jurisdictions, notably with respect to young offenders. New Zealand has gone further than most in putting restorative values into practice (Morris and Gelsthorpe, 2000, p.20). Among the most influential and widely celebrated examples of restorative justice initiatives across contemporary societies are the 'reintegrative shaming' initiatives often termed family group conferences. Family group conferences (FCGs) were first pioneered in New Zealand in 1989 and were adapted from traditional, communitarian systems of conflict resolution within Maori culture. They directly involve those people most affected by the offending, the offender, the victim and their families, in determining appropriate responses to it. The aim of FGCs is to hold offenders accountable for their actions and to take into account the interests of the victim. The most usual outcomes are apologies and community work (Maxwell and Morris, 1996). Conferences are held in two situations: first, where the police decide *not* to warn or otherwise divert the young person and want the young person dealt with by a judge in court, or second, where the police have arrested the young person. In the first situation, the young person will only be referred to court if the conference cannot otherwise deal with the offending. (Most of these cases do not proceed to court.) In the second situation, the young person appears in court but the judge cannot sentence the offender without first referring him or her to a conference which then makes a re-recommendation to the judge with regard to how the offender should be dealt with. What is worth pinpointing is that most judges follow these recommendations (Morris and Gelsthorpe, 2000, p.21). The role of the court is thus quite marginal to the work of family group conferencing in New Zealand.

family group conferences

FCGs involve a professional co-ordinator, dealing with both civil and criminal offences, who brings together the young person, their family and friends and victims to decide whether the young person is 'in need of care and protection'. Such conferences take place in informal settings, offering a greater voice for lay people, not least the victim and family of the offender. Since their introduction, supporters of FCGs claim that there has been an 80 per cent reduction of young people in care for welfare or criminal reasons. It is claimed that virtually all FGCs reach an agreement and advise on an active penalty, such as community work, reparation or apology (Hudson *et al.*, 1996). In New Zealand, conferences are held for only about 20 per cent of young offenders but it is the 20 per cent who have committed medium-serious and serious offences or who have persistently offended (Morris and Gelsthorpe, 2000, p.21).

Proponents of reintegrative processes such as the FGCs argue that it is not a 'soft option' for offenders. Such activities generally carry with them a degree of compulsion given that the reintegration of the transgressor back into the community will depend upon their compliance with the terms of the negotiated settlement. It is often claimed that they may be tougher than custodial disposals in that, with the latter, offenders are removed from acknowledging their wrong-doing and the harm that has resulted from their actions. In contrast, the techniques of reintegrative shaming, mediation and reparation used by FGCs work on the conscience of the harm-doer in ways that formal legal processes do not. In accord with the general drift of communitarian thought, restorative justice-based conferences do not shy away from recognizing that society's response to crime must be moralizing (but not rejecting). This 'tough' re-moralizing and responsibilizing agenda may in part help explain the international 'success' of both Braithwaite's work in general and FGCs in particular. As Rose (1999, pp.271–2) observes, a key reason for the current popularity of the technique of reintegrative shaming in many interagency programmes targeting, for instance, high-risk youth or the like lies in its reconfigured strategy of control through 'ethical reconstruction', which in turn should instil the capacity for self-management. The other key factor in the international 'success story' of FGCs is the evidence that participation in such conferences appears to reduce the chances of re-offending when compared to other modes of sanction and disposal (Maxwell and Morris, 1996).

According to supporters of FGCs, research findings from New Zealand show that they can meet restorative expectations. In Extract 6.2 below, the tone of Maxwell and Morris's (1996, p.108) conclusion to their overview of research findings in 1996 is upbeat:

Extract 6.2 Maxwell and Morris: Family group conferencing in New Zealand

The principles underlying family group conferences are new, radical and exciting. They emphasize diversion, restorative justice and responding to the needs of young people through strengthening families and acknowledging cultural differences. They have impacted considerably on practice. Diversionary outcomes have been achieved for the great majority of young offenders. At the same time, nearly all young people involved in offending that is considered sufficiently serious to warrant a family group conference are held accountable for their offences. Families are, for the most part, participating in the processes of decision-making and are taking responsibility for their young people. Extended families are also often becoming involved in the continuing care of their kin and as an alternative to foster care and institutions. Families, professionals and young people record high levels of satisfaction with outcomes. Greater acknowledgement is being given to the customs of different cultural groups and, in some instances, traditional processes have been used to reach agreements. Victims are also involved to a greater extent than they were before and than is customary elsewhere. And many of the victims involved in family group conferences report being satisfied with the outcomes.

However, critical questions have been raised about the fairness of the system, its potential coerciveness and its ability to achieve the ideals of diversion, restorative justice and cultural appropriateness. Although an examination of practice demonstrates, as might be expected, imperfections, it also demonstrates the potential of family group conferences to achieve these goals to a greater extent than the more traditional process of court hearings. Much depends on practice, resources and the systems that support the processes. Poor practice can fundamentally undermine outcomes, fiscal restraint can starve the system of the necessary resources in terms of both staff and services and inadequate structures can impede the delivery of quality services.

ACTIVITY 6.9

In the light of the criticisms of previous community-based initiatives related to the logics of welfare and rehabilitation noted in sections 3 and 4, try to think of the likely limitations and dangers of this latest moment of restorative justice.

Strong claims have been made for FGCs and their reintegrative shaming techniques as concrete examples of the positive 'success' of restorative justice. However, it is wise to be circumspect about their potential for creating the concrete and 'realistic' conditions for a progressive, community-based, non-discriminatory approach to justice. For example, it has yet to be shown that reintegrative shaming will not be mobilized against the most vulnerable sections of society or be employed for trivial offenders without any reduction in the use of traditional custodial sentences. Blagg (1998), commenting on reintegrative shaming experiments in Australia, has noted that the 'product' being 'franchised' in that country in the late 1990s was targeted at Aboriginal people and intensified rather than reduced police controls over this already victimized population. Meanwhile, Daly and Immarigeon's (1998) international review of the field of restorative justice suggested that, in terms of routine criminal justice practices, it is generally viewed as a set of alternatives *within* the system of formal justice, its function being to siphon off less serious cases and provide opportunities for victims and offenders to meet and perhaps make amends. There is also the issue of the extent to which restorative justice measures, administered in the penal-welfare complex and potentially subject to bureaucratic and professional capture, may extend the net of social control further into the community. Furthermore, the lack of accountability and the absence of protection for the offender in terms of appeals to legality and due process remain major areas of concern

5.3 Towards a new politics of community justice?

At the beginning of the twenty-first century in England and Wales, restorative justice schemes have been established nationally through the introduction of reparation orders in the 1998 Crime and Disorder Act. The thrust of the restorative initiatives in this Act has been to make juveniles more *responsible* (this appears to be at the root of its popular, communitarian appeal). These developments have promoted the greater use of reparation as a punishment for young offenders together with an enhanced role for local authority Youth Offender Teams (YOTs) in dealing with crime and disorder. These initiatives in part reflected the growing recognition in the late 1990s that some forms of community intervention could be successful in reducing *some* re-offending at *some* times. In general, it has been argued that programmes which address offending behaviour instead of processing through the courts and which are based in community rather than residential settings appear to have the highest chance of success. They also have the economic advantage of avoiding the high cost of formal court processing (Audit Commission, 1996; Goldblatt and Lewis, 1998).

In the White Paper, *No More Excuses* (Home Office 1997a: para. 9.21), great emphasis was placed on the need 'to reshape the criminal justice system in England and Wales to produce more constructive outcomes with young offenders'. The White Paper also referred to the need to build on the three 'R's: responsibility, restoration and reintegration.

ACTIVITY 6.10

You should now read the following extract from 'Tackling Youth Crime: A Consultation Paper (Home Office, 1997b).

Compare the analysis and aspirations in this extract from 'New' Labour with those of the Extract 6.1 taken from the 1964 Labour Party Study Group report, *Crime–A Challenge To Us All.*

Extract 6.3 Tackling Youth Crime: A Consultation Paper

Taking responsibility

Young people who commit crime must face up to the consequences of their actions for themselves and for others and must take responsibility for their actions. The Government proposes to:

■ modernize the archaic rule of 'doli incapax' which currently presumes – unless proved otherwise – that a child under 14 does not know the difference between right and wrong; and

■ give courts power to impose a new reparation order, requiring young offenders to make some form of reparation to their victims or to the community at large.

The parents of young offenders must also recognize their responsibility for the actions of their children. They have an important role to play in any further offending. The Government proposes a new parenting order to give courts powers to deal effectively with parents who wilfully neglect their responsibilities – or who need help and support in fulfilling them.

Tough on youth crime and its causes

When young people offend, the response of the youth justice system should be rapid, consistent and effective. No young person should be allowed to feel that he or she can offend with impunity. By intervening early and effectively before crime becomes a habit, we can prevent young offenders from graduating into adult criminals. ...

Punishment is important as a means of expressing society's condemnation of unlawful behaviour as a deterrent. Punishment should be proportionate to the offence but progressively tougher if young people continue to offend. To ensure the protection of the public, punishment for young offenders should be complemented by intervention to change their behaviour and prevent them offending again.

(Home Office, 1997b, pp.2–3)

As a result of the Crime and Disorder Act 1998, these 'responsibilizing' aspirations were given legislative substance. The 1998 Act introduced restorative justice through conferencing, reparation and action plan orders and by giving victims a greater say with respect to the content of certain orders (Goldson, 2000). Such measures clearly point to the importance of restoration and restitution in the delivery of youth justice.

Restorative justice in action? Offender doing 'community service' in the presence of the victim

The effects of the Crime and Disorder Act 1998 and the Youth Justice and Criminal Evidence Act 1999's promotion of specific restorative justice initiatives remain a matter for debate. Certain commentators such as Dignan (1999a, p.50) see signs of an establishment of 'some elements of the restorative approach as part of the mainstream response to offending by young people'. Dignan (1999b, p.123) also argues that there has been a move towards a more inclusive approach to criminal justice policy-making since the election of 1997 whilst also acknowledging that the legislation of the late 1990s encompasses 'a mixed bag of inclusive and restorative initiatives as well as measures more redolent of the punitive and exclusionary measures of the past. Despite his uncertainty over how this tension will be resolved, Dignan (1999b, p.3) suggests that 'the prospects for a more orderly and systematic integration of a restorative justice approach into the workings of the criminal justice system are undoubtedly better now than at any time since the recent revival of interest in the emerging concept began to take root in the late 1970s.' Other commentators are less optimistic about the prospects of restorative processes occupying a less marginal role in criminal justice. According to Morris and Gelsthorpe (2000, p.18), restorative justice processes in England and Wales will continue to sit on the margins until the values and practices of blaming and punishing are given considerably less emphasis and restorative values and practices are given significantly more weight. Morris and Gelsthorpe draw on the very different place occupied by, and importance given to, restorative processes in FGCs in New Zealand in making their negative assessment of the prospects for genuine restorative processes in the youth justice system in the UK.

Much of the discussion in this section suggests that at the beginning of the twenty-first century in the UK, we have witnessed the emergence of a moralizing and responsibilizing impulse associated with restorative justice initiatives. These initiatives are certainly consistent with communitarian principles. In the new 'ethico-politics' of 'governance through community' (Rose, 1999), the subject – in this case the offender – is addressed as a moral individual with bonds of obligation and responsibilities for his/her conduct, particularly to family and community. Accordingly, restorative justice-based reintegrative shaming programmes bring the offender face to face with the victim, in the presence of the offender's family and loved ones and explore in depth the consequences of the act for others. In doing so, they seek to inscribe awareness of the dire consequences of illegal acts for others directly into the ethical make-up of the offender (Rose, 1999, p.190). It remains debatable whether such strategies of moral reconstruction of the offender (delivered by means of community-based reintegrative shaming techniques and allied restorative justice initiatives) will have any lasting impact on the area of community sanctions in the UK in the first decade of the twenty-first century. What is more certain, however, is the prospect of continuing debate about the relative merits and limitations of the competing rationales of community sanctions, among which restorative justice is but the latest hybridized form.

6 Key issues

This section draws together the key issues raised by the discussion in the previous sections for wider developments in criminal justice and social control. In particular, we look first at the issue of the degree to which community sanctions are genuine alternatives to custody or mere additions to crime control. Second, we consider the extent to which we are witnessing a shift from an impossibilist 'nothing works' narrative on community sanctions to that of a more pragmatic, evidence-led one of 'some things work sometimes with some people'.

6.1 Alternatives or additions? Blurring boundaries

Much of the academic debate in criminology has tended to assume that the promotion of community-based disposals when compared with custodial sentences has a self-evidently benevolent objective. However, there are important dissenting voices which stand in opposition to this position. For critics such as Stanley **Cohen** (**1979**, 1985), the real effect of the 'decarceration' movement since the 1960s has been to increase the reach and intensity of state control – bringing about additions rather than alternatives to imprisonment – and in addition blur the boundaries between what was 'in' custody and what was 'outside' in the community. In particular, it was claimed by Cohen that the criminal justice system expanded and drew more people into its reach ('net widening'), that levels of intervention involving individualized treatment intensified ('net strengthening') and at the same time existing (custodial) institutions were rarely replaced but instead were supplemented by new forms of control and intervention (new, different nets of social control). The boundaries between the means of coercive control and non-justice agencies were also viewed as becoming increasingly blurred with the result that the social control network was extended to new institutional areas. This pursuit of community-based initiatives and disposals involved a greater role for non-criminal justice agencies such as social work, education and employment agencies in the extended web or continuum of control and correction. A dystopian vision of social control is conjured up whereby it has become increasingly impossible to determine just who is enmeshed in the extended social control network and who is not. There has been in effect what **Foucault (1977)** termed a 'dispersal of discipline'. According to some abolitionists, there is no point in breaking down the taken-for-grantedness of prison without breaking down the taken-for-grantedness of punishment. If punitiveness is not diminished but prisons are abolished, the pains of imprisonment will be infiltrated into the supposed alternatives to custody and the dispersal of discipline thesis will truly have come into being. As Hudson (1996, p.144) notes, some of the proposals for 'tough' and 'realistic' non-custodial sentences that have been put forward as alternatives to excessive imprisonment would seem to bear this out; in Hudson's words, 'electronically monitored home confinement often seems to be turning homes into prisons rather than keeping people out of "prison" and at "home"'.

> **blurring boundaries**

> **net widening**

> **dispersal of discipline**

This radical twist on totalitarianism has been contested on both empirical and theoretical grounds (Bottoms, 1983; McMahon, 1990). Different interpretations remain of the effects of supposedly destructuring reforms. It is likely that the plurality of interpretations reflects the differential strategies and contexts within which such initiatives are embedded. There is then no meta-narrative to explain the consequences of diversion, decarceration and other destructuring impulses in the community. However, the notion of the dispersal of discipline offers a useful organizing framework for further debate. For example, although there is a danger that its sweeping analysis forecloses the investigation of complex, uneven and unfinished processes, it remains valuable in alerting us to the possible discrepancies between 'well-intentioned' objectives and actual outcomes in the area of community sanctions. As a result of this radical critique, it is difficult to ignore the very real potential for supposed 'alternatives' to become 'additions', drawing groups and individuals into intensive forms of intervention whose offending behaviour does not warrant such responses. Furthermore, this critique also effectively dispels the notion that extending the use of community-based sanctions and disposals will necessarily result in the reduction of the use of custody. At the same time, it is important to note the danger of such criticisms of community-based initiatives serving to vacate the political space of the penal-welfare complex to those forces who want to increase the profile of retributive and custodial penalties yet further.

Other critics such as Barbara Hudson (1993) have alerted us to the evidence of sexual and racial discrimination in the use of community sanctions. Even the Home Office's figures chronicle the differential use of community-based sentences for different social categories. These point to discriminatory outcomes where categories of people are most likely to receive 'non-custodial' rather than custodial disposals. For example, women are less likely to get community sentences than men; overall, 5 per cent of female offenders receive community service orders compared to 9 per cent of male offenders (Worrall, 1997, p.96). This may reflect a sexist view of what is considered 'appropriate work' for women in comparison to men. Most of the work associated with community sentences is in traditional terms 'physical labour' such as clearing land or repairing and decorating houses, from which women have tended to be excluded historically. As we saw in Chapter 3, another social category subject to differential – and discriminatory – treatment with regard to community sanctions is that of ethnic minority groups. In 1997, 19 per cent of the prison population was made up of minority groups (who comprise 5.8 per cent of the general population). While ethnic minority groups are disproportionately more likely to be imprisoned, they are also less likely to be placed on probation and they tend to receive higher tariff alternatives to custody. In 1997, Afro-Caribbeans and Asians made up 7 per cent of those on probation and 10 per cent of those receiving community service orders and combination orders. What is the likely impact of such discriminatory processes and outcomes on the 'remnant' prison population who are viewed as unsuitable for community-based disposals? According to Hudson (1993, p.138), community-based sentencing does not reduce the penal population but rather 'restructures' it with the division between 'a young, white, hopeful penal population in the community, and a black, mentally disordered, homeless and hopeless population in the prisons'.

These criticisms and issues are vital ones for those who advocate the use of community sanctions on humanitarian rather than cost-cutting grounds. They also alert us to the fact that social policies can have latent as well as declared functions. Furthermore it is likely that a society as fragmented on the lines of age, gender and race as the UK is likely to reproduce inequalities of power and disadvantage in even its best-intended institutions unless positive steps are taken to combat this tendency.

(Brownlee, 1998, p.32).

Apart from the dangerous blurring of the 'public' and the 'private', the 'formal' and the 'informal' which commentators such as Cohen have highlighted, developments associated with the logic of community-based, restorative justice are also associated with a potentially less pernicious blurring of the criminal and civil law in many jurisdictions across the world. As **McLaughlin (2001)** notes with regard to debates on human rights and their violation, there is a growing international appeal to informal, restitutive mechanisms of conflict resolution, or 'alternative dispute resolution' (ADR), in, for example, such initiatives as the Peace and Reconciliation Tribunal in South Africa in the 1990s. These high-profile and politically volatile initiatives appear to share a similar logic to that associated with the management of the more mundane misdemeanours of young offenders in family group conferences. Such processes may be indicative of a significant flow of ideas across the globe whereby the hegemony of the criminal justice discourse is increasingly challenged and an alternative civil justice approach may be promoted.

6.2   From 'nothing works' to 'some things' work

The demise of the rehabilitative ideal saw the ascendancy of a pessimistic credo that 'nothing works'. This 'impossibilist' attitude towards rehabilitation has been superseded in turn by the claim and conviction (at least in some influential circles) that *some things work, with some people, some times.* As Mair (1997, p.1224) notes, 'the confidence that the "Nothing Works" dragon has finally been slain has engendered considerable optimism amongst those who work in community penalties'. There is an obsession across the public sector with 'evidence-based' evaluation of what works. This tendency is particularly to the fore in the realm of community punishments. However, we could ask what 'work' means in an exact sense of the word? Does it refer to the level of reoffending? There are limitations in using reconviction as a measure of success. For example, despite the intentional escalation in the seriousness of offenders with whom the probation service was dealing in the 1990s, almost three-quarters of all probation orders run their full course without breach for offending. A clear example of 'success' it would appear. Viewed more critically, this same finding can be read as showing that over a quarter of such disposals fail in terms of 'known' offending alone. There will thus continue to be controversy and contestations over how success is measured in terms of what does (or does not) work in non-custodial sanctions. In his review of the evidence regarding the effectiveness of community-based punishments in tackling recidivism, Brownlee (1998, pp.179–80) concludes that they are at least as effective as an institutional sentence and that, given what we know about some of the other advantages of punishment in the community (e.g. lower unit costs, the tendency to be less dehumanizing than custody), 'the lack of any demonstrable superiority on the part of institutional sentencing in controlling recidivism should mean

new penology

that it is the use of *custody* not community sentencing that has to be justified and defended'. Such debates are unlikely to be resolved in any definitive manner. Instead, the focus of both research and practice-based evaluations of the efficacy of non-custodial sanctions has shifted to the more pragmatic analysis of how risks may be best managed by targeted interventions informed by the rationale of what has been termed the new penology **(Feeley and Simon, 1992)**.

According to proponents of the new penology thesis, the last two decades of the twentieth century saw a paradigmatic shift in penal ideology and practice. The transformation has been most marked in the USA but there are similar trends emerging in the UK's criminal justice systems. It is argued that the main aim of the new penology is managerial rather than transformative. In other words, it does not seek to reform and re-socialize the offender through diagnosis and treatment but rather to identify, classify and manage categories of at-risk or risky groups by means of the notion of dangerousness. Rather than prescribing treatment, the new expertise is associated with how to calculate risk. This trend towards managerialism emphasizes the pragmatic, efficient and systemic regulation of deviance rather than its dramatic denunciation or therapeutic correction and the development of an 'actuarial' calculation of risk. Crime control systems like other services in the reformed public sector are to be judged by reference to cost-effectiveness. The key task of this reformed criminal justice system becomes that of differentiating on the basis of actuarial calculation of risk between different types of offender groups in terms of who might be rehabilitated or deterred and who would not, and in turn of providing appropriate and cost-effective levels of incapacitation according to the assessment of risk (Brownlee, 1998, p.81). This shift in the type and function of non-legal expertise in the social response to crime has been described as the move from disciplinary to actuarial practice (Hudson, 1996, p.154). As one of the leading theorists of the new penology, Jonathon Simon (1988, p.773), notes:

> I believe a genealogical analysis of the technologies through which power is exercised today would demonstrate that over the past half century we have been moving away from the disciplines and toward actuarial practices that are, in turn, more efficient in the use of resources and less dangerous in the political resistances they generate.

> Disciplinary practices focus on the distribution of a behaviour within a limited population. … This distribution is around a norm, and power operates with the goal of closing the gap, narrowing the deviation, and moving subjects towards uniformity. … Actuarial practices seek instead to maximize the efficiency of the population as it stands. Rather than seeking to change people ('normalize them', in Foucault's apt phrase) an actuarial regime seeks to manage them in place.

Much of our earlier discussion of the recent trends and transformations in community sanctions lends support to this broad sociological thesis of a paradigmatic shift in penology at the end of the twentieth century. It would appear that the risk which the criminal justice system now attempts to manage is that of victimization and that the main target is not the offender but the community of potential victims. It is also evident that there is now pressure to 'target' interventions more selectively and monitor and evaluate initiatives, so that future practice may be informed by 'evidence-based' decisions about 'what works', 'when' and 'for whom'. There is a broad consensus among most academic commentators that the 'criminal justice system harbours little or no ambition to "rescue" individuals; rather, aggregate populations must be differentiated, according to assessments of varying degrees of risk, and "managed" through the application of appropriate and affordable levels of incapacitation' (Brownlee, 1998, p.99). For example, Kemshall (1997) contends that the dominant *raison d'être* of the policies and practices of social service and probation agencies by the end of the twentieth century was increasingly concerned with the assessment, management and monitoring of risks. Hudson (1996, p.155) has also noted that there is a strong ideological strand in the new risk penology which stresses that there is a sizeable minority in late modern societies – the so-called 'underclass' – who are not going to change but instead are more likely to become more rather than less criminal (see **Murray, 1990**). As a consequence of this strand, actuarial regimes are generating techniques aimed at keeping segregated and under surveillance those who possess the factors associated with the risk of crime and disorder.

Whilst there are clear indications of a shift to the managerialized model based on risk assessment, its pervasiveness may be exaggerated. Indeed, Feeley and Simon (1995, p.149) have contended that there are limits to the 'success story' of the new penology, not least in terms of its influence on the popular, public discourse on crime. Furthermore, developments associated with restorative justice initiatives do not fit so neatly into the actuarialist discourse. Although such initiatives as FGCs and restitutive programmes are in crucial ways influenced by the cost-effective calculation of risk, such developments do not sit easily with the claim that there is an almost complete shift away from concerns with reformation and resocialization of the offender. Current developments in the field of community sanctions are unlikely to be the pure expression of an actuarialist logic and are more likely to be 'hybridized' in character. Reformative strategies have had a resurgence in the 'new rehabilitationism' (Robinson, 1999), but in the context of greater selectivity regarding their employment in terms of targeting interventions on those for whom they can be shown empirically to be effective in terms of positive response (McGuire, 1995; Audit Commission, 1996). Robinson (1999, p.430) has pointed out the dangers of overstating the dominance of the actuarial discourse and ignoring the parallel punitive and rehabilitative impulses at work in community-based penalties. Indeed, the 'old' and 'new' penologies appear in many respects mutually supportive. Robinson's work usefully questions the simple notion of a shift from (a) rehabilitation to (b) actuarial risk-management and instead points to a symbiotic relationship between the two whereby a hybrid form of rehabilitationism has been revived. It appears that rehabilitation is no longer the general all-purpose prescription of old but is instead targeted at those most likely to make 'cost effective' use of the expensive services of the penal complex. Rehabilitation thus gets re-inscribed in a regime organized around risk-management, acting now as a secondary concept and as a means to an end of risk reduction for some offenders.

7   Conclusion

Despite the different interpretations with regard to the future fate of any significant decentering of custodial punishment from its central place in the criminal justice system, it is unlikely that the appeals to greater informalism, community-based sanctions and 'solutions' will leave the political and policy arena in the first decades of the twenty-first century. In certain contexts, the rise of informalism may reflect efforts to recognize the (increasingly) polycentric nature of a society and accordingly the promotion of degrees of legal pluralism (such as in New Zealand and Canada). In other contexts, the rise of community justice initiatives such as victim–offender mediation may be more to do with the crisis of rigidly formal legal discourses and heightened problems associated with managing the urban crisis in what is perceived to be an increasingly globalized and atomized world. The offloading of the state's responsibility for crime control onto 'responsibilized' individuals and families in communities appears to be a crucial feature of policies and practices of crime control at the beginning of the twenty-first century. Are we witnessing the emergence of community-based punishment and justice as the new criminological 'imaginary'? The term 'community' has been increasingly deployed as a key rhetorical part of an increasingly severe penal climate by governments throughout the twentieth and early twenty-first century. As Tim May (1994, pp.881–2) notes, '"Community" would now appear to be a sphere in which punishment is legitimately enacted and visible'.

We are observing the continued reshaping of the criminal justice system and the wider network of social control strategies at the beginning of the twenty-first century in the UK. Much remains in flux. Certainly, the contemporary picture of community-based sanctions across many societies is confusing and messy. Many of these programmes and penalties are currently overlaid with contradictory objectives and concerns, including the questions of managerial cost-effectiveness, 'value for money' risk-management, public protection and community safety, just deserts, victim satisfaction, responsibility of the offender, as well as the vestiges of rehabilitation and the resurgence of restorative justice. One dominant impulse appears to be those of greater systematization and managerialization of the processes of sentencing and disposal of offenders. Much of this is driven by a rationale of actuarial risk-management. At the same time, there are notable attempts to increase 'community' participation in the work of crime and disorder reduction (see Chapter 7) and in the resolution of disputes and the punishment of the wrong-doer. This latter development closely chimes with the call for greater responsibility from offenders and their families and **responsibilization** communities for their actions – termed a strategy of responsibilization (Garland, 1996) – as well as the populist punitiveness of all British governments during recent decades. There is then a melting pot of contradictions, themes and rationales at work which arguably defy any easy description. What remains clear, however, is the reality that community sanctions continue to be practised in 'the shadow of the prison'. We seem incapable of conceptualizing other penalties except in terms of their relationship to imprisonment. This is perhaps why community-based sanctions and programmes continue to attract such popular suspicion despite the trend for non-custodial measures across the world to be increasingly concerned with the punitive restriction of liberty, surveillance and monitoring rather than welfare, rehabilitation and restorative justice. One final lesson to be drawn from our discussion of the competing logics of community sanctions is that strategies of crime control cannot be adequately understood in terms of the narrow technical questions regarding efficiency and effectiveness. Rather, they need to be connected to the debates on how the wider social and political formations are themselves subject to challenges and transformations at the beginning of the new millennium.

Review questions

- What are the main competing rationales of community sanctions and strategies?
- Are community sanctions an alternative to, or an adjunct of, penal custody?
- What are the implications of drawing the community into systems of crime control, justice and punishment?
- Are formal criminal justice systems the most appropriate and effective means of dealing with the 'troublesome'?
- Can any effective criminal justice system really jettison all traces and notions of welfare, rehabilitation and restorative justice?

Further reading

There is no one book that adequately addresses the range of issues which this chapter discusses. However, Cohen (1985) remains the most important analysis of the relationship of community sanctions and interventions to wider processes of social control in contemporary society. In most of the existing literature, the relationship of youth justice and probation to the competing logics of community sanctions are dealt with separately. May (1994) offers a good overview of community sanctions and probation and both Brownlee (1998) and Worrall (1997) offer detailed and accessible accounts of the recent history of both the probation service and community punishments in England and Wales. Muncie (1999) provides the best critical introduction to the study of youth justice in Britain whilst Goldson's (2000) edited collection, *The New Youth Justice*, provides a lively set of essays on the state of youth justice in the context of New Labour's reforms of the system. On restorative justice, see Daly and Immarigeon's (1998) useful overview of trends and debates in the area. On the new politics of community and strategies of crime control, see Rose (1999).

References

Audit Commission (1996), *Misspent Youth*, London, Audit Commission.

Blagg, H. (1998) 'A just measure of shame: Aboriginal youth and conferencing in Australia', *British Journal of Criminology*, vol.37, no.4, pp.481–501.

Bottoms, A. (1974) 'On the decriminalization of youth justice', in Hood, R. (ed.) *Crime, Criminology and Public Policy*, London, Heineman.

Bottoms, A. (1983) 'Some neglected features of contemporary penal systems', in Garland, D. and Young, P. (eds) *The Power to Punish,* London, Heineman.

Bottoms, A. (1995) 'The philosophy and politics of sentencing', in Clarkson, C. and Morgan, R. (eds) *The Politics Of Sentencing Reform*, Oxford, Clarendon Press.

Braithwaite, J. (1989) *Crime, Shame and Reintegration*, **Oxford, OUP. (Extract reprinted as 'Reintegrative shaming' in Muncie *et al.*, 1996.)**

Braithwaite, J. (1993) 'Shame and modernity', *British Journal of Criminology*, vol.33, no.1, pp.1–18.

Broad, B. (1991) *Punishment Under Pressure*, London, J. Kingsley Publishers.

Brownlee, I. (1998) *Community Punishment: A Critical Introduction*, Harlow, Longman.

Cavadino, M. and Dignan, J. (1997) *The Penal System: An Introduction*, 2nd edn, London, Sage.

Christie, N. (1977). 'Conflicts as property', *British Journal of Criminology*, vol.17, no.1, pp.1–15.

Christie, N. (1993) *Crime Control as Industry*, London, Routledge.

Clarke, J. and Newman, J. (1998) *The Managerial State*, London, Sage.

Cohen, S. (1979) 'The punitive city: notes on the dispersal of social control', *Contemporary Crises*, **vol.3, no.4, pp.341–63. (Extract reprinted in Muncie *et al.*, 1996.)**

Cohen, S. (1985) *Visions of Social Control*, Cambridge, Polity.

Crawford, A. (1997) *The Local Governance of Crime*, Oxford, Clarendon Press.

Cullen, F. and Gilbert, K. (1982) *Reaffirming Rehabilitation*, **Cincinnati, Anderson. (Extract reprinted as 'The value of rehabilitation' in Muncie *et al.*, 1996.)**

Daly, K. and Immarigeon, R. (1998) 'The past, present and future of restorative justice: some critical reflections', *Contemporary Justice Review*, vol.1, pp.21–45.

De Haan, W. (1991) 'Abolitionism and crime control: a contradiction in terms', in Stenson and Cowell (1991). (Extract reprinted as 'Abolitionism and crime control' in Muncie *et al*., 1996.)

Dignan, J. (1999a) 'The crime and disorder act and the prospects for restorative justice', *Criminal Law Review*, January, pp.48–60.

Dignan, J. (1999b) 'Restorative crime prevention in theory and practice', *Prison Service Journal*, May, no.123, pp.2–50.

Eaton, M. (1986) *Justice for Women*, Milton Keynes, Open University Press.

Feeley and Simon (1992) 'The new penology: notes on the emerging strategy of corrections and its implications', *Criminology*, **vol.30, no.4, pp.452–74. (Extract reprinted as 'The new penology' in Muncie** *et al.***, 1996.)**

Feeley and Simon (1995) 'True crime: The new penology and the public discourse on crime', in Blumberg, T.G. and Cohen, S. (eds), *Punishment and Control*, New York, Aldine De Gruyter.

Foucault, M. (1977) *Discipline and Punish,* **trans. Alan Sheridan, London, Allen Lane. (Extract reprinted as 'The Carceral' in Muncie** *et al.***, 1996.)**

Garland, D. (1985) *Punishment and Welfare: A History of Penal Strategies*, Aldershot, Gower.

Garland, D. (1996) 'The limits of the sovereign state: strategies of crime control in contemporary society', *British Journal of Criminology*, vol.36, no.4, pp.445–71.

Goldblatt, B. and Lewis, G. (1998) *Reducing Offending*, London, Home Office.

Goldson, B. (ed.) (2000) *The New Youth Justice*, Lyme Regis, Russell House.

Hamai, K., Ville, R., Harris, R., Hough, M. and Zvekvic, V. (eds) (1995) *Probation Round the World*, London, Routledge.

Harris, R. (1992), *Crime, Criminal Justice and the Probation Service*, London, Tavistock/Routledge.

Home Office (1962) *Report of the Departmental Committee on the Probation Service*, Cmnd 1650, London, HMSO.

Home Office (1990) *Crime, Justice and Protecting the Public*, CM 965, London, HMSO.

Home Office (1995a) *Strengthening Punishment in the Community*, CM 2780, London, HMSO.

Home Office (1995b) *Dealing with Dangerous People: The Probation Service and Public Protection, Report of a Thematic Inspection*, London, Home Office.

Home Office (1997a) *No More Excuses*, London, Home Office.

Home Office (1997b) *Tackling Youth Crime: A Consultation Paper*, London, Home Office.

Home Office (1999) *Cautions, Court Proceedings and Sentencing, England and Wales 1998*, London, Home Office Statistical Bulletin, Issue 21/99.

Hudson, A. (1988) 'Boys will be boys: masculinism and the juvenile justice system', *Critical Social Policy*, no.21, pp.30–48.

Hudson, B. (1993) *Penal Policy and Social Justice*, Basingstoke, Macmillan.

Hudson, B. (1996) *Understanding Justice*, Buckingham, Open University Press.

Hudson, J., Morris, A., Maxwell, G. and Galaway, B. (1996) *The Family Group Conferences: Perspectives on Policy and Practice*, Annandale, NSW, Federation Press.

Hughes, G. (1996) 'Communitarianism and law and order', *Critical Social Policy*, vol.16, no.4, pp.17–41.

Hughes, G. (1998) *Understanding Crime Prevention: Social Control, Risk and Late Modernity*, Buckingham, Open University Press.

Hughes, G. and Mooney, G. (1998) 'Community', in Hughes G. (ed.) *Imagining Welfare Futures*, London, Routledge.

James, A. and Raine, J. (1998) *The New Politics of Criminal Justice*, London, Longman.

Johnston, V. (1995) *The Rebirth of Private Policing*, Basingstoke, Macmillan.

Jordan, W. (1971) 'The probation service in the sixties', *Social and Economic Administration*, vol.5, no.2, pp.125–37.

Jordan, B. and Arnold, J. (1995) 'Democracy and criminal justice', *Critical Social Policy*, nos 44/45, pp.171–80.

Kemshall, H. (1997) 'Concepts of risk in relation to organizational structure and functioning within the personal social services and probation', *Social Policy and Administration*, no.31, pp.213–32.

Labour Party Study Group (1964) *Crime–A Challenge to Us All: report of the Labour Party Study Group*, London, Labour Party.

Labour Party (1996) *Tackling the Causes of Crime: Labour's Proposals to Prevent Crime and Criminality*, London, Labour Party.

Mair, G. (1997), 'Community penalties and the probation service', in Maguire, M., Morgan, R. and Reiner, R. (eds) *The Oxford Handbook of Criminology*, 2nd edn, Oxford, Clarendon Press.

Martinson, R. (1974) 'What works? Questions and answers about prison reform', *Public Interest*, vol.35, pp.22–54.

May, T. (1991) *Probation: Politics, Policy and Practice*, Milton Keynes, Open University Press.

May, T. (1994) 'Probation and community sanctions', in Maguire, M. *et al.* (eds), *Oxford Handbook of Criminology*, Oxford, Clarendon Press.

Maxwell, G. and Morris, A. (1996) 'Research on Family Group Conferences with young people in New Zealand', in Hudson, J. *et al.* (eds).

McAra, L. and Young, P. (1997) 'Juvenile Justice in Scotland', *Criminal Justice*, vol.15, no.3, pp.8–10.

McGhee, J., Waterhouse, L., Whyle, B. (1996) 'Children's hearings and children in trouble', in Asquith, S. (ed) *Children And Young People In Conflict With The Law*, London, Jessica Kingsley.

McGuire, J. (1995) *What Works: Reducing Offending*, Chichester, Wiley.

McLaughlin, E. (1998) 'Social work or social control? Remaking probation work', in Hughes, G. and Lewis, G. (eds) *Unsettling Welfare,* London, Sage.

McLaughlin, E. (2001) 'Political violence, terrorism and states of fear', in Muncie, J. and McLaughlin, E., ***The Problem of Crime*****, Milton Keynes, The Open University.**

McLaughlin, E. and Muncie, J. (2000) 'The criminal justice system: New Labour's new partnerships', in Clarke, J., Gewirtz, S. and McLaughlin, E. (eds) *New Managerialism, New Welfare?*, London, Sage.

McMahon, M. (1990) '"Net-widening": vagaries in the use of a concept', *British Journal of Criminology,* no.30, pp.121–49.

McWilliams, W. (1983) 'The mission to the English police courts 1876–1936', *Howard Journal*, no.22, pp.129–47.

McWilliams, W. (1985) 'The mission transformed: professionalization of probation between the wars', *Howard Journal*, no.25, pp.241–60.

McWilliams, W. (1987) 'Probation, pragmatism and policy', *Howard Journal*, no.26, pp.97–121.

Morris, A. and Gelsthorpe, L. (2000) 'Something old, something borrowed, something blue, but something new? A comment on the prospects for restorative justice under the Crime and Disorder Act 1998', *Criminal Law Review*, January.

Muncie, J. (1999) *Youth and Crime: A Critical Introduction*, London, Sage.

Muncie, J., McLaughlin, E. and Langan, M. (1996) (eds) *Criminological Perspectives: a Reader*, London, Sage in association with The Open University.

Murray, C. (1990) *The Emerging Underclass*, London, Institute of Economic Affairs. (Extract reprinted as 'The Underclass' in Muncie *et al.*, 1996.)

Nash, M. (1998) 'Enter the "polibation officer"', *International Journal of Police Science and Management*, vol.1, no.4, pp.360–8.

Newburn, T. (1998) 'Tackling youth crime and reforming youth justice: origins and nature of "New Labour" policy', *Policy Studies*, vol.13, nos. 3/4, pp.199–211.

Northern Ireland Review Group (1979) *Report of the Children and Young Persons Review Group*, Belfast, HMSO, Northern Ireland (the Black Report).

Pease, K. (1980) 'The future of the community treatment of offenders in Britain', in Bottoms, A.E. and Preston, R.H. (eds), *The Coming Penal Crisis*, Edinburgh, Scottish Academic Press.

Pitts, J. (1996) 'The politics of youth justice', in McLaughlin, E. and Muncie, J. (eds) *Controlling Crime*, London, Sage.

Pratt, J. (1989) 'Corporatism: the third model of juvenile justice', *British Journal of Criminology*, vol.29, no.3, pp.236–54.

Radzinowicz, L. (1958) 'Preface in Cambridge Department of Criminal Science', *The Results of Probation*, London, Macmillan.

Robinson, G. (1999) 'Risk-management and rehabilitation in the probation service: collison and collusion', *Howard Journal*, vol.38, no.4, pp.421–33.

Rose, N. (1999) *The Powers of Freedom*, Cambridge, Cambridge University Press.

Schichor, D. and Sechrest, D.K. (eds) (1998) *Three Strikes and You're Out: Vengeance as Public Policy*, California, Sage.

Scottish Home and Health Department and the Scottish Education Department (1964) *Report of the Committee on Children and Young Persons*, Cmnd 2306, Edinburgh, HMSO.

Simon, J. (1988) 'The ideological effects of actuarial practices', *Law and Society Review*, vol.22, no.4, pp.772–800.

Thorpe, D., Smith, D., Green, C. and Paley, J. (1980), *Out Of Care: The Community Support Of Juvenile Offenders*, London, Allen and Unwin.

Weeks, J. (1996) 'The Idea of a Sexual Community', *Soundings*, Issue 2, pp.71–84.

Williams, R. (1988) *Keywords*, Glasgow, Fontana.

Worrall, A. (1997) *Punishment in the Community: The Future of Criminal Justice*, Harlow, Longman.

CHAPTER 7

Community and Crime Prevention

by Sandra Walklate

Contents

1   Introduction

Historically, crime prevention in Britain was always considered to be the responsibility of the police. Indeed, this historical legacy is still keenly felt in the form of the dedicated Crime Prevention Officer and in police involvement in many crime prevention initiatives. However, the role of crime prevention in policework has always been accorded a somewhat lower status than other kinds of policework. There is evidence for this in the acceptance by many police forces that effective crime prevention can only be achieved through co-operation between the police and the community. Recognition of this fact raises important theoretical and practical questions: What, for example, do we understand by the concept of 'community'? What do we understand as constituting the central features of the policing task? How might we understand the relationship between the citizen and the state? What is meant by democratic participation in such processes? These questions underpin the discussion in this chapter concerning the relationship between crime prevention and the community.

A community-based understanding of crime prevention was given a definitive focus by the Conservative Party in the early 1980s. This reflected a change of emphasis not only in the nature of crime prevention, but also in the way in which the Conservative government perceived its role as a deliverer of public services. Home Office circular 8/84 stated that crime prevention was no longer, only or simply, an issue to be addressed by police forces. It argued that effective crime prevention could only be put into place on the basis of inter-agency co-operation. As the Scottish circular on the same issue states, 'Just as the incidence of crime can affect the whole community, so too its prevention is a task for the community' (quoted by Bottoms, 1990, p.4).

This change of emphasis – from police to community – in crime prevention policy reflects at least two different assumptions. The first concerns an understanding of the causes of crime and subsequently how it might be prevented (an issue which threads its way through this chapter). The second concerns an understanding of the nature of communities and parallels the political assertion by the Conservative Party of a role for the community in a range of policy activities, from health care through to education and crime, which de-emphasizes the role of the government in these matters. However, there are a number of more particular reasons why the role of the community in crime prevention should have been put to the fore in this way in the early 1980s. It will be useful for us to explore some of them.

First, the report by Lord Justice Scarman on the civil disturbances in inner-city areas in 1981 made a number of recommendations concerning police–community relations – such as the need for community consultative committees and lay visitors to police stations – which were intended to improve police–community contacts, lessen conflict between the police and the community, and harness support for police activity. In this way, the need for consensual community support for policing was reiterated. Second, the use of the British Crime Survey for the first time in 1982 suggested that law-breaking was about four times as high as that recorded by the police. While much of this was less serious crime, it clearly indicated that the police alone could not combat such a level of crime (see **Muncie, 2001**). Third, the Home Office Crime Prevention Unit, established in 1983, provided the opportunity for the development of a critical perspective on crime prevention policy. This perspective pointed to the ineffectiveness of using the criminal justice system alone as a deterrent to crime. Fourth, the government committed itself to looking for more cost-effective ways of delivering public services, including those services, such as the police, which have traditionally been regarded as being operationally free from government interference.

All of these factors pointed to the difficulties inherent in expecting the police to respond to the crime problem proactively, reactively and in a preventive capacity all at the same time, and the need to re-examine the role of the police in crime prevention especially (see Chapter 2). In this respect the case was strongly made for a wider sharing of the crime prevention role. It is useful to remember, however, that this assertion of a role for the community in crime prevention was as much a part of a wider political strategy permeating a whole range of policy areas in the early 1980s as it was rooted in any evidence that community-based responses to crime prevention might prove to be more effective. This community rhetoric constituted, in part, a search for a politically defensible policy while simultaneously demanding cutbacks in public expenditure. In other words, it represented one way of ensuring that aspects of the criminal justice system could be seen to work, if only in economic terms.

This chapter takes as its starting point the idea that communities have a role to play in crime prevention. It is important to note, however, that while such a role has been identified as desirable, its actual form and recommended content varies considerably. We shall therefore be concerned here to document such policy variations and to examine the different presumptions they make concerning both the nature of crime and the communities in which crime is seen to be a problem. It is also important to note that crime prevention policy has been active in a number of different contexts – from situational to social – since the early 1980s. This chapter will be concerned to locate community-based crime prevention policies within a broader spectrum of crime prevention activity.

2 Initiatives in crime prevention and crime reduction

Home Office circular 8/84, issued in 1984, constituted a significant moment in the development of crime prevention initiatives. This circular, with its emphasis on a multi-agency approach to crime prevention (or what, by the 1990s, was more commonly referred to as the 'partnership' approach) sparked a number of subsequent government-led initiatives.

In 1986 the Home Office Crime Prevention Unit established the Five Towns Initiative. This was intended to act as a demonstration of how the 1984 circular might work. The towns included in this project were Bolton, North Tyneside, Croydon, Swansea and Wellingborough. The project ran for 18 months, with some of the crime prevention projects it generated continuing beyond this initial period. After this, in 1988, the government launched the Safer Cities Programme. This was a bigger and more ambitious version of the Five Towns Initiative, with 16 cities chosen initially to participate in the scheme. This programme, again overseen by the Home Office, sponsored crime prevention projects in these cities for an initial three-year period, by which time it was expected that the schemes would have secured independent funding in order to continue their work. For example, Salford Safer Cities became Safer Salford in April 1994, sponsored by Marks and Spencer. Finally, in 1989 an organization called Crime Concern was established, again with Home Office money initially. This organization is now a registered charity whose main function is to disseminate good practice in the crime prevention field.

The Morgan Report (Home Office, 1991) constituted the moment at which the partnership approach to crime prevention became the underlying principle of policy in this arena. Under a New Labour government the Crime and Disorder Act (1998) has further enhanced this approach. That legislation made it a statutory requirement for local authorities and the police to develop community safety partnerships together. Local authorities have been required subsequently to conduct local crime audits and to produce planned crime reduction strategies in concert with other agencies including the police. Arguably this legislation articulates the extent to which the discourse around crime *prevention* has shifted into one concerned with crime *reduction* and community *safety*. This legislation also introduced a range of other measures with community safety in mind; for example the anti-social behaviour order. As Crawford (1998, p.60) observes, 'behind the various "community safety" and "protection" orders envisaged by the new government lurks a penal response' (see Chapter 5, and this theme within crime prevention policy will be returned to below).

This summary of developments clearly locates the responsibility for the development of crime prevention policy centrally within the Home Office. However, government departments other than the Home Office also support a range of crime prevention activity; for example the Department of the Environment through Priority Housing Estates and the Urban Aid Programme. Moreover, police forces, voluntary agencies and academics have all been involved in a variety of ways in developing and implementing crime prevention initiatives of different kinds. Many of these initiatives have taken as read the premise of the 1984 Home Office circular that the community has a key role to play in crime prevention. While this might be a common thread between such initiatives, they can vary considerably in content and style of implementation. Since such differences can sometimes feed into the potential effectiveness of a particular initiative, it will be useful to consider for a moment the different ways in which it is possible to think about, and implement, crime prevention policy.

2.1 Ways of thinking about crime prevention policy

Responses to crime and criminal victimization can vary widely. We have seen already, for example, that responses can be led by the police, government or more locally, perhaps involving voluntary organizations. The key questions are: What characterizes these responses? How are they formulated? How does this set the tone for their subsequent development? There are a number of different ways of thinking about responses to crime prevention. For example, Smith (1986), in discussing public responses to criminal victimization, distinguishes 'individual reactive protective' responses from 'collective reactive protective' responses. In this way she is attempting to alert us to the difference between individual prevention strategies and community ones, a distinction we shall build on below. Lewis and Salem (1986), on the other hand, draw our attention to different dimensions of crime prevention activity. In discussing responses to the fear of crime in particular, they identify policies characterized by either coercion or co-operation and/or empowerment, all of which may have a 'top-down' or a 'bottom-up' implementation style. The central role of the Home Office, as we have already seen, sets the general tone of policy and can thus be characterized as a top-down style. This distinction between top-down or bottom-up can sometimes be more apparent than real, but can play a crucial part in ensuring the support of a particular community in the implementation of an initiative.

Identifying the nature of policies in this way is useful. However, what is also important is to appreciate what kind of crime is being targeted by such policies. If we add to the distinctions identified above the usual distinctions made between 'crime of the streets', 'crime of the suites', and 'crime behind closed doors', it is perhaps easy to understand why it is difficult to adopt too simplistic an approach to analysing crime prevention. It is also perhaps easier to understand why, when faced with the question of 'what works?', the answer may inevitably be 'it depends!' Successful crime prevention policy will depend on how a policy is implemented, its style of implementation, its crime focus, and so on. In the context of community crime prevention policy, it may also depend on the nature of the community infrastructure, how far policy-makers and practitioners are sensitive to that infrastructure, and how a particular community or neighbourhood may be responding to crime independent of any formal policy process. In the following discussion we shall see that all of these questions have a bearing on the nature and extent of the success of community crime prevention policy. It will be useful therefore to ask what kind of crime is being targeted by the kind of policy under discussion, whether the policy has been implemented in a top-down or bottom-up style, whether it has been police-led, government-led or locally led, and whether it is targeted at individuals or the community in general.

Though the relationship between the community and crime prevention is the key focus of this chapter, there are other ways of responding to crime preventatively. In order to contextualize community-based responses to crime prevention, we shall consider briefly three other themes in crime prevention policy: offender-centred strategies, victim-centred strategies, and environment-centred strategies. We shall examine each of these in turn, but it is important to remember that these headings are really only a heuristic device to encourage critical thinking about the different policy themes it is possible to identify in this area. It may be that some of the initiatives discussed could fit under more than one heading. You should keep this in mind as you work through the rest of this chapter. But first a comment about the concepts of 'prevention' and 'reduction'.

2.2 Prevention or reduction?

Little theoretical work in the social sciences has examined the concept of prevention per se. In general, however, the extent to which late modern societies **prevention** have been presumed to be risk-avoidance societies has been well observed by Douglas (1992) and others. Overall it is possible to observe that prevention is seen to be a 'good' thing because social problems are 'bad' things (Freeman,

1992). As a concept it has been borrowed from debates on public health, yet even in that arena, what the notion of 'prevention' involves and how it might be explored are rarely examined. Crawford (1998) and Hughes (1998) offer critical and comprehensive accounts of recent developments in crime prevention policy and it is clear that most understandings of prevention entail the possibility of both predicting an outcome and intervening in that process to change the predicted outcome. This implies two separate processes if the ultimate aim of preventive policy is to make a difference to human behaviour or experience or both. In the context of crime prevention, it presumes that in the first instance we know, can agree upon and can identify the causes of crime. In the second instance it presumes that we know, can agree upon and can identify the appropriate policy responses that will inhibit crime. These, of course, reflect a long-standing debate which precedes the more current concern with the role of the community. As the remainder of this chapter illustrates, these are neither simple nor straightforward issues.

ACTIVITY 7.1

By the end of the 1990s, there was a shift of emphasis in the discourse on crime control from that of crime *prevention* to crime *reduction*. In 1998, the Home Secretary, Jack Straw, announced a Crime Reduction Programme supported by £250 million. According to Straw, this programme was 'based on concrete evidence of what is effective in reducing crime and tackling its causes, not just dealing with effects. It is the first sustained campaign in this country to reduce crime though investing in evidence and effectiveness' (Home Office, 1999, p.2). This programme grew out of a government-commissioned review of what is effective and cost-effective in reducing offending (Goldblatt and Lewis, 1998).

A leading Home Office researcher, Paul Ekblom has contended that crime *prevention* is 'future orientated' and is concerned with 'reducing the risk of occurrence and the potential seriousness of crime and disorder events, by intervening in their causes'. On the other hand, crime *reduction* is 'present and future orientated' and is concerned with 'reducing the number of crime and disorder events and the seriousness of their consequences, by intervening directly in the events and in their causes'. Ekblom (2000, p.60) goes on to contend that a key rationale of crime reduction policy, either within the national Crime Reduction Programme or local Community Safety/Crime Reduction partnerships (both established since 1998), is how to make best use of the resources currently available to bring about a diminution in the volume and consequences of crime: 'For this, it is necessary to examine cost effectiveness, in this context, the amount of crime reduction that can be achieved by a particular activity, for a given resource input (usually expressed as money).'

Bearing in mind the above comments, what are the likely attractions of adopting both the language and practice of crime reduction rather than prevention for both national government and local government bodies? Are there any limitations in this shift from prevention to reduction for proponents of community safety?

3   Offender-centred strategies

Offender-centred strategies for crime prevention presume a deterrent effect of policing and prison and can be found in a number of different guises. In October 1993, for example, the Home Secretary, Michael Howard, made an impassioned statement to the Conservative Party conference. This was reported by *The Guardian* under the headline 'Prison Works!' In his speech Howard argued that prison works as a deterrent to crime, because it incapacitates offenders from further offending and because it also serves the purpose of retribution (see also Chapter 5). Emphasizing the role of the prison system as a preventive strategy proved to be very popular at the conference. The strategy is an expensive option, and it is not particularly novel. Similar strategies historically have either taken the form of the prevention of recidivism (through, at best, rehabilitation or, at worst, incapacitation), or the mobilization of support for what Elias (1986) has called 'enforcement crackdowns'. The notion that 'prison works' fits easily under this latter heading.

Enforcement crackdowns can enjoy the support of a broad spectrum of political viewpoints. These can be divided primarily into two broad camps: those who adopt a tough stance on law and order, and those who favour a softer approach. Those arguing for a tough stance on crime are really invoking the use of the criminal justice system as a deterrent, and the constituencies sharing this viewpoint can be very varied. Elias (1986) names the Victims Committee of the International Association of Chiefs of Police, and Victim Advocates for Law and Order (VALOR) in the USA as examples of victim groups who espouse the view that more prosecutions, convictions and punishments will prevent crime. Victim groups expressing such views are also to be found in the United Kingdom. For example, Victims of Violence, started on Merseyside and led by Joan Jonkers, is an organization known for expressing similar views. Such views also find frequent support in different police organizations, such as the Police Federation. Moreover, feminists in both the UK and the USA have been known to adopt a tough stance on crimes of sexual violence. Many of these organizations invoke the image of the victim in support of their views. Such an image has been used frequently in the UK by politicians advocating a strong stance on law and order.

Enforcement crackdowns can, however, encapsulate a 'softer' edge. At this 'softer' end of offender-centred strategies lies the view that prisons are about rehabilitation, not punishment. Initiatives such as Intermediate Treatment for potential juvenile offenders and latterly mediation and reparation projects, encouraged by the 1998 Crime and Disorder Act (see Chapters 3 and 6), are designed with a preventive/rehabilitative goal in mind. This approach takes the view that offenders are educable, trainable and supervisable, and through these processes those known to be criminal, or thought to be at risk of offending, can be targeted and redirected in their behaviour.

Whether 'hard' or 'soft', both of these approaches assume that the cause of offending behaviour lies within the individual, who, once having learned the 'error of their ways', will cease to offend in the future. Indeed, there is some evidence to suggest that factors such as personality, attitudes and moral sense predispose some individuals to commit crime. As a consequence, offender-centred strategies have been shown to be more or less effective with particular offenders at particular times. As crime prevention strategies, however, their effectiveness is significantly limited by the presumption that the cause of crime lies within individual pathology. Moreover, there is considerable evidence to suggest that the causes of crime are more social in origin, and, of course, it is those social dimensions which offender-centred strategies are not designed to address.

4   Victim-centred strategies

As has already been suggested, the victim of crime became a symbolically important feature of law and order rhetoric during the 1980s. The emergence of the image of the victim to some extent coincided with the emergence of Victim Support, established nationally in 1979, as *the* organization speaking for, and offering support to, victims of crime. It is possible to argue that this imagery has become so powerful that crime prevention literature and strategies have become deeply embedded in a discourse of victimization avoidance – a discourse that has proceeded in the absence of little critical comment.

Victim Support

Every year I in 5 people becomes a victim of crime. **Victim Support** is the national charity for crime victims. Our volunteers provide **practical help and emotional support** to people affected by crime.

Our service is confidential and free.

Victim Support working for victims of crime.
Patron: HRH The Princess Royal.

BT
Community Programme

However, victim-centred strategies, rather like offender-centred strategies, can take a number of different forms. The victim of crime may, of course, be an individual human being, an animal, or an individual property or business. However, victimization avoidance as a way of thinking about crime and crime prevention has permeated a range of different organizational responses to crime. For example, insurance companies can now lay down fairly strict crime prevention criteria before offering household insurance in some postcode areas. They are thus able to dictate what kinds of locks should be fitted and where. Should the householder fail to put the relevant hardware in place, the insurance company does not have to pay out on a claim. This clearly places the responsibility for the prevention of burglary on the householder and implies that failure to do so is tantamount to inviting the crime to happen. Such a 'target hardening' approach to crime

Since its establishment in 1979, Victim Support, together with similar organizations, has ensured a higher profile for the interests of victims in criminal justice and criminological matters

prevention is one feature of what has been referred to as situational crime prevention (discussed more fully in section 5 below) but shares the underlying presumption of a victim-centred approach. As a crime prevention strategy it clearly implies that the *precipitative* behaviour or lack of action on the part of the victim is the clue to understanding why crime occurs.

Focusing on the precipitative behaviour of the victim has been used as a way of explaining homicide and rape by victimologists. The concept of victim precipitation was originally formulated by Wolfgang in the 1940s. As a lawyer-cum-criminologist, he was concerned to understand the nature of the culpability for a crime. The connections between culpability and victim precipitation have been made explicit by the courts on more than one occasion, especially in the context of rape, and have been translated as 'contributory negligence' (Jeffreys and Radford, 1984). However, in more general terms, focusing on the precipitative behaviour of the victim is a way of thinking about crime and criminal victimization which has very deep roots. With respect to crime prevention advice to women in particular, the translation of this precipitative view into a victimization avoidance policy strategy, and the victim-blaming connotations that this subsequently implies, are worthy of further consideration.

victim precipitation

4.1 Avoiding sexual danger

Crime prevention advice to women can range from taking self-defence classes to avoiding 'risky' places after dark. Much of this advice locates the responsibility for taking precautions with the potential victim of crime. So, for example, women are advised not to walk in poorly lit areas, to avoid walking on their own late at night, or, if drivers, to lock themselves in their car when driving alone. The basic message is: be prepared and know how to deal with an attack. But, the irony in all of this advice is, as Stanko (1990) has cogently argued (but see also Crawford *et al.*, 1990), that women do not need to be told about taking such precautions. They have devised many of their own. Moreover, as Stanko observes,

> Crime prevention advice revolves around public crime. And while the police and criminal justice system are slowly becoming involved, private violence is still seen as something different than public violence. Crime prevention advice, including much of the advice about avoiding sexual assault, focuses on the public domain. It is easier to give advice about checking the back seat of your car for intruders, or advising against standing at dimly lit bus stops, than finding ways of advising women not to trust so-called 'trustworthy' men.

(Stanko, 1990, p.4)

This brief discussion draws our attention to a number of important issues concerning crime prevention activity and its targets. Thinking about the advice offered to women on avoiding sexual danger, as Stanko rightly points out, encourages us to think about what kind of criminal victimization is being privileged in the crime prevention literature. In other words, it draws our attention to the presumption that the key source of danger to women is strangers – that is, men they do not know as opposed to men they do know. Yet there is a wealth of evidence from feminist research and other sources that women are in greatest danger from men they know (see **Saraga, 2001**). From this experience women are well practised, indeed expert, at devising strategies for their personal safety. So much so that women's self-regulation becomes part of their own (and others) 'governing of the soul' (Stanko, 1997). This highlights the way in which 'top-down' strategies can miss the mark by telling people to do what they are already well practised at! Such remedies encourage us to think that the cause of crime lies with the victim's own behaviour, rather than with that of the perpetrators. In this particular instance it places the responsibility for women's experiences of sexual violence with women rather than with men. With this in mind, you might like to consider the two crime prevention leaflets shown below, issued by the Greater Manchester Police Authority.

Simple Advice to Women

ON SEXUAL VIOLENCE

THERE ARE LOTS OF PAMPHLETS, BOOKS AND OTHER INFORMATION ABOUT HOW WOMEN CAN AVOID OR DEAL WITH RAPE, SEXUAL ATTACKS OR HARASSMENT.

THE PURPOSE OF THIS LEAFLET IS SIMPLY TO REAS-SURE WOMEN ABOUT THEMSELVES AND SET OUT WHERE YOU CAN GET ADVICE AND ASSISTANCE IF YOU NEED IT.

FEELING OF GUILT

If you are raped or sexually attacked, assaulted or harassed, you should not feel guilty about it or believe that you are to blame. The rapist or sexual attacker is always to blame. You are entitled to the full support of the law and society if you call upon their assistance.

YOUR BEHAVIOUR

How you dress, and how you act is your own business. No man is entitled to draw any conclusions from it about your willingness to have sex or your worth as a person. Once you say "no", at any stage of the activity or association, a man must accept his advances are not acceptable and stop.

MAKE YOUR ASSUMPTIONS

Some men are different from others. There are often no tell tale signs in a man's behaviour to show if he is one of the nice ones that won't try to attack you sexually or otherwise or one of the dangerous ones that will. If you are not sure, do not place yourself in potentially dangerous situations.

Greater Manchester Police Authority
Telephone : 061 793 3127

WHAT IF IT'S SOMEONE I KNOW

The previous points hold true in your home. Many rapes are carried out by men known to women and in their own home - even close relatives. You must make no assumptions about them and you should not feel guilty or responsible for anything that happens. The fault lies with them if you are assaulted or raped.

THE POLICE ARE THERE TO PROTECT YOU

Every woman is entitled to demand that anyone who rapes or attacks her is prosecuted. You are entitled to call on the police for protection if you are attacked or if you reasonably fear an attack. If, after you have called the police, you want to withdraw an accusation, you can do so, but you should not do this because of threats from anyone.

There are a large number of women officers in the Greater Manchester Police and you can ask to speak to a woman officer if you feel easier doing so.

WHAT YOU CAN DO

The Greater Manchester Police Authority have produced this leaflet and its counterpart "Simple Advice to Men to avoid Sexual Violence to Women" in an attempt to curb violent crimes against women. The Authority hope that the leaflets will reach all the public of Greater Manchester via Police/Community Liaison Panels, colleges, schools and places of work. You can make your contribution to the Authority's campaign by encouraging the men and boys whom you come into contact with to discuss this leaflet and the mens leaflet with their workmates and school mates in a sensible and supportive way. By doing so, you could be saving yourself or your mother, sister or daughter from a vicious and humiliating attack.

Although this leaflet makes it clear that men are always to blame for any rape or sexual attack or other violence, it is advisable to take reasonable precautions to avoid attacks and there are a number of leaflets available giving advice about this.

Simple Advice to Men

VIOLENCE AGAINST WOMEN IS A CRIME

VIOLENCE AGAINST WOMEN IS A CRIME

WHEN THE SUBJECT OF SEXUAL VIOLENCE TO WOMEN IS RAISED, A LOT OF MEN TREAT IT AS A JOKE. IT IS NO JOKE — IT IS DEADLY SERIOUS. RAPE AND SEXUAL ATTACKS RUIN THE QUALITY OF LIFE FOR MANY WOMEN — AND MANY MEN TOO, WHO ARE THE HUSBANDS, FATHERS, BOY FRIENDS, SONS OR FRIENDS OF WOMEN VICTIMS.

THIS LEAFLET SETS OUT GUIDELINES TO BE FOLLOWED WHEN YOU ARE IN THE COMPANY OF A WOMEN OR GIRL OR WITH OTHER MEN.

YOU ARE RESPONSIBLE IN LAW

Remember, "no" means "no".
Any sexual contact which you have with a woman or girl without her clear consent given freely without any threat or pressure is a serious criminal offence. No matter how much you may have or may think you have been encouraged or provoked, if she says "stop" or "no" you alone are fully responsible for any further sexual contact which is criminal and you could be sent to jail for it.

If you try to get a woman's "consent" because of the threat of your greater physical strength, position of power at work, or by intimidation, threats, or harassment, you are still wholly, morally and legally responsible for your behaviour.

DON'T DRAW CONCLUSIONS

A woman is entitled to dress or behave in any way she likes. You cannot assume that because she may look provocative or sexy that she wants sex with you or anyone else. You should not draw conclusions that she wants or consents to any sexual contact from what she says. A woman may speak to you on any topic. You should not assume that this means she wants to have sex with you.

WATCH YOUR LANGUAGE

How you behave when other men talk about sexual violence could affect the life of your mother, sister, girl friend or daughter. If you talk in such a way as to give the impression that men are entitled to sex and women are required to provide it, you could be beginning a chain reaction which results in someone being raped or murdered. This is equally true if you appear to support or agree with other men talking in that way.

YOUR BIGGEST RESPONSIBILITY IS AT HOME

The previous advice holds good in relation to women or girls whom you live with — your wife, girl-friend, daughter, step-daughter or sister. You have a special responsibility to women and girls whom you can easily dominate because of family circumstances. The fact that violence against women in the home is a crime is now generally accepted by both society and the police.

TAKE ALL COMPLAINTS SERIOUSLY

In every society people depend on each other. You can help by taking action if a woman is being raped, attacked, or assaulted, whether inside or outside the home.

You should always call the police, or arrange for them to be called. If a woman comes to you in fear of attack, all you need to do is take her seriously, stay with her, and call the police.

ALL WOMEN AND GIRLS DESERVE RESPECT ....

One of the most basic human rights is the right to freedom from fear of violence. One of the most basic human responsibilities is to respect one another equally and not make women feel anxious or afraid because of your behaviour. Any conduct in the company of women which they find frightening, threatening or unpleasant is a breach of that responsibility; so is "touching up" or unwanted attention.

Greater Manchester Police Authority crime prevention leaflets

ACTIVITY 7.2

Visit your local police station and ask for a sample of their crime prevention literature. Consider what advice, if any, is given regarding personal safety. If such advice is given, compare and contrast the literature you have gathered with the advice leaflets offered to both women and men in Greater Manchester. Ask yourself the following questions:

1 Who is presumed to be responsible for violence towards women in this literature?

2 What specific advice is offered to women?

3 Does the advice offered make sense to you?

4 How does the advice compare or contrast with your own precautionary strategies?

5 If you are a woman, what ways have you adopted of keeping yourself safe?

6 How, and under what circumstances, do you think such advice might work – how might it prevent criminal behaviour?

This discussion is not intended to deny the 'good sense' offered in crime prevention literature for women, nor is it intended to deny that the public domain is not a significant arena for crime prevention activity as far as women are concerned. Indeed, the public domain is also an important arena of crime prevention advice for men, but one wonders what would happen if men were told to stay off the streets at night. Moreover, some local authorities have attempted to take gender issues seriously in respect of crime prevention in the public domain. So, for example, improved street lighting (Painter, 1988), the introduction of women-only taxi services, late-night bus services for women, and all-female sessions at leisure centres (all examples cited by the research organization Comedia, 1991) may have improved the quality of life for those women who have used them. Perhaps the most significant point of this discussion is that it reminds us that communities are *gendered*. Communities are, at a minimum, spaces occupied by men and women (also adults *and* children, young *and* old, and people from ethnic minorities). In this sense it is important to consider such questions as 'whose crime?' and 'whose community?'. Answers to these questions may vary, of course, according to whose interests are being privileged by the policy-making process.

Victim-centred strategies can be about empowerment – enabling people to engage in activities or go to places which they otherwise would not; or they can be about blaming – looking for a way of reducing crime by encouraging individuals to change their behaviour in less positive ways, for example staying in rather than going out. In each case, it could be argued that they share a concern to reduce the opportunities for crime to occur. Reducing the opportunities for crime was the objective of one of the major crime prevention strategies of the early 1980s, namely situational crime prevention – here referred to more generally as environment-centred strategies.

5 Environment-centred strategies

situational crime prevention

Environment-centred strategies include both the specific targeting associated with situational crime prevention and the more general approach of 'designing out crime'. Clarke and Mayhew (1980) define situational crime prevention measures as:

- being directed at specific crimes;
- managing, designing or manipulating the immediate environment in which such crime occurs;
- ensuring that these measures are systematic and permanent;
- reducing overall opportunities for crime.

target hardening

Bottoms (1990) suggests that such opportunity-reducing measures could include target hardening (for example more secure doors and windows), removing the means for criminal activity (for example screening devices at airports), or increasing surveillance (for example closed-circuit television (CCTV) cameras in shopping malls and high streets).

A surveillance camera maintains a watchful eye in Liverpool

Targeting specific offences in this way has met with some success. Hough and Mo (1986) suggest, on the basis of British Crime Survey data, that attempted burglaries are prevented from being completed burglaries by the presence of crime prevention hardware. Obviously such findings need to be compared with what burglars themselves say will deter them: some research has shown that they rate the chance of being seen much more highly than the presence of hardware as an effective deterrent (Bennett and Wright, 1984). However, the work of Allatt (1984a and 1984b) on 'target hardening' on a 'hard to let' housing estate seems to point to some success with these kinds of initiative (see Clarke, 1992).

Manipulating the environment in order to prevent and/or reduce crime has also been explored as a more general strategy. These approaches stem largely from the work of Newman (1972), and have been taken up most extensively in the UK by Coleman (1985). This view of crime prevention implies a form of architectural determinism; in other words, the built environment provides the precipitative framework in which crime can be made more or less easy. The aim of these crime prevention programmes is to restructure the environment in order to reduce the opportunities for crime to occur. This may involve, for example, the disassembling of concrete walkways, which often permit numerous routes of unsurveyed access and egress on some housing estates, so as to make it harder for criminals to move around an estate unseen and unhindered. However, whether we define situational crime prevention narrowly as in specific target hardening, or whether we define it more generally as in environmental design, these strategies share a common problem. They raise the question of what happens to the potential criminal behaviour. This is referred to as the problem of displacement.

Theoretically, displacement can take a number of different forms. Barr and Pease (1992), citing Hakim and Rengert (1981), list four possible displacement effects:

displacement

- temporal – committing the intended crime at a different time;

- spatial – committing the intended crime at a different place;

- tactical – committing the same crime in a different way;

- target – committing a different crime from that originally intended.

How and under what circumstances these different types of displacement occur is not a clear-cut issue. Barr and Pease (1992) point out that the basic premise underlying situational crime prevention initiatives was derived from evidence relating to suicide. The change from toxic to non-toxic domestic usage of gas appeared to lead to a reduction in the suicide rate. However, the extent to which such opportunity reduction has an effect in the context of crime means identifying what kind of displacement occurs, how much, and when. Understanding whether an offender chooses to offend at a different place, a different time, or chooses to commit a different crime, is quite a complex process. It cannot merely be assumed that target hardening pushes one kind of offending somewhere else. Indeed, for the more 'professional' burglars, for example, target hardening a business may mean that they simply become more adept at negotiating those harder targets! In effect few situational crime prevention strategies have seriously evaluated these possibilities. As a consequence Barr and Pease (1992) prefer to talk of crime *deflection* rather than displacement. In other words, situational measures may move crime from a chosen target rather than reduce crime overall.

As was stated earlier, any preventive strategy makes certain presumptions about the possible explanations for, and the possibility of, predicting crime. In the case of offender-centred strategies and victim-centred strategies the locus of the cause of crime is clearly self-evident: it lies either with the individual offender or with a lack of vigilance on the part of the individual victim. In environment-centred strategies the locus of the cause of crime lies within a certain kind of architecture (Kinsey *et al.*, 1986). Environmental strategies view behaviour in general, and criminal behaviour in particular, as a product of the opportunities presented by physical structures. This view of crime causation implies that offenders engage in a rational decision-making process prior to offending and clearly connects with a neo-classical, conservative approach to criminology. In other words, it is assumed that offenders weigh up the relative risks and advantages of committing a certain offence under certain circumstances and decide on a course of action in the light of this: that is, they choose to offend or not on the basis of their rational assessment of the opportunities presented to them (see **Clarke, 1980**). To what extent this view can account for different kinds of law-breaking behaviour is highly problematic.

There is no doubt that the presence of opportunities can make crime easier. For example, a significant proportion of burglaries are facilitated by doors and windows being left open when property is unoccupied. The operative word here, however, is facilitated. As Bright (1991) points out, the fact remains that most people do not burgle houses or steal cars. He goes on to comment: 'While situational crime prevention, theoretically, can reduce the estimated 70 per cent of *recorded* crime that is thought to be opportunistic, it is unable to prevent many violent crimes such as some categories of assault, domestic violence, child abuse and racially motivated crime' (Bright, 1991, p.66). In other words, at best it is a very limited crime prevention strategy addressing a limited range of crimes with potentially limited impact.

Facilitation, then, does not equate with causation. However, the effect, in policy terms, of making things harder for the criminal has led to very particular ways of thinking about crime prevention. First, it encourages us to think of crime prevention in terms of technical expertise: fit the infra-red burglar alarm, install a CCTV camera, or remove the walkways from a housing estate and the crime problem is solved. Second, target hardening can have disastrous repercussions when individuals, or individual housing estates, develop a 'fortress mentality' in dealing with their routine day-to-day lives (Davis, 1990; **Graham and Clarke, 2001**). In other words, many environment-centred crime prevention strategies also have wider social and community consequences.

6 Community-centred strategies

To argue that certain crimes occur in some areas with greater frequency than in others is not new. Police statistics, while problematic in their structure and interpretation, have always shown this. What is relatively new perhaps is the impetus that has been given to this phenomenon through the use of the criminal victimization survey (Reiss, 1986). Such surveys, whether sponsored by the Home Office or by local authorities (and therefore by definition geographically focused), have consistently revealed that people living in certain areas, especially inner-city areas and poorer council housing estates, suffer disproportionately from both street crime and household crime. Recognition of this phenomenon, in crime prevention terms, has taken the form of an emphasis on and development of community crime prevention strategies. Hope and Shaw (1988a) offer two reasons for this emphasis: first, an increasing awareness of the impact of the fear of crime and an increasing belief that such fear is having a deleterious effect on 'community life'; and second, an increasing awareness that many people are affected by crime either as victims or as friends of victims. However, while the idea of the potential effectiveness of community strategies has been invoked since the early 1980s, we need to be clear about what is meant by 'community' in this context.

6.1   What is a community?

In some ways this is the sociological question *par excellence*. As with the concept of prevention, there is a presumption that communities are a 'good thing'. This is deeply embedded not only in popular consciousness, but also in much sociological thinking. That thinking, which has attempted to map the changing trajectories of modernizing societies, commonly assumes that traditional communities, together with extended family ties, neighbourliness, a sense of belonging and a personal sense of place and identity, have been destroyed by the processes of modernization. Indeed, so great was the sociological concern about the impact of the processes of modernization on community life that during the 1950s a whole generation of sociological work had 'the community' as its central focus (see, for example, Willmott and Young, 1962). Though this work produced a wealth of information about the nature of modern communities, their local networks and the kind of family ties that were being constructed, the concept of 'community' itself has remained relatively underdeveloped. Yet it is clear that as a concept it is used in different ways with different meanings. As Crawford (1995, p.98) points out, while the concept of community does not have a fixed meaning, especially in the crime prevention debate, it is certainly 'both a signifier and referent around which complex and contradictory effects, meanings and definitional struggles coalesce'. New Labour's adoption of communitarianism is one way in which community has been given contemporary meaning.

Borrowing from Etzioni's (1997) understanding of the need to reinvent communities of the past who spoke with one sense of morality and one sense of public interest, New Labour have embraced this version of community in their desire to *Bring Britain Together* (Social Exclusion Unit Report, 1998). This is not the place to discuss fully the strengths and weaknesses of this stance, but it does raise some interesting questions concerning 'whose community' to which we shall return (for a fuller discussion see Chapter 6 and Hughes, 1998).

Hope and Shaw (1988a) identify two main ways in which the concept of 'community' has been invoked in criminological thought: the disorganized community and the disadvantaged community. The notion of the disorganized community emanates from the work of Shaw and McKay, who were influential in the Chicago School. Portraying the city in ecological terms emanated from a concern with the 'zone of transition', a 'community' which is continuously inhabited by new immigrants and characterized by the absence of shared norms (see **Graham and Clarke, 2001**, and **Bottoms and Wiles, 1992**). In this view the absence of shared norms was seen to be the key to understanding offending behaviour. Moreover, securing and fostering social organization through the

disorganized community

socialization process was seen to be the crime prevention solution. In other words, it was the failure of community life that fostered crime. The second concept of community identified by Hope and Shaw (1988a), the disadvantaged community, emerged much later from the work of writers such as Cloward and Ohlin (1960). These writers argued that juveniles turned to delinquency as a result of frustration: that is, as a result of their desire to aspire to economic advance being met with the reality that this was not achievable. More recently, Hope (1995) has identified a third strand in the criminological use of community: the frightened community, associated with the harnessing of support for such policies as the Neighbourhood Watch schemes of the 1980s discussed below.

These first two images of community were derived from criminological thought that originated in North America. In empirical terms they found little validity in the UK at the time they were proposed. However, it is clear that given some of the consistent patterns of unemployment and social deprivation in some communities, there is some mileage, for example, in resurrecting a notion of the disadvantaged community. Indeed, a version of this can be found in the writing of Young and others who espouse a left realist agenda for criminology (see **Lea and Young, 1984** and **Young, 1986**). Using the term 'relative deprivation' rather than 'disadvantage', and focusing on 'lived realities', Young (1992, p.38) states: 'Crime is one form of sub-cultural adaptation which occurs when material circumstances block cultural aspirations and where non-cultural alternatives are absent or less attractive.' In many housing estates and inner-city areas, these are the kinds of conditions that exist and in which certain kinds of crime thrive. It is also these kinds of communities that have been differently targeted with varying degrees of success by the community crime prevention industry, in which, Willmott (1987) has observed, community is a 'seductive word'.

Willmott suggests that it is useful to distinguish between the 'territorial community' (those people who live in a particular area), the 'interest community' (those people who have something in common over and above the geographical area in which they live), and the 'attachment community' (people who have a sense of belonging to a place). Of course, the way in which we experience living in our 'communities' may comprise any one or a mixture of these categorizations at any moment, or it may change over time. Moreover, these experiences may not be coterminous with one another. Viewing 'communities' experientially, however, is not necessarily the focus of policy initiatives, though policies too may be differently informed by each of the categories identified above. Such policies may differ in other respects, as we shall see.

disadvantaged community

frightened community

ACTIVITY 7.3

At this juncture it would be useful to think about your own 'community'. What do you understand by that term? Is this a concept that has relevance for you? Are you thinking about where you live, your neighbourhood, your locality, or some other, perhaps larger, unit? Is your thinking informed by your feelings about where you live, or have you constructed some geographical boundary in your head? How do these thoughts interconnect? How might a crime prevention policy-maker think about your community, and how far might such thinking match with your own understanding of your community?

Given the central importance of the appeal to the concept of community in recent crime prevention policy rhetoric and practice, the following discussion, implicitly and explicitly, addresses these questions:

- What do you understand by the concept of community, and how might different definitions of community lead in different directions with respect to crime prevention?

- What do you understand by crime prevention, and to what extent have crime prevention initiatives been subjected to fashionable policy and political influences?

- Are there different kinds of community crime prevention initiatives; if so, what do they comprise?

- What kind of community crime prevention initiatives are likely to succeed, for whom, where, and under what circumstances?

- What might communities of the future look like, given current crime prevention trends?

It is possible to identify the emergence of two main crime prevention strategies during the 1980s, and these invoke the image of the community in differing ways. The first, Neighbourhood Watch, invokes the *citizen* as a member of the community and invites greater citizen participation in crime prevention. The second, multi-agency co-operation, invokes the community through the greater co-operation of the various agencies who work in an area.

6.2 Neighbourhood Watch: the eyes and ears of the police?

Neighbourhood Watch schemes take their lead from the USA. The first **Neighbourhood** Neighbourhood Watch scheme in the UK was established in 1982, and by **Watch** 1994 there were reported to be 115,000 schemes (*The Guardian*, 6 April 1994). They have been defined as the 'mobilization of informal community controls' directed 'in the defence of communities against a perceived predatory threat from outside' (Hope and Shaw, 1988a, p.12). In crime prevention terms there are two arguments which commend them as possible policy strategies. First, they propose an opportunity reduction view of crime – they presume that increased surveillance will deter criminals by encouraging citizens to be the eyes and ears of the police on the street. Second, they propose to reduce the 'incivilities' of urban life through creating and harnessing social cohesion by increasing contact between neighbours, in the hope that this will lead to a greater trust between citizens and a consequent reduction in the fear of crime.

It is clear that the growth and development of Neighbourhood Watch schemes across the UK has been remarkable; what is less certain is what such schemes actually achieve. The 1984 British Crime Survey afforded an opportunity to examine the development of these schemes a little more closely. Having analysed the data, Hope (1988, p.159) states: 'Where the strongest spontaneous support for Neighbourhood Watch resides is in those communities where people are sufficiently worried about crime, where they feel the need to do something about it, and where they feel positively towards their neighbours and to the community in general.' He goes on to add that those people who appear to be willing to involve themselves in these schemes are white, middle-aged, and lower-middle/middle-class. These findings seem to concur with other research which has been concerned to measure the overall effectiveness of the schemes. Collectively, these findings point to the fact that Neighbourhood Watch schemes are most likely to achieve some of their objectives (primarily fear reduction) among white, middle-class homeowners (Bennion *et al.*, 1985; Donnison *et al.*, 1986; Bennett, 1987).

Neighbourhood Watch seems to be popular in areas where worry about crime is likely to be high, but where the risk from residential crime is relatively low: that is, in areas where crime is likely to be perceived as being a threat external to the community. On the other hand, in areas where the recorded crime rate is higher, that is in areas of poorer public sector housing, poorer older terraced housing and multi-racial areas, Neighbourhood Watch is less popular. In these areas it is likely that the crime problem is not seen or experienced as a threat from outside the community, but one with which members of the community routinely live. One study suggests that up to 60 per cent of offenders live less than a mile away from the scene of their crime (Cooper, 1989). People may see and hear what is going on, but do not necessarily possess the local trust and support from their neighbours should they report such incidents. Indeed, some may be positively intimidated from doing so.

There are, of course, a number of problems in assuming that all the registered Neighbourhood Watch schemes work effectively and in line with their objectives. There is a suspicion that many are inactive or exist only on paper. Moreover, a significant input of police time is required for them to work effectively, and this can be a key variable in the overall achievement of objectives (Bennett, 1987). Why they have proved to be so popular in the leafy suburbs tells us more about the willingness of people living in such areas to participate generally than it does about the success of the schemes themselves.

Of course, none of these issues necessarily means that the idea of Neighbourhood Watch is in itself misplaced. As Bright (1991, p.78) suggests, difficulties such as these raise a number of important questions:

- What can be done to sustain the interest and involvement of scheme members?
- How should schemes be managed and supported (given the demands it places on the police)?
- How can their potential be developed in high crime areas?

None of these questions necessarily presumes, for Bright, that Neighbourhood Watch can effectively reduce crime. However, as Bright points out, its popularity could be capitalized upon through, for example, the development of a national network of organizations in which good practice could be shared, and by expanding the remit of schemes to include strategies designed to enhance the quality of life (refuse, dog nuisance, play facilities, and so on). Bright's analysis suggests that many schemes have already begun to diversify in this way, and consequently have the potential to keep the membership active as well as improve the quality of life. This view highlights the constructive potential for locally based schemes. But Bright is not the only one to have highlighted their potential.

A private street-patrol officer on duty in Sedgefield, County Durham; the force is funded and operated by the local council

At a Neighbourhood Watch conference in 1994 the idea was mooted that the remit of Watch schemes could be expanded to include crime prevention patrols. This was met with some criticism and resistance by those committed to the basic Watch principles. Yet community patrols of various kinds are clearly on the increase.

ACTIVITY 7.4

Read the descriptions of three Neighbourhood Warden Schemes reproduced as Extract 7.1. Then answer the following questions:

1   What do you think are the key similarities and differences between Warden Schemes and Neighbourhood Watch?

2   What questions do both developments raise concerning the idea of community? What are the dangers inherent in this idea?

3   In what ways, if any, could either of these developments be identified as vigilantism? Do you think this is a potential problem? If so, why?

4   What relationship between citizen and state is envisaged by developments such as these? What are their respective responsibilities in crime prevention?

Extract 7.1 Jacobson and Saville: 'Neighbourhood Warden Schemes in Swansea, Sedgefield and Newport'

Swansea Estate Wardens and Neighbourhood Support Unit

Focus and aims

In 1994 an 'Estate Warden Scheme' covering Townhill North Estate was established, and was extended in 1997 with the establishment of the Neighbourhood Support Unit by the local authority Housing Department. This covers all council housing in Swansea City and Council (approximately 17,000 properties). It employs 20 Neighbourhood Support Workers who provide a 24 hour on-site landlord presence, and have responsibility for maintaining high visibility patrols and installing and monitoring alarms in empty properties.

The driving force behind the original Estate Warden Scheme was the Housing Department's reaction to thefts of heating systems from void properties. Concerns with increasing levels of anti-social behaviour on local authority estates, as well as with void security, led to the establishment of the Neighbourhood Support Unit. A tenant consultation forum was set up to promote tenant involvement, and newsletters continue to keep residents informed of developments.

Staffing and partnership

The role of the Neighbourhood Support Workers includes installing, maintaining and responding to radio alarms; carrying out foot and mobile patrols; witness protection; information gathering; observing antisocial behaviour; reporting crime; communicating with tenants; and court attendance. Training for the staff, provided by the Council and the South Wales Police Authority, covers issues such as offences; civilian powers; communication skills; conflict management and the Crime and Disorder Act.

The Neighbourhood Support Workers do not hold any additional powers to those held by normal citizens. However, as members of the Neighbourhood Support Unit they are able to gather information enabling the local authority to sanction anti-social tenants, for example through evictions.

The scheme has helped to establish stronger working relationships between the Housing Department and many other statutory agencies including the police, Social Services, the Environmental Health Department, the Legal Department, the Youth Justice Team, the Drugs Project and the public at large. The most striking improvement since the inception of the scheme has probably been in terms of the relationship with the police. The collaboration has involved training for local authority staff, the enforcement of housing injunctions and co-operation in problem resolution.

(Jacobson and Saville, 1999, p.12

Newport Estate Ranger Service

Focus and aims

The Newport Estate Ranger Service was established in 1994 by the Borough Council, in response to the growing problems of anti-social behaviour on estates and the increasing number of complaints from tenants. It is dedicated to preventing anti-social behaviour – such as excessive noise, threatening behaviour, joy-riding, vandalism and neighbour disputes. Incidents of crime are immediately reported to the police; therefore the activities of the rangers filter out those incidents where a police presence is not required or is not an appropriate use of resources.

The service was originally restricted to Council estates (approximately 12,500 properties), and has been expanded to include Charter Housing Association estates (a further 1,600 properties). The service therefore caters for about 25 per cent of the Borough population.

Staffing and partnership

A team of 12 Rangers operates 2 shifts per day, 7 days a week, from 8am to midnight. The rangers wear a low-key uniform, and patrol in Council vehicles. They can be diverted to incidents by radio messages sent from a centralised control centre.

Sedgefield Borough Community Force

Focus and aims

The Sedgefield Community Force is a local authority run force charged with conducting a 24 hour uniformed patrol of the public streets of the local authority area. Sedgefield is a Borough Council with a population of more than 90,000 over 54,000 acres. The introduction of the Force in 1994 was the first stage of a community safety strategy designed by the Council's Community Safety Officer, and was initiated in response to comments from electors during a local election about fear of crime.

The stated objectives of the Force are as follows:

To provide a community patrol to increase public safety and reassure the public.

To consult with local residents regarding anti-social problems in their area.

3 To consult with local police regarding crime trends and problems, and how the Force can assist in combating them.

4 To provide advice and information to local residents on crime prevention.

5 To obtain and provide evidence of anti-social behaviour in order to assist the relevant enforcement agencies or departments of the Council.

6 To ensure the safety of Council employees whilst undertaking their normal duties.

7 To provide security checks/patrols of Council properties.

8 To generally advise regarding security issues.

Staffing and partnership

The Force consists of 11 patrolling officers and 1 senior patrolling officer, who patrol in marked vehicles and on foot. They operate from a council depot and are in constant radio contact with a control room. They have no special powers, and maintain a non-confrontational policy of 'observe and report only'. They therefore aim to act as the eyes and ears for the public police, and they immediately inform the police of any incidents.

The officers undergo two weeks of theoretical training and two weeks of practical training. The subjects covered include basic legal knowledge, health and safety, first-aid, situation management and crime prevention. County Durham Constabulary support this training by providing instruction in evidence gathering, scene of crime protection and procedures for bomb threats.

(Jacobson and Saville, 1999, pp.14–15)

which accepts calls from the public. Staff receive a two week induction course, and on-going training under qualified supervision.

The Rangers aim to prevent anti-social behaviour through their presence, and to stop the escalation of incidents through informal persuasion. Furthermore, evidence is gathered on anti-social tenants for the Housing Officer who can take legal action if required. The Rangers have no special powers, and aim to nip problems of anti-social behaviour in the bud without showing an excessive reaction in order to improve the atmosphere on the estates.

The relationship of the scheme with the police is very effective; informal liaison takes place at all levels but most commonly in the form of Ranger/Constable interaction. A formal protocol has recently been drawn up with the police which allows for the passing of information on specific cases. There is also informal liaison with community groups including Neighbourhood Watch groups.

(Jacobson and Saville, 1999, p.22)

The discussion of Neighbourhood Watch, and the exercise you have just completed, have alerted us to a number of issues. First, harnessing citizen support for community crime prevention strategies of this kind is fraught with difficulties. In terms of implementation, ensuring active participation across a full range of communities has yet to be achieved. Second, in terms of effectiveness, Neighbourhood Watch and Warden Schemes appear to have achieved some success in making people feel better about the crime problem in their local area. However, there appears to be little evidence to support a view that such initiatives have resulted in a reduction in crime. Finally, the core role of Neighbourhood Watch and Warden Schemes is unclear: to prevent crime, promote intolerance of disorder, improve the physical environment, promote community solidarity or rid local areas of those deemed 'unwanted'? The thin dividing line between some of these roles and vigilantism serves to remind us that community-based initiatives may not always, by definition, be a 'good thing'.

Taken together, the issues outlined above raise an underlying problem for community-based initiatives of this kind. That problem relates to their central purpose: is it to reduce crime or to reduce the fear of crime? If it is the former, then as a policy initiative it shares many of the same assumptions about the causes of crime as the environmentally based initiatives discussed earlier: they all articulate an opportunistic view of crime. Not only does this raise the question of displacement but, perhaps more importantly in this particular context, it raises questions about the assumptions being made concerning the communities themselves. It has already been stated that Neighbourhood Watch schemes fit most readily with a view of crime which sees it as a threat from outside the community. In addition, however, they assume a very static image of the community, although we know that communities change, people grow up, new people move in, others move out, and so on. All of these processes can have an impact on crime independently of any crime prevention strategy. Finally, all of these schemes take as their central focus 'public' crime – that which occurs on the streets or against property. Yet, for many people, especially women, most of the crime they experience directly takes place in the private domain and involves victims and offenders who are typically known to each other. However, the extent to which the gendered nature of communities is taken on board may be dependent upon the resources available to target what kind of crime with what kind of initiative.

6.3   Multi-agency co-operation

multi-agency co-operation

The second strand to community crime prevention that emerged in the 1980s took the form of multi-agency co-operation. Hope and Shaw define the purpose of multi-agency co-operation as follows:

> In as much as crime within local communities is likely to be sustained by a broad range of factors – in housing, education, recreation, etc. – the agencies and organisations who are in some way responsible for, or capable of, affecting those factors, ought to join in common cause so that they are not working at cross purposes or sustaining crime inadvertently.

> (Hope and Shaw, 1988a, p.13)

This approach to crime prevention endeavours to take Home Office circular 8/84 to heart. However, as an approach to crime prevention it has been researched relatively little. The most important piece of work in this area was sponsored by the Economic and Social Research Council (ESRC) in the mid 1980s and conducted by a research team based at the University of Lancaster and Middlesex Polytechnic (Sampson *et al.*, 1988).

Sampson *et al.* identified two traditional ways of thinking about multi-agency co-operation at a theoretical level: the *benevolent* and the *conspiratorial*. The benevolent sees the idea of forming a consensus between different organizations with different goals as unproblematic. The conspiratorial view, usually associated with those on the political left, sees such developments as an extension of the coercive role of the state. Sampson *et al.*'s own research on the process of implementing multi-agency strategies points to the inadequacy of both of these positions and to the importance of developing a 'more socially nuanced understanding which is alive to the complexities of locally based crime prevention initiatives and of power differentials running between state agencies, as well as to the competing sectional interests within existing communities' (Sampson *et al.*, 1988, p.482).

This does not mean, of course, that multi-agency work is non-problematic. On the contrary, there are dilemmas to be faced by agencies participating in such initiatives. As a policy process they may be less than democratic – that is, dominated by the expert status of the police (Kinsey *et al.*, 1986). They may also compromise the role of other agencies, for example by determining the nature of social work with young people or probation work with ex-offenders (Blagg *et al.*, 1988). Issues such as these led Bottoms (1990, p.16) to ask a number of important questions about the multi-agency approach:

- Do different agencies have different amounts of power in inter-agency crime prevention forums, and does it matter?

- How much autonomy is it necessary for each agency to lose for the sake of the collective good, and are they willing to lose it?

- To what extent is it right to recognize that different agencies (such as the police and social work departments) have different assigned functions, and that these functions will necessarily limit the extent to which co-operation between agencies may properly (and ethically) occur?

The question remains, of course, as to what multi-agency co-operation might achieve with respect to crime prevention and the community. Sampson *et al.*'s research cited above offers us two possibilities. The first constitutes a broadening of the focus of what had been traditionally conceived of as crime prevention business. For example, Blagg *et al.* state:

> What is most striking is the contrast between the neglect of domestic violence as a site upon which to enact measures of crime prevention (in other words to regard such violence as crime) or to invoke the concept of inter-agency co-operation when set against the elaborate liaison apparatus which is arranged around child protection.
>
> (Blagg *et al.*, 1988, p.217)

Viewed over a decade later this is a particularly astute observation, as we shall see in section 6.8 below. Suffice it to say at this stage that multi-agency co-operation has indeed become one of the by-words of responses to 'domestic' violence, especially in the wake of Home Office circular 60/1990. That circular reminded all chief constables of the potential power of arrest in domestic situations, made it clear that 'domestic' violence was to be taken as seriously as violence occurring in the street, encouraged the use of arrest for the perpetrators of 'domestic' violence, and advised police forces of the need to support the victim. However, Blagg *et al.* were rightly drawing attention to the way in which the crime prevention agenda had, until this time, assumed a vision of the crime problem as being located solely in the public domain.

The second possibility exposed by Blagg *et al.* lay in the view that communities were not necessarily being consulted about their concerns with respect to crime. This points to the tensions that exist between statutory agencies (who have the power to define the local problem and allocate resources to it) and the local communities in which they are working. These tensions may sometimes result in decisions being taken in the face of local opposition and/or demands for a different problem to be addressed with a different resource allocation. Such a top-down implementation style can also result in the further stereotyping of a community and/or the overlooking of problems genuinely felt by people living in a particular locality. These tensions point to the need for closer and more effective consultation with communities for such implementation styles to work.

ACTIVITY 7.5

Make a list of the main limitations of community-centred strategies as you now understand them.

Neighbourhood Watch, Warden Schemes and multi-agency co-operation, as conventionally understood, are limited by the fact that they tend to be police-led and they tend to operate with a focus on property crime, street crime, or 'nuisances'. They are also initiatives which primarily reflect a territorial definition of the community where crime is seen as an external threat or is recognized as a problem internal to the community and may result in the further stereotyping of that community. In addition, both tend to operate with a top-down implementation style, often neglecting less formal groups and glossing over the problems of trying to create 'social cohesion' as a crime prevention strategy. Moreover, there is a sense in which the kinds of communities successfully targeted by both of these policy initiatives are those communities in which some semblance of social cohesion already exists: the leafy suburbs, or those areas in which the statutory agencies still find some basis of co-operation. However, there is a third strand to community-centred crime prevention which runs somewhat contrary to these first two. This strand is informed by the concept of community safety rather than crime prevention per se, and can be identified in the work of the National Association for the Care and Resettlement of Offenders (NACRO) and the Safer Cities Programme. The work of NACRO in particular focuses on a very different kind of community from that discussed so far.

6.4 Community safety

6.4.1 The NACRO framework

Bottoms (1990) suggests that the most ambitious social crime prevention programmes in the UK to date have been established by NACRO, a voluntary organization which set up a Crime Prevention Unit in 1979 and a Safe Neighbourhood Unit in 1980. The initiatives emanating from this organization frequently include elements of both situational and social crime prevention. Social crime prevention, as opposed to situational crime prevention, endeavours to address the root causes of crime. The initiatives are focused primarily on multiply deprived housing estates in high crime-rate areas. These projects involve active consultation with the local community 'to tease out possible solutions to the problems from their knowledge of the area' (Whiskin, 1987). They are based on a concept of community safety whose origins can be located not only in the work of NACRO but also in the work of the police monitoring groups that emerged in some police authority areas following the Scarman Report in 1981.

social crime prevention

community safety

Bright (1987, pp.49–50) outlines the NACRO framework as including:

- strategies for the involvement of local councils
- services for victims of crime
- strategics for protecting those most at risk (women, ethnic minorities, children)
- schemes for involving the police
- schemes tailored to different residential areas

Although, as Whiskin (1987) states, a framework of this kind is not strikingly original, it does draw attention to a number of critical features of the community crime prevention industry which are, arguably, neglected by both multi-agency approaches and Neighbourhood Watch schemes.

First, the framework starts from the premise that tackling criminal victimization and the fear of such victimization is the responsibility of a broad base within the community: formal agencies, informal agencies, and community networks. This implies that it is necessary not only to ensure community participation, but also to establish mechanisms to ensure that participation is both facilitated and representative. Second, it is a framework within which the definition of the crime problem incorporates an understanding of criminal victimization that takes into account the structural variables of age, ethnicity and sex – facets of community crime prevention which are not commented on explicitly in the initiatives discussed above. Third, it proposes a genuinely co-operative approach to community crime prevention. This moves close to the idea of empowerment. Taken together, the features of the NACRO framework for crime prevention come closest to resonating with all three definitions of community identified by Willmott (1987) and discussed earlier.

empowerment

The NACRO framework requires the formulation of a locally based action plan, and an implementation process usually involving a complex mixture of situational/environmental measures and social strategies. Because of the complexity of these initiatives it has proved difficult to evaluate their effectiveness. As Rock (1988) comments, while it may be clear that NACRO interventions have an effect, the reason why is uncertain. Indeed, there is some controversy concerning the overall effectiveness of the NACRO approach to crime prevention and reduction (see, for example, Poyner *et al.*, 1986). Nevertheless, NACRO projects present a view of crime prevention which has had a considerable impact on policy thinking and from which, Bright (1991) argues, a number of lessons have been learned.

First, NACRO initiatives illustrate that the best projects are multi-focused in housing estates with multiple problems. This often means that evaluation has to be long-term before any effects can be noted. It also means that issues like estate design, play provision, employment opportunities, policing and estate management need as much attention as crime prevention itself. Second, NACRO schemes show that residents will only become involved in such initiatives if the local council and local police are both seen to be using their resources and their power to address local problems. Third, the schemes clearly suggest that resources are needed to improve the environment (to tackle vandalism and poor street lighting, for example) alongside the need for community participation and multi-agency co-operation. Bright (1991) argues that the variable availability of resources during the 1980s was frequently a factor in what was achievable or not within these projects.

However, the rhetoric of community safety has not been confined solely to NACRO projects: the Safer Cities initiative launched by the government in the 1980s shares the use of this terminology.

6.4.2   Safer Cities

The Safer Cities Programme was the Home Office contribution to the Action for Cities initiative introduced by the government in 1988. Building on the knowledge acquired from the earlier Five Towns Initiative and the associated demonstration projects, Safer Cities aimed to: reduce crime, lessen the fear of crime, and 'create safer cities where economic and community life can flourish' (Tilley, 1993). Having established a locally based programme designed to achieve these aims, each Safer Cities initiative expected to do one of two things: either to end community involvement having met the original aims, or to have established an alternative source of funding to that provided by the Home Office in order to continue working. As a programme, then, it shared the partnership approach to crime prevention. In this case, however, the partnership was between central government in the main and local projects. The brief of local projects was to forge multi-agency contacts, especially in the formation of their steering committees. The realization of such a partnership was obviously a key variable for projects not guaranteed permanent status. It is of interest to our discussion to explore what is meant by 'community safety' in this context, since this has not always been made clear (see Extract 7.2).

In his evaluation of the Safer Cities initiative Tilley (1992) comments that the terms 'community safety' and 'crime prevention' appeared to be used interchangeably. He suggests that, in practice, schemes have concerned themselves with issues beyond the usual target hardening or Neighbourhood Watch approach to crime prevention but have perhaps not gone so far as to include issues like noise or pollution which might be associated with community safety. So the aims of Safer Cities were broad, and it is interesting to note in

partnership

particular the emphasis on the role of crime prevention in relation to the business community within each scheme area. Moreover, Safer Cities schemes have funded projects in schools, in relation to domestic violence, as well as the more usual target hardening work.

Extract 7.2 The Morgan Report: 'Crime prevention and community safety'

3.1 Early on, the Working Group noted the absence of a definition of crime prevention in Circulars 8/84, 44/90 and the accompanying booklet, *Partnership in Crime Prevention*. Although none of the responses submitted by Chief Constables or local authority Chief Executives attempted a definition, the Association of Chief Police Officers (ACPO), in a separate document entitled *The Role of the Force Crime Prevention Officer*, defined crime prevention as: 'the anticipation, recognition and appraisal of a crime risk and the initiation of the pre-emptive action to remove or reduce it'.

3.2 A somewhat different perspective informs the Association of District Councils' report *Promoting Safer Communities*. This comments: 'More and more the phrase crime prevention is understood to be about promoting community safety and examining wider social issues'.

3.3 Responses from local authorities and police forces made use of such terms as '*crime reduction strategies and policies*', '*situational crime prevention*', '*social crime prevention policy*' and '*community safety*', which covered a wide variety of activities and perspectives. However, for the most part, crime prevention was perceived in terms of schemes for reducing the opportunities for crime.

3.4 It is the view of the Working Group that the social aspects of crime prevention, which seek to reduce those influences which lead to offending behaviour, and the fear of crime, need to receive attention at least equal to that given to the situational aspects of crime prevention, in which efforts are made to reduce opportunities and '*harden*' potential targets for crime.

3.5 We have been impressed by the need identified by the leading organizations for a broad spectrum of activities, ranging from the prevention of opportunity through deterrence to more social aspects of crime prevention. These include diversion of existing and potential offenders, dealing with offenders after sentence, and more general attention to youth activity. We have also been impressed by the stress placed by both Ministers and officials of the Home Office and other government Departments on the need for crime prevention measures which address the causes of offending.

3.6 The term '*crime prevention*' is often narrowly interpreted and this reinforces the view that it is solely the responsibility of the police. On the other hand, the term '*community safety*' is open to wider interpretation and could encourage greater participation from all sections of the community in the fight against crime.

3.7 We see community safety as having both social and situational aspects, as being concerned with people, communities and organizations including families, victims and at risk groups, as well as with attempting to reduce particular types of crime and the fear of crime. Community safety should be seen as the legitimate concern of all in the local community.

(Home Office, 1991, p.13)

Evaluation was built into the Safer Cities Programme, but it is important to consider what is being evaluated: the programme as a whole, individual projects, or individual schemes within projects? Each of these different levels of evaluation suggests a rather complex evaluative model. Tilley's (1992) work offers some comments on the implementation process of the programme as a whole. His analysis draws attention to a number of issues for the schemes, including the difficulties of:

- placing crime prevention as a central issue on local authority agendas, where lack of recognition at worst, or lack of a coherent response at best, are key problems to address;
- being faced with a lack of credibility, especially from other agencies well established in local communities;
- the absence of an expected 'blueprint for action' from central government;
- the danger of the police or some other powerful local agency taking the lead in setting the local agenda.

Tilley (1992) highlighted the crucial role played by the co-ordinators and their assistants, who by definition were required to be members of the local community, in steering a constructive course through these difficulties, and their role in ultimately establishing an exit strategy – that is, a plan of action for disengaging from the community. Tilley also provides a useful overview of the kinds of strategies that have been put in place under the auspices of Safer Cities (see Table 7.1).

Commenting on this range of interventions, Tilley suggests that, all other things being equal and providing that funds are available, difficulties increase going from left to right and from top to bottom. The bottom right-hand corner constitutes the most threatening strategy to existing agency practices.

ACTIVITY 7.6

Table 7.1 presents some useful concrete examples of the kinds of crime prevention work conducted by Safer Cities. Using this chart, make notes on the following questions:

1   How do you think this view of community crime prevention compares with that proposed by the NACRO model?
2   What kind of definition of the 'community' is assumed by Safer Cities and NACRO? How do these definitions compare? Who is included and who is excluded by these definitions?
3   Compare and contrast the implementation styles of each version of community safety. Which do you think is most likely to succeed?

Tilley goes on to state:

> Even though in a fully fleshed-out Community Safety Strategy it may not be appropriate that the police and local authority have the dominant voices, it is clear that their co-operation is a *sine qua non* of any longer term community safety/crime prevention strategy. If the agreement of either of these to participate is not forthcoming, no workable strategy can develop.

(Tilley, 1992, p.18)

Table 7.1   Examples of interventions by scope and level of penetration

Level of intervention	Physical intervention	Social intervention
First level: conduct of new dedicated initiatives	Examples: • installation/provision of door locks • window locks • fencing • blocking or creating alleyways • lighting • creation of curtilage parking • personal alarms • burglar alarms • CCTV • aspects of risk management in schools and hospitals	Examples: • schemes for those at risk of offending such as youth facilities or parent support groups • victim or potential victim schemes such as advice centres • offender-based programmes such as motor projects or careers advice • training for staff in public houses in dealing with violence • aspects of risk management in schools and hospitals • Neighbourhood Watch, Pub Watch, etc.
Second level: incorporation into new, potentially relevant initiatives	Examples: • design of new housing estates • shopping complexes • public buildings such as schools, colleges and hospitals • siting of banks and post offices	Examples: • new school curriculum contents • management of new commercial concerns
Third level: re-examination of existing patterns of practice	Examples: • council repair practices for burgled properties • council policies for removal of graffiti • rubbish collection practices • provision of screechers to female employees and students	Examples: • school culture and management • methods of running children's homes • patterns of service delivery in health visiting • housing allocation policies • styles of policing high-crime areas • service delivery by police to crime victims • victim support for offender victims • recruitment policies for victim support • employment services to ex-offenders • policies relating to race and gender relations in public and private sector institutions

Source: Tilley, 1992, p.29

Thus within the Safer Cities Programme we are faced with a similar organizational dilemma to that found in other initiatives that have a different emphasis. There is a clear strain within any crime prevention programme towards a top-down style stemming from the necessary involvement of both the police and the local authority. This observation, of course, does not necessarily imply that such initiatives are doomed to failure or by definition will only ever have limited success. It does, though, beg a number of questions concerning how the needs of people living in those communities that have been targeted for action are identified, taken account of, and/or indeed met. How these processes are or are not achieved is more often than not a matter of political vision, and in the context of crime prevention, as elsewhere, criminologists differ both theoretically and politically as to how best to achieve success in the crime prevention arena (see section 6.6).

6.5 Mixed-policy community strategies

Implicitly and explicitly, community-centred crime prevention programmes frequently advocate a mixture of both situational and social crime prevention initiatives. Two projects in particular point to the potential for success of such mixed strategies: the Kirkholt Burglary Prevention Project in Rochdale and the Hilldrop Project in Islington, north London.

The Kirkholt Burglary Project, influenced by Canadian research, was predicated on evidence of repeat or multiple victimization. In other words, built into the prevention programme was the knowledge that the chances of a house being burgled within six weeks of an initial incident were very high. The main preventive activity was therefore focused on the recently victimized. The measures introduced included: the removal of pre-payment meters, more rapid repairs after a burglary, the target hardening of property, a property-marking scheme, a security survey, and the establishment of so-called 'cocoon' Neighbourhood Watch schemes involving the victimized house and immediate neighbours. The results of this programme were impressive, with a large reduction in burglary and only minimal evidence of displacement (Forrester *et al.*, 1988). It is, of course, difficult to say which, if any, of the measures produced this effect. However, it is clear that the considerable resource investment of different kinds that took place in this community certainly had an impact.

The Hilldrop Project also deployed a mixture of crime prevention measures, but adopted a different way of gauging the crime prevention needs of the community. Following a local crime survey of the people living in the area, a team of researchers and policy-makers devised a list of crime prevention priorities for the area. These included target hardening, women's self-defence classes, increased beat policing, curriculum activity in schools, and the development of a form of Neighbourhood Watch scheme (Lea *et al.*, 1988).

It is interesting that both of these projects incorporated a version of Neighbourhood Watch into their programmes, perhaps validating the need to rethink what such schemes can achieve and how they might best deliver some form of success. It is also interesting to note that as projects they were differently sponsored (the first by the Home Office, the second by a local authority) and that they bear the hallmarks of different political flavours to the crime prevention policy process.

6.6 Community crime prevention: beyond left or right?

The community crime prevention initiatives we have so far discussed target different factors as the cause of criminal behaviour. One of the key differences between these initiatives is the extent to which social factors such as social deprivation, poor housing and unemployment are highlighted as factors which need to be taken into account in crime prevention policy. The NACRO initiatives have come closest to constituting *social* crime prevention programmes in this sense. The extent to which such social factors are seen to contribute to crime is clearly connected to political visions of the crime problem. The denial that unemployment is a contributory factor to crime, for example, has been a characteristic of the response to crime of those on the right. It comes as no surprise, then, to observe that those communities in which crime is seen as an internal rather than an external threat are also those in which there are other social problems; they consequently demand more resources as well as the political will to devise and introduce policies that take those factors on board.

Since the early 1980s, government policy has put much effort into supporting community responses to crime prevention. These responses, primarily Neighbourhood Watch and Safer Cities, have relied on communities that comprise citizens with the personal and economic resources, free of intimidation, to put such policies to good effect. The available evidence clearly illustrates how, where and when success has been achieved by these policies and the ongoing difficulties in measuring success! The question remains as to whether left-wing strategies would look any different.

In many respects those on the left invoke the same rhetoric as those on the right concerning the need for a role for the community in crime prevention. How that community is to be approached, harnessed and encouraged in its organization of crime prevention is clearly different, as perhaps the NACRO definition of community safety illustrates. Left realism makes much of putting the victim of crime at the centre of any policy agenda, but in the context of a democratic process. As Lea (1987, p.369) states, 'The maximization of democratic participation is ultimately the solution both to the problem of what is crime and to the problem of how to deal with it'. Lea further argues that an important feature of a realist approach to crime prevention would involve a real plurality of agencies, both formal and informal, centrally and locally organized. Crawford *et al.* (1990) describe such an agenda in more detail. They identify five crime prevention strategies:

- individual crime prevention
- crime reduction
- crime detection
- crime deterrence
- victim support

All of these need to take account of specific local problems, types of crime, the environment (including the quality of life), multi-agency approaches, consultation, political will and the evaluation of effectiveness. This vision of crime prevention espouses a view of policy-making as a *process* (as negotiated between bottom-up and top-down styles). It is also concerned to empower communities through co-operation. This is in contrast to the more right-wing stance, which is more top-down in style and makes consultation less of a feature. Indeed, the question of *effective* partnership is highlighted by the Audit Commission's Report *Safety in Numbers* (1999) yet has nevertheless become a statutory requirement in the flagship legislation of the 1998 Crime and Disorder Act implemented under New Labour. However, the extent to which empowerment is practically realizable is very different. Jefferson *et al.* (1988) point out the difficulties of implementing policies that are sensitive to the questions of participation, representation and the community. While these practical problems need to be acknowledged, such an ideal endeavours to take the interests of various groups into account. This raises the question: which groups?

Many of the initiatives we have discussed so far have adopted either situational or social crime prevention as their main focus (or indeed have devised strategies that combine the two). Currie (1988) neatly sidesteps this bifurcation in his analysis of crime prevention activity. He identifies two 'phases' in community crime prevention activity, and argues that:

> Their views of what it means to strengthen a community in order to fight crime differ sharply. Moreover, they differ in their view (and even more in their practice) on what kinds of communities should receive most attention, and similarly, on what kind of crime should be most heavily targeted by community prevention – or indeed whether reducing crime is the main priority at all. By the same token, the two 'phases' differ in the degree to which they are concerned with the offender, or potential offender, as a focus of intervention. Finally, they differ on the balance to be struck between public and private responsibility for crime prevention and more generally for the enhancement of community life.
>
> (Currie, 1988, p.280)

Currie goes on to state:

> There is no sense, for example, that the people you are dealing with might include a neighbour's kid who has a learning problem and hangs about on the corner because he is afraid to go to school, or your sister's abusive husband – hardly a stranger – but an intimate member of a local household.
>
> (Currie, 1988, p.281–2)

Currie refers to these contradictions as emanating from a 'lack of structural awareness' (see also **Currie, 1991**). In some respects the concerns he identifies can be redefined as reflecting a need to emphasize a *public* sense of well-being (Taylor, 1991) over and above a private one. This raises a crucial question concerning the way in which communities targeted by the crime prevention policy discussed here can be understood as *gendered* communities.

6.7 Whose crime? Whose community?

Currie's (1988) analysis makes explicit a number of assumptions concerning community crime prevention in particular, and crime prevention in general. The explication of those assumptions not only draws our attention to what kind of communities are targeted for crime prevention work, but also to who is targeted within those communities. The general rhetoric concerning citizen involvement in community crime prevention presumes, of course, that we can identify and agree upon who the citizens are who make up a community and what the crime concerns are for such citizens. Such presumptions can render certain groups and their needs more or less visible (see Metropolitan Police poster below).

There are now 5 more reasons to report racist crimes.

1 Combating racist crime now has one of the highest priorities in the Metropolitan Police Operational Plan.

2 The Police in every London borough are being trained to recognise and to react vigorously to racist crime.

3 If a crime is racially motivated, the criminal may now be sentenced to serve up to 2 additional years in jail.

4 If you do not report a racist crime, you may be encouraging the criminal to commit further racist acts.

5 The Police are actively targeting racist criminals. Your information may contribute to solving related racist crimes.

If you have been a victim of racist crime then contact your local police station.

If you have any information regarding a racist criminal then call **CRIMESTOPPERS** ANONYMOUSLY

METROPOLITAN POLICE   POLICING DIVERSITY   *protect and respect*   **0800 555 111**

In the aftermath of the inquiry into the murder of Stephen Lawrence, police forces committed themselves to prioritizing racist violence

In the context of crime prevention directed at women, as we have seen already, this has frequently meant regarding their personal crime prevention behaviour as a focus for concern. If, however, we were to examine more closely the kinds of crime that affect women and the kind of crime prevention activity that is increasingly being adopted to address such crime, the question of the role of the community in the context of crime prevention might be framed somewhat differently. We shall examine these issues in the particular context of 'domestic' violence (the use of inverted commas here indicates the highly problematic nature of the meaning of 'domestic' violence – see Edwards, 1989).

335

6.8   Responding to 'domestic' violence

Home Office circular 60/1990, which was issued to all chief constables (and other chief executives of various service delivery agencies), urged police forces to treat 'domestic' violence as seriously as violence occurring between strangers in the street. The circular reminded chief constables in particular of the range of statutory and common law powers they have available to them to arrest perpetrators of violence, and encouraged them to consider the establishment of dedicated 'domestic' violence units as part of their policy response to support the victims. This circular offered a twofold approach to 'domestic' violence: a 'presumption to arrest' policy, backed by a policy framework supportive of the 'victim'.

In some respects this circular has been very influential. As Radford and Stanko (1991) have commented, police forces appear to have been competing with one another to see who can put the most imaginative policy response into practice. This is not the place, however, to discuss the document's strengths and weaknesses. Suffice it to say that this policy constitutes a partial translation to the UK of an essentially North American response to 'domestic' violence (Morley and Mullender, 1991). This in itself poses some difficulties without addressing whether or not as a policy it constitutes an adequate or effective way of responding to the complex needs of women. The central concern here is: what does such a policy response represent in relation to the question of crime prevention?

In many ways, as a preventive response, the strategies recommended and adopted following circular 60/1990 represent an 'enforcement crackdown' policy (Elias, 1986). It rests on the assumption that treating 'domestic' violence like other incidents of violence will have a preventive effect. In other words, by treating such behaviour as an offence and using the available legal framework to arrest the perpetrator, two consequences will emerge: it will convey the general message that such behaviour is no longer acceptable, while the act of arresting the perpetrator will have a deterrent effect on that individual engaging in similar behaviour in the future. A number of questions arise from this kind of policy stance.

First, as a policy it rests on the presumption that arrest does have a deterrent effect in these circumstances. The evidence for this is partial and inconclusive, and in some circumstances arrest may actually make the situation worse for the victim (Berk and Sherman, 1984; Sherman, 1992). Second, this policy also presumes that the normative response of police officers is to arrest the offender in non-domestic incidents of violence. As Chatterton (1983) and others have shown, the decision to arrest is a far more complex process. These presumptions are particularly interesting given the patent failure of arrest to deter persistent offenders from committing other kinds of crime. Why, then, should it be presumed that arrest is a 'reasonable deterrent strategy' in 'domestic' incidents?

Asking this question does not imply that such a strategy should either be abandoned or not taken seriously. Any strategy which affords some protection for a woman in a violent relationship, for however short a period, has to be acknowledged as offering something and, perhaps more important, conveying the message that her needs are being taken seriously. What emerges, however, is the individualistic offender-centred nature of this policy – a policy in which the rhetoric of community is notable by its absence. Such an absence is all the more remarkable given the sheer weight of its presence in policy responses across a broad spectrum of issues since the early 1980s. In addition, the North American evidence (on which policies in this area appear to draw so heavily) indicates that a 'presumption to arrest' policy is at its most effective when put in place alongside a range of community-based initiatives such as refuge facilities for women and children, counselling initiatives for men, and so on (Jaffe *et al.*, 1986).

As this policy initiative has unfolded in practice, what has not been absent has been a focus on a multi-agency approach to co-ordinate common local practices. Characterized in some areas by the establishment of Domestic Violence Forums, in which both statutory and voluntary agencies meet to co-ordinate policy, this is the kind of approach heralded as possible by the work of Blagg *et al.* (1988) (see section 6.3).

The foregoing discussion presumes that one of the goals of this policy initiative on 'domestic' violence was crime prevention, which may, of course, not necessarily be the case. Indeed, there is some evidence to suggest otherwise. It may make some sense, for example, to view this particular policy direction as constituting one element in a range of processes occurring within policing to do with 'value for money', efficiency and

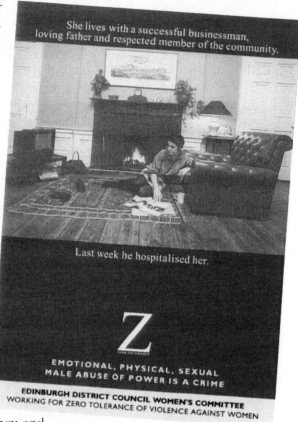

A poster issued by the Edinburgh Zero Tolerance Campaign against 'domestic' violence

the securing of consent, rather than as necessarily being a crime prevention policy. Yet this policy does convey a preventive message: arrest the offender and support the victim. Such a message raises some fundamentally contradictory questions for crime prevention policy for women in general. Why, for example, does so much crime prevention literature focus on the threat to women from strangers, when women know that those most likely to be troublesome to them are so-called 'trustworthy' men? (Stanko, 1992). And why do so many community crime prevention initiatives presume that the community in which they are working is a coherent one in which all individuals share the same or similar concerns about the same or similar law-breaking activity? The issue of 'domestic' violence clearly encourages us to think much more carefully about what is both visible and invisible in the community crime prevention industry. It also encourages us to think about communities as a gendered experience in relation to crime and how that might be best addressed (see **Saraga, 2001**).

It is important to note the extent to which this multi-agency approach to crime prevention has permeated responses to 'crime behind closed doors' as well as 'crime of the streets'. Moreover, it is pertinent to examine some of the underpinning characteristics of that multi-agency work across the spectrum of crime prevention activity. Indeed, it is valuable to reflect on the extent to which the acceptance of multi-agency strategies has also implicitly involved an acceptance of the need to disrupt the traditional barriers between those services considered to be under the auspices of public provision and those considered to be more appropriately provided from within the private sphere. As Crawford (1994) observes, local agency forums on crime prevention frequently bring together people from a diversity of agencies and groups not easily categorized as public or private. Moreover, as Loveday (1994) comments, such activities have also frequently ensured the further marginalization and sometimes exclusion of local authorities. As Crawford (1994) goes on to argue, these characteristics, often couched in terms of partnership, herald the development of corporatism at the local level. Such a development makes it very difficult to draw any lines between the responsibilities of the state and those of civil society as boundaries between organizations become increasingly blurred in the search for co-ordinated policy and action. Some of this may become clearer as the implementation process of the 1998 Crime and Disorder Act continues to unfold. However, questions concerning who is actually setting the local policy agenda are becoming increasingly difficult to resolve.

Processes such as these can have a number of effects. They can result in the construction of a crime prevention policy agenda for a particular community, on which all the agencies can agree but which may gloss over the needs of that local community, including the needs of the various 'publics' within it (for example women, minority ethnic groups, children, the elderly). Indeed, and perhaps more important, such policy constructions may gloss over the conflicts that exist within a particular community and between neighbouring communities. As Crawford (1995, p.105) has commented, an assumption is frequently made in appealing to the community that 'more community equals less crime' – a view which implicitly denies that the community itself may be criminogenic. Yet it is important to recognize that, as Campbell (1993) has observed, some of Britain's 'dangerous places' are also among some of Britain's most economically deprived areas. These areas are also assessed to be the most crime-ridden, and some of that crime is produced and sustained within those areas themselves (see **Graham and Clarke, 2001**). In other words such policies may gloss the lived reality of communities, leading to a further set of questions: whose policy, whose process?

7   Whose policy? Whose process?

The discussion which follows draws on findings from a longitudinal study of two communities' responses to their experience of living in high crime areas during the 1990s. That study demonstrated that these two areas (referred to as Oldtown and Bankhill), whilst seemingly so similar on official indicators, and geographically less than two miles apart, were actually exhibiting very different responses to their situation. These differences have been described as, on the one hand, Oldtown being an example of a 'defended community' (that is, an ordered community: not disordered as the Chicago school would suggest), trusting (of those who are local) and, whilst certainly disadvantaged, well defended from interference from 'outsiders'. On the other hand, Bankhill has been described as an example of a 'frightened community', socially disordered, where there was an absence of the trust of 'being local' found in Oldtown, and where there was no general collective community infrastructure. The residents of Bankhill do, however, offer generalized trust to the official agencies (see Evans and Walklate, 1996; Evans, 1997; Walklate, 1998). Such dynamics reflect the differing and differential relationship people living in these areas have in relation to crime and, as a consequence, feed and fuel particular policy possibilities.

It has been argued that the processes that underpin the surface manifestation of these community dynamics reflect different kinds of trust relationships. These relationships demonstrate the salience of the questions of: who can you trust?, how do you trust?, how much can you trust?, and when can you trust? (Nelken, 1994). The sense of well-being that individuals construct for themselves in these two high crime areas is mediated by their understanding of where they find themselves in relation to a 'square of trust' (Evans *et al.*, 1996; Walklate, 1998; Walklate and Evans, 1999).

trust

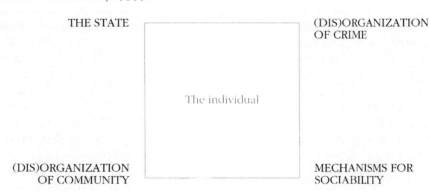

THE STATE

(DIS)ORGANIZATION OF CRIME

The individual

(DIS)ORGANIZATION OF COMMUNITY

MECHANISMS FOR SOCIABILITY

Figure 7.1 The square of trust (Source: Walklate and Evans, 1999, p.135)

In these two high crime areas trust relationships were certainly differently constituted in relation to the four points of this square (see Figure 7.1). In one, Oldtown, trust relationships meant not trusting state officials to sort things out in favour of expecting the more locally organized criminal gangs (organized crime) to do something. In the absence of the gang doing anything other issues might be managed as a result of the presence of kinship and family networks (the organization of the community); for instance, knowing someone's father or brother. Both processes, arguably, contributed towards local social solidarity (mechanisms for sociability). In the other area, Bankhill, trust relationships meant offering a generalized trust to state officials to sort things out but with little expectation that this might happen and moreover with little to put in the place of an official response (an absence of organized crime or an organized community resulting in weak mechanisms for sociability). A detailed analysis of the way in which these trust relationships manifest themselves is discussed in Walklate and Evans (1999). So what are the implications of raising the questions whose policy, and whose process?

8   Conclusion: crime prevention and communities of the future?

Raising the questions of 'whose policy?' and 'whose process?' draws attention to the need to challenge the separation of the public from the private which is presumed in crime prevention policy. Challenging this separation has a number of consequences.

First, it constitutes a challenge to understanding who or what counts as 'the public' in a particular community. This may mean that it is necessary to consider how, and in what ways, gender (or ethnicity or age) acts as a mediating variable, enhancing or inhibiting the success of any initiative. As an illustration of the potential value in doing this, a survey conducted in Tayside relating to women and safety identified the potentially complex interrelationship between where you live and how safe you feel (Tayside Women's Forum, 1988). Thus a person's sense of well-being in public may be mediated not only by their 'private' experiences, but also by their interconnectedness with their local community.

Second, with respect to community crime prevention initiatives per se, this challenge suggests that we do not know, and as yet do not take enough account of, the infrastructure of communities and what may or may not work within them. The consensus view that the multi-agency approach is a 'good thing' may in fact add to the routine daily problems being faced by people in some economically deprived areas, whether that be in peripheral council estates or in inner-city areas. In some of these areas, as our discussion has demonstrated, some people may feel more protected by the power that the local gang asserts on their streets (in keeping hard drugs out of their area, for example) than by any multi-agency initiative. Raising these fundamental questions about the infrastructure of communities may lead us to the conclusion that if we are to take the crime problem seriously, in all its forms but especially as a gendered experience, it may be necessary to target the behaviour of men in general and young men in particular (Campbell, 1993).

Third, understanding communities as gendered communities with their own infrastructure and conflicts may also mean that we have to reconsider who feels safe and what this means for men/women, young/old, etc. For example, how do we begin to understand the more recent developments in the technology of crime prevention, such as the increased deployment of CCTV and other styles of surveillance in city centres? One interesting feature of these developments has been the extent to which women in particular have supported the introduction of such surveillance techniques in spite of the civil liberties issues that they raise.

While such situational strategies might be attracting some 'public' support in city centres, it has to be said that the continued and persistent emphasis overall on situational crime prevention at the expense of paying more attention to what might be achieved by social crime prevention may have unintended and deleterious effects on the quality of life for everyone. For example, Davis states that:

> The dire predictions of Richard Nixon's 1969 National Commission on the Causes and Prevention of Violence have been tragically fulfilled: we live in 'fortress cities' brutally divided between 'fortified cells' of affluent society and 'places of terror' where the police battle the criminalised poor … In many instances the semiotics of so-called 'defensible space' are just about as subtle as the swaggering white cop.
>
> (Davis, 1990, pp.225–6)

Davis is commenting here on the changing urban landscape of Los Angeles, where the privately policed shopping mall and the privately policed suburban developments ensure that the wealthy move safely and unthreatened from one secure environment to another. Thus we are beginning to see, in the USA at least, real physical as well as economic and social boundaries between the wealthy and the poor. Such an effect is clearly possible in the UK, as the social and economic gap grows between those communities which have (and are relatively crime-free) and those communities which have not (and are relatively crime-soaked) (Hutton,

1994). Understanding the effects of these processes, their relationship with law-breaking behaviour, and the subsequent effects that crime has on communities unprotected by private police and technological hardware is the real challenge of community crime prevention policies. Such an understanding raises another real challenge in the contemporary British context: whose partnership?

To return to the two communities (Oldtown and Bankhill) discussed earlier. At the time this research was conducted in Bankhill there was a great willingness on the part of the community to work for change. Such willingness was expressed in both the desire to work with the 'authorities' and the trust and expectation invested in them to be able to make things happen. In return, people in Bankhill wanted their concerns, which may appear petty and trivial (criminal damage and vandalism), to be taken seriously by the 'authorities'. Consequently, in an area like this, the local authority and the police may be able to take a lead in local developments and will find support for them so doing in the local community. This support may be best harnessed by exploring interpretations of the notion of partnership above and beyond the more normatively prescribed multi-agency approach.

This kind of strategy implies the view that crime is a local problem to be *managed* locally, not necessarily prevented or reduced. So the result may not be crime prevention or even crime reduction, but management; that is, ensuring that people feel better about, and more in control of, what is going on in their area. By implication this vision of the relationship between partnership and crime embraces the importance of managing incivilities, as highlighted by the much maligned 'broken windows' thesis (Wilson and Kelling, 1982), with the local authority or local community groups being responsible for that process rather than the police.

On the other hand, in Oldtown the crime problem was already being managed, not by a community safety partnership strategy, but through the (fragile) equilibrium between the police, the local community, and the organized nature of crime in that area – a very different conception of what might constitute a partnership! Yet the processes underpinning these relationships, in allowing people to feel all right about living in their locality, seem to work for most of the people living there most of the time. Of course, relationships such as these make agency-led interventions a difficult prospect in areas like Oldtown. Moreover, in different localities in this ward, very local problems have been managed by local residents working together, sometimes with official aid coming afterwards, sometimes with that aid not coming at all.

In other words, partnerships in areas like Oldtown might well be formed but they may not have any of the characteristics of conventional organizational (voluntary or otherwise) allegiances; such partnerships may be with strategically placed individual residents, for example. Again, understanding the problem may be primarily about management; the desired result may not be crime prevention or crime reduction but restoring local equilibrium and the opportunity to discover what such an equilibrium might look like.

The implications of this discussion suggest that it is necessary to move away from universalistic and/or simplistic solutions to crime in localities like Oldtown and Bankhill. The alternatives may be more complex (though not necessarily more expensive); they may have different outcomes from those valued by the crime prevention industry; and they may challenge conventional views of what is, or is not, acceptable as a crime problem. In addition, they raise the questions of not only whose policy and whose process is crime prevention but also the question of what is democratically acceptable at a local as well as a national level. Locally informed and locally formulated policy responses may need to take account of the diversity of views which exist and which are acceptable. Moreover, the meaning of 'locally' may need to be reinterpreted and redefined in terms of quite small units (maybe at the level of the street in some localities) in order to formulate policies which make sense to local people and therefore stand a chance of working.

It is important to note that Oldtown and Bankhill are not unusual places. Each urban (and, increasingly, rural) area has its equivalent Oldtowns and Bankhills. These are predominantly white areas, where the traditional working class historically coexisted with the 'social scum' and those who were endeavouring to better themselves as market forces permitted. Oldtown and Bankhill may be at different points on a socio-economic trajectory (which the research was not designed to accommodate); but this trajectory is suggestive (almost) of an ecological, historically driven process which Oldtown has found a way of managing and Bankhill is in the process of so doing. Such a process is characterized by a number of features, one of which is the changing mechanisms of social inclusion and exclusion, especially in a context in which the nature of work is changing:

> ... your *place* in relation to crime *places* you in a community of belonging and exclusion ... It is consequently important to recognize who is seen to be protecting you and how: for many people it is not the police or the council but local families and/or the Salford Firm. Moreover, it is the absence of confidence in the formal agencies which creates the space for those other forces to come into play.
>
> Evans *et al.*, 1996, p.379)

This quotation refers to Oldtown; a locality from which the state had, for the most part, withdrawn. It was apparent that parts of Bankhill were also in the process of suffering a similar fate. There are other similar localities throughout the United Kingdom, as Campbell's (1993) analysis suggests; some of them peopled by ethnic minorities; just as many peopled by Caucasians. They are all areas which have been ripped apart by the market forces of the last two decades and which have suffered disproportionately as the gap between rich and poor has grown (Hutton, 1994). To reiterate, a critical reflection on the findings produced by this research reveals much about the ways in which the mechanisms of social inclusion and exclusion have operated and been managed at a local level. The question remains as to how much responsibility we should assume, collectively, for the most vulnerable in our society, however we might choose to define that vulnerability.

ACTIVITY 7.7

The statutory framework of the Crime and Disorder Act clearly indicates those considered responsible for community safety. Figure 7.2, from the Audit Commission Report, outlines the key requirements of the Crime and Disorder Act (1998), and some of the key problems facing those working in this area. Given what you have read about Oldtown and Bankhill consider:

1   The likely success of statutory partnerships in: (a) Oldtown; (b) Bankhill.

2   How the difficulties identified by the Audit Commission might be overcome in: (a) Oldtown; (b) Bankhill.

3   What alternative strategies might be put in place for effective community partnership in: (a) Oldtown; (b) Bankhill.

Problems	Causes
Poor grounding in local people's views	• Failure to give sufficient weight to local views • Failure to develop an overall communications strategy • Difficulty in reconciling bottom-up and top-down views
Poor grasp of causes of and solutions to community safety problems	• Insufficiently thorough mapping and analysis of problems • Lack of understanding of 'what works' • Insufficient monitoring and evaluation
Under-investment in prevention	• Reliance on external funding • Difficulty in identifying spending on community safety • Under-investment in people
Unclear rationale for partnership	• Difficulty in establishing clear ownership and accountability • Complex reporting links to delivery
Lack of integration of community safety with mainstream agencies	• Mainstream agencies and departments do not see relevance to their work • Crowded corporate agendas • Emphasis on situational project approaches bypassing mainstream departments

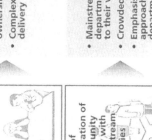

Crime and Disorder Act Statutory Framework

Local authorities and police forces are required to:

- *form statutory partnerships* with other prescribed authorities (health authorities, probation, magistrates courts, CPS and the voluntary sector) at the level of the district or unitary council. The Act requires the chief constable and the chief executives of the local authorities to form the partnership as joint leaders. In addition to those prescribed authorities, they can invite others – such as existing partnerships and voluntary agencies – on to the partnership at their discretion;

- *conduct an audit* of crime and disorder across the local authority area, using the relevant data from partner agencies;

- *consult the public* at key stages in strategy development, notably on the results of the audit and on identifying the targets for agencies to aim for;

- *draw up three-year community safety strategies* with short and long-term targets for reducing crime and disorder; and

- *monitor and evaluate* this work systematically; all initiatives are to be monitored, but with selective evaluation so as to learn from new types of initiatives without reinventing the wheel.

Figure 7.2   Community safety – statutory requirements, problems and possibilities (Source: Audit Commission, 1999, pp.21, 53)

It is clear that, whilst the relationship between the citizen and the state has changed in emphasis in the UK since 1945, there are also strong historical continuities in that relationship – historical continuities informed by notions of a distinction between the deserving and undeserving, the principle of less eligibility, and the notion of the dangerous classes. These dangerous classes, of course, provide the criminal justice system with much of its work, so for that reason alone it is important to have a clear understanding of how and why these processes happen in the way that they do.

In a different context, Currie (1997, p.147) has discussed the marketization of violence. By that he is referring to the processes whereby the 'pursuit of private gain' is 'likely to breed high levels of violent crime'. In this context, that same pursuit seems to have produced communities which, when left to devise their own management strategies, have found ways of making life all right for themselves: the marketization of trust. The consequences of these processes are there to be seen (*inter alia*) in the Social Exclusion Unit Report (1998). That report highlights communities for whom not only crime, but health, education, housing and so on, still constitute issues for serious concern. In the foreword to that document the Prime Minister states: 'Our goal is simple: to bridge the gap between the poorest neighbourhoods and the rest of Britain. Bridging that gap will not be easy. It will require imagination, persistence, and commitment.' The argument presented here certainly supports the view that bridging this gap will not be easy. Those who are socially excluded, and have found ways of managing that exclusion, will not be easily persuaded that it is in their interests to manage differently.

So, the question remains as to whether or not the proposed policy strategies to tackle social exclusion are imaginative, persistent and committed enough to face social reality, 'to think the unthinkable', and work with that in meaningful ways; as the Oldtown/Bankhill research also clearly demonstrates, there are opportunities for that to happen. If the lived experiences of those people in high crime areas are taken into account, there is clearly another layer of questions to be considered concerning what works, for whom, how, why, where and when. However, in order for such accounting to occur it is important that academics, politicians, policy makers and the locally powerful pay constant vigilant attention to the questions of whose policy and whose process. As Giddens (1998, p.88) states: 'In order to work, partnerships between government agencies, the criminal justice system, local associations and community organizations have to be inclusive – all economic and ethnic groups must be involved. ... To be successful, such schemes demand a long-term commitment to social objectives.' As he goes on to point out, such an approach does not necessarily mean denying any link between unemployment, poverty and crime; but it does mean that policies need to be co-ordinated with common goals and objectives. They also need to be resourced: an issue remarkably absent from the implementation process of the 1998 Crime and Disorder Act.

However, to reiterate, above all else, a genuine desire for policy to work for change needs to be cognisant of the importance of the local context in which that policy is set. This desire needs to work with rather than against the historical and socio-economic circumstances which structure that local context. Such a desire does demand imagination, commitment and persistence. It also requires that the desire for policy to work be both authentic, relevant and genuine for the communities themselves.

Review questions

- What have been the key developments in crime prevention policy since 1980?
- How might crime prevention policy be informed by questions of gender?
- What do you understand by community and how might different understandings of community influence crime prevention policy?
- What do you understand by partnership in crime prevention policy and how might that be differently structured?
- What is community safety?

Further reading

A solid overview of the development of community crime prevention is given in the collection of essays edited by Hope and Shaw (1988b), while Bottoms (1990) is another useful reference. Campbell (1993) offers an interesting insight into understanding some of the processes at play in some economically deprived communities and the provocative questions that these processes raise for crime prevention. Looking to the future, one challenging image of the community is presented by Davis (1990). For an introduction to situational crime prevention see **Clarke (1980)**. **Currie (1991)** provides a more radical vision of what should be involved in effective social crime prevention strategies in market societies. Hope (1995), Crawford (1998), Hughes (1998) and Ballintyne *et al.* (2000) offer more contemporary analyses and critiques of the development of the crime prevention industry.

References

Allatt, P. (1984a) 'Residential security: containment and displacement of burglary', *Howard Journal of Criminal Justice*, vol.23, no.2, pp.99–116.

Allatt, P. (1984b) 'Fear of crime: the effect of improved residential security on a difficult to let estate', *Howard Journal of Criminal Justice*, vol.23, no.3, pp.170–182.

Audit Commission (1999) *Safety in Numbers: Promoting Community Safety*, Abingdon, Audit Commission Publications.

Ballintyne, S., Pease, K. and McLaren, V. (eds) (2000) *Secure Foundations: Key Issues in Crime Prevention, Crime Reduction and Community Safety*, London, Institute of Public Policy Research.

Barr, R. and Pease, K. (1992) 'The problem of displacement', in Evans, D.J., Fyfe, N.R. and Herbert, D.T. (eds) *Crime, Policing and Place: Essays in Environmental Criminology*, London, Routledge and Kegan Paul.

Bennett, T. (1987) *An Evaluation of Two Neighbourhood Watch Schemes in London: Executive Summary. Final Report to the Home Office Research and Planning Unit*, Cambridge, Institute of Criminology.

Bennett, T. and Wright, R. (1984) *Burglars on Burglary*, Aldershot, Gower.

Bennion, C., Davies, A., Hesse, B., Joshua, L., McGloin, P., Munn, C. and Tester, S. (1985) 'Neighbourhood Watch: the eyes and ears of urban policing?', *Occasional Papers in Sociology and Social Policy*, no.6, Guildford, University of Surrey.

Berk, R.A. and Sherman, L.W. (1984) 'The specific deterrent effects of arrest for domestic assault', *American Sociological Review*, vol.49, pp.261–72.

Blagg, H., Pearson, G., Sampson, A., Smith, D. and Stubbs, P. (1988) 'Inter-agency co-ordination: rhetoric and reality', in Hope and Shaw (1988b).

Bottoms, A.E. (1990) 'Crime prevention facing the 1990s', *Policing and Society*, vol.1, no.1, pp.3–22.

Bottoms, A.E. and Wiles, P. (1992) 'Explanations of crime and place', in Evans, D.J., Fyle, N.R. and Herbert, D.T., *Crime, Policing and Place*, London, Routledge and Kegan Paul. (Extract reprinted in Muncie *et al.*, 1996.)

Bright, J. (1987) 'Community safety, crime prevention and the local authority', in Willmott, P. (ed.) *Policing in the Community*, London, Policy Studies Institute.

Bright, J. (1991) 'Crime prevention: the British experience', in Stenson and Cowell (1991).

Campbell, B. (1993) *Goliath: Britain's Dangerous Places*, London, Virago.

Chatterton, M. (1983) 'Police work and assault charges', in Punch, M. (ed.) *Control in the Police Organisation*, Cambridge, Mass., MIT Press.

Clarke, R.V. (1980) '"Situational" crime prevention: theory and practice', *British Journal of Criminology*, vol.20, no.2, pp.136–47. (Reprinted in Muncie *et al.*, 1996.)

Clarke, R.V. (1992) *Situational Crime Prevention: Successful Case Studies*, New York, Harrow and Heston.

Clarke, R.V. and Mayhew, P. (eds) (1980) *Designing Out Crime*, London, HMSO.

Cloward, R.A., and Ohlin, L.C. (1960) *Delinquency and Opportunity*, Glencoe, Ill., Free Press.

Coleman, A. (1985) *Utopia on Trial*, London, Hilary Shipman.

Comedia (1991) *Out of Hours: Summary Report*, London, Calouste Gulbenkian Foundation.

Cooper, B. (1989) *Management and Prevention of Juvenile Crime Problems*, Home Office Police Research Group Crime Prevention Unit paper, no.20, London, HMSO.

Crawford, A. (1994) 'The partnership approach to community crime prevention: corporatism at the local level?', *Social and Legal Studies*, vol.3, pp.497–519.

Crawford, A. (1995) 'Appeals to community and crime prevention', *Crime, Law and Social Change*, vol.22, pp.97–126.

Crawford, A. (1998) *Crime Prevention and Community Safety*, London, Longman.

Crawford, A., Jones, T., Woodhouse, T. and Young, J. (1990) *The Second Islington Crime Survey*, Middlesex University, Centre for Criminology.

Currie, E. (1988) 'Two visions of crime prevention', in Hope and Shaw (1988b).

Currie, E. (1991) 'Social crime prevention strategies in a market society', in *International Developments in Crime and Social Policy*, London, NACRO. (Extract reprinted in Muncie *et al.,* 1996.)

Currie, E. (1997) 'Market, crime and community', *Theoretical Criminology*, vol.1, no.2, pp.147–72.

Davis, M. (1990) *City of Quartz: Excavating the Future in Los Angeles,* London, Verso.

Donnison, H., Skola, J. and Thomas, P. (1986) *Neighbourhood Watch: Policing the People*, London, The Libertarian Research and Education Trust.

Douglas, M. (1992) *Risk and Blame: Essays in Cultural Theory,* London, Routledge.

Edwards, S. (1989) *Policing 'Domestic' Violence*, London, Sage.

Ekblom, P. (2000) 'The conjunction of criminal opportunity', in Ballintyre, S., Pease, K. and Mclaren, V. (eds) *Secure Foundations: Key Issues in Crime Prevention, Crime Reduction and Community Safety*, London, IPPR.

Elias, R. (1986) *The Politics of Victimization*, Oxford, Oxford University Press.

Etzioni, A. (1997) *The New Golden Rule*, London, Profile Books.

Evans, K. (1997) '"It's alright round here if you're local" – Community in the inner city', in Hoggett, P. (ed.) *Contested Communities*, Bristol, Policy Press.

Evans, K. and Walklate, S. (1996) *Community Safety, Personal Safety and the Fear of Crime*, End of Project Report, ESRC.

Evans, K., Fraser, P. and Walklate, S. (1996) 'Whom do you trust? The politics of grassing on an inner city housing estate', *Sociological Review*, vol.44, no.3. pp.361–80.

Forrester, D., Chatterton, M., and Pease, K. (1988) *The Kirkholt Burglary Prevention Project*, Crime Prevention Unit Paper 13, London, HMSO.

Freeman, R. (1992) 'The idea of prevention: a critical review', in Scott, S., Williams, G., Platt, S. and Thomas, H. (eds) *Private Risks and Public Dangers*, Aldershot, Avebury.

Giddens, A. (1998) *The Third Way*, Oxford, Polity.

Goldblatt, P. and Lewis, C. (eds) (1998) *Reducing Offending*, Home Office Research Study, No.187, London, HMSO.

Graham, P. and Clarke, J. (2001) 'Dangerous places: crime and the city', in Muncie and McLaughlin (2001).

Hakim, S. and Rengert, G.F. (1981) *The Crime Spill Over*, Beverly Hills, Sage.

Home Office (1991) *Safer Communities: The Local Delivery of Crime Prevention Through the Partnership Approach*, Report of the Standing Conference on Crime Prevention (the Morgan Report), London, HMSO.

Home Office (1999) *Reducing Crime and Tackling its Causes*, London, HMSO.

Hope, T. (1988) 'Support for Neighbourhood Watch: a British Crime Survey analysis', in Hope and Shaw (1988b).

Hope, T. (1995) 'Community crime prevention', in Tonry, M. and Farrington, D.P. *Building a Safer Society, Crime and Justice*, vol.19, Chicago, IL, University of Chicago Press.

Hope, T. and Shaw, M. (1988a) 'Community approaches to reducing crime', in Hope and Shaw (1988b).

Hope, T. and Shaw, M. (eds) (1988b) *Communities and Crime Reduction*, London, HMSO.

Hough, M. and Mo, P. (1986) 'If at first you don't succeed', *Home Office Research Bulletin*, no.21, pp.10–13.

Hughes, G. (1998) *Understanding Crime Prevention*, Buckingham, Open University Press.

Hutton, W. (1994) 'A question of relativity', *Search*, no.20, summer.

Jacobson, J. and Saville, E. (1999) *Neighbourhood Warden Schemes: An Overview*, Crime Reduction Research Series, paper 2, London, HMSO.

Jaffe, P., Wolfe, D.A., Telford, A. and Austin, G. (1986) 'The impact of police laying charges in incidents of wife abuse', *Journal of Family Violence,* vol.1, pp.37–49.

Jefferson, T., McLaughlin, E. and Robertson, L. (1988) 'Monitoring the monitors: accountability, democracy and policewatching in Britain', *Contemporary Crises*, vol.12, no.2, pp.91–106.

Jeffreys, S. and Radford, J. (1984) 'Contributory negligence or being a woman? The car rapist case', in Scraton, P. and Gordon, P. (eds) *Causes for Concern*, Harmondsworth, Penguin.

Kinsey, R., Lea, J., and Young, J. (1986) *Losing the Fight Against Crime*, Oxford, Blackwell.

Lea, J. (1987) 'Left realism: a defence', *Contemporary Crises*, vol.11, pp.357–70.

Lea, J. and Young, J. (1984) *What Is To Be Done About Law and Order?*, Harmondsworth, Penguin. (Extract reprinted as 'Relative deprivation' in Muncie *et al.*, 1996.)

Lea, J., Jones, T., Woodhouse, T., and Young, J. (1988) *Preventing Crime: The Hilldrop Environmental Improvement Survey: First Report*, Middlesex University, Centre for Criminology.

Lewis, D.A. and Salem, G. (1986) *Fear of Crime: Incivility and the Production of a Social Problem*, New Brunswick, NJ, Transaction.

Loveday, B. (1994) 'Government strategies for community crime prevention programmes in England and Wales: a study in failure?', *International Journal of the Sociology of Law*, vol.22, pp.181–202.

Morley, R., and Mullender, A. (1991) 'Preventing violence against women in the home: feminist dilemmas concerning recent British developments', paper presented to the British Criminology Conference, July.

Muncie, J. (2001) 'The construction and deconstruction of crime', in Muncie and McLaughlin (2001).

Muncie, J. and McLaughlin, E. (eds) (2001) *The Problem of Crime*, 2nd edn, London, Sage in association with The Open University.

Muncie, J., McLaughlin, E. and Langan, M. (eds) (1996) *Criminological Perspectives: A Reader*, **London, Sage in association with The Open University.**

Nelken, D. (1994) 'Whom can you trust?', in Nelken, D. (ed.) *The Futures of Criminology*, London, Sage.

Newman, O. (1972) *Defensible Space*, New York, Macmillan.

Painter, K. (1988) *Lighting and Crime Prevention: The Edmonton Project*, Middlesex Polytechnic, Centre for Criminology.

Poyner, B., Webb, B. and Woodall, R. (1986) *Crime Reduction on Housing Estates: An Evaluation of NACRO's Crime Prevention Programme*, London, Tavistock Institute of Human Relations.

Radford, J. and Stanko, E.A. (1991) 'Violence against women and children: the contradictions of crime control under patriarchy', in Stenson and Cowell (1991).

Reiss, A. (1986) 'Official statistics and survey statistics', in Fattah, E.A. (ed.) *From Crime Policy to Victim Policy*, London, Macmillan.

Rock, P. (1988) 'Crime reduction initiatives on problem estates', in Hope and Shaw (1988b).

Sampson, A., Stubbs, P., Smith, D., Pearson, G. and Blagg, H. (1988) 'Crime, localities and the multi-agency approach', *British Journal of Criminology*, vol.28, pp.478–93.

Saraga, E. (2001) 'Dangerous places: the family as a site of crime', in Muncie and McLaughlin (2001).

Sherman, L.W. (1992) *Policing Domestic Violence: Experiments and Dilemmas*, New York, Free Press.

Smith, S. (1986) *Crime, Space and Society*, Cambridge, Cambridge University Press.

Social Exclusion Unit (1998) *Bringing Britain Together*, London, Home Office.

Stanko, E.A. (1990) 'When precaution is normal: a feminist critique of crime prevention', in Gelsthorpe, L. and Morris, A. (eds) *Feminist Perspectives in Criminology*, Buckingham, Open University Press.

Stanko, E.A. (1992) Plenary address, Violence Against Women Conference, Manchester, May.

Stanko, E.A. (1997) 'Safety talk: conceptualizing women's risk assessment as a "technology of the soul"', *Theoretical Criminology*, vol.1, no.4, pp.479–99.

Stenson, K. and Cowell, D. (eds) *The Politics of Crime Control*, London, Sage.

Taylor, I. (1991) *Not Places in Which You'd Linger: Public Transport and Well-Being in Manchester*, University of Salford, Department of Sociology.

Tayside Women's Forum (1988) *Women and Safety: Survey Report*, Dundee, Tayside Regional Council.

Tilley, N. (1992) *Safer Cities and Community Safety Strategies*, Crime Prevention Unit Series, Paper 38, Home Office Police Research Group, London, HMSO.

Tilley, N. (1993) 'Crime prevention and the Safer Cities story', *Howard Journal of Criminal Justice*, vol.32, no.1.

Walklate, S. (1998) Crime and community: fear or trust?, *British Journal of Sociology*, vol.49, no.4, pp.550–69.

Walklate, S. and Evans, K. (1999) *Zero Tolerance or Community Tolerance? Managing Crime in High Crime Areas*, Aldershot, Ashgate.

Whiskin, N. (1987) 'Crime prevention: an inter-agency approach at neighbourhood level', in Junger-Tas, J., Rutting, A. and Wilzing, J. (eds) *Crime Control in Local Communities in Europe*, Lochem, J.B. van den Brink.

Willmott, P. (1987) 'Introduction', in Willmott, P. (ed.) *Policing and the Community*, London, Policy Studies Institute.

Willmott, P. and Young, M. (1962) *Family and Kinship in East London*, Harmondsworth, Penguin.

Wilson, J. and Kelling, G. (1982) 'Broken windows', *Atlantic Monthly*, March, pp.29–37.

Young, J. (1986) 'The failure of criminology', in Matthews, R. and Young, J. (eds) *Confronting Crime*, London, Sage. (Extract reprinted in Muncie et al., 1996.)

Young, J. (1992) 'Ten points of realism', in Young, J. and Matthews, R. (eds) *Rethinking Criminology: The Realist Debate*, London, Sage.

Acknowledgements

Grateful acknowledgement is made to the following sources for permission to reproduce material in this book:

Text

Chapter 2: 'Guns won't protect the police', *The Independent on Sunday*, 24 October 1993. **Chapter 3:** Griffiths, J.A.G. (1991) *The Politics of the Judiciary*, HarperCollins Publishers Ltd; Travis, A. (1999) 'Thousands will lose the right to trial by jury', *The Guardian*, 19 May 1999, © Guardian Newspapers Ltd; Macpherson, W. (1999) *The Stephen Lawrence Inquiry*, Report of an Inquiry by Sir William Macpherson of Cluny, Cm 4264, © Crown Copyright. Reproduced with the permission of the Controller of Her Majesty's Stationery Office; Travis, A. (1994) 'Courts "lenient toward women"', *The Guardian*, 20 May 1994, © Guardian Newspapers Ltd; Lightfoot, L. and Anderson, A. (1995) 'Courts condemn women to tougher sentences than men', *The Sunday Times*, 9 April 1995, © Times Newspapers Ltd. **Chapter 4:** *Punishment and Social Structure* by Georg Rusche and Otto Kirchheimer, copyright © 1939 by Columbia University Press, reprinted with permission of the publisher. **Chapter 5:** The Rt Hon Justice Woolf and His Honour Judge Stephen Tumin (1991) *Prison Disturbances April 1990*, © Crown Copyright. Reproduced with the permission of the Controller of Her Majesty's Stationery Office; Greig, G. (1995) 'Jails to become hell on earth', *The Sunday Times*, 12 March 1995, © Times Newspapers Ltd, 1995. **Chapter 7:** Jacobson, J. and Saville, E. (1999) *Neighbourhood Warden Schemes: An Overview*, Crime Reduction Research Series Paper 2, Home Office, Policy and Reducing Crime Unit, Research, Development and Statistics Directorate, © Crown Copyright. Reproduced with the permission of the Controller of Her Majesty's Stationery Office; Independent Working Group under the Chairmanship of James Morgan (1991) *Safer Communities: The Local Delivery of Crime Prevention Through the Partnership Approach*, August 1991, © Crown Copyright. Reproduced with the permission of the Controller of Her Majesty's Stationery Office.

Figures

Figure 2.1: Courtesy of the Association of Chief Police Officers of England, Wales and Northern Ireland; *Figures 2.2, 2.3*: Audit Commission (1993) *Helping With Enquiries: Tackling Crime Effectively*, Audit Commission Publications; *Figure 2.5*: Jones, S. (1986) *Policewomen and Equality: Formal Policy versus Informal Practice*, Macmillan Ltd; *Figure 5.1*: adapted from 'The penal estate', *The Guardian*, 8 October 1991, Copyright © 1999 *The Guardian*; *Figure 5.2*: Cullen, C. and Minchin, M. (2000) *Research Findings No. 111, The Prison Population in 1999: A Statistical Review*, Home Office, Research, Development and Statistics Directorate, © Crown Copyright. Reproduced with the permission of the Controller of Her Majesty's Stationery Office; *Figure 5.3*: Barclay, G.C. and Tavares, C. (eds) (1999) *Digest 4*, Home Office, Research, Development and Statistics Directorate, © Crown Copyright. Reproduced with the permission of the Controller of Her Majesty's Stationery Office; *Figure 5.4*: Mathiesen, T. (1990) *Prison on Trial: A Critical Assessment*, figure 1.1, Sage Publications Ltd, © Thomas Mathiesen 1990; *Figure 5.5*: Box, S. (1987) *Recession, Crime and Punishment*, figure 5.1, Macmillan Press Ltd; *Figure 6.1*: Sisson, S. *et al.* (1999) *Home Office Statistical Bulletin*, Issue 21/99, 11 November 1999, Research, Development and Statistics Directorate, © Crown Copyright. Reproduced with the permission of the Controller of Her Majesty's Stationery Office; *Figure 6.2*: Home Office (1999) *Cautions, Court Proceedings and Sentencing, England and Wales 1998*, Home Office Statistical Bulletin, Issue 21/99, © Crown Copyright. Reproduced with the permission of the Controller of Her Majesty's Stationery Office; *Figure 7.1*: Walklate, S. and Evans, K. (1999) *Zero Tolerance or Community Tolerance? Managing Crime in High Crime Areas*, Ashgate; *Figure 7.2*: Audit Commission (1999) *Safety in Numbers: Promoting Community Safety*, Audit Commission Publications.

Tables

Tables 1.1, 1.2: adapted from Palmer, S.H. (1988) *Police and Protest in England and Ireland 1780–1850*, Cambridge University Press; *Table 2.1*: Jordan, P. (1998) 'Effective policing strategies for reducing crime', in Goldblatt, P. and Lewis, C. (eds) *Reducing Offending: An Assessment of Research Evidence on Ways of Dealing With Offending Behaviour*, Home Office Research Study 187, © Crown Copyright. Reproduced with the permission of the Controller of Her Majesty's Stationery Office; *Table 3.1*: adapted from Home Office (1999) *Criminal Statistics, England and Wales 1998*, Cm 4649, © Crown Copyright. Reproduced with the permission of the Controller of Her Majesty's Stationery Office; *Table 3.2*: Farrington, D.P. and Morris, A. (1983) 'Sex, sentencing and reconviction', *British Journal of Criminology*, 23 (3), July 1983, reprinted by permission of Oxford University Press; *Table 4.1*: Cohen, Professor S. (1985) *Visions of Social Control: Crime, Punishment and Classification*, pp.16–17, Polity Press; *Table 4.2*: Matthews, R. (1999) *Doing Time: An Introduction to the Sociology of Imprisonment*, Macmillan Press Ltd, copyright © Roger Matthews 1999; *Table 5.1*: Cullen, C. and Minchin, M. (2000) *Research Findings No. 111, The Prison Population in 1999: A Statistical Review*, Home Office Research, Development and Statistics Directorate, © Crown Copyright. Reproduced with the permission of the Controller of Her Majesty's Stationery Office; *Table 6.1*: adapted from Black Committee (1979) *Report of the Children and Young Persons Review Group*, HMSO, © Crown Copyright. Reproduced with the permission of the Controller of Her Majesty's Stationery Office; *Table 7.1*: Tilley, N. (1992) *Safer Cities and Community Safety Strategies*, Police Research Group Crime Prevention Unit Series: Paper No. 38, Home Office Police Department, © Crown Copyright. Reproduced with the permission of the Controller of Her Majesty's Stationery Office.

Photographs

pp.15, 41 (right): courtesy of the Metropolitan Police Museum; *p.16*: by courtesy of the National Portrait Gallery, London; *p.17*: reproduced by permission of the Public Record Office, HO 61/9 June–July 1833 PRO, London; *p.18*: Greater Manchester Police Museum; *p.29*: courtesy of the Metropolitan Police Service; *p.34*: photograph from the January 1991 issue of *Special Beat*, source unknown; *p.35*: courtesy of Cambridge University Library; *p.39*: Hulton-Deutsch/Fox; *p.41 (left)*: Bildarchiv Preussischer Kulturbesitz; *p.41 (centre)*: Roger-Viollet; *p.58*: reproduced by kind permission of Mrs Warner and the Estate of Jack Warner. Photograph: BBC Photo Library; *p.59*: courtesy of John Thaw/copyright Central Broadcasting Ltd; *p.63*: courtesy of The Metropolitan Police Service; *p.69*: David Hoffmann; *p.70*: Martin Godwin; *p.72*: Eamonn McCabe/*The Guardian*; *p.78*: Richard Pohle; *p.81*: courtesy of The Police Federation; *p.90*: Marc Burden Photography; *p.103*: Press Association/Martin Keene; *p.120*: Universal Pictorial Press & Agency Ltd; *p.122*: Popperfoto/Reuter; *p.125*: David Hoffmann; *p.168*: from the Bentham Papers, University College, London; *p.169 (top)*: Mansell Collection; *p.171*: from Mayhew, H. and Binney, J. (1862) *The Criminal Prisons of London and Scenes of Prison Life*, London, Griffin Bohn and Company; *p.175*: Guildhall Library, Corporation of London/photograph by Geremy Butler; *p.209*: Yorkshire Post Newspapers Ltd; *p.213*: Central Office of Information; *p.218*: courtesy of the Press Office, The Prison Service; *p.221 (top)*: Mercury Press Agency; *p.221 (bottom)*: Denis Thorpe/*The Guardian*; *p.230*: Daniel Portnoy/Associated Press; *p.239*: Press Association; *pp.262, 290*: Mark Harvey/iD.8 Photography Library; *p.271*: Clare Marsh/John Birdsall Photography/NACRO. from *Safer Society*, 2, February 1999, p.9; *p.272*: North News Pictures; *p.280*: Paula Illingworth/Associated Press Ltd; *p.284*: News Team International; *p.285*: News Team International; *p.310*: Victim Support; *p.312*: extracts from leaflets on sexual violence towards women: courtesy of the Greater Manchester Police Authority; *pp.314 and 321*: Don McPhee/*The Guardian*; *p.335*: Courtesy of The Metropolitan Police Service; *p.337*: Edinburgh District Council Women's Unit, Zero Tolerance Division/copyright the Estate of Franki Raffles.

Every effort has been made to locate all copyright owners, but if any have been overlooked the publishers will make the necessary arrangements at the first opportunity.

Index